DOSTOEVSKY
&
GOGOL

TEXTS AND CRITICISM

Edited by

PRISCILLA MEYER
&
STEPHEN RUDY

ARDIS / / / ANN ARBOR

Dostoevsky and Gogol: Texts and Criticism

Edited and translated by Priscilla Meyer
and Stephen Rudy

Introduction by Priscilla Meyer and Stephen Rudy

Copyright©1979 by Ardis.

Published by Ardis,
2901 Heatherway,
Ann Arbor, Michigan 48104.

Manufactured in the United States of America.

ISBN 0-88233-315-1

Library of Congress Catalog Card No.: 79-51642

ACKNOWLEDGEMENTS

Grateful acknowledgement is made to the following for permission to quote from copyright material:

Fyodor Dostoevsky: "Uncle's Dream." Excerpts reprinted from *An Honest Thief and Other Stories*, translated by Constance Garnett, by permission of Macmillan Publishing Co., Inc., New York. Copyright ©1916 by Macmillan.

Fyodor Dostoevsky: *The Idiot.* Excerpts reprinted from *The Idiot*, translated by David Magarshack, by permission of Penguin Books Ltd., London. Copyright © 1955 by David Magarshack.

Fyodor Dostoevsky, *Netochka Nezvanova.* Excerpts reprinted from *Netochka Nezvanova,* translated by Ann Dunnigan, by permission of Prentice-Hall, Inc., Englewood Cliffs, New Jersey. Copyright © 1970 by Ann Dunnigan.

Boris Eikhenbaum: "How Gogol's 'Overcoat' is Made." Reprinted from "The Structure of Gogol's 'The Overcoat,'" translated by Beth Paul and Muriel Nesbitt, by permission of *The Russian Review*, Stanford, California. Copyright © 1963 by *The Russian Review*.

Nikolai Gogol: *The Collected Tales and Plays of Nikolai Gogol.* Excerpts reprinted from the *Collected Tales and Plays of Nikolai Gogol*, translated by Constance Garnett and Leonard Kent, by permission of Random House, Inc., New York. Copyright ©1964 by Random House.

Nikolai Gogol: *Dead Souls.* Excerpts reprinted from *Dead Souls*, translated by B.G. Guerney, by permission of Holt, Rinehart and Winston, Inc., New York. Copyright © 1942 by The Reader's Club.

Mikhail Bakhtin: "Discourse Typology in Prose." Excerpts reprinted from *Readings in Russian Poetics*, edited by L. Matejka and K. Pomorska, by permission of M.I.T. Press, Cambridge, Mass. Copyright © 1971 by M.I.T.

Gogol: *Selected Passages from a Correspondence with Friends.* Excerpts reprinted from *Selected Passages from a Correspondence with Friends*, translated by Jesse Zeldin, by permission of Vanderbilt University Press, Nashville, Tennessee. Copyright © 1969 by Vanderbilt University Press.

Thomas Mann, *Doctor Faustus.* Excerpts reprinted from *Doctor Faustus,* translated by H.T. Lowe-Porter, by permission of A.A. Knopf, New York. Copyright © 1948 by A.A. Knopf.

CONTENTS

Ĺᴏᴦᴵ

PREFACE

This collection provides materials for understanding how Dostoevsky began his career as a writer by confronting Gogol's literary heritage. The topic is one that has occupied a central place in Russian literary criticism during the last century and served as the impetus for some of the most outstanding works of Formalist, as well as of more traditional, literary scholarship. Our purpose in translating the criticism included here is to make available to the English-speaking reader the best of the factually and methodologically rich heritage of Russian criticism on this topic.

Dostoevsky's early works (from the publication of *Poor Folk* in 1846 to his exile to Siberia in 1849) provide an exemplary model for a discussion of literary evolution in the context of a crucial period in Russian literature. In order to understand Dostoevsky's work fully, both close readings of the texts and the study of Russian literary evolution from the 1820s to the 1840s are essential. Neither has been possible in English criticism because of the absence of accurate translations of both Gogol and Dostoevsky and the ignorance of the Russian literary tradition, a situation which this collection, we hope, will amend.

We pay particular attention to the stories about the poor clerk, which respond to Gogol's later work, only alluding briefly in the foreword to the second stage of Dostoevsky's early period, which relates to Gogol's earlier writing. This anthology may be used as a companion to Dostoevsky's first two novels, *Poor Folk* and *The Double*. It is unfortunate that they are too long to be included here, because the existing translations do not convey the peculiarities of the heroes' speech, which is riddled with diminutives, folk sayings, and idiosyncratic juxtapositions of stylistic levels. We have translated quotations from these two novels ourselves, providing letter and chapter references respectively. For citations from other works we refer the reader to existing English translations, but in most cases we have substantially revised them. Hitherto the imprecision of the translations of the stories we include has made it impossible for the English reader to appreciate their style. We have made an effort to preserve Gogol's deliberate awkwardness of construction, his alliterations, redundancies and illogicalities, which are usually smoothed over or ignored. The same is true in our renderings of Dostoevsky's stories, especially where he imitates Gogol. This enables the reader to verify the stylistic analyses here given by consulting the English versions.

The texts we have used for Gogol's stories are those of the Academy of Sciences edition (1938) in which the parts originally censored, omitted in most translations, have been restored. The new Academy of Sciences edition (1971) of Dostoevsky's work is the source for "Mr. Prokharchin" and "Polzunkov." The translations of prose by Gogol and Dostoevsky are by Priscilla Meyer; the critical articles, unless otherwise specified, are translated by Stephen Rudy.

For a chronology of Gogol's work we refer the reader to *The Collected Tales of Nikolai Gogol*, edited by Leonard Kent. Konstantin Mochulsky's *Dostoevsky, His Life and Work* provides a complete biography and chronology.

In the body of the text the system of transliteration, with minor exceptions, is that used in D.S. Mirsky's *History of Russian Literature*, which the reader may wish to consult for general background information as well. In the scholarly apparatus we use a modified Library of Congress system. This makes pronunciation easier for non-Russian-speakers without sacrificing accuracy for those doing research in Russian.

We would like to thank Wesleyan University and the Ford Foundation for generous grants which made our work possible. We are grateful to the late Dmitry Chizhevsky for permission to include his article, and to Peter Stetson for his fine translation of Bem's article. Thanks are also due to Nancy Martin for typing the manuscript. We are particularly indebted to Greta Slobin, Michael Holquist, Vadim Liapunov, Krystyna Pomorska and Roman Jakobson for their invaluable aid and comments. Roger, Bill, Ilona and Krista provided crucial patience and support.

INTRODUCTION

I

Influence studies have been in ill repute among literary scholars for at least the last half century—and deservedly so. The dangers inherent in such an approach are reason enough for this fact. It is impossible in most cases to prove conclusively the existence of a given influence, inasmuch as external features of style and theme are most often the common property of an entire generation of writers and too easily deceive the overeager investigator into mistaking convergences or coincidences for the direct influence of one writer on another.[1] Furthermore, a given influence, even if firmly established by literary and extraliterary documentation, may prove quite irrelevant for the total scheme of a writer's work and merely add to the catalogue of disconnected literary facts. Finally, there are "deep psychological and personal influences which are not reflected on the literary level at all."[2] But beyond these inherent dangers, the distrust of this particular avenue of research reflects a larger shift in the methodology of literary studies that has rendered the question of influences as such a marginal or insignificant problem.

This shift in methodology owes much to the heritage of Russian Formalism. The early Formalists attempted to establish a concrete poetics that would investigate individual works with the aim of determining the specific, intrinsic characteristics of verbal art: the emphasis was on "art as device" and on how particular works are made. This immanent approach reflected their insistence on the autonomy of literary studies and their rejection of social criteria and psychologism in the analysis of literature. Eikhenbaum's study, "How Gogol's 'Overcoat' Is Made," is an exemplary work of early Formalism in this respect. Rejecting the prevalent "social" interpretation of Gogol's short story and in particular of its so-called "humane" passage, Eikhenbaum focuses on the narrative devices that determine the composition of "The Overcoat" and examines the function that the "humane" passage fulfilled within that overall compositional system. The conclusions he reaches about the grotesque nature of the story could be generalized to include the writer's entire work, a point that Slonimsky was later to make in examining *Gogol's Comic Technique*,[3] or be seen in terms of Gogol's evolution as a writer (which Vinogradov criticizes him for failing to do—see p. 181 below), but Eikhenbaum limits himself primarily to the material at hand. His primary interest is an exhaustive investigation of a specific text as it relates to one area of poetics, namely the theory of the grotesque.[4]

The "immanent" method was developed by the Formalists in their pursuit of the object of literary science, the object here being taken as the "literariness" of a work, its specifically literary devices. While this method was valid in its attempt at descriptive adequacy and its avoidance of the value judgments that characterize traditional literary criticism, it was inadequate because of the splendid isolation it imposed on literary works, not only from the social and cultural context, but even from the context of literary history. Tynyanov, who grasped the historical nature of "literariness," asked: "Is the so-called 'immanent' study of a work as a system possible outside its correlation with the system of literature?"[5] He concluded that it was impossible, even in respect to contemporary literature. Even if individual works were understood not merely as sum totals of their devices but as systems, i.e. functional interdependencies of elements hierarchically ordered and with a "dominant," the dynamic and functional nature of literature as a whole could not be appreciated:

> It is exclusively in terms of its evolution that we shall be able to arrive at an analytical "definition" of literature. . . . Literature . . . is a dynamic verbal construction. The requirement of incessant dynamism is what brings evolution about, seeing that every dynamic system necessarily becomes automatized and a constructional principle of an opposite kind dialectically comes into play.[6]

Evolution was to become the primary factor in understanding literary processes that had previously been examined, more often than not statically, under the rubric of "influences."[7]

This concern with the dynamism of literary works underlies Tynyanov's essay on "Dostoevsky and Gogol." His primary concern is to demonstrate that Gogol's influence on Dostoevsky is a much more complicated problem than literary historians, content with tracing motifs or stylistic features, would have us believe. The question is not simply the circle of devices that Dostoevsky "borrowed" from Gogol, but what use he put them to and what his very selection can tell us about his work. Tynyanov circumscribes the problem of influence by pointing out the larger theoretical issue that subsumes it, namely the problem of literary polemics. Literary works do not exist in a vacuum; they are dynamic works which respond to the literary system preceding them. Tynyanov proposes two theoretical factors to use in analyzing what an author does with the devices he borrows from his predecessors: stylization and parody. The latter notion, which Tynyanov understands in its broad sense, is a fundamental characteristic of almost any literary work that challenges a given tradition. In the case of Dostoevsky it proves to be the determining characteristic of his early work.

The emphasis in later Formalism on the "evolutionary" dynamism underlying the structure of literary works and on their functional significance is apparent throughout Viktor Vinogradov's *The Evolution of Russian Naturalism* and particularly in the essay translated here, "The School of Sentimental Naturalism (Dostoevsky's *Poor Folk* against the Background of the Literary Evolution of the 1840s)." Vinogradov approaches Dostoevsky's first novel from two points of view which he labels the "functional, immanent" and the "retrospective, projective" approaches.[8] The first examines the work as a "self-contained system of stylistic interrelations, the functional basis of which is the immanent goal realized in the creation of the work"; the second "sketches the structuration of an artistic work against the background of chronologically contiguous, homogeneous literary structures, as the realization of a new synthesis of the forms presented in them and, consequently, as their transformation, or as an act of destroying the ruling styles by reviving and creatively regenerating outlived forms." Vinogradov finds the first method indispensible for the construction of a comprehensive "literary theory" or poetics, the second for a "literary history," but, as he stresses, the two approaches are "mutually interdependent and inseparable."

Vinogradov pays a great deal of attention to the "secondary" writers of the period in an attempt to elucidate the common "language of literature"[9] confronted by Dostoevsky at the beginning of his career. He makes a particular point of emphasizing that the devices and even the combinations of devices used by Dostoevsky that are often cited as the direct "influence" of Gogol are "collective—like the grammatical categories of a language; they are the accomplishment of a literary school."[10] Gogol's own work was misread by his contemporaries, who saw it only in the perspective of the school which it was thought to represent and therefore failed to discern its true evolutionary pattern. Vinogradov goes so far as to assert that "influence has no place" in a history of literature that is concerned with the "evolution of literary systems," since each system contains "in microcosm . . . the reflection of the forms of previous literary traditions and the potential tendencies of future transformations" into new systems. Devices which might be taken as influences because of external similarities "turn out to be internally motivated by the immanent evolution of the system," and "the principle of influence is superfluous for an historical elucidation" of these devices. As Victor Erlich has stated in his study of the Formalists' concern with "literary dynamics," the Formalists discovered that the essential thing in questions of influence was often "not what the 'lender' does best, but what the 'borrower' needs most."[11] Vinogradov's study is a fine analysis of how the system of a literary work fits into the system of literature of its time and exemplifies the type of literary history that the Formalists attempted to construct, one that would not simply "review a chaos of manifold phenomena and orders of phenomena."[12]

The final stage of Formalist literary theory was concerned with the problem of relating purely literary systems to social, psychological and cultural systems. The so-called "Bakhtin School," a group of scholars who tried to integrate Formalist methods with Marxist criticism, laid the groundwork for a solution of this problem.[13] They attempted to construct a general theory of discourse that could show how the various functions of language operate vis-à-vis the roles of "author," "reader," and "hero" in structuring the "ideology" (that is, the system of value judgments) of a literary work. Bakhtin's essay included here is from his book *Problems of Dostoevsky's Poetics* (first edition 1929), in which Bakhtin elaborated such a typology of discourse and applied it to Dostoevsky's works. The particular section deals with Dostoevsky's first two novels, *Poor Folk* and *The Double*, and it is interesting to see how Bakhtin extends the analyses of literary functions made by Tynyanov and Vinogradov within the wider framework of the social and psychological functions implicit in a work of literature. Bakhtin's book is one of the best pieces written about Dostoevsky, both from a critical and theoretical standpoint.

The one genuine "influence study" included here is by A.L. Bem, a sensitive literary critic who was not content with mere "juxtapositions" of themes and stylistically coincident passages. Bem examines the function of Gogol's "The Nose" as a subtext for Dostoevsky's *The Double*, using the method of "close reading." The fact of influence here is placed within the larger framework of Dostoevsky's polemic with Gogol, the theoretical basis for which was provided by the studies of Tynyanov and Bakhtin contained in this volume.

II

The early 1830s marked a crucial turning point in the history of Russian literature. Poetry, which had its "Golden Age" in the first quarter of the century, was giving way to prose. This shift can be at least partly explained by the fact that verse had been cultivated to such a point of excellence that even the mediocre poetry of the late 1820s was being written in a well-formed poetic language (in terms of vocabulary, syntax, meter, genres, etc.). Prose, on the other hand, was in a chaotic state and completely lacked norms of style and genre. It was split between two unreconciled poles: that of antiquated bookish language, which, despite Karamzin's reforms, basically dated to the XVIIIth century and was suitable only for "lofty" topics; and that of conversational speech, too crude to be used as a basis of the literary language. The crucial task of the literature of the time was to establish a prose language that could bridge the gap between the "high" and "low" level of Russian and serve as a basis for elaborating a range of genres and normative styles.[14]

The experiments of the late 1820s and the early 1830s in Russian prose ran the gamut from writing influenced by foreign models, especially in terms of syntax, to the stylized and folksy language of Dahl's fairytales[15] or the historical novels of the time. The latter, a return to Old Russian, was clearly impossible ("We should learn to speak in Russian and not just in fairy-tales," as Pushkin said).[16] By the beginning of the 1830s two types of prose had emerged: one which opposed itself to poetry by its simplicity and exact-ness of expression (best exemplified by the prose of the poet Pushkin); the other, "ornamental" prose that was oriented on verse, using rhythmic and declamatory patterns of speech. Boris Eikhenbaum puts it as follows: "As in France the line extending from Chateaubriand to Hugo is opposed to that ex-tending from Mérimée to Stendhal, so in Russia the prose of Marlinsky and Gogol, in part going back to the prose of Karamzin . . . is opposed to that of Pushkin."[17] "Ornamental" prose had the more immediate impact, since it permitted a greater range of styles.[18]

This opposition is strikingly illustrated by the appearance in 1831, a few months apart, of Pushkin's *Tales of Belkin* and Gogol's *Evenings on a Farm Near Dikanka*. Both were short-story cycles using the "frame" device, most likely derived from Walter Scott's "Tales of My Landlord,"[19] of having a fictitious "publisher or editor" introduce a group of stories written down by a central narrator and gathered from various "storytellers."

While Pushkin used anecdotal plots and concentrated on normalizing the prose style of his narrator, Gogol played the role of a "Russian Walter Scott" and submerged his readers in the "ethnography" of the Ukraine. His "Ukraine" was an amalgam of folklore and local legend and the German *Kunstmärchen* tradition,[20] with stereotyped figures from the Ukrainian pup-pet-theatre *(vertep)* acting out mechanical love intrigues, the interest of which was not in the situation but in the *telling*. The latter fact causes the comic side of the diabolic and fantastic to far outweigh their tragic side, as the concern with narrative devices and absurdities of everyday, vulgar language dominate every aspect of these tales.

Gogol's primary device in the *Evenings* was the *skaz*, narration pre-sented by a narrator distinct from the author and endowed with a verbal man-ner characterizing his personality and social milieu.[21] The formal features of this type of narration are amply demonstrated by "The Tale of Captain Ko-peykin" from Gogol's *Dead Souls* (1842), parts of which are quoted by Chi-zhevsky in his discussion of "The Overcoat" (see below, p. 142). In *Evenings* the comic effects of the *skaz* are as much a product of the context as of its formal characteristics. The narrator presents his story to a set of listeners who are part of a close circle of acquaintances. Many of his asides are elliptical, taking for granted his audience's comprehension, or, on the contrary, are elaborate and amplify details that would be of interest *only* to that audience. Yet the story is being read by a reader foreign to that circle, thus creating a comic disparity between the events of the "little" world of the provincial storyteller and their lack of significance in terms of the "greater" world of the educated reader. This is the germ of the grotesque as it will appear eleven years later in Gogol's "The Overcoat": "The situation or event described [is] contained in a world, small to the point of the fantastic, of artificial experiences . . . completely cut off from the larger reality" (Eikhenbaum, p. 132 below; cf. Chizhevsky on the same point, p. 150 below). This disparity between two sets of perceptions, the reader's and the narrator's, gives the author full scope to play with the larger disharmony between things as they exist and as they are spoken about. The anomalies of language, the seemingly innocent slips and mannerisms of the "storyteller's" speech, his play with words, mask the author's more purposeful and often more sinister play with the world.

In *Evenings* the *skaz* is motivated characterologically. The "publisher," Rudy Panko the Beekeeper, introduces his narrators with characterizations that serve to justify the varieties and types of style employed in the tales. Yet Gogol's *skaz* often sparkles with a display of verbal fireworks that cannot possibly be subsumed under the image of any one narrator: the author shows his hand. One finds in *Evenings* the two styles that are the earmark of Gogol's entire creative output. Vasily Rozanov was the first to isolate and describe these styles: "The features of the one rise infinitely upward, those of the other [descend] downward"—an opposition of "endless *lyricism*" and the "dead fabric" of naturalistic "waxen language."[22] In *Evenings* the "endless lyricism" is most apparent in the nature descriptions (as it will be in all of Gogol's works from the first volume of *Evenings* to the second volume of *Dead Souls*), which are based on the metaphorical rhetoric of late romanticism, with a particularly sentimental, idealistic tinge. This lyricism is also present in Gogol's imitations of the style of folk poetry, which have more in common with rhetorical, ornamental prose than they have with the folk tradition. One contemporary critic, Polevoy, labelled this element of Gogol's style "soaringly incomprehensible flights" of words. The other element, which has been characterized as Gogol's naturalistic style, is based on the rambling dialectal speech of his storytellers, whose inability to express themselves often borders on verbal pathology. In Gogol's mature style, naturalistic description is so extreme that it results in a confusion between people and things, between the animate and the inanimate. When Gogol transfers this latter style from the field of folklore plots to the novella-farce based on a grotesque anecdote, as in "The Tale of How Ivan Ivanovich Quarreled with Ivan Nikiforovich" (referred to henceforth as "The Two Ivans"), the first stylistic layer, that of "endless lyricism," is downgraded and deliberately misapplied. The narrator's style has by this point lost what little characterological motivation it had, and disintegrates

xvi

into a succession of verbal masks. This hybrid of inverted naturalism and lyricism distorts the fictional universe, and this in turn casts doubt upon reality itself.

In *Mirgorod* (1835), Gogol turns to a variety of different genres in his effort to transcend the limitations placed on him by material from the Ukrainian milieu. Besides "The Two Ivans," the volume contains "Old World Landowners," in which Gogol parodies the ancient and still popular sentimental genre of the idyll by introducing comic and ironic motifs that undercut the "idyllic" life of the old couple who are its heroes. The denouement, death in the shape of a black cat summoning Pulkheria Ivanovna, illustrates "the tragedy of insignificant events," which had been treated on a more vulgar, comic level in "The Two Ivans." In "Viy," Gogol uses the folkloristic demonology of *Evenings*, but describes the terrifying visions of the seminarian at the end of the story in such detail that contemporary reviewers were offended. The rhetoric of the story clearly shows the influence of that late and short-lived branch of French romanticism called the "école frénétique"[23] (see Vinogradov, p. 162 ff. below). The same is present to a lesser degree in Gogol's historical novel, *Taras Bulba*, particularly in the depiction of tortures and executions.

In 1835 Gogol also published *Arabesques,* a collection of assorted "odds and ends," including essays on history and culture and earlier attempts at historical fiction in the mode of the *école frénétique*, as well as three of Gogol's best stories: "The Portrait," "Nevsky Prospect," and "The Diary of a Madman." "The Portrait," a variation on the romantic *Kunstnovel*, is the weakest of the three. It traces the rise and fall of an artist who has ruined his talent through ambition and by "selling out to the Devil," with a rather facile "prehistory" in the second part explaining the origin of the demonic force of the portrait and the fantastic events that have issued from it. The second of the group, "Nevsky Prospect," is a masterpiece in which Gogol successfully completes the transition from the Ukrainian milieu of his earlier works to the Petersburg setting in a synthesis of his two lines of attack on the poetics of romantic idealization: "High" genres are subtly overturned and "low" genres portray the seamy side of life in a farcical manner. The story is constructed on the basis of two contrasting parallel plots. The first traces the unfortunate "Petersburg artist" Piskaryov's pursuit of a "perfect Bianca of Perugino" whom he encounters on Nevsky Prospect and who turns out to be a common prostitute; he cannot bear the disillusionment and kills himself. Here the *Kunstnovel* of Hoffmann and German Romanticism is mingled with motifs from the urban novels of the *école frénétique* and the incidental motif of opium derived from De Quincey.[24] The other plot is the story of Lieutenant Pirogov, who is out for easier prey, but instead gets involved with the wife of a solid (and drunken) German workman. It is basically a reworking in a vaudeville vein of an officer's anecdote about an unsuccessful seduction, with one farcical scene which mocks the romantic sources of the first plot (the quarrel between the two German workmen named Schiller and Hoffmann). These two plots are framed by a description of Nevsky Prospect inspired by the journalistic feuilleton then in vogue.[25] (This genre, which became popular when the *école frénétique* shifted from historical to urban settings, was the germ of the Russian "physiological sketch" that was to become the standard genre of the Natural School—cf. Vinogradov, p. 166ff. below.) In "Nevsky Prospect," Gogol reworks all three of these traditions—the romantic *Kunstnovel,* the urban novel of the *école frénétique*, and the journalistic feuilleton—and unifies them by the pervasive motif of delusion. The numerous demonic figures of the Ukraine have been transformed into the unobtrusive yet omnipresent demon of the capital who tempts its inhabitants according to their characters and "infatuations." As Andrei Bely quipped, *"Chort 'Vecherov' stal chertoi"* ("the devil of the *Evenings* became a trait").[26]

The last of these stories from *Arabesques* is "The Diary of a Madman." The original title of the story was to have been "The Diary of a Mad Musician," and there is little doubt that it was conceived at first as a romantic *Kunstnovel* about a mad artist. This theme, embodied most successfully in Gogol's Piskaryov, the "victim of a frantic passion" in "Nevsky Prospect," was a theme Gogol found most attractive. He was enthusiastic about his friend Prince V. Odoevsky's[27] projected cycle *The House of Madmen* and knew the stories published separately that were to have been included in it: "Beethoven's Last Quartet" (1831, in an issue of *Northern Flowers*[28] that also contained an early sketch by Gogol under the influence of Walter Scott and the *école frénétique*), "Opere del Cavaliere Giambatista Piranesi" (1832), and "The Improvissatore" (1833). All three were tales of madmen obsessed with an *idée fixe* based on their art, the best example being Piranesi and his unrealizable architectural dreams. In his unfinished comedy "The Order of St. Vladimir of the Third Class," Gogol used the romantic theme of the *idée fixe* while downgrading it by making his hero a petty official whose obsession is the attainment of a particular medal (the appropriate surrogate in the case of a man whose "art" is that of bureaucracy). In the play the hero ends up being metamorphosed in his fantasy into the object of his desires: he imagines himself to be "The Order," in a typically Gogolian reversal of the categories of animate and inanimate.

The hero of "The Diary of a Madman" is also a civil servant obsessed with status. His madness is sparked, however, not by his lack of success in obtaining a medal but by the hopelessness of his love for the daughter of the Director of his department. Yet this love is based precisely on his obsession with rank. It is presented not as a spontaneous love prohibited by his low position in life; rather, the cause of his love is the "exalted" status of the object of his passion. Poprishchin's obsession with rank is hinted at from the very beginning of the story. He announces: "Yes, I confess, it it weren't for the respectability [*blagorodstvo*: the word suggests "nobility"] of the work, I "tragic" for his characters consists only in their loss of prestige or the blow to their pride caused by the strange events: the "soul" remains unaffected, since it does not exist or has already been lost.

Viktor Vinogradov has amply demonstrated Gogol's indebtedness to the "nosological" literature of the first quarter of the nineteenth century, where "cut-off, baked, suddenly disappearing and reappearing noses constantly flashed before the reader's eyes."[32] This craze was launched in Russian literature by the publication in 1804-1807 of the Russian translation of Lawrence Sterne's *The Life and Opinions of Tristram Shandy* ("Slawkenbergius's Tale" in Book IV is particularly relevant), where the nose is the subject of absurd debate, an object of envy or ridicule, and the basis for puns with veiled sexual reference. The many idioms and paronomastic set phrases of the Russian language which contain the word "nose"[33] were combined by Gogol with the literary traditions of "nosology" and served as the basis of the story's events. In fact, the central event could be described as a literal "realization" of a witticism by Pushkin using one such idiom: "And thus you surely will be 'with the nose' [i.e., "in hot water," "made a fool of"] when you find yourself without a nose."[34] (This epigram has a sexual connotation, namely that the nose's loss is due to venereal disease, and this is one of the "real" explanations of the event that Gogol plays on in the story through his hints about Kovalyov's amorous exploits). The primitive adventure novel with an exotic setting suitable for relating the adventures of cut-off noses or heads (Persia was a favorite place of action) provides the basic motif for the plot of the first part of "The Nose," the tale of the cut-off and baked nose (cf. "The Story of the Baked Head" in chapter XLV of James Morier's *The Adventures of Hajji Baba of Ispahan*), but the setting is shifted to everyday St. Petersburg and the central exotic event is treated quite naturalistically: Ivan Yakovlevich and his wife are less astounded by the fantastic nature of the event than they are afraid of its practical consequences. Gogol uses, as well, anecdotal material from the journalistic "miscellany" *(smes')* of the period for various subplots. Several articles had appeared in the journals during the twenties and early thirties about the new branch of medicine called "rhinoplastics" (plastic surgery on noses), which reported the facts of the medical procedure in a semi-humorous vein using nose puns. They are the source for the episode in which Kovalyov appeals to the "medic" for aid in "attaching" his nose, but Gogol comically negates the possibility of such an operation by the absurd reply of the doctor, who informs Kovalyov that the nose "can, of course, be attached; I could, probably, attach it right now for you; but I assure you that it would be worse for you." The mock "panegyrics" to the nose, another, strictly humorous, variant of journalistic "miscellanies" of the time involving noses, treated the nose as a personification of the virtues of a man and as a "sign of his honor": Kovalyov's reactions to the loss of his nose follow precisely such a rationale, and the energy with which he goes about attempting to retrieve his nose outdoes that of the most mortally offended romantic hero.

The grotesque nature of the story rests on the absurdity of the initial premise that a nose can belong simultaneously to the category of things and of animate beings. The first part of the story portrays it as a "cut-off" nose and ends with it being tossed into the Neva by the barber Ivan Yakovlevich. The second part relates the exploits of the nose, disguised in the uniform of a State Councillor, Kovalyov's unsuccessful efforts to pursue and retrieve it or at least seek justice (he appeals first to a newspaper office and only then to the police), the nose's capture, and finally Kovalyov's attempt to put it back (which is as unsuccessful as his earlier attempt in the Kazan Cathedral to put the "Nose" in his proper place). The illusion of a connection between these two parts of the story is created by the formal indication in each of them that the nose in question is precisely that of Major Kovalyov and by the parallelism of the beginning and ending of each part (awakening, horror, action; "all is shrouded in fog"). But no firm connection is ever established, nor is any explanation given of how the nose came to be in either of its estranged forms. Instead, the only episode in which it seems that the two plots will merge into one and the nose's disconcerting metamorphosis will finally be explained only intensifies the absurdity by piling on yet another irrelevant fact. The police officer who has apprehended the "Nose" just as he was about to escape to Riga with a false passport returns the "nose," neatly wrapped up in a rag in his pocket, to Kovalyov. His comment—that luckily he had his glasses on at the time of the capture and was thus able to tell that it was no "gentleman" but a "nose"—in no way accounts for the transformation that must have occurred for the "Nose" to be in his pocket.

The final resolution (Part III) is as inexplicable as the initial event: the nose reappears suddenly "in its proper place." Major Kovalyov is led out of the labyrinth which the author had constructed around him and goes on his merry, philistine way. We see the heroes of Part I and II, the barber and Kovalyov, together in the shaving scene in which neither mentions what has transpired. The story ends with the author, after confessing that there is "much that is improbable" in his narrative, justifying the "reality" of the absurd events he has detailed: ". . . and after all, where aren't there incongruities? . . ." The plane of the fantastic and the plane of the real are completely merged in this "extraordinarily strange" everyday tale.

"The Nose" thereby attacks not only the thematics, but the very form of the fantastic literature of late romanticism, in which the planes of the real and the supernatural were placed in graceful parallelism and the transition one to the other carefully, if ambiguously, motivated.[35] In Hoffmann's "The Sandman" or Pushkin's "The Queen of Spades" (1834), which Dostoevsky was later to call "the pinnacle of the art of the fantastic,"[36] the essence of the fantastic lies precisely in the hesitation between an interpretation of the events that rationally explains their apparently supernatural character and one conceding the existence of the supernatural. Dostoevsky writes in regard to Pushkin's "The Queen of Spades": "You believe that Hermann really had a vision, and precisely in accordance with his world view, and yet at the end of the story, that is, having read it through, you don't know what to think. Did this vision emerge from the nature of Hermann, or is he really one of those who have come into contact with another world, [a world] of spirits evil and hostile to mankind? . . . Now this is art!"[37] The art Dostoevsky so admired was the author's ability to maintain the illusion of the impossible while offering sufficient motivation for its occurrence, in a way that forces the reader simultaneously to doubt and to believe in it.

Gogol's story is not a fantastic tale in essence, because of the absurd premise and the lack of hesitation between the real and the unreal. Although Gogol has his narrator or characters mention all the standard motifs used in the fantastic romantic short story to "explain the supernatural" (wine, rumor, dream, madness), he rejects them outright or plays with reversals of them. One such reversal is the catalogue of rumors that circulate about Kovalyov's story at the end of Part II. The usual function of rumors was to discredit the supernatural event (the rumors prove false or questionable) or to detail the real consequences of the character's folly after the event had proved a delusion; Gogol introduces rumors which themselves are called into doubt with particularly sharp irony. By debunking the rumors issuing from the fantastic event, he asserts the event's reality, which should have been more in question than the truth of rumors circulating in its wake. The total effect of the tale is not the hesitation between the real and the supernatural but the creation of a fictional universe terrifying in its detailed similarities to "vulgar," everyday reality yet impenetrable to the laws of common sense. Vinogradov catches much of the essence of the tale when he labels it a "naturalistic grotesque." "The Nose" contains in extreme form the essence of Gogol's later fiction, summarized by D.S. Mirsky in a few eloquent lines: "He made vulgarity reign where only the sublime and beautiful had reigned. This was *historically* the most important aspect of his work. Nor was the younger generation's general concept of him as a social satirist entirely unjustified. He did not paint (and scarcely knew) the social evils of Russia. But the caricatures he drew were, weirdly and terribly, *like* the reality around him; and the sheer vividness and convincingness of his paintings simply eclipsed the paler truth and irrevocably held the fascinated eye of the reader."[38]

"The Overcoat" is so thoroughly discussed in the articles by Eikhenbaum and Chizhevsky included here that it would be superfluous to treat the structure of the story or its place in Gogol's work in any more detail. It should be noted, however, that the story differs in many ways from *Dead Souls*, which was published the same year (1842). The *skaz* in *Dead Souls*, like that in "The Overcoat," has no consistent narrator. But the naturalistic presentation of "reality" is considerably heightened in *Dead Souls* by the careful delineation of the speech of the characters. The "verbal masks" that the characters wear are constructed in so convincing a manner and supported by so detailed a presentation of their gestures and environment that the reader fails to notice that they are just as much the narrator's "marionettes" as was Akaky Akakievich. In fact, hostile contemporary critics did not object to Gogol's treatment of his characters in *Dead Souls*, as they had in the case of Akaky Akakievich, but to his selection of such "low" types. (This was a continuation of Gogol's experiments in drama, e.g., *The Inspector General* [1836], where the illusion of the reality of characters was achieved by the convincingness of their spoken manner.)

The other respect in which the *skaz* in *Dead Souls* differs from that of "The Overcoat" is in its authorial digressions, which assume a consistency of theme and style that renders them a voice on a par with that of the characters. What results is a "verbal mosaic" of often antithetical elements. The main antithesis, that between the naturalistic descriptions and the sentimental "effusions" of the author, is intensified rather unsuccessfully in the chapters salvaged from the uncompleted Part II of *Dead Souls*. The increasingly moralistic tone of the author, couched in sentimental terms, was simply too grating against the background of the "low" themes and their naturalistic embodiment. In Part I of *Dead Souls*, the "verbal mosaic" held together because of Gogol's mastery in constructing various integral verbal masks (those of characters and narrator) in a polyphonic array; in Part II, it fell apart because of the predominance of one of those masks, that of the narrator-author's moralistic voice.

In Part II of *Dead Souls*, Gogol, whose entire work had been a polemic designed to undermine sentimentalism and romanticism, tried unsuccessfully to revive and reconcile sentimentalism with the naturalistic style, its "low" themes and characters, in whose name he had earlier rejected it. Dostoevsky, confronted by the heritage of Gogol's work as well as the extremes to which it had been taken by his imitators, succeeded in *Poor Folk* in accomplishing precisely what Gogol failed to do: a synthesis of naturalism and sentimentalism. The prevailing motivation in Gogol's case, his religious and moralistic orientation, had led to endless contradictions (cf. Tynyanov on the style of *Selected Passages from a Correspondence with Friends*, pp. 109 ff. below). Dostoevsky, for whom sentimentalism was merely a vehicle to transcend the limitations of crude naturalism, was able to combine naturalism and sentimentalism to achieve greater social and psychological depth, providing the foundations for the realistic prose of the second half of the century.

III

Dostoevsky led an isolated childhood, and early began to immerse himself in the world of fiction. His parents took him to see *The Robbers* when he was ten, as a result of which he conceived a passionate enthusiasm for Schiller. He read Derzhavin, Karamzin and Pushkin, and revelled in the novels of Walter Scott, which opened up a new exotic world to him. In "Petersburg Visions in Verse and Prose" (1861), Dostoevsky writes:

> . . . in my youthful fantasy I loved to imagine myself at times Pericles, or Caius Marius, or a Christian at the time of Nero, or a knight at the tournaments, or Edward Glendinning from Walter Scott's novel *The Monastery*, etc. etc. And what didn't I dream of in my youth. . . . There were no moments more full, holy and pure in my life. I was so lost in dreaming that I let my whole youth slip by me.[39]

Dostoevsky was intensely interested in literature, and his first works are predominantly concerned with literary reality. His early reading was mostly romantic, but around 1843 his tastes began to change, and while he was writing his first novel, *Poor Folk*, he was deeply impressed by Gogol's work. It was as a result of Gogol's vision of St. Petersburg which he found in "Nevsky Prospect" ("Everything is an illusion; everything is a dream") that Dostoevsky suddenly saw his surroundings with new eyes, as he later described in "Petersburg Visions":

> It seemed . . . that all this world, with all its inhabitants, both the strong and the weak, with all their habitations, whether beggars' shelters or gilded palaces, at this hour of twilight resembled a fantastic, enchanted vision, a dream which in its turn would instantly vanish and waste away as vapor into the dark blue heaven.[40]

Dostoevsky had come to perceive contemporary reality to be as fantastic as any romantic tale, and it is the task of his first stories to integrate the disparate literary world views of idealistic romanticism and Gogol's grotesque naturalism. The final result was what he called the "realism in a higher sense," the "fantastic realism" of his great novels.

The evolution that *Poor Folk* underwent in its three successive revisions from 1844 to April 1845, if Bem's hypothesis is correct,[41] contains in microcosm this movement away from romanticism towards naturalism. Dostoevsky started to write the novel in the typically romantic form of the confession of the young, wronged and helpless Varenka, possibly under the influence of Karamzin's sentimental tale *Poor Liza*, and only subsequently created the naturalist figure of Devushkin, whereupon the heroine's sentimental tale was restricted to Varenka's diary and assumed a secondary role. Similarly, in all of Dostoevsky's works written prior to his exile to Siberia in 1849, he performs a series of experiments in combining various elements of the sentimental and romantic traditions with naturalist themes and styles.

Dostoevsky's own evolution anticipated a turning point in the Natural School as a whole. The early physiological sketches which had provided the basis for the development of the Natural School were initially limited to the description of social groups, isolated by profession ("The Watercarrier," "The Organgrinders"), geographic location ("Petersburg Summits," "Moscow Markets"), or customs ("Weddings in Moscow," "Tea in Moscow"). The dominant focus was on the social milieu rather than on the individuals populating it.[42] Character was merely an adjunct of social type. But at the same time (around 1845), partly as a reaction against Gogol's epigones who had taken the comic short story to extremes of superficiality, and partly as a reaction against the limitations of "physiology," there was a reinfusion of sentimental elements which resulted in greater attention to the characters and less to their surroundings (see Vinogradov, p. 180 below). Using the later Gogolian model provided in "The Overcoat" and *Dead Souls*, and influenced by French philanthropic literature, the Natural School produced an offshoot called "sentimental naturalism" which attempted, often quite superficially, to inject notes of pathos into what remained essentially naturalist sketches. One group of writers, finding this view insufficient, called for a depiction of man based on his inner essence rather than on his external surroundings.[43] The leaders of this group, who belonged to the Petrashevsky circle, grounded their poetics in the philosophy of Utopian Socialism, and advocated the transformation of the physiological approach. Their literary-aesthetic principles were formulated in their most extreme form by Valerian Maikov, who, like the influential radical critic Belinsky, asserted that the role of belletristic literature was the popularization of socially important ideas. As opposed to Belinsky, however, Maikov and another member of the Petrashevsky circle, the poet Pleshcheev, advocated the examination of the depths of the soul in order to show how the social milieu formed and distorted human nature, in contradistinction to the "daguerrotype" sort of static depiction which gave no explanation of how the heroes became what they are. This approach followed from the utopian socialist principle of the innate goodness of man: in order to undo the damage wrought on the individual by society, one had to understand the mechanism at work.

> The sight of any sore is disgusting; but when you meet it not in the illustrations of a medical article . . . but on the body of a live person in whom you recognize your brother, a second self, —no matter what class he belongs to . . . —love will awaken in you, you will feel that sore on yourself, you will seize your own breast and feel with your own nerves that same pain which brings spasms to the limbs of your brother.[44]

It is utopian socialist ideology that motivates Dostoevsky's reinterpretation of Gogol. As a youth Dostoevsky had read the novels of George Sand

and Balzac which raised social questions, and the ideas of French Utopian Socialism were being discussed in the journals he read by the second half of the 1830s. His association with Belinsky, whom he met in May of 1845, when the critic read the manuscript of *Poor Folk* and acclaimed it as the first Russian social novel, reinforced Dostoevsky's literary concern with social questions. In his own words, he at first "passionately accepted all [Belinsky's] teachings."[45] But Belinsky's atheism quickly alienated Dostoevsky, who in 1847 became a member of the Petrashevsky circle, the members of which based their socialism on the ideal of Christian brotherhood. Like Fourier, Saint-Simon and Lamennais, they believed in a kind of religious humanism in which the highest values were man's right to equality and dignity. These ideals of the brotherhood of man are at the basis of Dostoevsky's tales about the poor clerk.

Another contributing factor to Dostoevsky's rethinking of naturalist poetics was Hoffmann's work. During the craze of Russian Hoffmannism in the 1820s, which continued into the 1830s,[46] Hoffmann's influence was primarily thematic and formal. Dostoevsky returns, however, to the psychological dimension of the fantastic in Hoffmann, which had been previously explored by Pushkin in "The Queen of Spades." Dostoevsky had read all of Hoffmann in German and/or Russian by the time he was seventeen, and in his early period, particularly in *The Double* and *The Landlady*, reinterprets Gogol's treatment (whether serious, as in "A Terrible Vengeance," or parodic, as in "The Nose") of romantic themes using Hoffmann's psychologism. Like Hoffmann, Dostoevsky makes use of the fantastic within a realistic setting, and achieves grotesque effects by the juxtaposition of the extraordinary to the everyday. But in Hoffmann's Berlin stories the fantastic takes the form of events whose reality is ambiguous, accepted by some characters whose sanity is in question and rejected by others who take a "practical" view. The author reserves judgment and leaves the reader vacillating on the borderline between reality and fantasy. For Dostoevsky, however, the fantastic results from the refraction of reality through the abnormal consciousness of the hero. The grotesque in Dostoevsky is a product of the tension between the external world as seen through another's eyes and the inner reality of the hero's consciousness.[47] And to emphasize the inherent disparity between these two views, Dostoevsky portrays abnormal consciousnesses which are distorted either by physical disease (delirium is the source of the unconscious in its purest state, as in "Mr. Prokharchin," *The Landlady*, and later, *Crime and Punishment*), or by mental disorders. The heroes in *The Double* and "A Faint Heart" go insane, while Devushkin and the dreamer in *White Nights* simply have distorted views of the world, the result of injured pride (Devushkin) or bookish isolation (the Dreamer).

Dostoevsky's first three works, *Poor Folk, The Double,* and "Mr. Prokharchin" (all published in 1846), take the naturalist theme of the petty clerk and reinterpret it, using sentimental and romantic elements to add the moral and psychological dimensions Dostoevsky found contained in Utopian Socialism and in Hoffmann's work. *Poor Folk* uses the sentimental form of the correspondence between two lovers, *The Double* combines the mock heroic epic (via Gogol's "Two Ivans" and *Dead Souls*) with the German romantics' favorite theme of the double and attendant madness, and "Mr. Prokharchin" also uses a romantic theme, that of the miser whose "bedscreens are the walls of his castle" while his treasure chest stands "deep below" (under his bed).[48] In each case the implicit juxtaposition to the earlier tradition is used to motivate the naturalist thematics, and the embodiment of these thematics Dostoevsky finds in Gogol's work.

The choice of Gogol is of course an obvious one, as he dominated literature at the time Dostoevsky was forming his style, but there are more specific reasons as well. Gogol had taken the theme of the petty clerk, which had become a mere comic convention, and made it into a moral allegory by the reinfusion of sentimental elements. In the process, he touched on a set of motifs central to Dostoevsky's thoughts about the clerk's psychology, as in "Diary of a Madman." Dostoevsky rejects the taxonomic and comic treatments of Petersburg "low life" to return to Gogol and extract what Dostoevsky saw as the essence of his predecessor's writing.

Dostoevsky replaces Gogol's religious morality with the ideology of Utopian Socialism. Gogol pits his poor clerk against representatives of power who assume allegorical status—The Important Personage, The General; Dostoevsky presents the clerk's social milieu less allegorically by surrounding his heroes with an array of secondary characters—Pokrovsky, Gorshkov—whose similar fates serve to generalize the hero's experience.[49] As Valerian Maikov put it, "For [Gogol] the individual is important as a representative of a given society or circle; for [Dostoevsky] the society itself is interesting for its influence on the personality of the individual."[50] Gogol had applied motifs used in the high genre of German romanticism, "imposture," schizophrenia and ambition, to the figure of the "little man." But Gogol characteristically renders animate objects inanimate: his use of metonymy transforms people into mere appendages of their clothing, facial features, or names, using grotesque verbal masks to obliterate human personality. Dostoevsky also wanted to rework the same romantic motifs using the poor clerk. Repelled by Gogol's depersonalization of his heroes, who were typically inarticulate, Dostoevsky had his characters reveal themselves through their verbal manner. Thus while it is possible to say that Dostoesky was "correcting" Gogol by humanizing his heroes, it is also true that Dostoevsky saw himself as continuing Gogol's attempts at adding greater depth to the comic convention of the poor clerk.

Central to Dostoevsky's interpretation of the utopian socialist ideal of the integrity of the individual is the concept of pride, which is the motivating factor at the deepest level in his early clerk stories and later assumes metaphysical scope in the great novels. His downtrodden clerks, deprived of their human dignity by the hierarchical bureaucratic system, develop an exaggerated sense of pride, which they feel they are not "permitted" by their station, and to which they therefore react, consciously or unconsciously, by assuming a meek stance or deliberately humiliating themselves. This alternation between pride and humility, between arrogance and submissiveness, can also be found in Gogol's petersburg tales. Poprishchin, on the one hand, is in awe of aristocracy, but on the other, he rebels in his madness against his limitations by becoming one of the authorities—in fact, the highest possible—the King of Spain. Major Kovalyov too aspires to rise in the ranks, but is obsequious to his Nose, who has achieved its owner's ambition. But Dostoevsky finds Gogol's treatment lacking in motivation, and sets himself the task of analyzing the psychology of the clerk: how is this disorder brought about and how does it manifest itself?

Factors impinging upon the clerk's sense of dignity, which Gogol had treated externally, Dostoevsky reexamined from the point of view of the clerk himself. The subordinate's relationship to his superiors is of course a determining element in his view of self, and Dostoevsky emphasizes the degree to which the clerk is deprived of equal status even by his superiors' benevolence. In *Poor Folk*, Dostoevsky responds to "The Overcoat" on this point: while Akaky is destroyed by being "raked over the coals " by the Important Personage, Devushkin is shown to be morally and psychologically destroyed by his superior's kind gift of a hundred rubles. His very gratitude betrays an acceptance of a system in which one man may humiliate another by bestowing charity on him. That the victim of the order of things may praise his exploiter for humiliating him and not even notice it demonstrates the degree to which he has been convinced that he is undeserving of human dignity. This idea is taken to extremes in "A Faint Heart" (1847), in which the poor clerk Vasya Shumkov goes mad partly as a result of his employer's "benevolence." Yulian Mastakovich gives Shumkov some papers to copy for extra pay and the clerk's anxiety over failing to meet the deadline drives him insane. He feels guilty toward his superior, whom he regards "as a father," imagining that the authorities will punish him by inducting him into the army. Mastakovich, in fact, underpays him, but Shumkov's mere perception of benevolence, which is again the product of feelings of inferiority, destroys him and is used by his superior to exploit him. As Dostoevsky notes, it is "pleasant for the authorities" to have their subordinates relate to them as a father.[51]

The concept of pride is further explored in the theme of the poverty that dooms the poor man to humiliation. Dostoevsky analyzes poverty in terms of its psychological effects on the poor. He has Devushkin himself comment on the hypersensitivity of the poor man:

He, the poor man, is exacting. He even views God's world differently and looks askance at each passerby while at the same time he casts about an embarrassed glance and listens attentively to every word—aren't they talking about him? Aren't they asking why he's such an unsightly sort? (Letter of August 1)

Poverty is synonymous with lack of power: it renders one helpless, and hence intimidated and submissive. Dostoevsky's poor clerks differ from the clerk traditionally portrayed in naturalist stories in that they all intuitively understand their oppressed position and the factors determining it. Furthermore, they attempt to preserve some sense of psychological integrity, of "a place of one's own," and their personal tragedies result from their need to do so.

Makar Devushkin, Mr. Golyadkin and Mr. Prokharchin are rebels. They try to assert themselves against the overwhelming forces that govern their lives at the same time as they guiltily deny doing so. Each rebels in a different way, and is punished for his transgression by ruin, madness or death. Devushkin rebels against the social definition of himself that he finds in Gogol's depiction of Akaky Akakievich, and does so through literature: he rejects the role of the inarticulate soulless automaton suggested by Akaky and asserts his personality through his letter-writing. His letters to Varenka are as concerned with their own literary quality as with communication. His love for Varenka is more a literary manifestation than a real love; almost all of their association takes place on paper. Devushkin needs her not as a woman but as the literary character she is: the recipient of love letters in a romantic novel. For Devushkin she is the reason to write, his muse, his inspiration, without whose implicit response his letters would lose their meaning and hence fail as a means of confirming his spiritual dimension. His last letter talks as much of letter-writing as of their parting:

> "It simply can't be that this is the last letter. How can it be suddenly, precisely, absolutely the last! No, I'll write, and you write . . . . And just now when my style was taking shape. . . . Akh, my dear, what is style! Right now I don't know what I'm writing, I don't know at all, I don't know anything, and I'm not rereading it, and I'm not correcting the style, but I'm writing just to write, just to write to you a little more. . . ."

The end of his correspondence signifies the end of his life as a full human being, and we surmise that he will probably drink himself to death in the corner of his kitchen. It is his guilt over his protest, his "free-thinking," opposing the "natural order of things," that prevents Devushkin from transcending his grief.

The question of guilt plays a more prominent role in *The Double*, where

Mr. Golyadkin's rebellion is both more total and more pathological than Devushkin's. Unable to attain a position of respect and ashamed even to admit that he has such aspirations, he develops a schizoid self in order to realize them. The irony of his wanting to become one of his oppressors is demonstrated by having him be persecuted by his very success: his double is a parody of his superiors and of his aspirations. His guilt about his "ambition"—his pursuit of position and the boss's daughter—is manifest in his constant denial of it, in all his hints about masks and imposture. He knows, at some level, that he himself is the impostor, that like Grishka Otrepiev (the False Dmitri) he wants to snatch the crown under false pretenses. The oscillation between extreme humility and inflated pride is nowhere better shown than in Golyadkin's monologue to Dr. Rutenspitz in Chapter II:

> I, Krestyan Ivanovich, have nothing to hide from you. I'm a little man, you know yourself, but, to my good fortune, I don't regret that I am a little man. Even the reverse, Krestyan Ivanovich, and, to say it all, I am even proud that I am a little man, and not an important one.

In *The Double*, Dostoevsky elaborates the tragic dimension of the problem Gogol treated comically in "The Nose": that of the human personality faced with conflicting personal and social pressures. The basis of Golyadkin's ambition is the desire for power; the allusions to the False Pretender are the remnants of an idea that Dostoevsky removed from his final version (cf. Bem, p. 245 below).

"Mr. Prokharchin" also contains elements of social protest, but these are very obscure because the story was severely mutilated by the censor; even the word *chinovnik*, "civil servant" or "petty clerk," was removed from the manuscript. Nicholas I was said to have based his bureaucratic hierarchy on five thousand department heads; therefore Prokharchin's fear that his job will be eliminated and his entire department shut down could be read as a suggestion of the instability of Nicholas I's regime.[52]

Prokharchin is also a rebel, but whereas Devushkin rebelled through literature and Golyadkin through position, he rebels using money. His hoarding, like Golyadkin's careerism, is the bid of a helpless puppet for power. The point of the story is revealed when Mark Ivanovich asks Prokharchin if he thinks he is Napoleon. The "idea of Napoleon," later developed more fully in *Crime and Punishment*, is the transgression of moral law. Prokharchin tries to overstep his decreed bounds by grasping for the power that money bestows and is reassured by the simple knowledge that he possesses his fortune. But unlike Raskolnikov, he is only unconsciously aware that he has transgressed against humanity by refusing to share its lot: while Raskolnikov wants to become Napoleon by his theft (of another hoarded treasure), Prokharchin is horror-stricken when the idea is made explicit. In Prokharchin's delirious dream, he understands his guilt, which is essentially the same as Raskolnikov's: he has cut himself off from his fellow man. Raskolnikov does this by his crime, also a product of exaggerated pride; Prokharchin by his isolation behind his screens, by hoarding, and by another form of imposture, his pretended poverty.

Like Devushkin and Golyadkin, Prokharchin is ruined by his attempt to transcend the limitations imposed on him by society. He goes mad from fear of his own "free-thinking," imagining—like Vasya Shumkov in "A Faint Heart"—that he will be conscripted into the army. His rebellion, like Golyadkin's, is perverted by the pathological fear instilled in him by his hopeless situation, and the ambivalence both feel about achieving their goals drives them insane.

"Polzunkov" (1848), while it does not belong to this "trilogy," as Terras calls the first three stories,[53] has thematic similarities to them. Polzunkov too oscillates between pride and its opposite, which here takes the form of self-humiliation. Polzunkov is the prototype of Dostoevsky's "voluntary buffoon," the predecessor of Marmeladov in *Crime and Punishment*, who seeks to abase himself by provoking others to laugh at him, thereby attempting to expiate his guilt. Polzunkov, like the three previous clerks in Dostoevsky's work, attempts to challenge the authorities: he tries to gain power over his superior by blackmail. Like Golyadkin and Poprishchin before him, he seeks the hand of the boss's daughter. And he too is thwarted and left in his lowly and frustrating position.

The themes discussed above are common to Dostoevsky's early stories about the clerk. But it is Dostoevsky's style that contains the more radical innovations and conveys the essence of his philosophy. As Bakhtin has shown,[54] the ideology underlying Dostoevsky's style consists in his making the hero the subject of literature, rather than its object. This is the key to Devushkin's reaction to "The Overcoat": he is enraged by the image of Akaky not because he perceives him as a lifeless marionette—on the contrary, he readily recognizes himself in him ("What if I do tiptoe at times to save my boots?")—but because he feels that the author has exposed him by describing him from an unsympathetic, condescending point of view. Hence his positive evaluation of a story about another pitiable "little man," Pushkin's "The Stationmaster" from the *Tales of Belkin*. Samson Vyrin's poverty and humiliation are no less than Akaky's or Devushkin's but Pushkin's narrator is not only sympathetic, he places no distance between himself and Vyrin.[55] Vyrin is viewed as an equal, whereas Akaky is examined through the eyes of "the other."

This principle of the author's democratic relationship to his characters is the basis of Dostoevsky's stylistic and architectonic experiments in his early work. It is the motivation for Devushkin's first person self-revelation in his letters, and for the complex system (see Bakhtin, pp. 255-65 below) of narration in *The Double* which compels the reader to be both inside and outside Mr. Golyadkin's mind simultaneously. But the final product is a reality which can only be understood through the consciousness of the hero. The seemingly unanswered questions about the reality of Golyadkin's correspondence, of what actually happened with the ten fish pastries in the coffee house, are all resolved if one understands the entire novel as the representation, the transcription, of Golyadkin's unconscious. Even the stylistic parody of the mock heroic narration can be understood as the voice of "the other," so feared that it has become internalized by Golyadkin as a commentary on the battle he sees himself waging against the enemy. Precisely this portrayal of the character's unconscious was misunderstood by contemporary critics, whose scathing response so upset Dostoevsky that he was moved to answer them in "Mr. Prokharchin," not, as has been suggested, by greater economy of expression,[56] but by simplifying this stylistic device.[57] He does this by isolating the voices of Prokharchin's unconscious instead of merging them in the narration. What had been Golyadkin's self-justifications in *The Double* are put in the mouth of Prokharchin's alter ego Zimoveykin. Golyadkin says "I'm pure, I'm straightforward, orderly, pleasant, gentle"(Ch. 6), whereas Zimoveykin tells Prokharchin: "You're not a touchy person, you're attractive, amiable! You're simple, you're virtuous. . . ." In "Mr. Prokharchin," each element is attributed to a separate character, a principle which Dostoevsky was to develop to enormous complexity in his novels. Thematically, the elements are simplified: the mask is reduced to pure pretense—Prokharchin claims to be poor; imposture is stripped of the attributes of rank and position and simplified to the pure bid for power through money. Mark Ivanovich assumes the role of the accuser, and his speech is markedly differentiated from all the others; it is a parody of high style,[58] just as the voice of the narrator in *The Double* at times parodies the high style of the heroic epic. It is Mark Ivanovich who conducts the investigation into Prokharchin's motivations, just as Porfiry torments Raskolnikov by playing upon his guilt. The taunts of the "other" are separated from Mark Ivanovich's probes, and are taken up by the chorus of lodgers. They contribute to Prokharchin's demise by teasing him with false rumors, which contain the image of what Prokharchin is supposed to be, an image which hinges upon belonging to a social world which he has deliberately cut himself off from. And true to Dostoevsky's philosophy, Prokharchin himself reveals his own unconscious in his delirium, since, like Akaky Akakievich, he lacks a conscious dimension. Here his full guilt before suffering humanity is described: the nightmare scene in which the unfortunate are gathered contains the people Prokharchin has wronged, whether actually (the cabbie he cheated) or indirectly (the coworker whose plight is even more dire than Prokharchin's own). And it contains a parody of Prokharchin's shameless niggardliness in the person of the woman who worries about her own misfortunes while she is surrounded by others' disasters.

"Mr. Prokharchin" contains Dostoevsky's first fictional embodiment of the buffoon, the "mooching boozer" Zimoveykin, who is Prokharchin's cohort in debauchery, the one responsible for having led him astray. Zimoveykin is clearly intimately involved in Prokharchin's rebellion, because he is able to terrorize him with the threat of giving him away and "telling all." His having lost his job "for the truth" suggests that he too may have been guilty of "free-thinking." This hypothesis may be supported by the close relationship Zimoveykin bears to the "green gentleman," also a "boozer," who appears in Nekrasov's "Petersburg Lodgings,"[59] published the year before "Mr. Prokharchin" was written. The boozer was fired from one job "for writing poetry," then fired from the next for his drunkenness and replaced by a "married man," and there are a number of other details relating Nekrasov's story to Dostoevsky's. The "green gentleman" bears a marked resemblance to Marmeladov. He speaks in high-flown language, tries to preserve his lost dignity and at the same time drinks in order to humiliate himself by way of self-punishment. The character of Prokharchin contains the seeds of Raskolnikov, and he is closely connected to Zimoveykin, who will evolve into Marmeladov. Like Raskolnikov and Marmeladov, Prokharchin and Zimoveykin are connected to each other as variations on the theme of crime and punishment.

"Mr. Prokharchin" may be read as another response to "The Overcoat." In *Poor Folk*, Dostoevsky had replaced the stammering Akaky Akakievich with an articulate clerk. Mr. Prokharchin, however, is even more dehumanized than Akaky, scrimping on food and laundry in the name of his obsessional goal, but Gogol's concept of an "infatuation" dominating his heroes' psyches in a demonic way is here recast by Dostoevsky as the problem of diseased consciousness obsessed with an "idea." The terror felt by the "little man" at his helplessness that ultimately drives Prokharchin mad can be seen in Akaky's dumb-struck reaction to Petrovich's announcement that he needs a new overcoat. The essence of the underlying principle is revealed: money, as a representation of power, becomes an abstract symbol of the self-affirmation Dostoevsky's early heroes crave. But because the means become obsessional, the desire for self-affirmation itself is distorted into a thirst for power which will sacrifice everything to attain its goal. In Pushkin's "Queen of Spades," Hermann's fanatical hunger for money in the name of power leads him to kill an old lady. In the character of Raskolnikov, Dostoevsky develops this motif, adding the "idea of Napoleon": although Raskolnikov is confused about his motivation for killing the pawnbroker, once again money is connected with a pathological desire to rise above one's fellow man, which isolates the hero and drives him to delirium. In "Mr. Prokharchin," Dostoevsky had likewise taken the concept of the miser "with an idea" from Pushkin, whose "Covetous Knight" cuts himself off from his son and the world around him in the name of his treasure.[60] Prokharchin's "treasure" with its "inheritance" of useless trash, like Akaky's "legacy" of old buttons discovered at his death, illustrates the material and spiritual poverty of the hero's life, but for Prokharchin, the trunk is a decoy masking his "Napoleonism."

After the resounding failure of "Mr. Prokharchin," which seemed to critics a step backwards because of its extreme elaboration of the comic grotesque, Dostoevsky abandoned that particular Gogolian mode. He himself felt he had exhausted the variations on the poor clerk theme combining sentimental and romantic elements and Utopian Socialism with the grotesque of Gogol's Petersburg tales. His next story, "Polzunkov," tempers the grotesque in order to present the theme of the brotherhood of man more effectively.

The descriptive sketches of the Natural School tradition all presented the low hero through the eyes of an educated narrator, and Dostoevsky uses this form to advance once again the ideals of Utopian Socialism. In "Polzunkov," the educated narrator, rather than being implicitly condescending to his hero, points out his intrinsic worth and "goodness of heart." And just as Devushkin had spoken for himself, Polzunkov tells his own tale in a folksy, pun-ridden *skaz* which is highlighted by the bland, educated speech of the narrator. But while Devushkin only imagines the voice of the foreign "other," in "Polzunkov" this "other" is embodied in the mocking audience whom Polzunkov panders to, telling a story at his own expense precisely for their benefit. Polzunkov is the second fictional incarnation of Dostoevsky's "voluntary buffoon," and the motive for his drive to self-humiliation is not provided. Dostoevsky was simultaneously working on what he intended to be his first full-scale novel, *Netochka Nezvanova,* in which the buffoon figure is more fully elaborated in the person of Efimov, the direct predecessor of Marmeladov in *Crime and Punishment,* both of whom are guilty of ruining their families. Polzunkov's guilt is of a more anecdotal nature, in the same vein as other short stories Dostoevsky turned out in 1848 to pay his debts ("Another Man's Wife," "A Christmas Tree and a Wedding"). One of these stories, however, continues the direction of "Polzunkov" in moving further away from the grotesque towards the sentimental. "An Honest Thief" has the same narrative structure of a story within a story: a framing tale introduces a second narrator who tells a tale about a lower-class hero, the buffoon and "honest thief" Yemelyan. The sympathy of this narrator for Yemelyan, unlike the grotesque relationship between Polzunkov and his audience, evokes pity for the hero. These two stories, and the experiments with the authorial first person Dostoevsky conducts in the four journalistic feuilletons known as the "Petersburg Chronicle" (1847), consitute a transitional stage in which sentimental elements come to outweigh the grotesque.

The Gogolian devices Dostoevsky applied in his first works caused the critics to overlook his humanism. Golyadkin's tragedy did not show through the comic grotesque narration clearly enough for contemporaries to distinguish *The Double* from other stories which had made comic use of the *doppelgänger* motif, just as they did not understand the full implications of Hoffmann's tales. Dostoevsky saw that the naturalist grotesque had undermined his intentions in both "Mr. Prokharchin" and *The Double*, and abandoned this style, as well as the theme of the poor clerk, in favor of a more emotionally expressive mode in his next work, *The Landlady* (1847). Here he reinterprets the folk poetic and thematic elements of Gogol's Ukrainian tales by placing them in the setting of St. Petersburg. As Andrei Bely put it, "The early Dostoevsky flowed out of the style of the mature Gogol, while late Dostoevsky came from the thematics of early Gogol brought down from the clouds: life."[61]

In *The Landlady* Dostoevsky analyzes the problem of the strong personality's domination of the weak using the thematics of Gogol's "A Terrible Vengeance."[62] Katerina's story in *The Landlady* is the same as Katerina's in "A Terrible Vengeance," but whereas Gogol's version of incest between father and daughter is put in terms of the supernatural, Dostoevsky provides the psychological underpinnings. Gogol's sorcerer summons his daughter's soul during her sleep, but Murin's power is psychological, and the daugher's participation in ousting her mother as a rival is underlined when her mother curses Katerina for her betrayal.

Dostoevsky develops the folk element of "A Terrible Vengeance" not only by setting Katerina's tale on the Volga, but in her speech as well. Like Devushkin, who writes in a distinctive blend of office jargon, folk sayings, diminutives and misused words from literary language,[63] like Golyadkin, whose speech reflects the dynamic of his schizophrenia, and like Prokharchin with his occasional outbursts of disconnected particles, the character of Katerina is formed by her melodic, rhythmic verbal image. Dostoevsky had first sketched the outline for such a female folk figure in the character of another "landlady," Ustinya Fyodorovna, in "Mr. Prokharchin," who is also distinguished by her cooing folk intonation. And as in "Mr. Prokharchin," the hero is revealed through his delirium. Bem's convincing hypothesis that much of the action, especially the erotic scenes between Katerina and Ordynov, is the "dramatization of [Ordynov's] delirium" helps to explain contemporary critics' inability to comprehend *The Landlady*: once again they had misunderstood Dostoevsky's portrayal of the unconscious and read him literally. In "A Terrible Vengeance," it is Katerina who is unconscious of her true motivations; in *The Landlady* the heroine understands herself and the focus is shifted to the hero's developing self-awareness.

Ordynov has led the isolated life of a "dreamer," a type Dostoevsky first describes in his "Petersburg Chronicle":

They settle themselves for the most part in a deep solitude, in inaccessible corners, as though trying to hide themselves from people and from the world, and in general when one first glances at them, something melodramatic strikes the eye. . . . They love to read [. . .] but usually after the second or third page they lay the reading aside, for they are completely satisfied. Their fantasy, animated, soaring, light, is already stimulated, an impression has been fashioned; and an entire dream world with its joys, with its sorrows, with heaven and hell, with captivating women, with heroic exploits, with noble pursuits, always with some sort of gigantic struggle, with crimes and all sorts of horrors, suddenly seizes possession of the dreamer's whole being. The room disappears, and space as well; time comes to a halt or flies so quickly that an hour seems as though it were but a minute.

The dreamer becomes dependent on his own fantasies and divorced from reality:

At last [. . .] he completely loses that moral instinct by means of which a person is capable of appreciating all the beauty of the real, [. . .] and in his state of apathy lazily folds his hands and does not want to know that human life is the continual contemplation of self in nature and in day-by-day reality [. . .] And is not such a life a tragedy! Is it not a sin and a horror! Is it not a caricature![64]

"Mr. Prokharchin" presents a "low" comic-grotesque variant of the dreamer; Ordynov represents the romantic "elevated" dimension of the type, which explains the extreme emotionalism of this Petersburg version of the romantic "tale of terror," in which Belinsky saw a synthesis of "Marlinsky and Hoffmann, with a little Gogol thrown in."[65] The motif of two "faint hearts" struggling to free themselves from the domination of a stronger father figure may well have been suggested to Dostoevsky by Hoffmann's story, "The Mistake," in which the young Baron Theodor, also a dreamer, is, like Ordynov, not strong enough to free the heroine from her captivity. Dostoevsky, however, provides the motivation: as Murin explains, "Let him have his sweet will, the weak individual; he'll wrap it up himself, he'll carry it back to you." Like the Grand Inquisitor, Murin understands the terrible burden of freedom.

Whether the specific use of Gogol and Hoffmann is unconscious or not, it is clear that Dostoevsky deliberately chose the romantic mode to convey the elevated dimension of some ideas he had already broached. Katerina is more Ordynov's projection born of his bookish intensity than she is a real character, just as Varenka was a literary phenomenon for Devushkin. The idea of the dreamer gains substance in Ordynov who, immersed in his solitary work, is endowed with some of Dostoevsky's own experience, and who, unlike Prokharchin, is aware that he is isolated in his own fantasy. Dostoevsky's next serious work explores the character of the dreamer further but without the fantastic coloration and hyperbolic emotionalism that had caused the failure of *The Landlady*.

Subtitled "a sentimental novel," *White Nights* (1848) follows the romantic tradition of breaking the tale into "nights." It is written in the form of a confession by a first-person narrator who develops out of the authorial persona of the "Petersburg Chronicle," a character as closely autobiographical in a literal sense as any in Dostoevsky's work, and whose next incarnation is Ivan Petrovich, the author of a book resembling *Poor Folk*, in *The Insulted and Injured*. The dreamer hero has none of Ordynov's hysteria; of all Dostoevsky's early works, *White Nights* is the freest from grotesque elements of either high or low type. While the importance of the dreamer's very personal perception of the Petersburg setting relates him to Gogol's Piskaryov in "Nevsky Prospect," *White Nights* is closer to German romantic idealism in its confessional form, ornamental language, and thematics of the dreamer than any other of Dostoevsky's works. The idea of the dreamer was a favorite theme in Hoffmann and other romantics, but the stress on its negative aspect was Dostoevsky's. By giving oneself over to fantasy, one cuts oneself off from one's fellow man, when all men should share equal responsibility for each other. This idea contributes to the ruin of another dreamer, Vasya Shumkov of "A Faint Heart"; he is about to get married, but feels undeserving of his sudden happiness. As his friend says, Vasya wants there to be "no unhappy people on earth when he gets married." He cannot allow himself to be happy because he will no longer be sharing the lot of his fellow men, and this, mixed with his guilt before his employer, drives him insane. Shumkov, modeled on Yakov Butkov,[66] dreams of an ideal brotherhood of man, reflecting Dostoevsky's involvement with Utopian Socialism during that period.

Netochka Nezvanova, Dostoevsky's last major work of his early period, was conceived in the spring of 1846, but Dostoevsky was unable to find time to work on it, so that only the first part appeared by February 1849 and the novel was left unfinished after his arrest. The first episode of Part I, in particular, is interesting in the context of Dostoevsky's relationship to the Natural School. He was writing *Netochka* at a time when he was disenchanted with the Natural School, and therefore chose a romantic theme which had been used by Hoffmann, Odoevsky, Polevoy and others, that of the mad musician. The novel is written in the form of Netochka's confession, and it is possible that, after the shattering failures of *The Double*, "Prokharchin," and *The Landlady*, Dostoevsky was returning to his only success, *Poor Folk*. His first novel, the autobiography of an unfortunate girl who loses her mother, was originally to have taken the form of Varenka's confession, written in a sentimental style. Netochka's tale follows this basic scheme, but here the heroine remains the central figure both stylistically and thematically. The naturalist figure of Devushkin in the role of romantic lover is replaced by the naturalist figure of Netochka's violinist-stepfather Efimov in the role of the romantic mad musician. The focus is shifted from the hero to the heroine, and *Netochka* describes a young girl's growing self-awareness, just as *Poor Folk* told of an old man's. The romantic narrative and thematics contain naturalist elements: the first section takes place in one of the Petersburg garrets where she lives with her mother and stepfather. Efimov induces Netochka to steal money from her mother to buy him drink; when her mother dies of consumption, Efimov plays his violin over her corpse and then runs away from Netochka in scenes as grotesque as the climax of "Mr. Prokharchin." Dostoevsky was attempting to go beyond the confines of the naturalist grotesque which dominated his early stories, but he reworked elements of it within new contexts throughout his writing career. In fact, in the early 1860s he began to write a novel called *The Drunkards* which told the story of Marmeladov, whose character and circumstances are almost exactly analogous to Efimov's (except for the theme of the artist-failure), in the naturalist style. The material of *The Drunkards* was worked into *Crime and Punishment* where it retained its naturalist coloration in the midst of the new style which Dostoevsky developed to accommodate the thematics of his mature period. While he had outgrown the thematics of the poor clerk and the literary polemics associated with it, he used the material related to the insulted and humiliated poor in sub-plots within his great novels, from Marmeladov to Captain Snegiryov *(The Brothers Karamazov).*

Dostoevsky began to write at a crucial turning point in Russian literature. His early period was spent experimenting with various combinations of naturalist thematics, Gogol's later low comic-grotesque and earlier high romantic style, Hoffmann's psychologism, and the ideology of Utopian Socialism. He points to the nature of the reinterpretation he is attempting by a wealth of allusions, both specific and general, to other writers and traditions. But after ten years of Siberian exile, Dostoevsky's ideas had gained depth and demanded autonomy from any existing schools. He returned to literature in 1859 to create his own unique synthesis. In the process of transcending the figure of Gogol, Dostoevsky completed the foundation for the Russian realist novel of the 19th century, which Pushkin, Lermontov and Gogol had only so recently prepared.

Priscilla Meyer and Stephen Rudy

DOSTOEVSKY
&
GOGOL

THE DIARY OF A MADMAN

October 3rd

An extraordinary incident occurred today. I got up rather late in the morning, and when Mavra brought me my cleaned boots I asked what time it was. Hearing that it had already long ago struck ten, I hurried to dress as quickly as possible. I confess, I wouldn't have gone to the department at all, knowing in advance what a sour face the chief of our division would make. For a long time he's been saying to me: "How come, brother, your head's always in such a muddle? Sometimes you run around like a lunatic, you get your work so tangled up that Satan himself couldn't make it out, you write a small letter in the heading, you don't put in either the date or the number." The damn heron! He probably envies me for sitting in the director's study and sharpening quills for his Excellency. In a word, I wouldn't have gone to the department if it weren't in the hope of seeing the treasurer and somehow getting even a little of my salary in advance out of that Jew. What a creature! For him ever to give money a month in advance—my God, the Judgment Day will come sooner. Beg him, tear your hair, be desperate—he won't give it, the gray-haired devil. But at home his own cook slaps him in the face. The whole world knows that. I don't understand the advantages of serving in my department. There are absolutely no resources. In the provincial civil and treasury offices it's a completely different matter: there, you look, someone is squeezed into a tiny corner and writing. His wretched frockcoat is vile, his snout makes you want to spit, but just look at the dacha he rents! Don't bring him a gilded porcelain cup: "That," he'll say, "is a present for a doctor," but give him a pair of trotters, or a droshky, or a beaver coat at three hundred rubles. He looks so quiet, speaks so tactfully: "Lend me your little knife to sharpen my little quill," and then he'll so clean out a petitioner that he'll leave him only his shirt. True, our work on the other hand is respectable, there is such cleanliness everywhere as a provincial office will never see: the tables are mahogany, and all the superiors use the formal form of address to us. Yes, I confess, if it weren't for the respectability of the work, I would have long ago left the department.

I put on my old overcoat and took my umbrella because it was pouring rain. There was no one on the streets; I saw only peasant women covering their heads with their skirts and Russian merchants under umbrellas, and coachmen. As for the respectable classes, only a fellow clerk was plodding along. I saw him at the intersection. As soon as I saw him I said to myself: "Aha! No, my dear, you're not going to the department, you're hurrying after that woman who's running along ahead of you and you're looking at her legs. What a beast our fellow clerk is! I swear to God, he's worse than any officer: some female goes by in a little hat and he's bound to attach himself. While I was thinking this, I saw a carriage drive up to the store I was passing. I recognized it at once: it was our director's carriage. But he has no reason to go to the store, I thought: probably it's his daughter. I pressed myself against the wall. A footman opened the doors, and she fluttered out of the carriage like a little bird. How she glanced left and right, how she flashed her brows and eyes.... My God! I was lost, completely lost. And why did she have to go out at such a rainy time? Now try to tell me women don't have a great passion for all those rags. She didn't recognize me, and anyway I deliberately tried to wrap myself up as much as possible, because I had on a very dirty overcoat, and an old-fashioned one at that. Now they wear cloaks with long collars but mine were little short ones one on top of the other; besides, the cloth wasn't at all rainproof. Her little dog, not managing to leap in the door of the store, remained on the street. I know that little dog. They call her: Madgie. I hadn't been there a minute when I suddenly heard a thin little voice: "Hello, Madgie!" How do you like that! Who's speaking? I looked around and saw two ladies walking under umbrellas: one an old lady, the other a young one; but they had already passed, while near me again sounded: "Shame on you, Madgie!" What the devil! I saw that Madgie was exchanging sniffs with the little dog which had been following the ladies. Aha! I said to myself, hang on, am I drunk? Only that, it seems, rarely happens to me. "No, Fidèle, you're wrong to think that," I myself saw Madgie say, "I was, bow wow! I was bow wow wow! very sick." Oh you little dog! I confess, I was very surprised to hear her speaking human language. But later, when I thought this all out thoroughly, I stopped being surprised. Actually, a great number of such things have already happened in the world. They say that in England a fish swam up which said two words in such a strange language that scholars have been trying to identify it for three years already and still to this day haven't discovered a thing. I also read in the papers about two cows that came into a shop and asked for a pound of tea. But, I confess, I was much more surprised when Madgie said: "I did write to you, Fidèle; Polkan probably didn't bring you my letter!" Well I'll forfeit my salary! Never yet in my life have I heard of a dog that could write. Only a nobleman can write correctly. Of course, some shopkeeper-bookkeepers and even serfs do a little writing sometimes, but their writing is mostly mechanical: no commas, no periods, no style.

This surprised me. I confess, recently I've begun to hear and see such things sometimes as no one has seen or heard before. I think, I said to myself, I'll follow that little dog and find out what she is and what she thinks. I folded up my umbrella and set off after the two ladies. They crossed to Gorokhovoy, turned into Meshchansky, then to Stolyanny, finally to Kokushkin

4

Bridge and stopped in front of a large house. I know this house, I said to myself. This is the Zverkov house. What a thing! What people live in it: how many cooks, how many Poles! and our fellows, the clerks, sit one on top of the other like dogs. I have a friend there who plays the trumpet well. The ladies went up to the fifth floor. Good, I thought: I won't go in now, but I'll remember the place and won't fail to make use of it at the first opportunity.

October 4th

Today is Wednesday, and therefore I was in our chief's study. I deliberately arrived a bit early and, having sat down, sharpened all the quills. Our director must be a very intelligent man. His whole study is lined with books. I read the titles of some of them: all scholarliness, such scholarliness that for one of my ilk there's no approaching it: it's all either in French or in German. And when you look him in the face: foo, what importance glows in his eyes! I have never yet heard him say a superfluous word. Only perhaps when you give him a paper, he'll ask: "What's it like out?" "Damp, Your Excellency." Yes, not a match for our ilk! A statesman. I've noticed, though, that he particularly likes me. If only the daughter too...ekh, rascalry!... Never mind, never mind, silence! I read *The Bee*. What a stupid people the French are! Well, what do they want? I'd take them all, I swear to God, and birch them! There I also read a very pleasant description of a ball written by a Kursk landowner. Kursk landowners write well. After that I noticed that it had already struck twelve-thirty, but our man hadn't come out of his bedroom. But around one-thirty an incident occurred which no pen can describe. The door opened, I thought it was the director, and I leapt from my chair with some papers; but it was she, she herself! Holy fathers, how she was dressed! Her dress was white as a swan: foo, how luxurious! And how she gazed: the sun, I swear to God, the sun! She bowed and said, "Has Papa been here?" Ai, ai, ai! What a voice! A canary, really, a canary! Your Excellency, I wanted to say, don't command me to be executed, but if you want me executed, execute me with your little aristocratic hand. Yes, the devil take it, somehow my tongue wouldn't obey and I only said: No, Miss. She looked at me, at the books, and dropped her handkerchief. I rushed after it, slipped on the damn parquet and almost knocked my nose off, however, I recovered myself and got the handkerchief. Saints, what a handkerchief! The most delicate, batiste— ambergris, absolute ambergris! It simply exudes aristocracy. She thanked me and smiled slightly so that her sweet little lips almost didn't move, and after that she went out. I sat for another hour when suddenly a footman came in and said: "Go home, Aksenty Ivanovich, the master has already gone out." I can't stand the footman set; they're always lounging around the front hall and won't even make the effort to nod to you. As if that weren't enough:

5

once one of these beasts took it into his head, without even getting up from his place, to offer me some snuff. Do you know, you stupid serf, that I'm a clerk, I'm of noble origin. However, I took my hat and put on my coat myself, because these gentlemen will never help you on with it, and went out. At home I mostly lay on my bed. Then I copied out some very good little verses:

> *Not having seen my love an hour,*
> *I thought at least a year had passed;*
> *And finding that my life'd grown sour,*
> *Do I not live in vain, I asked.*

Must be Pushkin's work.* In the evening, wrapped up in my overcoat, I walked to the entrance of Her Excellency's house and waited for a long time to see if she wouldn't come out to get into her carriage so that I could have another little look at her—but no, she didn't come out.

November 6th

The chief of the division was furious today. When I arrived at the department, he called me in and began to talk to me like this: "Well, tell me please, what are you doing?" "What do you mean what? I'm not doing anything," I answered. "Well, think it over carefully! After all, you're over forty, it's time you got smart. Who do you think you are? You think I don't know all your tricks? You're chasing the director's daughter! Well, look at yourself, just think, what are you? You're a zero, nothing more. You don't have a cent to your name. Just take a look in the mirror at your face, how can you think about that!" The devil take it, just because he has a face that looks a little like a druggist's bottle, and a clump of hair on his head curled into a pompadour, holds his head in the air and smears it with some kind of rosette oil, he thinks that only he can do anything he wants. I understand, I understand why he's angry at me. He's jealous; maybe he's seen the preferential signs of approbation shown me. Well I spit on him! So what if he is a court councillor! He gets a gold chain for his watch, orders boots at thirty rubles—and the devil take him! Am I some plebian, some tailor or subaltern's child? I'm a nobleman. I can rise in the service too. I'm still forty-two—the time when service only really begins. Just wait, friend! We too will become a colonel, or maybe, if God's willing, something a little higher. We too will get ourselves a reputation even better than yours. How did you get it into your head that except for you there just isn't a single decent person? Just

---

*[In fact by N.P. Nikolev (1758-1815).]

give me a fashionable frockcoat tailored by Ruch and let me put on a tie just like yours—then you won't hold a candle to me. I have no means—that's the problem.

November 8th

Was at the theater. They did the Russian fool Filatka. Laughed a lot. There was also some vaudeville with amusing verses about clerks, especially about a certain collegiate registrar, quite freely written, so that I was surprised that the censorship let it through, and they say right out about merchants that they deceive the people and that their sons are debauched and climb into the nobility. There was also a very amusing couplet about journalists: that they love to rail against everything and that the author requests protection from the audience. Very funny plays authors are writing nowadays. I love going to the theater. As soon as there's a penny in your pocket—you can't keep from going. But among our fellow clerks there are such swine: he absolutely won't go to the theater, the peasant; only maybe if you give him a free ticket. One actress sang very well. I remembered the one who... ekh, rascalry!... Never mind, never mind...silence.

November 9th

At eight o'clock I set off for the department. The head of the division pretended he hadn't noticed my arrival. I too for my part, as if there had been nothing between us. I looked over and folded some papers. Went out at four o'clock. Passed the director's apartment but no one was in sight. After dinner mostly lay on my bed.

November 11th

Today I sat in our director's study, sharpened 23 quills for him, and for her, ai! ai...for Her Excellency four quills. He really likes a lot of quills around. Ooh! What a brain he must be! Always silent, but in his head, I bet, always deliberating. I would like to find out what he thinks about most; what's going on in that head. I would like to have a closer look at the life of these gentlemen, all these equivoques and court doings, what they're like, what they do in their set—that's what I'd like to find out! Several times I've thought of starting a conversation with His Excellency, only, the devil take it, my tongue just doesn't obey: you only say it's cold or hot out, and you absolutely won't get out anything more. I would like to get a glimpse of the living room, which you only sometimes see through into still another room.

7

Ekh, what rich decor! What mirrors and porcelain. I'd like to get a glimpse of the half where Her Excellency is, that's what I'd like to see! The boudoir, how all those little jars and bottles are arranged, such flowers that it's terrifying even to breathe on them, how her dress lies thrown down there, looking more like air than a dress. I'd like to get a glimpse of the bedroom...there, I bet, are marvels, there, I bet, is a paradise such as is not even to be found in the heavens. To have a look at the little stool she stands on getting out of bed, at her little foot, at how she puts on her little stocking white as snow on her little foot...ai! ai! ai! never mind, never mind...silence.

Today however it came to me in a flash: I remembered that conversation between the two dogs that I heard on Nevsky Prospect. Fine, I thought to myself: Now I'll find out everything. I have to seize the correspondence those rotten little dogs were carrying on. There I'll probably find out something. I confess, I once even called Madgie over and said: "Listen, Madgie, here we are alone now, if you want, I'll even lock the door so no one will see, tell me everything you know about your mistress, what's she like? I swear to you I won't tell anyone." But the sly dog tucked her tail under her, doubled up and quietly went out as if she hadn't heard a thing. I have long suspected that dogs are much smarter than people; I was even sure that they can talk, but that they just have a kind of stubbornness in them. They're exceptional politicians: they notice everything, a person's every step. No, no matter what, tomorrow I'll go to the Zverkov house, interrogate Fidèle and, if possible, seize all the letters Madgie wrote her.

November 12th

At two o'clock in the afternoon I set out to see Fidèle without fail and to interrogate her. I can't stand cabbage, the smell of which pours out of all the small shops on Meshchansky; furthermore such hellishness wafts out from under the gates of every house that I wrapped up my nose and ran as fast as I could. What's more, the foul craftsmen let out such a quantity of soot and smoke from their workshops that it's absolutely impossible for a respectable person to take a walk here. When I made my way up to the sixth floor and rang the bell, a not completely bad-looking girl with little freckles came out. I recognized her. It was the same one who had been walking with the old lady. She blushed a bit, and I suspected at once: you, dearie, want a fiancé. "What do you want?" said she. "I need to speak with your dog." The girl was stupid! I knew at once she was stupid! At that moment the dog ran up with a bark; I wanted to grab her but, the vile thing, she almost grabbed me by the nose with her teeth. However, I saw her basket in the corner. Ah, that's just what I need! I went up to it, rummaged in the straw in the wooden box and, to my singular satisfaction, pulled out a small packet of little papers. The loathesome dog, seeing this, first bit me on the calf, and then when she had sniffed out that I'd taken the papers, began to whine and fawn, but I said: "No, dearie, goodbye!" and ran off. I think the girl took me for a madman, because she was extraordinarily frightened. Having come home, I wanted to get to work at once and decipher those letters because I see a little badly by candlelight. But Mavra decided to clean the floor. These stupid Finns are always inappropriately clean. And therefore I went to take a walk and think over this occurrence. Now I'll finally find out all their affairs, designs, all those springs, and I'll finally get to the bottom of everything. These letters will reveal everything to me. Dogs are an intelligent lot, they know all the political relationships and therefore probably everything will be there: a portrait and all the affairs of that husband. There'll also be something about her...never mind, silence! Towards evening I came home. Mostly lay on my bed.

November 13th

Well, let's see: the letter is pretty legible. However, there's something sort of doggy in the handwriting. Let's read it:

Dear Fidèle, I just can't get used to your bourgeois name. Couldn't they have given you a better one? Fidèle, Rose—what vulgar taste, however, that's beside the point. I'm very glad we decided to write to each other.

The letter is written very correctly. The punctuation and even the spelling is right everywhere. Even our division chief couldn't write that simply, though he says he studied in a university somewhere. Let's look further:

I think that sharing one's thoughts, feelings and impressions with another is one of the great blessings in the world.

Hm! The thought is taken from some composition translated from the German. I don't recall the title.

I say this from experience, although I haven't been around the world further than the gates of our house. Doesn't my life flow pleasurably? My mistress, whom Papa calls Sophie, loves me madly.

Ai, ai!...never mind, never mind. Silence!

Papa also pets me very often. I drink tea and coffee with cream. Akh, ma chère, I should tell you that I just don't see the pleasure of the big gnawed

9

bones which our Polkan gobbles in the kitchen. The only good bones are from gamebirds, and then only when no one has sucked the marrow out of them yet. It's very good to mix several sauces together, only without capers and without greens; but I don't know of anything worse than the custom of giving dogs little balls rolled out of bread. Some gentleman or other sitting at the table who's held all sorts of trash in his hands will start mashing bread with these hands, call you over and shove a little ball in your teeth. To decline is somewhat impolite, so you eat it; with disgust, but you eat it....

The devil only knows what that is. What nonsense! As if there weren't a better subject to write about. Let's look on another page. Maybe there'll be something a bit more sensible.

I'm quite ready and willing to inform you about all the events going on at our house. I've already told you something about the chief gentleman, whom Sophie calls Papa. He's a very strange person.

Ah! At last! Yes, I knew it: they have a political view of every subject. Let's see what Papa is like:

. . . a very strange person. Mostly he is silent. He speaks very seldom; but a week ago he talked to himself incessantly: Will I get it or won't I get it? He would take a paper in one hand, close the other empty one and say: Will I get it or won't I get it? Once he even turned to me with the question: What do you think, Madgie? Will I get it, or won't I get it? I couldn't understand anything at all, I sniffed his boot and went away. Then, ma chère, a week later, Papa came home overjoyed. All morning gentlemen in uniforms came to see him and congratulated him for something. At the table he was merrier than I've ever seen him, told anecdotes, and after dinner held me up to his neck and said: "Look, Madgie, what's this?" I saw some little ribbon. I sniffed it, but found absolutely no aroma; finally, on the sly, I licked it: a little salty.

Hm! That little dog, I think, is a bit too...she ought to be whipped! Ah! So he's ambitious! This must be taken into account.

Farewell, ma chère! I must run and so on...and so on.... Tomorrow I'll finish the letter. Well, hello! Now I'm back again. Today my mistress Sophie...

Ah! well, let's see what Sophie is like. Ekh, rascalry! Never mind, never mind...we will continue.

. . . my mistress Sophie was in an extraordinary flurry. She was going to

Ma chère Fidèle, forgive me for not writing for so long. I have been in utter ecstasy. Truly did some writer say that love is a second life. Furthermore, there are big changes at our house. The court chamberlain is here every day now. Sophie is madly in love with him. Papa is very gay. I even heard from our Grigory who sweeps the floor and almost always has conversations with himself, that soon there'll be a wedding; because Papa absolutely wants to see Sophie marry either a general or a court chamberlain, or a colonel....

The devil take it! I can't read any more.... Everything's either a court chamberlain or a general. Everything that's best in the world, everything goes to court chamberlains or generals. You find yourself some poor treasure, you think it's within arm's reach—and a court chamberlain or a general grabs it from you. The devil take it! I'd like to become a general myself, not to win her hand and so on. No; I'd like to be a general only in order to see how they dangle around doing all these various court routines and equivoques, and then tell them I spit on both of you. The devil take it. It's irritating! I tore the stupid dog's letters to bits.

December 3rd

It can't be. Rumors! There won't be a wedding! What if he is a court chamberlain? After all that's nothing more than a position; not some visible thing you could hold in your hands. After all, just because you're a court chamberlain you don't get a third eye in your forehead. After all his nose isn't made of gold, but it's just like mine, like everyone's; after all he uses it to smell with, and not to eat with, to sneeze with, not to cough with. I've wanted several times to figure out where all these differences come from. Why am I a titular councillor and why should I be a titular councillor? Maybe I'm some count or general, and only seem to be a titular councillor? Maybe I don't know myself who I am. After all there are so many examples in history: there's some simple guy, not quite a noble, but simply some bourgeois or even a peasant—and suddenly it's discovered he's some magnate, and sometimes even a ruler. When a peasant sometimes turns out like that what might a noble turn out to be? Suddenly, for example, I come in in a general's uniform: an epaulette on my right shoulder and an epaulette on my left shoulder, a blue ribbon across my chest—what'll happen? What tune will my beauty sing then? What will Papa himself say, our director? Oh, what an ambitious man! A mason, certainly a mason, although he pretends to be this and that, but I noticed at once that he's a mason: if he gives someone his hand, he only sticks out two fingers. And can't I this very minute be appointed governor general or commissary or some other thing? I'd like to know why I'm a titular councillor? Why precisely a titular councillor?

13

Today I read the newspapers all morning. Strange things are going on in Spain. I couldn't even really figure them out. They write that the throne is vacant and that they are having difficulty trying to choose a successor and therefore insurrections are taking place. This seems extraordinarily strange to me. How can a throne be vacant? They say that some donna is supposed to ascend the throne. A donna can't ascend the throne. She just can't. A king should be on the throne. But they say there is no king. It can't be that there is no king. A government can't be without a king. There is a king, only he's incognito somewhere. It might be that he's right there, but either some family reasons or threats on the part of neighboring powers, France and other lands, are somehow forcing him to hide, or there are some other reasons.

December 8th

I was quite ready to go to the department, but various reasons and considerations kept me. I just can't get the Spanish affairs out of my head. How can it be that a donna should become a queen? They won't permit that. And, in the first place, England won't permit it. And furthermore political affairs of all Europe: the Austrian emperor, our sovereign...I confess, these events have so exhausted and shaken me that I absolutely couldn't do anything all day. Mavra kept remarking to me that I was exceptionally distracted at the table. And actually, it seems I threw two plates on the floor out of absent-mindedness which instantly broke. After dinner I walked up to the hills. Couldn't get anything instructive out of it. Mostly lay on my bed and thought about the Spanish affairs.

Year 2000 43rd of April

Today is a day of the greatest jubilation! There is a king in Spain. He has been found. I am this king. Only just today did I find out about this. I confess, it struck me suddenly like lightning. I don't understand how I could think and imagine that I was a titular councillor. How could this mad thought get into my head? It's a good thing no one thought of putting me in the madhouse at the time. Now everything has been revealed to me. Now I see everything clear as day. But before, I don't understand, before everything was in a kind of fog before me. And it all, I think, comes from the fact that people imagine that the human brain is located in the head; not at all: it is brought by the wind from the direction of the Caspian Sea. At first I revealed who I am to Mavra. When she heard that the King of Spain was standing before her, she threw up her hands and almost died of fright. The stupid woman had never seen a King of Spain before. However, I tried to calm her and tried to assure her in gracious words of my good favor, and that I wasn't the least angry that she sometimes cleaned my boots badly. After all they're a benighted lot. They can't talk about lofty subjects. She was frightened because she is convinced that all kings in Spain look like Philip II. But I explained to her that there is no resemblance between me and Philip and that I don't have a single Capuchin.... Didn't go, to the department. The devil with it! No, friends, you won't entice me now; I'm not about to copy your foul papers!

Marchtober the 86th
Between day and night

Today our messenger came to get me to go to the department since I haven't been going to work for more than three weeks already. I went to the department just for kicks. The division chief thought that I'd bow to him and start apologizing but I looked at him indifferently, not too angrily and not too graciously, and sat down in my place as if not noticing anyone. I gazed at the whole office scum and thought: What if you knew who's sitting among you.... My God! What a hubbub you'd raise, and the division chief himself would start bowing low to me the way he now bows to the director. They put some papers before me for me to do an extract of them. But I didn't even lift a finger to them. After a few minutes everything flew into a flurry. They said the director was coming. Many clerks ran up and vied with each other to show themselves to him. But I didn't budge. When he passed through our division everyone buttoned up their frock coats; but I didn't do a thing! What's a director! I'm supposed to stand up for him—never! What kind of director is he? He's a cork, not a director. An ordinary cork, a simple cork, nothing more. The kind they stop bottles with. What amused me most was when they thrust a paper at me to sign. They thought that I'd write on the very bottom of the sheet: clerk so-and-so, what else? But in the most important place where the director of the department signs, I wrote: "Ferdinand VIII." You should've seen what an awed silence reigned; but I just waved my hand, saying: "No signs of allegiance are necessary!"—and went out. From there I went straight to the director's apartment. He wasn't home. A footman didn't want to let me in, but I said such things to him that he simply gave up. I made my way straight to her dressing room. She was sitting before a mirror; she leapt up and retreated from me. However, I didn't tell her that I was the King of Spain. I only said that such happiness awaited her as she couldn't even imagine and that, despite the machinations of our enemies, we would be together. I didn't want to say anything more and went out. Oh, what a perfidious creature is woman! Only now have I comprehended what woman is. Until now no one has yet discovered whom she's in love with: I'm the first to discover it. Woman is in love with the devil. Yes, no joking. Physicists write stupidities, that she's this and that—she loves only the Devil. You see over there, in the first tier of boxes, she's focussing her lorgnette. You think she's looking at that fat man with the medal? Not at all, she's looking at the Devil who's standing behind his back. Now he's hiding in his medal. Now he's beckoning to her with his finger! And she'll marry him. She will. And all these people, all their high-ranking fathers, all these who fawn in all directions and climb into court circles, and say they're patriots and this and that: rents, rents are what these patriots want! They'd sell their mother, father, God for money, ambitious creatures, Christ-sellers! It's all ambition and ambition comes from a little bubble under the tongue and in it there's a small worm the size of the head of a pin, and it's all done by some barber who lives on Gorokhovaya. I don't remember his name; but it's certainly true that he and a certain midwife want to spread Mohammedanism throughout the whole world and therefore, they say, the majority of the people in France already profess the faith of Mahomet.

No date at all.
The day was dateless.

I walked incognito along Nevsky Prospect. The imperial sovereign drove by. The whole city took off their hats and I did too; however, I gave no sign whatsoever that I was the King of Spain. I considered it indecorous to reveal myself right there in front of everyone because my tall confrère would probably have asked why the King of Spain had not yet been presented at court. And indeed one should present oneself at court first. The only thing that stopped me was that I still don't have a king's raiment. At least if I could get a royal mantle. I wanted to order it from the tailor, but they're complete asses, besides they're utterly careless with their work, they're addicted to fraud and mostly cobble stones on the street. I decided to sew myself a royal mantle out of my new uniform which I'd only worn twice. But so that those scoundrels couldn't ruin it, I decided to sew it myself, locking the door so that no one would see. I cut it all up with the scissors because it was necessary to redo it entirely and give the whole cloth the appearance of ermine tails.

Don't remember the date.
There was no month either.
Devil knows what there was.

The royal mantle is completely ready and sewn. Mavra screamed when I put it on. However, I still haven't decided to present myself at court. There's still no delegation from Spain. It's improper without deputies. There'll be no weight to my dignity. I expect them any hour.

The 1st date

The extraordinary slowness of the deputies surprises me. What reasons could be detaining them? Not France? Yes, that's the most unfavorably disposed power. I went to the post office to find out if the Spanish deputies hadn't arrived. But the postmaster was extraordinarily stupid, he doesn't know anything: no, he says, there aren't any Spanish deputies here, but if you want to write letters, we'll take them at the established rate. The devil take it! What's a letter? A letter's nonsense. Druggists write letters....

Madrid. Februarius the thirtieth

And so I'm in Spain, and it happened so quickly that I could hardly regain my senses. This morning the Spanish deputies came to me and I got into a carriage with them. The extraordinary speed seemed strange to me. We drove so fast that in half an hour we reached the Spanish border. However, there are now castiron roads all over Europe and steamboats go extraordinarily fast. Spain is a strange land: when we entered the first room I saw a number of people with shaved heads. However, I guessed that these must be either Dominicans or Capuchins because they shave their heads. The conduct of the State Chancellor who led me by the arm seemed extraordinarily strange to me; he pushed me into a small room and said: Sit here and if you keep calling yourself King Ferdinand I'll beat that whim out of you. But, knowing this was nothing more than a test, I answered negatively, for which the Chancellor hit me twice with a stick on the back so painfully that I almost screamed, but I restrained myself, remembering that this was a custom of the knights on entering high rank, because in Spain even to this day knightly customs are maintained. Remaining alone, I decided to occupy myself with affairs of state. I discovered that China and Spain are absolutely one and the same country, and it's only from ignorance that they're considered different nations. I advise everyone to write down Spain on paper, and it'll come out China. But I was exceptionally grieved by an event which will take place tomorrow. Tomorrow at 7 o'clock a terrible phenomenon will be accomplished:

17

the earth will mount the moon. The famous English chemist Wellington writes about it. I confess, I felt real anxiety when I imagined the unusual delicacy and frailty of the moon. The moon after all is usually made in Hamburg; and is most poorly made. I'm surprised that England pays no attention to this. A lame cooper makes it, and it's clear the fool hasn't the least conception of a moon. He used tarred rope and part olive oil; and therefore there's a terrible stench all over the earth so that you have to hold your nose. And therefore the moon itself is such a delicate sphere that people simply can't live there and now only noses live there. And that's why we can't see our own noses, for they're all on the moon. And when I realized that the earth is a heavy substance and by mounting could grind our noses into flour, such anxiety possessed me that, putting on my shoes and socks, I hurried into the State Council hall in order to give an order to the police not to let the earth mount the moon. The Capuchins of whom I found a great number in the State Council hall were a very intelligent lot and when I said: "Gentlemen, let us save the moon; because the earth wants to mount it," everyone at once ran to carry out my monarchal will and many climbed the wall in order to get the moon; but at that time the great Chancellor came in. Seeing him, everyone scattered. I, as the King, remained alone. But the Chancellor, to my surprise, struck me with a stick and chased me into my room. Such power do folk customs have in Spain!

January of the same year,
occurring after February

I still don't understand what kind of a country Spain is. The folk customs and court etiquette are quite unusual. I don't understand, I don't understand, I absolutely don't understand anything. Today they shaved my head, despite the fact that I shouted with all my might about my unwillingness to be a monk. But I can't even remember anymore what happened to me when they began to drip cold water on my head. I have never felt such hell. I was ready to fly into a frenzy, so that they could hardly restrain me. I just don't understand the significance of that strange custom. The custom is stupid, senseless! The folly of the kings who haven't yet abolished it is incomprehensible to me. Judging by all probabilities, I wonder: haven't I fallen into the hands of the Inquisition, and the one I took for the Chancellor, isn't he the Grand Inquisitor himself? Only I still can't understand how a king could be subject to the Inquisition. It's possible, true, on France's part and especially Polignac's. Oh, that beast Polignac! He's sworn to harm me to the death. And now he pursues and pursues me; but I know, friend, that you're being led by the Englishman. The Englishman is a great politician. He bustles about everywhere. It's already known to the whole world that when England

18

takes snuff France sneezes.

date 25th

Today the Grand Inquisitor came to my room but, hearing his steps when he was still at a distance, I hid under the chair. Seeing that I wasn't there, he began to call me. At first he shouted: "Poprishchin!" I didn't say a word. Then: "Aksenty Ivanov! Titular councillor! Nobleman!" I keep silent. "Ferdinand VIII, King of Spain!" I was about to stick out my head, but then I thought: No, brother, you won't fool me! We know you: you're going to pour cold water on my head again. However, he saw me and chased me out from under the chair with a stick. The damn stick hits extraordinarily painfully. However, today's discovery rewarded me for all that: I found out that every rooster has a Spain, that it is found under his feathers. The Grand Inquisitor, however, left me in a rage and threatening me with some punishment. But I completely disregarded his impotent malice, knowing that he is acting like a machine, as a tool of the Englishman.

Da 34 te Mth yrae. ʎɹɐnɹqǝℲ 349

No, I have no more strength to endure it. God! What they're doing to me! They pour cold water on my head! They don't listen to, don't see, don't hear me. What did I do to them? Why are they tormenting me? What do they want from poor me? What can I give them? I don't have anything. I don't have strength, I can't bear all their torments, my head burns and everything whirls before me. Save me! Take me away! Give me a troika with horses swift as a whirlwind! Take your seat, my coachman, ring, my bells, soar up, steeds, and bear me away from this world! Further, further, so that nothing, nothing is visible. There the heavens swirl before me; a little star twinkles in the distance; the forest rushes past with dark trees and the moon; a blue-gray fog spreads out beneath my feet; a chord rings in the fog; on one side the sea, on the other—Italy; over there Russian huts can be seen. Is that my house showing blue in the distance? Is that my mother sitting at the window? Mother, save your poor son! Shed a tear on his sick head! Look how they torment him! Press your poor orphan to your bosom! There is no place for him in the world! They're chasing him away! Mother! Have pity on your sick child!... And did you know that the Dey of Algiers has a bump right under his nose?

1835

THE NOSE

I

On March 25th in Petersburg an extraordinarily strange occurrence took place. The barber Ivan Yakovlevich, who lives on Voznesensky Avenue (his surname has been lost, and even on his signboard—where a gentleman is depicted with a soaped cheek and the inscription: "We also let blood"—nothing more is stated), the barber Ivan Yakovlevich woke up rather early and detected the smell of hot bread. Raising himself up a bit in his bed, he saw his wife, a rather respectable lady who was very fond of drinking coffee, taking from the oven some freshly baked rolls.

"Today, Praskovya Osipovna, I will not drink coffee," said Ivan Yakovlevich, "but instead I would like to eat a bit of hot bread with onion." (That is, Ivan Yakovlevich would have liked both the one and the other, but knew that it was quite impossible to ask for two things at once: for Praskovya Osipovna very much disliked such whims.) "Let the fool eat bread; so much the better for me," thought his wife to herself, "there'll be an extra portion of coffee left." And she threw one roll on the table.

For decency's sake Ivan Yakovlevich put his tailcoat on over his nightshirt and, sitting down at the table, sprinkled salt, prepared two onions, took a knife in hand and, assuming a significant expression, proceeded to cut the bread. Having cut the bread into two halves, he looked into the middle and, to his surprise, saw something white. Ivan Yakovlevich poked carefully with the knife and felt with his finger. "Solid!" he said to himself, "what sort of thing could it be?"

He thrust in his fingers and pulled out—a nose!... Ivan Yakovlevich was dumbfounded; he began to rub his eyes and to feel it: a nose, precisely, a nose! And furthermore, it seemed to belong to someone he knew. Horror was expressed on Ivan Yakovlevich's face. But this horror was nothing next to the indignation which seized his wife.

"Where did you cut off a nose, you beast?" she shrieked with rage. "Scoundrel! Drunkard! I'll denounce you to the police myself. What a bandit! I've already heard from three people that you yank their noses so hard while shaving them that they hardly stay on."

But Ivan Yakovlevich was more dead than alive. He realized that the nose belonged to none other than the collegiate assessor Kovalyov whom he shaved every Wednesday and Sunday.

"Wait, Praskovya Osipovna! I'll wrap it in a rag and put it in the corner. Let it lie there a little bit, and later I'll take it away."

21

"I won't hear of it! I'm supposed to let a cut-off nose lie around my room? You dried-out bread crust! He only knows how to strop his razor, but soon he won't be in a condition to fulfill his duty at all, the rake, the good-for-nothing! I'm supposed to answer to the police for you?... Oh you filth, you blockhead! Out with it! Out! Take it where you want! Don't let me set eyes on it again!"

Ivan Yakovlevich stood exactly as if he had been beaten. He thought and thought—and didn't know what to think. "The devil knows how that happened," he said at last, scratching behind his ear with his hand. "Whether I came home drunk yesterday or not, I really can't say for sure. But by all indications it should be an impossible occurrence: for bread is a baked affair, while a nose is something entirely different. I can't make anything of it!..." Ivan Yakovlevich fell silent. The thought that the police would discover the nose on him and indict him threw him into a total frenzy. The crimson collar beautifully embroidered in silver, the sword, already flashed before him... and he shook all over. At last he got his underwear and boots, put on all this rubbish and, accompanied by the unlovely remonstrations of Praskovya Osipovna, wrapped the nose in a rag and went out onto the street.

He wanted to slip it somewhere: either into the post by the gate, or simply to drop it accidently somehow and then turn into a side street. But to his misfortune some acquaintance or other kept happening along who would begin immediately with the inquiry: "Where are you going?" or "Whom are you going to shave so early?"—so that Ivan Yakovlevich couldn't find the right moment. On another occasion he actually dropped it, but a policeman at some distance off pointed to it with his halberd, saying: "Pick it up! You've dropped something there!" And Ivan Yakovlevich had to pick up the nose and hide it in his pocket. He was seized with despair, all the more since the crowd on the street constantly increased as the stores and shops began to open.

He decided to go to the Isakievsky bridge: wouldn't he manage somehow to fling it into the Neva?... But I am somewhat remiss in that up to now I have said nothing about Ivan Yakovlevich, an honorable man in many respects.

Ivan Yakovlevich, like every decent Russian workman, was a terrible drunkard. And although every day he shaved other peoples' chins, his own was forever unshaven. Ivan Yakovlevich's tailcoat (Ivan Yakovlevich never wore a frockcoat) was motley, that is, it was black, but covered with brownish-yellow and gray blotches; the collar shone, and instead of the three buttons only threads dangled. Ivan Yakovlevich was a great cynic, and when the collegiate assessor Kovalyov would say to him as usual while he was being shaved: "Ivan Yakovlevich, your hands always stink!" Ivan Yakovlevich would reply with the question: "Why should they stink?" "I don't know, brother, only they stink," the collegiate assessor would say, and Ivan Yakovlevich, having taken a pinch of snuff, would soap him for this both on the cheek and under the nose and behind the ear and under the beard, in a word, wherever he wanted.

This respectable citizen found himself already on the Isakievsky Bridge. First of all he looked around; then he leaned over the railing as if to look under the bridge to see whether there were many fish running, and stealthily flung in the rag with the nose. He felt as if five hundred pounds had fallen off him at once; Ivan Yakovlevich even grinned. Instead of going to shave officials' chins, he started off for an establishment with the sign "Food and Tea" to ask for a glass of punch, when he suddenly noticed at the end of the bridge a police inspector of noble appearance with full sidewhiskers, in a three-cornered hat, with a sword. He froze; however, the inspector crooked his finger at him and said:

"Come here, my good man!"

Ivan Yakovlevich, knowing good form, took off his cap when he was still at a distance, and, approaching gracefully, said:

"I wish your honor good health!"

"No, no, brother, not your honor; say, what were you doing standing on the bridge?"

"I swear to God, Sir, I was going to shave someone, and I only looked to see if the river was flowing quickly."

"You're lying! You're lying! You won't get off with that. Kindly answer!"

"I'm prepared to shave your grace two times a week or even three, without any objection," answered Ivan Yakovlevich.

"No, friend, that's a trifle! Three barbers shave me, and furthermore they consider it a great honor. But now kindly tell me what you were doing there?"

Ivan Yakovlevich paled.... But here the event is entirely covered in fog, and of what happened further, absolutely nothing is known.

II

The collegiate assessor Kovalyov woke up rather early and went "Brrr" with his lips, which he always did when he woke up, although he himself could not explain for what reason. Kovalyov stretched, and ordered the small mirror standing on the table to be brought to him. He wanted to look at the pimple which had popped up on his nose the evening before, but to his great amazement, he saw that instead of a nose, there was an entirely smooth space! Taking fright, Kovalyov ordered water to be brought and rubbed his eyes with a towel: precisely, no nose! He began to feel with his hand to ascertain: isn't he asleep? It seems he's not asleep. The collegiate assessor

Kovalyov leapt out of bed and shook himself: no nose! He ordered his clothes to be brought at once and flew off directly to the chief of police.

But meanwhile it is essential to say something about Kovalyov, so that the reader might see what sort of collegiate assessor he was. The collegiate assessors who receive that title with the help of academic certificates may in no way be compared with those collegiate assessors who used to be appointed in the Caucasus. These are two entirely distinct breeds. Learned collegiate assessors.... But Russia is such a wondrous land, that if you talk about one collegiate assessor, all collegiate' assessors from Riga to Kamchatka are sure to take it personally. Of course the same is true of all titles and ranks. Kovalyov was a collegiate assessor from the Caucasus. He had so far only enjoyed that title for two years and therefore couldn't forget it for a minute; but in order to give himself nobility and weight, he never called himself a collegiate assessor, but always a major.* "Listen, my dear," he would usually say upon meeting a woman selling shirtfronts on the street, "you come to my house; my apartment is on Sadovaya; just ask: Does Major Kovalyov live here? Anyone will show you." If he met some pretty little thing, he would give her a secret instruction as well, adding: "You ask, my sweet, for Major Kovalyov's apartment." For this very reason we too will henceforth call this collegiate assessor "major."

Major Kovalyov had the habit of strolling along Nevsky Prospect every day. The collar of his shirtfront was always exceptionally clean and starched. His whiskers were of the sort which even now can still be seen on provincial and district surveyors, architects and regimental doctors, also on the directors of various police functions and in general on all those men who have full, ruddy cheeks and play Boston very well: these whiskers go along the very middle of the cheek and go straight up to the nose. Major Kovalyov wore a quantity of seals; cornelian, and with crests, and those on which was engraved: Wednesday, Thursday, Monday, and so on. Major Kovalyov had come to Petersburg on business, namely to look for a position befitting his title: if he were successful, a vice-governor's, if not—an executor's in some conspicuous department. Major Kovalyov was not against even marrying, but only on the condition that the bride come with two hundred thousand in capital. And by this the reader can now judge for himself what was the situation of this major when he saw instead of a rather attractive and moderate nose a ridiculous, level and smooth space.

To his misfortune, not one coachman showed up on the street and he had to go on foot, wrapped in his cloak and covering his face with a handkerchief, giving the impression that he was bleeding. "But maybe I just imagined it: it's impossible that a nose would disappear out of sheer stupidity,"

---

*[The equivalent military rank to the civil service title of "collegiate assessor."]

24

he thought and went into a pastry shop expressly in order to look in the mirror. Fortunately there was no one in the pastry shop; little boys were sweeping the rooms and arranging the chairs; some with sleepy eyes were bringing out hot meat pies on trays: yesterday's coffee-spattered newspapers were scattered around on the tables and chairs. "Well, thank God no one's here," he said, "now I can have a look." He shyly approached the mirror and looked. "The devil with it, what rubbish!" he said, spitting. "At least if there were something in place of a nose, but nothing!..."

Biting his lip with annoyance, he went out of the pastry shop and decided, contrary to his habit, not to look at anyone or to smile at anyone. Suddenly he stopped by the doors of a house as if rooted to the spot; before his eyes an inexplicable phenomenon occurred: a carriage stopped in front of the entrance; the doors opened; bending over, a gentleman in a uniform jumped out and ran up the stairs. What was the horror and at the same time astonishment of Kovalyov when he realized that this was his own nose! At this unusual spectacle it seemed to him that everything whirled before his eyes; he felt that he could hardly stay on his feet; but he, all trembling as if in a fever, decided at any cost to wait until the nose returned to his carriage. In two minutes the nose did in fact come out. He was in a uniform embroidered in gold with a high-standing collar; he wore buckskin breeches, at his side a sword. From his plumed hat one could conclude that he held the rank of state councillor. From everything it was evident that he was going visiting somewhere. He looked to both sides, shouted to the coachman: "Let's go!" got in and drove off.

Poor Kovalyov almost went out of his mind. He did not know how even to think about such a strange occurrence. How could it be, indeed, that a nose, which just yesterday was on his face, couldn't ride or walk—was in uniform! He ran after the carriage, which, fortunately, did not drive on very far and stopped before the Kazan Cathedral.

He rushed into the cathedral, made his way through a row of old beggar women with wrapped-up faces with two holes for the eyes, whom he used to laugh at so, and went into the church. There were few worshippers inside the church; they all stood just by the entrance in the doorway. Kovalyov was in such a distressed state that he had no strength whatsoever to pray, and he cast his eyes about all the corners in search of that gentleman. At last he saw him standing to one side. The nose had entirely hidden his face in the high-standing collar and was praying with an expression of the greatest piety.

"How to go up to him?" thought Kovalyov. "From all appearances, from the uniform, from the hat, it's evident that he is a state councillor. The devil knows how to do it!"

He began to cough a bit in his vicinity; but the nose did not for a minute abandon his pious attitude and kept bowing low.

"My dear sir..." said Kovalyov, inwardly forcing himself to take courage, "my dear sir...."

"What do you want?" answered the nose, turning around.

"I'm surprised, my dear sir, it seems to me...you should know your place. And suddenly I find you, and where?—in church. You must agree...."

"Excuse me, I cannot make sense of what you are pleased to be talking about...explain yourself."

"How am I to explain to him?" thought Kovalyov, and, summoning his courage, began: "Of course I...however, I am a major. For me to go around without a nose, you will agree, is unseemly. Some marketwoman who sells peeled oranges on Voskresensky Bridge can sit around without a nose; but I, having the intention of attaining...furthermore being acquainted with ladies in many good families: Chekhtaryova, the state councillor's wife, and others... Judge for yourself.... I don't know, dear sir.... (At this Major Kovalyov shrugged his shoulders.) Excuse me.... If one looks at this according to the rules of duty and honor...you yourself can understand...."

"I understand absolutely nothing," answered the nose, "explain yourself more satisfactorily."

"My dear sir..." said Kovalyov with a sense of his own dignity, "I don't know how to understand your words.... The whole matter, it seems, is perfectly obvious.... Either you want...why, you are my own nose!"

The nose looked at the major, and his brows knit somewhat.

"You are mistaken, dear sir. I'm on my own. Furthermore there cannot be any close relations between us. Judging by the buttons on your uniform, you must work in another department." Having said this, the nose turned away and continued to pray.

Kovalyov was utterly confused, not knowing what to do and even what to think. At this moment the pleasant sound of a woman's dress was heard; a middle-aged woman came up, all done up in lace, and with her a slim little thing, in a white dress very prettily describing her slender waist, in a pale-yellow little hat, light as a pastry. Behind them a tall footman with big side-whiskers and a whole dozen collars stopped and opened his snuffbox.

Kovalyov drew nearer, stuck out the batiste collar of his shirtfront, arranged his medals dangling on a golden chain and, smiling to all sides, turned his attention to the light little lady who, like a spring flower, inclined slightly and brought her little white hand with its semi-transparent fingers to her brow. The smile on Kovalyov's face spread still further when he saw from under her hat her little round chin of bright whiteness and part of a cheek flushed with the color of the first spring rose. But suddenly he leapt back as if burned. He remembered that in place of a nose he had absolutely nothing, and tears came to his eyes. He turned around in order to say straight out to the gentleman in the uniform that he was only posing as a state councillor, that he was a swindler and a scoundrel and that he was nothing more than merely his own nose.... But the nose was already gone: he had managed to gallop off, probably again to visit someone or other.

This plunged Kovalyov into despair. He went back and stopped for a minute under the colonnade, attentively looking in all directions in case the nose might turn up somewhere. He remembered distinctly that the hat he was wearing had a plume and his uniform was embroidered in gold; but he hadn't noticed his overcoat, nor the color of his carriage, nor the horses, nor even whether he had some kind of servant in the rear and in what livery. Furthermore such a quantity of carriages flew back and forth, and with such speed, that it was difficult even to distinguish them; but even if he had distinguished one of them, he would have had no means whatsoever of stopping it. The day was fine and sunny. On the Nevsky it was thick with people; an entire flowery waterfall of ladies flowed along the whole sidewalk, from the Police to the Anichkin Bridge. There went a court councillor he knew whom he called "colonel," particularly if they happened to meet in the presence of outsiders. There too was Yaryzhkin, the head clerk in the senate, a great friend, who always lost at Boston when he bid eight. There too was another major who had received his assessorship in the Caucasus, waving his hand so that he would come up to him....

"Oh, the devil take it!" said Kovalyov. "Hey coachman, take me straight to the chief of police!"

Kovalyov got into the droshky and merely shouted to the coachman, "Full speed ahead!"

"Is the chief of police in?" he cried, entering the hall.

"Not at all," answered the doorman, "he just left."

"How do you like that!"

"Yes," added the doorman, "not even so long ago, but he left. If you had come just a minute earlier, then, perhaps, you would have found him at home."

Kovalyov, not taking the handkerchief from his face, got into the carriage and shouted in a despairing voice:

"Let's go!"

"Where?" said the coachman.

"Straight ahead!"

"What do you mean straight ahead? There's a turn here; right or left?"

This question stopped Kovalyov and made him think again. In his position he ought first of all to consult the Board of Security, not because it had direct connection with the police, but because its disposition of the affair might be much quicker than in other places; to seek satisfaction from the heads of the place in which the nose claimed to work would be senseless, because from the nose's own answers one could already see that for this person nothing was sacred and he could be lying in this case as he had lied in asserting that he had never associated with him. So, Kovalyov was already going to order the coachman to drive to the Board of Security, when the thought again

27

came to him that this swindler and cheat who already at their first meeting had acted in such an unscrupulous manner, could again, conveniently making use of the time, somehow slip out of town, and then all searches would be in vain or could continue, which God forbid, for a whole month. Finally, it seemed, heaven itself brought him to his senses. He decided to go straight to the newspaper office and place a timely ad with a detailed description of all the specifications so that anyone meeting the nose could at that very minute present him to him or at least let him know of his whereabouts. So, having decided on this, he ordered the coachman to drive to the newspaper office and didn't stop pummelling him on the back with his fist, the whole way repeating "Faster, you scoundrel, faster, you rogue!" "Ekh, master!" the coachman would say, shaking his head and lashing with the reins at the horse whose coat was as long as a lapdog's. The droshky at last stopped, and Kovalyov, gasping for breath, ran into a small reception room where a gray-haired clerk in an old tailcoat and glasses sat at a table and, holding a pen in his teeth, was counting the small change that had been brought in.

"Who here takes notices?" shouted Kovalyov. "Oh, hello!"

"My respects," said the gray-haired clerk, raising his eyes for a minute and lowering them again to the distributed piles of money.

"I wish to print...."

"If you please. Kindly wait a bit," said the clerk, marking a figure on the paper with one hand and advancing two beads on the abacus with the fingers of his left hand. A servant with gold braid and an appearance showing he lived in an aristocratic house stood by the table with a note in his hands, and saw fit to show his worldliness. "Would you believe it, sir, that the mutt isn't worth eight kopeks, that is I wouldn't even give eight kopeks for her, but the countess loves her, I swear to God she loves her, and so the one who finds her gets a hundred rubles! To put it decently, that is, the way you and I are now conversing, people's tastes are entirely incompatible; if you're a hunter then keep a pointer or poodle; don't spare five hundred, pay a thousand, but at least let it be a good dog."

The worthy clerk listened to this with a significant air and at the same time made up the estimate: how many letters were there in the note brought in. At the sides stood a quantity of old ladies, merchant assistants and porters with advertisements. In one it was advertised that a coachman of sober conduct was released for service; in another—a little-used carriage imported in 1814 from Paris; there a housemaid of nineteen experienced in laundering, suitable also for other kinds of work, was available; a solid droshky missing one spring; a firey young dapple-gray horse seventeen years old; new turnip and radish seeds received from London; a dacha with all conveniences: with two stalls for horses and a place where one could start an excellent birch or pine grove; there too was a summons to those wanting to buy old shoe soles with the invitation to appear at the bidding every day from eight to three

28

o'clock in the morning. The room in which all this company was contained was small, and the air in it was exceptionally thick; but collegiate assessor Kovalyov couldn't smell anything because he covered himself with the handkerchief and because his actual nose was God knows where.

"Dear sir, allow me to ask you...I badly need..." he said at last with impatience.

"Right away, right away!... 2 rubles 43 kopeks! In a minute! One ruble 64 kopeks!" the gray-haired gentleman was saying, throwing advertisements in the faces of the old ladies and the porters. "What do you want?" he said at last, turning to Kovalyov.

"I beg you..." siad Kovalyov, "a swindle or a hoodwinking has occurred, I am still quite unable to find out which. I ask you only to print that he who presents that scoundrel to me will receive a suitable reward."

"Permit me to ask, what is your name?"

"No, why my name? I can't tell it. I have many acquaintances: Chekhtaryova, the state councillor's wife, Pelageya Grigorievna Podtochina, the staff officer's wife...they might find out, God forbid! You can simply write: collegiate assessor, or still better, one being of the rank of major."

"And the one who ran off was your house serf?"

"What house serf? That wouldn't even be such a big swindle! What ran off was...my nose...."

"Hm! What a strange name! And did this Mr. Nosov steal a large sum from you?"

"My nose, that is...you don't understand! My nose, my own nose, has disappeared somewhere unknown. The devil wanted to play a joke on me!"

"But in what way did it disappear? There's something I can't quite understand."

"But I can't tell you how; the main thing is that he's now driving all over town and calling himself a state councillor. And therefore I ask you to announce that anyone capturing him should immediately present him to me as soon as possible. Judge for yourself, after all, how am I to go around without such a prominent part of the body? It's not as if it were some little toe which I can stick in a boot—and no one will see if it's missing. I go to the state councillor's wife Chekhtaryova on Thursdays: Podtochina Pelageya Grigorievna, the field officer's wife, and she has a very pretty daughter, are also very close acquaintances, and you yourself can judge how I feel now.... Now I can't show myself to them."

The clerk pondered this, which his firmly compressed lips attested.

"No, I cannot place such an advertisement in the papers," he said at last after a long silence.

"What? Why?"

"Because. The newspaper might lose its reputation. If everyone starts writing that his nose has run away, then.... Even so they already say that a lot

29

of absurdities and false rumors are printed."

"But in what way is this matter absurd? Here, it seems, there is nothing of the sort."

"It seems to you that there isn't. But last week there was just such a case. A clerk came in, the same way you came in now, brought in an advertisement, the bill came to 2 rubles 73 kopeks, and the whole advertisement consisted in the fact that a poodle with a black coat had run away. You'd think, what could be the harm in that? But it turned out to be a libel: that poodle was a treasurer, I don't remember of what department."

"But after all I'm not asking you to advertise about a poodle, but about my own nose: that is, almost the same thing as about me myself."

"No, I can in no way put in such an announcement."

"Even when my nose has, precisely, disappeared!"

"If it has disappeared, then it's a doctor's affair. They say that there are such people who can stick on any kind of a nose you want. However, I remark that you must be a man of merry nature who loves to have a joke in society."

"I swear to you, as God is holy! Perhaps, if it's come to that, I'll show you."

"Why trouble yourself!" continued the clerk, sniffing snuff. "However, if it's no trouble," he added with a gesture of curiosity, "then it would be desirable to have a look."

The collegiate assessor took the handkerchief from his face.

"Indeed, extraordinarily strange!" said the clerk, "an entirely smooth space, as if it were a freshly-fried pancake. Yes, flat to an incredible degree!"

"Well, are you going to argue even now? You see for yourself that it's impossible not to print it. I will be particularly grateful to you; and I'm glad that this incident has given me the pleasure of meeting you...." The major, as is evident from this, decided on this occasion to be a little low.

"Printing it, of course, is a trivial affair," said the clerk, "only I don't foresee any advantage for you in it. If you really want, give it to someone who has an artful pen to describe it as a rare phenomenon of nature and print the little article in *The Northern Bee* (here he again took a pinch of snuff) for the edification of youth (here he wiped his nose) or simply for general curiosity."

The collegiate assessor felt completely hopeless. He lowered his eyes to the bottom of the newspaper where the information about performances was; his face was already ready to smile on encountering the name of an actress, very attractive, and his hand felt for his pocket: did he have a five ruble note on him, because field officers, in Kovalyov's opinion, should sit in the best seats—but the thought of his nose ruined everything!

The clerk himself, it seemed, was touched by Kovalyov's difficult position. Wishing to lighten his grief somewhat, he saw fit to express his sympathy in a few words: "It is, to be sure, very distressing to me that such a funny thing should have happened to you. Wouldn't you like to take a pinch of snuff? It dispells headaches and melancholy moods: it's good even in regard to hemorrhoids." Saying this, the clerk offered his snuffbox to Kovalyov, rather deftly opening the lid with a portrait of some lady in a hat.

This thoughtless action made Kovalyov lose all patience. "I don't understand how you can see fit to joke," he said with feeling, "can't you see that I don't have precisely that with which I could sniff? The devil take your snuff! I can't even look at it now, and not only at your wretched *Beryozinsky*, but even if you offered me rapé itself." Having said this, he went out of the newspaper office deeply vexed, and set off for the district police superintendent, an extraordinary lover of sugar. In his house the whole foyer, it and the dining room, was stacked with sugar loaves which merchants had brought him out of friendship. The cook at that moment was taking off the district superintendent's regulation Wellington boots; his sword and all his martial armor already hung peaceably in the corners, and his three-year-old son was already fingering his formidable three-cornered hat; and he, after a fierce fighting life, was preparing to taste the pleasures of peace.

Kovalyov went in to him at the moment when he stretched, grunted, and said, "Ekh, I'll sleep gloriously for two hours!" And therefore one could predict that the arrival of the collegiate assessor was entirely mistimed. And I don't know, if he had even brought him several pounds of tea or some cloth at this time, he would not have been received too joyfully. The superintendent was a great patron of all arts and manufacturings, but he preferred the government banknote to everything. "That's the thing," he would usually say, "there's nothing better than this thing: it doesn't ask for food, takes up little space, will always fit in the pocket, you drop it—it won't break."

The superintendent received Kovalyov rather drily and said that after dinner was not the time to carry on an investigation, that nature herself had ordained that, having eaten, one should rest a bit (from this the collegiate assessor could see that the pronouncements of the ancient wise men were not unknown to the district superintendent), that they don't pull the nose off a respectable man and that there are plenty of all sorts of majors in the world who don't even have their underwear in decent condition and who hang around all sorts of indecent places.

That is, right between the eyes! It is necessary to remark that Kovalyov was a man exceptionally easy to offend. He could forgive anything which might be said about himself, but he could not forgive it at all if it related to rank or profession. He even considered that in theatrical presentations one could permit anything which related to field officers, but one ought not to attack superior officers in any way. The reception of the superintendent so disconcerted him that he shook his head and said with a sense of dignity, somewhat spreading his arms: "I confess, after such insulting remarks on your part, I have nothing to add..." and went out.

He came home scarcely able to stand on his feet. It was already dark. His apartment seemed sad or exceedingly disgusting to him after all these unsuccessful searches. Entering the foyer he saw on the dirty leather divan his servant Ivan, who, lying on his back, was spitting at the ceiling and kept hitting the same spot rather successfully. The indifference of the man enraged him; he struck him on the forehead with his hat, saying: "You pig, you're always doing stupid things!"

Ivan leapt up suddenly from his place and rushed full speed to help him off with his cloak.

Going into his room, the major, tired and sad, threw himself into an armchair and at last after several sighs, said: "My God! My God! Why such a misfortune? Were I without an arm or a leg—it would still be better; were I without ears—wretched, but still more bearable; but without a nose a man is the devil knows what: neither fish nor fowl; simply take him and throw him out the window! And at least if it had been cut off at war or in a duel, or if I myself had been the cause: but it actually disappeared for no reason at all, disappeared for nothing, not for a kopek!... Only no, it can't be," he added, having thought a bit. "It's incredible that a nose should disappear; incredible by any means. This, probably, is either a dream or simply a daydream; perhaps somehow by mistake I drank the vodka I rub my beard with after shaving instead of water. Ivan, that fool, didn't take it away and I, probably, picked it up." In order really to convince himself that he wasn't drunk, the major pinched himself so painfully that he shrieked. This pain completely convinced him that he was acting and living in a waking state. He stealthily approached the mirror and at first shut his eyes tight with the thought that perhaps the nose would appear in its place; but at this very minute he leapt back, saying: "What a libellous appearance!"

This was, precisely, incomprehensible. If a button had disappeared, a silver spoon, a watch or something like that; but to disappear, and from whom to disappear? And furthermore in his own apartment!... Major Kovalyov, weighing all the circumstances, considered it almost the closest of all to the truth that the blame for this should belong to none other than the field officer's wife Podtochina, who wished him to marry her daughter. He himself liked to flirt with her, but he avoided a final resolution. When the field officer's wife announced to him straight out that she wanted to marry her to him, he quietly weighed anchor with his compliments, saying that he was still young, that he had to serve for about five years so that he would be exactly forty-two. And therefore the field officer's wife, probably for revenge, had decided to ruin him and hired some kind of peasant sorceresses for this, because it was in no way possible to suppose that the nose had been cut off—no one came into his room; the barber Ivan Yakovlevich shaved him only on Wednesday, and all during Wednesday and even all Thursday his nose was

32

whole—this he remembered and knew very well; besides he would have felt pain, and, without doubt, a wound wouldn't heal so fast and be flat as a pancake. He made plans in his head; either to summon the field officer's wife to court in the formal manner or to go to her himself and expose her. His deliberations were interrupted by a light shining through all the chinks of the door which indicated that the candle in the foyer had already been lit by Ivan. Soon Ivan himself appeared, carrying it in front of himself and brightly illuminating the whole room. Kovalyov's first gesture was to grab the handkerchief and cover the place where yesterday his nose had still been, so that the stupid man would not indeed start gaping, seeing such a peculiarity in his master.

Ivan hadn't managed to go off to his lair when an unfamiliar voice was heard in the foyer saying, "Does collegiate assessor Kovalyov live here?"

"Come in—Major Kovalyov is here," said Kovalyov, leaping up quickly and opening the door.

There entered a police officer of handsome appearance, with side-whiskers not too light and not too dark, with rather full cheeks, the very same one who at the beginning of the story stood at the end of the Isakievsky Bridge.

"You were pleased to lose your nose?"

"Just so."

"It is now found."

"What did you say?" cried Major Kovalyov. Joy made him lose his tongue. He stared at the officer standing before him, on whose full lips and cheeks the flickering light of the candle flashed brightly. "How?"

"By a strange coincidence: they caught him almost on the road. He had already gotten into a stagecoach and wanted to go to Riga. And his passport has been issued long ago in the name of a certain official. And the strange thing is that I myself at first took him for a gentleman. But, fortunately, my glasses were with me, and I at once saw that this was a nose. You see, I'm nearsighted and if you stand in front of me, I see only that you have a face, but I notice neither nose nor beard nor anything. My mother-in-law, that is, the mother of my wife, doesn't see anything either."

Kovalyov was beside himself.

"Where is he? Where? I'll go at once."

"Don't trouble yourself. I, knowing that you needed it, brought it with me. And the strange thing is that the chief accomplice in this affair is that scoundrel the barber on Voznesensky Avenue, who is now sitting in prison. I have long suspected him of drunkenness and thievery and only the day before yesterday he filched a dozen buttons in a certain shop. Your nose is exactly as it was." With this the officer dipped into his pocket and took out the nose wrapped in a piece of paper.

"That's it!" cried Kovalyov, "exactly it! Have a cup of tea with me today."

"I would consider it a great pleasure, but I couldn't possibly: from here I have to drop in on the House of Correction.... The high prices of all supplies have risen very greatly.... I have living in my house both my mother-in-law, that is, the mother of my wife, and the children; the eldest especially gives great promise: a very smart little boy, but there are absolutely no means whatsoever for his education."

Kovalyov caught on and, grabbing a ten-ruble note from the table, thrust it into the hands of the policeman who, having bowed, went out the door and almost at that very moment Kovalyov already heard his voice on the street, where he was admonishing with his fists a certain stupid peasant who had ridden right onto the boulevard with his wagon.

The collegiate assessor, upon the departure of the policeman, for some minutes remained in a kind of undefinable state and after some minutes hardly regained the ability to see and feel, to such oblivion had the unexpected joy reduced him. He carefully took the restored nose in both cupped hands and once again inspected it attentively.

"That's it, exactly it!" said Major Kovalyov. "Here is even the pimple on the left side which popped up yesterday." The major almost burst out laughing from joy.

But there is nothing enduring in this world, and therefore even joy in the second minute is already not as acute as in the first; in the third minute it becomes still weaker and finally merges unnoticeably with the usual condition of the soul, as a circle on the water, caused by the fall of a pebble, finally merges with the smooth surface. Kovalyov began to think and realized that the affair was still not finished: the nose was found, but after all it had to be attached, put in its place.

"And what if it won't stay put?"

At such a question, posed to himself, the major paled.

With a feeling of inexpressible terror he dashed to the table, brought the mirror over in order not to somehow put the nose on crooked. His hands trembled. Carefully and cautiously he laid it on its former spot. Oh, horror! The nose wouldn't stick!... He brought it to his mouth, warmed it slightly with his breath and again applied it to the smooth spot situated between his two cheeks; but the nose would in no way stay on.

"Come on, come on now, get on, you fool!" he said to it. But the nose was as if wooden and fell on the table with such a strange sound, as if it were a cork. The major's face contorted spasmodically. "Will it really not grow back on?" he said in fright. But however many times he brought it to its proper place, his efforts were unsuccessful as before.

He called Ivan and sent him for the doctor who rented the best apartment in the same house on the ground floor. This doctor was a fine-looking man, had beautiful pitch-black sidewhiskers, a fresh, healthy wife, ate fresh apples in the morning and kept his mouth in a state of unusual cleanliness, rinsing it every morning for almost three quarters of an hour and brushing his teeth with five different sorts of brushes. The doctor appeared right away. Having asked how long ago the misfortune occurred, he lifted Major Kovalyov by the chin and gave him a flick with his thumb in the very place where his nose had formerly been, so that the major had to throw his head back with such force that he hit the back of his head against the wall. The medic said that this was nothing, and, advising him to move away from the wall a bit, ordered him to bend his head at first to the right side and, having felt the place where his nose had formerly been, said: "Hm!" Then he ordered him to bend his head to the left side and said: "Hm!" And in conclusion again gave him a flick with his thumb so that Major Kovalyov jerked his head like a horse whose teeth are being inspected. Having performed this experiment, the medic shook his head and said:

"No, it's impossible. You had better just stay like that, because it might make it even worse. It can, of course, be attached; I could, probably, attach it right now for you; but I assure you that it would be worse for you."

"That's a fine thing! How am I to remain without a nose?" said Kovalyov. "It can't be any worse than it is now. This is simply the devil knows what! Where can I show myself with such a libel? I have important acquaintances: even today I have to be at parties in two houses. I am acquainted with many: the state councillor's wife Chekhtaryova, Podtochina the field officer's wife...although after her present action I have no further business with her other than through the police. "Do me a favor," said Kovalyov in a pleading voice, "isn't there a way? Stick it on somehow; even if not so nicely, just so it would hold; I can even prop it up slightly with my hand in dangerous situations. Furthermore I don't even dance, which might harm it by some careless motion. As regards appreciation of the visit, rest assured, as much as my means permit...."

"Would you believe," said the doctor in a voice neither loud nor soft, but exceptionally persuasive and hypnotic, "that I never practice out of self-interest? That is against my principles and my art. True, I take money for my visits, but solely in order not to offend by refusal. Of course, I could attach your nose; but I assure you on my honor, if by now you don't believe my word, that it will be much worse. Better leave it to the action of nature herself. Wash more often with cold water, and I assure you that you, not having a nose, will be just as healthy as if you had one. And the nose I advise you to put in a bottle with spirits or still better to pour in two tablespoons of strong spirits and heated vinegar, and then you can get considerable money for it. I'll even take it myself, if you don't set too high a price."

"No, no! I won't sell it for anything!" shrieked the despairing Major Kovalyov. "Better let it disappear!"

"Excuse me!" said the doctor, bowing his farewell, "I wanted to be of help to you...what can one do! At least you have seen my effort."

Having said this, the doctor walked out of the room with a majestic air. Kovalyov didn't notice even his face and in deep numbness saw only the cuffs of his shirt, white and clean as snow, peeking out of the sleeves of his black frockcoat.

The next day he decided, before registering a complaint, to write to the field officer's wife to see if she would agree without a fight to return him what was proper. The letter was of the following content:

Dear Madam,
    Alexandra Grigorievna!
    I cannot understand this strange action on your part. Rest assured that, acting in this way, you will gain nothing and will in no way force me to marry your daughter. Believe that the affair relating to my nose is completely known to me, equally as is the fact that you are the chief accomplice in this, and no one else. Its sudden separation from its place, its escape and masquerade, first in the form of a certain official, and then finally in its own form, is nothing more than the consequence of sorcery effected by you or by those who practice similar noble pursuits. I for my part consider it my duty to forewarn you that if the above-mentioned nose is not in its place this very day, I will be obliged to seek the defense and protection of the law.
    However, with complete respect for you, I have the honor to be

Your faithful servant
Platon Kovalyov

Dear Sir,
    Platon Kuzmich!
    Your letter surprised me exceedingly. I, I confess to you openly, in no way expected this, in particular as regards the unjust reproaches on your part. I wish to inform you that I have never received the offical whom you mentioned in my house either masquerading or in his real form. It is true that Filipp Ivanovich Potanchikov has been coming to my house. And although he, precisely, sought the hand of my daughter, being himself of good, sober conduct and great erudition, I never gave him any hope. You also mention a nose. If you mean by this that I wanted to lead you by the nose, that is to give you a formal refusal, then it surprises me that you yourself speak of this when I, as you know, was of the entirely opposite opinion, and if you pledge yourself to my daughter in legal fashion right now, I am ready to satisfy you at once, for this has always been the object of my most heartfelt desire, in the hope of which I remain always at your service

Alexandra Podtochina

"No," said Kovalyov, having read the letter. "She is clearly not guilty. It can't be! The letter is written in a way a person guilty of a crime couldn't write." The collegiate assessor was an expert in this because he had several times been sent on investigations when still in the Caucasus. "By what means, then, by what fates did this happen? Only the devil can make this out!" he said at last, in despair.

Meanwhile rumors about this extraordinary occurrence were spreading around the entire capital and, as always, not without certain additions. At that time everyone's minds were particularly disposed to the extraordinary: recently experiments with the effects of hypnotism had been occupying the whole town. Furthermore the story of the dancing chairs in Konyushennaya Street was still fresh, and therefore there is nothing surprising in the fact that they soon began to say that collegiate assessor Kovalyov's nose takes a stroll on Nevsky Prospect exactly at three o'clock. A multitude of curious people flocked there every day. Someone said that the nose was to be found in Junker's store; and next to Junker's there was such a crowd and a press that even the police had to intervene. One speculator of respectable appearance, with sidewhiskers, who sold assorted dry pastries at the entrance to the theatre, purposely set up excellent solid wooden benches on which he invited the curious to stand for 80 kopeks per visitor. One estimable corporal left his house early just for this purpose and with great difficulty made his way through the crowd; but, to his great indignation, he saw in the window of the store, instead of a nose, an ordinary woolen sweater and a lithograph which depicted a girl adjusting her stocking, and a dandy with an open waistcoat and a small beard looking at her from behind a tree—a picture which had been continually hanging in the same place for already more than ten years. Walking away, he said with annoyance: "How can one fool people with such stupid and improbable rumors?" Then the rumor went around that Major Kovalyov's nose was strolling not on Nevsky Prospect, but in the Tauride Gardens, that he had already been there a long time, that when Khozrev-Mirza* still lived there he used to be very surprised by this strange trick of nature. Some of the students of the surgical academy set off thither. One aristocratic, respectable lady asked the keeper of the garden in a special letter to show her child this rare phenomenon with, if possible, an explanation instructive and informative for the young.

Exceptionally delighted by all these events were all the men about town, the indispensable frequenters of soirées, who liked to amuse the ladies and whose resources at that time were entirely exhausted. A small portion of respectable and well-intentioned people was exceptionally dissatisfied. One gentleman said with indignation that he didn't understand how in our present enlightened century absurd inventions could spread, and that he was surprised that the government paid no attention to it. This gentleman, as is evident, be-

---

*[A Persian prince, in Petersburg in 1829 in connection with the murder in Persia of the Russian ambassador, the writer A.S. Griboedov. He stayed in the Tauride Palace.]

longed to the number of those gentlemen who would like to involve the government in everything, even in their daily fights with their wives. Following this...but here again the whole event is covered in fog, and what happened next is absolutely unknown.

III

Perfect nonsense goes on in the world. Sometimes there is absolutely no plausibility whatsoever: suddenly that very nose which had been riding around with the rank of state councillor and caused so much fuss in the town showed up again, just as if nothing had happened, in its place, that is, precisely between the two cheeks of Major Kovalyov. This happened already on the seventh of April. Waking up and inadvertently glancing in the mirror, he sees: his nose! Feel it—a nose exactly! "Ehe!" said Kovalyov and in his joy almost danced the gopak all around his room barefoot, but Ivan coming in deterred him. He ordered him to give him his washing things at once and, washing, glanced again in the mirror: a nose. Wiping himself with the towel he again glanced in the mirror: a nose!

"Look, Ivan, it seems I have sort of a pimple on my nose," he said, meanwhile thinking, "It would be awful if Ivan said: Oh no, sir, not only no pimple, but there's no nose!"

But Ivan said: "It's nothing, sir, no pimple: a clean nose!"

"Great, the devil take it!" said the major to himself and snapped his fingers. At that moment the barber Ivan Yakovlevich peeked in the door, but as timidly as a kitten which has just been whipped for stealing lard:

"Tell me first: are your hands clean?" Kovalyov shouted to him when he was still at a distance.

"Clean."

"Liar!"

"I swear to God they're clean, sir."

"Well, look out."

Kovalyov sat down. Ivan Yakovlevich covered him with a napkin and in one instant, with the help of a brush, turned his whole beard and part of a cheek into cream such as they serve at merchants' name-day parties. "Look at that!" said Ivan Yakovlevich to himself, looking at the nose, and then he turned his head to the other side and looked at it sideways. "There it is! How do you like that!" he continued and looked at the nose for a long time. At last lightly, with a caution which can only be imagined, he raised two fingers in order to seize it by the tip. Such was Ivan Yakovlevich's system.

"Now, now, now, look out!" screamed Kovalyov. Ivan Yakovlevich simply dropped his hands, stopped dead, and grew embarrassed as he had never been embarrassed. At last he carefully began to tickle him under the beard with the razor, and although it was difficult and not at all handy for

38

him to shave without holding onto the olfactory part of the body, nonetheless, somehow or other bracing himself with his rough thumb against the Major's cheek and lower jaw, he at last overcame all obstacles and finished shaving him.

When everything was ready, Kovalyov hurried to dress right away, took a cab and drove straight to the pastry shop. Entering, he called out still from a distance: "Boy, a cup of chocolate!" and the same minute turned to the mirror: there's the nose. He gaily turned around and with a satiric expression looked, somewhat squinting, at two soldiers, one of whom had a nose not the least bit bigger than a vest button. After this he set off for the office of the department where he was soliciting a vice-governor's job, or in case of failure, an executor's. Going through the reception room he glanced in the mirror: there's the nose. Then he went to see another collegiate assessor or major, a great scoffer, to whom he often said in answer to various nosy remarks: "Well, you, I know you, you're a sharp one!" On the way he thought: "If even the Major doesn't burst out laughing on seeing me, then it's a sure sign that everything, whatever it be, sits in its own place." But the collegiate assessor didn't say anything. "Great, great, the devil take it," thought Kovalyov to himself. On the way he met the field officer's wife Podtochina together with her daughter, bowed to them and was met with joyous exclamations, it must be all right, he hadn't undergone any damage. He talked with them for a very long time, and deliberately taking out his snuffbox, kept stuffing his nose at both entrances for an extremely long time in front of them, adding to himself, "There you are, womankind, stupid hens! And all the same I won't marry the daughter! Simply for fun, *par amour*—by all means!" And from then on Major Kovalyov went about as if nothing had happened, on Nevsky Prospect, to the theatres, and everywhere. And the nose too, as if nothing had happened, sat on his face, not giving even the appearance that it had been running around elsewhere. And thereafter Major Kovalyov was always seen in a good humor, smiling, pursuing absolutely all the pretty ladies and even stopping on one occasion in front of a stall in the Gostiny Dvor and buying the ribbon of some order, it is not known for what reason, because he himself was not the chevalier of any order.

That's the kind of incident that happened in the northern capital of our vast empire. Only now, on thinking it all over, we see that there is much that is implausible in it. Not to mention the really strange supernatural separation of the nose and its appearance in various places in the form of a state councillor—how could Kovalyov not realize that one cannot advertise for a nose through the newspaper office? I don't here mean it in the sense that it seemed to me a lot to pay for the advertisement; that's nonsense, and I am not at all one of those mercenary people. But it's indecent, indelicate, improper! And then again—how did the nose appear in a baked bread and what about Ivan Yakovlevich himself?.. No, I don't understand this at all, I absolutely don't understand! But what is stranger, what is least comprehensible of all, is how authors can choose such subjects. I confess, this is entirely inconceivable, it's exactly...no, no, I don't understand at all. In the first place, it is of absolutely no benefit to the fatherland; in the second place...but even in the second place there's also no benefit. I simply don't know what it is....

But yet with all this, although, of course, one may admit this, that and the other, may even...and after all, where aren't there incongruities? But all the same, when you think about it, there is something, really, in all this. No matter what anyone says, such things happen in the world; rarely, but they happen.

1836

THE OVERCOAT

In the department...but it's better not to say in which department. There is nothing more touchy than all sorts of departments, regiments, offices, and, in a word, all sorts of official bodies. Nowadays every private individual considers all of society insulted in his person. They say quite recently a petition circulated from a certain police inspector, I don't remember from which town, in which he clearly states that the government institutions are perishing and that his holy name is being pronounced absolutely in vain. And in proof he appended to the petition the hugest volume of some romantic composition, in which, every ten pages, a police inspector appears, in places even in a completely drunken state. And so, to avoid any unpleasantness, we had better call the department in question *a certain department*. And so, in *a certain department* served *a certain clerk*, a clerk one couldn't call very remarkable: of short stature, a little bit pocky, a little bit ruddy, even, to look at, a little bit squinty, with a small bald spot on top, with wrinkles along both sides of his cheeks and with a complexion that is called hemorrhoidal.... What can one do! The Petersburg climate is to blame. As regards rank (for among us before everything one must declare one's rank), he was what they call a perpetual titular councillor, about which, as is well known, various writers who have the praiseworthy habit of attacking those who can't bite back have japed and jibed their fill. The clerk's surname was Bashmachkin. By the very name it is already apparent that it at one time came from *bashmak*, shoe; but when, at what time and in what way it came from *bashmak*, nothing is known about this. The father and the grandfather and even the brother-in-law, and absolutely all the Bashmachkins went around in boots, only changing the soles about three times a year. His name and patronymic were Akaky Akakievich. Perhaps it will seem a bit strange and contrived to the reader, but it can be demonstrated that they didn't contrive it at all, but that such circumstances occurred of themselves that made it quite impossible to give him any other name, and it happened precisely like this: Akaky Akakievich was born, if only my memory doesn't deceive me, in the early hours of March 23rd. The late mother, a clerk's wife and a very good woman, arranged as is proper to christen the child. The mother still lay on the bed opposite the doors, while on her right hand stood the godfather, a most excellent person, Ivan Ivanovich Yeroshkin, who served as head clerk in the senate, and the godmother, the wife of a police officer, a woman of rare virtues, Arina Semyonovna Belobryushkova. They presented the mother with the choice of any three that she wanted to choose; Mokkiya, Sossiya, or to call the child after the martyr Khozdazat. "No," thought the late mother,

41

"those are all such names." To satisfy her, they opened the calendar in another place; again three names turned up: Trifily, Dula and Varakhasy. "What an affliction," said the old lady, "what names they all are, I really never heard the like. At least if it were Varadat or Varukh, but Trifily and Varakhasy!" They turned another page—Pavsikaky and Vakhtisy turned up. "Well, I see already," said the old lady, "that clearly such is his fate. If it's like that, better let him be called after his father. The father was Akaky, so let the son be Akaky too." In this way Akaky Akakievich came about. They christened the baby, at which he burst out crying and made such a grimace, as if he foresaw that he would be a titular councillor. And so, that's the way all this came about. We mentioned this so that the reader could see for himself that this happened entirely by necessity and to give any other name was quite impossible. When and at what time he entered the department and who appointed him, this no one could recall. However often directors and all sorts of superiors were changed, he was always seen at one and the same place, in the same position, in the same post, the same copying clerk, so that later they were convinced that he, evidently, was born into this world already entirely finished, in a uniform and with a bald spot on his head. In the department he was shown no respect whatsoever. The porters not only did not get up from their places when he passed by, but didn't even glance at him, as if a simple fly had flown through the reception hall. Superiors treated him somehow coldly and despotically. Some department head's assistant would thrust papers right under his nose, not saying even: "Copy it," or, "Here's a nice little interesting case," or something pleasant, as is done in well-bred offices. And he would take it, looking only at the paper, not noticing who presented it to him and whether he had the right to. He would take it and right away get set to copy it. The young clerks laughed at him and made jokes about him to the degree that clerk wit permitted; right in front of him they told various stories that had been made up about him; about his landlady, a seventy-year-old lady, they said she beat him, asked when their wedding would be, scattered bits of paper on his head, calling it snow. But not one word would Akaky Akakievich answer to this, just as if nobody were in front of him; it didn't even affect his work: among all these annoyances he would not make a single mistake in writing. Only when the joke was too unbearable, when they jogged his elbow, keeping him from doing his work, he would say: "Leave me alone, why do you insult me?" And something strange was contained in the words and in the voice in which they were pronounced. In it resounded something so evoking of pity that one recently appointed young man who, by the example of the others, was on the verge of permitting himself to laugh at Akaky, suddenly stopped as if transfixed, and from that time on it was as if everything had changed for him and appeared in another form. Some preternatural force alienated him from the comrades he had become acquainted with, having taken them for decent, well-bred people. And long

42

after, at the gayest moments, the short little clerk with the bald spot on top would appear to him with his penetrating words: "Leave me alone, why do you insult me?" And in these penetrating words rang other words: "I am your brother." And the poor young man would cover his face with his hands, and many times later in his life he would shudder, seeing how much inhumanity there is in man, how much fierce coarseness is hidden in refined educated breeding, and, God! even in the very man whom the world deems noble and honorable.

Hardly anywhere could one find a man who so lived for his work. It is too little to say he worked zealously, no, he worked with love. There, in this copying, he saw a certain special varied and pleasant world all his own. Delight was expressed on his face; some letters were his favorites, and when he would come upon them he would be beside himself, chuckle, wink and work them along with his lips, so that on his face, it seemed, one could read every letter his pen produced. If they had rewarded him in proportion to effort, he, to his own amazement, perhaps might have even landed among the state councillors; but he earned, as the wits, his comrades, expressed it, a button in his buttonhole, and netted hemorrhoids in another hole. However, it cannot be said that no attention whatever was paid him. A certain director, being a kind man and wishing to reward him for his long service, ordered that he be given something a little more important than the usual copying; namely, he was told to readdress an already prepared case to another office; it was only a matter of changing the main heading and of here and there changing the verbs from the first person to the third. This gave him such difficulty that he broke into an utter sweat, wiped his brow and at last said: "No, better let me copy something." From then on they left him to copying forever. Outside of this copying, it seemed, nothing existed for him. He didn't think at all about his dress: his uniform was not green, but of some reddish-floury color. The collar on it was narrow and low so that his neck, although it wasn't long, seemed, coming out of the collar, unusually long, like on those plaster kittens with bobbing heads whole dozens of which foreign peddlers carry on their heads in Russia. And something or other was always sticking to his uniform: either a piece of straw or some thread or other; furthermore he possessed the rare talent, walking along the street, of arriving under a window precisely at the very time when someone was throwing all sorts of rubbish out of it, and therefore he perpetually carried away watermelon and cantaloupe rinds and similar trash on his hat. Not once in his life had he paid attention to what is done and what goes on every day on the street, at which, as is well-known, his brother, the young clerk, will always look, sharpening his alert gaze to such acuity that he will even notice whose trouser strap has come undone on the other side of the pavement, which always summons a sly smile to his face.

But Akaky Akakievich, even if he had looked at something, would have

43

seen over everything his clean lines written out in level handwriting, and only possibly if, coming from who knows where, a horse's muzzle settled on his shoulder and let out a whole blast on his cheek through its nostrils, only then would he notice that he was not in the middle of a line, but rather in the middle of the street. Arriving home, he would at once sit down at the table, quickly gulp his cabbage soup and eat a chunk of beef with onion, not noticing their taste in the least, eat all this with flies and with whatever God would send at the moment. Noticing that his stomach was beginning to swell, he would get up from the table, take out a little pot of ink and would copy papers he had brought home. If there didn't happen to be any, he would deliberately take, for his own enjoyment, a paper to copy for himself, particularly if it were remarkable not for beauty of style but for being addressed to some new or important personage or other.

Even at those hours when the gray Petersburg sky completely darkens and all the clerk folk have eaten their fill and dined, each as he can, according to the salary he receives and his own whim—when everything has already had a rest after the departmental scratching of pens, after rushing about, after their own and others' essential affairs, and after all of that which indefatigable man voluntarily assigns himself even more than is necessary—when the clerks hurry to dedicate the remaining time to pleasure: the more lively one dashes off to the theater; another out onto the street, to devote the time to the inspection of certain stupid little hats; another to a party to waste the time in complimenting some comely girl, the star of a small clerk circle; another, and this happens most frequently, simply goes to his fellow clerk on the third or fourth floor, to two small rooms with a hall or kitchen and certain modish pretensions, a lamp or another article which has cost many sacrifices, goings without dinner or outings; in a word, even at that time when all the clerks scatter among the little apartments of their friends to play military whist, sipping tea from glasses with kopek crackers, drawing smoke from long chibouks, telling during the dealing some gossip that has drifted down from high society, from which a Russian can never and under no circumstances desist, or even, when there's nothing to talk about, retelling the eternal anecdote about the Commandant who was told that the tail of the horse on Falconet's monument* had been chopped off—in a word, even when everyone was trying to distract himself, Akaky Akakievich wouldn't yield to any distraction. No one could say that they had ever seen him at any party. Having written his fill, he would go to bed, smiling in advance at the thought of the next day: what would God send him to copy tomorrow? Thus flowed the peaceful life of a man who could be satisfied with his lot on a salary of four hundred, and it would perhaps have flowed on into advanced old age if there weren't various disasters strewn along the path of life not only of titular but even of privy, actual, court and all sorts of councillors, even

---

*[The equestrian statue of Peter the Great, which stands on the banks of the Neva.]

those who don't give anyone counsel or take it from anyone themselves.

There is in Petersburg a powerful enemy of everyone receiving four hundred rubles a year or thereabouts in salary. This enemy is none other than our northern frost, although, by the way, they do say it's very healthy. From eight to nine in the morning, precisely at the hour when the streets are covered with those going to the department, it begins to give such hard and prickly flicks on all noses indiscriminately that the poor clerks positively don't know where to put them. At this time, when the foreheads of even those who occupy higher posts ache from the frost and tears come to their eyes, the poor titular councillors are sometimes defenseless. The only salvation consists in running through five or six streets as fast as possible in a scraggy little overcoat and then stamping one's feet thoroughly in the cloakroom until, in this way, all the frozen abilities and gifts for dispatching one's duty thaw out. Akaky Akakievich had for some time begun to feel that his back and shoulder had somehow begun to be seared particularly forcibly, despite the fact that he tried to run across the usual space as fast as possible. He wondered, at last, whether there weren't certain faults in his overcoat. Having looked it over thoroughly at home, he discovered that in two or three places, namely on the back and on the shoulders, it had become exactly like cheesecloth: the broadcloth was so worn that it was transparent, and the lining was falling apart. One should know that Akaky Akakievich's overcoat also served as an object of merriment for the clerks; they took away even its honorable name of overcoat and called it a housecoat. Indeed, it had a certain strange demeanor: its collar diminished more and more with every year, for it served for patching the other parts. The patching showed no signs of the tailor's art, and it all came out quite baggy and unattractive. Seeing what the matter was, Akaky Akakievich decided that it would be necessary to take the overcoat over to Petrovich, the tailor, who lived somewhere on the fourth floor on a back stairway, who, despite his one eye and the pockmarks all over his face, engaged rather successfully in the repair of clerks' and all other sorts of trousers and tailcoats, of course, when he was in a sober state and not nourishing some other notion in his head. One ought not to say much, of course, about this tailor, but since it is already established that the personality of every character in a story should be described completely, there's nothing to be done, let's have Petrovich too. At first he was called simply Grigory and was a serf of some landowner; he began to call himself Petrovich when he received his freedom and began to drink rather heavily on all the holidays, at first on the big ones and then, indiscriminately, on all church holidays, wherever there was a little cross on the calendar. In this respect he was true to the traditions of his grandfathers and, arguing with his wife, would call her a worldly woman and a German. Since we have already let slip something about the wife, it will be necessary to say a couple of words about her too; but, unfortunately, not much was known about her, except that Petrovich had a wife, that she even wore a cap and not a kerchief; but she could not boast, it

45

appears, of her beauty; at least, on meeting her, only soldiers of the guard would peek at her under her cap, twitching a whisker and emitting some peculiar sound.

Making his way up the stairway leading to Petrovich's, which, to do it justice, was all soaked with water and slops and saturated through and through with that ammoniac smell which eats at the eyes and, as is well known, is inevitably present on all the back stairs of Petersburg houses—making his way up the stairway, Akaky Akakievich was already speculating how much Petrovich would ask, and mentally determined not to give him more than two rubles. The door was open, because the mistress, preparing some fish, had filled the kitchen with so much smoke that it was impossible to see even the very cockroaches. Akaky Akakievich went through the kitchen, unnoticed even by the mistress herself, and at last entered the room where he saw Petrovich sitting on a broad wooden unpainted table and crossing his legs under him like a Turkish pasha. His feet, as is the custom of tailors sitting at their work, were bare. And the first thing to strike the eye was his big toe, very well known to Akaky Akakievich, with a sort of deformed nail, thick and strong as the shell on a tortoise. Around Petrovich's neck hung a skein of silk and threads, while on his knees were some sort of rags. Already for about three minutes he had been aiming the thread at the needle's eye, not hitting it, and therefore was very angry at the darkness and even at the thread itself, muttering under his breath "She won't go in, the little barbarian; you've worn me out, you rascal!" Akaky Akakievich was distressed that he had come precisely at a moment when Petrovich was angry: he liked to order things from Petrovich when the latter was already a little under the influence, or, as his wife expressed it, "glutted with rotgut, the one-eyed devil." In this state Petrovich usually very willingly gave in and agreed, he even bowed and thanked one every time. Later, it's true, his wife would come in crying and say that her husband was drunk and therefore had let him off cheap; but usually you added one ten kopek piece, and the cat was in the bag. Now Petrovich was, it seemed, in a sober state, and therefore curt, intractable and eager to demand the devil knows what prices. Akaky Akakievich sensed this and already was about, as they say, to beat a retreat, but the business had already been begun. Petrovich screwed up his one eye at him very intently, and Akaky Akakievich involuntarily blurted out: "Greetings, Petrovich!"

"I greet you, sir," said Petrovich and squinted his eye at Akaky Akakievich's hands, wanting to make out what manner of booty he carried.

"I just came to you, Petrovich, sort of...." One should know that Akaky Akakievich expressed himself for the most part in prepositions, adverbs, and finally, in such particles as have absolutely no meaning whatever. And if the matter was very difficult, he even had the habit of not finishing the sentence at all, so that quite often, having begun a speech with the words: "That, really, is completely sort of..." but then there was nothing, and he

46

himself would forget, thinking he had already said everything.

"What is it?" said Petrovich and at the same time inspected Akaky's whole uniform with his one eye, from the collar to the sleeves, the back, the coattails and the buttonholes, all of which was very familiar to him, because it was his own work. Such is the habit of tailors; that's the first thing he does on meeting one.

"Well I just sort of, Petrovich...my overcoat, the broadcloth...just look, everywhere in other places it's quite strong, it's gotten a bit dusty and seems old, but it's new, and, see, only in one place it's a little bit sort of...in the back, and also here on one shoulder it's a bit worn, and just on this shoulder a bit—see, that's all. Only a little work...."

Petrovich took the housecoat, first laid it out on the table, looked it over for a long time, shook his head and groped with one hand at the window for a round snuffbox with the portrait of some general, precisely which is not known, because the place where the face was had been punched out with a finger and then pasted over with a square scrap of paper. Having taken some snuff, Petrovich spread out the housecoat in his hands and examined it against the light and again shook his head. Then he turned it lining upwards and again shook his head, again took off the lid with the general pasted over with paper, and, having stuffed some snuff in his nose, closed it, put away the snuffbox and finally said:

"No, it's impossible to fix: a rotten garment!"

At these words Akaky Akakievich's heart skipped a beat.

"Why impossible, Petrovich?" said he, almost in the pleading voice of a child, "It's really only that it's worn at the shoulders, you really must have some little scraps or other...."

"Sure you can find scraps, scraps can be found," said Petrovich, "but you can't sew 'em on: the thing's completely rotten, touch it with a needle— and it'll fall apart."

"Let it fall apart, and you put a patch on right away."

"But there's nothing to put a patch on, there's nothing for it to hang on to, it's had an awful lot of wear and tear. You can call it broadcloth, but just let the wind blow and it'll fly to pieces."

"Well, so, just reinforce it. How can it be, really, sort of!..."

"No," said Petrovich decisively, "it's impossible to do anything. A bad business altogether. Better make yourself leg cloths out of it when the winter cold spell comes, because a sock doesn't keep you warm. The Germans thought that up to get more money for themselves (Petrovich liked on occasion to take a poke at the Germans); but obviously you'll have to have a new overcoat made."

At the word "new" Akaky Akakievich's vision grew foggy, and everything in the room began to jumble before him. The only thing he saw clearly was the general with the face pasted over with paper on the lid of Petrovich's snuffbox.

"What do you mean, new?" he said, still as if in a dream. "But I really don't have the money for that."

"Yes, new," said Petrovich with barbaric calm.

"Well, if a new one had to,.. how would it sort of...."

"That is, what will it cost?"

"Yes."

"Three fifties plus will have to be got together," said Petrovich, and he compressed his lips at this significantly. He very much liked strong effects, he liked suddenly somehow to perplex one completely and then steal a peek at what kind of face the perplexed one would make after such words.

"One hundred and fifty rubles for an overcoat!" shrieked poor Akaky Akakievich, shrieked, perhaps, for the first time in his life, for he had always been distinguished by the quietness of his voice.

"Yessir," said Petrovich, "and it also depends on what kind of overcoat. If you put marten on the collar, and add a hood with a silk lining, then it might even get up to two hundred."

"Petrovich, please," said Akaky Akakievich in a pleading voice, not hearing and not trying to hear the words Petrovich said and all his effects, "fix it up somehow so that it will do just a little longer."

"No, it'll end up: you both waste the work and spend money for nothing," said Petrovich, and after these words Akaky Akakievich went out completely destroyed. And after his departure Petrovich kept on standing a long time, significantly compressing his lips and not getting to work, satisfied that he had neither lowered himself nor betrayed the tailor's art.

Having gone out onto the street, Akaky Akakievich was as if in a dream. "There's a business there," he said to himself, "I, really, didn't even think that it would turn out sort of..."—and then, after a certain silence, he added—"So that's how it is! That's what finally turned out, but I, really, couldn't have even at all supposed that it was like that." After this a long silence again followed, after which he said: "So that's it! What a really completely unexpected sort of...wouldn't have at all.... What a situation!" Having said this, he, instead of going home, went in the entirely opposite direction, not suspecting it himself. On the way a chimneysweep brushed him with his whole unclean side and blackened his whole shoulder; an entire hatful of lime spilled down on him from the roof of a house being built. He didn't notice any of this, and only later, when he bumped into a policeman who, standing his halberd next to himself, was shaking some snuff out of a horn onto his calloused fist, only then did he come to a bit, and then because the policeman said: "Whad're you bashing right into my snout for, don't you have the whole sideworkh?" This made him look around and turn homewards. Only now he began to collect his thoughts, saw his position in a clear and realistic light, began to talk to himself, no longer spasmodically, but reasonably and openly, as with a sensible friend with whom one can discuss the most tender and intimate matter. "Well, no," said Akaky Akakievich, "it's impossible to talk sense with Petrovich now: now he's sort of...his wife, clearly, had given him a beating or something. But it's better if I go to see him on Sunday in the morning: after Saturday night he'll be squinting and groggy so he'll need the hair of the dog, but his wife won't give him the money, and then I'll sort of put ten kopeks into his hand, and he'll be more agreeable, and then the overcoat sort of...." Thus Akaky Akakievich reasoned with himself, encouraged himself and awaited the next Sunday, and, seeing from a distance that Petrovich's wife was going out somewhere, went straight to him. After Saturday Petrovich was in fact squinting strongly, holding his head towards the floor, and completely groggy; but despite all this, as soon as he learned what the matter was, it was just as if the devil had given him a shove. "Impossible," he said, "kindly order a new one." Akaky Akakievich here thrust the ten kopeks at him. "I thank you, sir, I'll fortify myse¹f a wee bit to your health," said Petrovich, "but kindly don't distress youself about the overcoat; it won't serve any service. We'll sew you a glorious new overcoat, I guarantee you that."

Akaky Akakievich was still about to go on about repairing it, but Petrovich didn't hear him out and said, "I'll sew you a new one without fail, kindly depend on it, we'll make every effort. It could even be in the latest fashion, the collar will fasten with silver appliquéd clasps."

Here Akaky Akakievich saw that it was impossible to get by without a new overcoat, and his spirits fell completely. How indeed, on what, on what money to have it made? Of course, he could depend in part on a future bonus for the holidays, but this money had already long ago been distributed and disbursed in advance. He needed to acquire new pants, to pay the shoemaker an old debt for putting new vamps on his old boot-tops, and he ought to order from the seamstress three shirts and a couple of that article of linen which it is indecent to name in print, in a word: absolutely all the money had to be spent, and even if the director were to be so kind as to designate, instead of a forty-ruble bonus, forty-five or fifty, all the same some utter nonsense would remain which would be a drop in the ocean of the overcoat capital. Although, of course, he knew that Petrovich was subject to the whim of suddenly asking the devil knows what exhorbitant price, so that even his wife herself was unable to keep herself from shrieking: "Have you gone crazy, you fool! Another time he'll take work for nothing, but now the evil spirit's possessed him to ask such a price as he's not worth himself!" Although, of course, he knew that Petrovich would take the work even for eighty rubles, however, all the same where to get these eighty rubles? He could find half of it: a half could be unearthed; perhaps even a little bit more; but where to get the other half? But first the reader should know where the first half came from. Akaky Akakievich had the habit, from every ruble he spent, of putting

49

aside half a kopek in a small box locked with a key, with a little hole cut in the lid for throwing money in. At the end of every half year he would review the accumulating copper sum and replace it with silver change. Thus he continued for a long time, and in this way in the course of some years the accumulated sum turned out to be more than forty rubles. And so, half was in his hands; but where to get the other half? Where to get the other forty rubles? Akaky Akakievich thought and thought and decided that it would be necessary to cut down his usual expenditures, at least for one year; to give up using tea in the evenings, not to light candles in the evenings, and if something had to be done, to go to the landlady's room and work by her candle; when walking along the streets to step as lightly and carefully as possible on the cobblestones and paving stones, almost on tiptoe, in order in this way not to wear out his soles rapidly; to give his linen to the laundress to wash as seldom as possible, and, so that it wouldn't get dirty, to throw it off every time he came home and remain in only his cotton bathrobe, which was very ancient and spared even by time itself. The truth must be told that at first it was somewhat difficult for him to get used to such limitations, but then he somehow got used to it and all went well; he even entirely mastered going hungry in the evening; but on the other hand he was nourished spiritually, carrying in his thoughts the eternal idea of the future overcoat. From this time on it was as if his very existence had become somehow fuller, as if he had gotten married, as if some other person were with him, as if he were not alone, but some pleasant female life companion had agreed to travel life's road together with him—and that companion was none other than that same overcoat with the thick quilting, with the strong lining which wouldn't wear out. He became somehow livelier, even firmer in character, like a man who has already defined and set a goal for himself. Doubt, indecision, in a word, all the vacillating and indefinite traits, disappeared by themselves from his face and actions. At times a fire would show in his eyes, the most daring and audacious thoughts even flashed through his head: shouldn't he actually put marten on the collar? Deliberations about this almost brought him to absentmindedness. Once, copying a paper, he even almost made a mistake, so that he cried, "ookh!" almost out loud and crossed himself. In the course of every month he, at least once, would visit Petrovich to discuss the overcoat, where it was better to buy broadcloth, and what color, and at what price, and although somewhat anxious, he always returned home satisfied, thinking that finally the time would come when all this would be bought and when the overcoat would be made. The business went even faster than he anticipated. Contrary to every expectation, the director awarded Akaky Akakievich not forty or forty-five but a whole sixty rubles: whether he had a premonition that Akaky Akakievich needed an overcoat, or whether it happened like that by itself, nonetheless through this he found himself with an extra twenty rubles. This circumstance accelerated the pace of the business.

Some two or three months more of slight starvation and Akaky Akakievich would have actually collected about eighty rubles. His heart, usually quite calm, began to pound. On the very first day he set off with Petrovich for the store. They bought some very good broadcloth—and it wasn't hard, because they had thought about it half a year ahead and it was a rare month that they didn't drop into the stores to compare prices; furthermore Petrovich himself said that better broadcloth didn't exist. For the lining they chose calico, but so durable and solid, that in Petrovich's words, it was even better than silk and even dressier and glossier in appearance. They didn't buy marten, because it was really expensive, but instead they chose cat, the best that could be found in the store, cat which from a distance one could always take for marten. Petrovich fussed over the overcoat two weeks in all, because there was so much quilting, but otherwise it would have been ready sooner. For labor Petrovich took twelve rubles—less was quite impossible: everything was solidly sewn with silk, with a fine double seam, and Petrovich went over every seam with his own teeth, impressing various configurations with them. It was...it's hard to say on exactly what day, but, probably, on the most triumphant day of Akaky Akakievich's life, that Petrovich finally brought him the overcoat. He brought it in the morning, just before the time when he had to go to the department. The overcoat could never have arrived at a more appropriate time, because rather heavy frosts were already beginning and, it seemed, threatened to intensify even more. Petrovich appeared with the overcoat as a good tailor should. On his face was displayed such a significant expression as Akaky Akakievich had never yet seen. It seemed he felt in full measure that he had done no small deed and that he had suddenly demonstrated to himself the abyss which divides tailors who only put in linings and do repairs from those who sew from scratch. He took the overcoat out of the handkerchief he had brought it in; the handkerchief had just come from the laundress; he then folded it and put it in his pocket to use. Having taken out the overcoat, he looked at it quite proudly, and, holding it in both hands, threw it quite deftly over Akaky Akakievich's shoulders; then he pulled and smoothed it down in the back with his hand; then he draped Akaky Akakievich with it slightly opened. Akaky Akakievich, as a person of a certain age, wanted to try it with the sleeves on: Petrovich helped him to put the sleeves on—it came out handsome with the sleeves on too. In a word, it turned out that the overcoat was a total and perfect fit. Petrovich didn't lose the opportunity of saying at this point that he'd done it only because he lived without a signboard on a small street and besides had known Akaky Akakievich for a long time, that's why he'd taken the work so cheaply; but on Nevsky Prospect they would have charged him seventy-five rubles for the labor alone. Akaky Akakievich didn't want to debate this with Petrovich and even feared all the high prices with which Petrovich liked to throw dust in one's eyes. He paid him, thanked him, and went right out in the new overcoat to the department.

51

Petrovich went out after him and, remaining on the street, kept looking at the overcoat for a long time from a distance and then deliberately went out of his way so that, catching up by a curving side street, he could run out again onto the avenue and take another look at his overcoat from the other side, that is, head on. Meanwhile Akaky Akakievich walked along feeling in a most festive mood. He felt every moment of the minute that his new overcoat was on his shoulders, and several times he even smiled from inner satisfaction. Indeed, there were two benefits: one, that it was warm, and the other, that it was good. He didn't notice the walk at all and suddenly found himself at the department; in the cloakroom he took off the overcoat, inspected it all over and entrusted it to the special care of the porter. It is not known in what way everyone in the department suddenly found out that Akaky Akakievich had a new overcoat and that the housecoat no longer existed. Everyone ran out to the cloakroom at the same moment to look at Akaky Akakievich's new overcoat. They began to congratulate him, to greet him, so that at first he just smiled, but then even became embarrassed. And when everyone, coming up to him, began to say that one should drink to the new overcoat and that he should at least give them all a party, Akaky Akakievich got completely flustered, didn't know what to do, what to answer and how to get himself out of it. After a few minutes he, blushing all over, was even on the verge of insisting rather simply that it was not a new overcoat at all, that that's how it was, that it was his old overcoat. Finally one of the clerks, some assistant, even, of the head clerk, probably in order to show that he wasn't a snob in the least and even associated with those inferior to himself, said "So be it, I will give a party instead of Akaky Akakievich and request everyone to come to my house for tea: today, as if by plan, is my name day." The clerks, naturally, at once congratulated the assistant department head and eagerly accepted the invitation. Akaky Akakievich was about to get himself out of it, but everyone began to say that it was disrespectful, that it was simply shameful, and he was in no way able to refuse. Furthermore, he later grew pleased when he remembered that because of this he would have occasion to go around in his new overcoat even in the evening. This entire day was really the greatest triumphant holiday for Akaky Akakievich. He returned home in a most happy frame of mind, took off the overcoat and hung it carefully on the wall, again admiring the broadcloth and the lining, and then specially dragged out, for comparison, his former housecoat, which had entirely disintegrated. He glanced at it, and even burst out laughing: there was such a vast difference! And still long afterward at dinner he kept smiling as soon as the condition the housecoat was in would come to his mind. He dined gaily and after dinner wrote nothing more, no papers, but just played the sybarite a little on his bed until it got dark. Then, not prolonging the matter, he got dressed, put his overcoat on his shoulders, and went out onto the street. Where exactly the clerk who had invited him lived, unfortunately we cannot say: our memory begins to deceive us greatly, and everything in Petersburg, all the streets and houses, have so merged and mingled in our head that it is quite difficult to get anything out of it in a decent state. However that may be, it is at least true that the clerk lived in the best part of the city, and therefore not very close to Akaky Akakievich. At first Akaky Akakievich had to pass through some deserted streets with feeble lighting, but the streets became livelier, more populous, and brighter lit in proportion to the proximity to the clerk's apartment. Pedestrians began to show up more often, ladies too began to appear, beautifully dressed, beaver collars appeared on the men, Vankas with their wooden sledges studded with little gilded nails were met with less frequently, on the contrary, daredevil cabdrivers in raspberry velvet hats kept appearing with laquered sleighs, with bear rugs, and carriages with decorated boxes flew across the street, squeaking their wheels on the snow. Akaky Akakievich gazed at all this as a novelty. He hadn't gone out on the street in the evenings for several years. He stopped with curiosity in front of the illuminated window of a store to examine a painting where some beautiful woman was depicted taking off her shoe, thus baring her whole foot, not a bad one at all; and behind her back, from the doors of another room, some man with sideburns and a handsome Van Dyck thrust out his head. Akaky Akakievich shook his head and smiled, and then went his way. Why did he smile, because he had encountered a quite unfamiliar object, but one about which, however, everyone nonetheless cherishes some feeling, or did he think, like many other clerks, the following: "Oh these French! There's nothing to be said, if they want something like that, then it's really sort of...." Or perhaps he didn't even think that—after all, it's really impossible to crawl into a man's soul and find out everything he thinks. At last he reached the house in which lodged the assistant department head. The assistant department head lived in great style: a light shone on the stairway, the apartment was on the second floor. Having entered the front hall, Akaky Akakievich saw whole rows of galoshes on the floor. Among them, in the middle of the room, stood a samovar, hissing and emitting puffs of steam. On the walls everywhere hung overcoats and cloaks, among which some even had beaver collars or velvet lapels. On the other side of the wall noise and talk was audible, which suddenly became clear and ringing when the door opened and a footman came out with a tray filled with emptied glasses, a creamer, and a basket of crackers. It was obvious that the clerks had already long ago assembled and drunk a first glass of tea. Akaky Akakievich, having hung up his overcoat himself, entered the room and before him all at once flashed candles, clerks, pipes, card-tables and fluent conversation rising from all sides and the noise of tables being moved confusedly struck his ear. He stopped entirely awkwardly in the middle of the room wondering and trying to think up what he should do. But they had already noticed him, received him with a shout, and everyone instantly went into the front hall and inspected his overcoat afresh. Although

53

Akaky Akakievich was becoming a bit embarrassed, he, being a simple-hearted man, could not but rejoice, seeing how everyone praised his overcoat. Then, of course, everyone abandoned both him and his overcoat, and turned, as usual, to the tables set up for whist. All this—the noise, the talk and the crowd of people—all this was somehow wondrous for Akaky Akakievich. He simply didn't know how to behave, where to put his hands, his feet and his whole body; finally he sat down with the players, looked at the cards, kept glancing at the faces of this one and that one and after a while began to yawn, to feel bored, the more so since the time had already long since arrived at which he, according to custom, went to sleep. He wanted to say goodbye to the host, but they wouldn't let him go, saying that they absolutely had to drink a glass of champagne in honor of the renovation. After an hour they served dinner, consisting of vinaigrette, cold veal, pâté, pastries and champagne. They made Akaky Akakievich drink two glasses, after which he felt that it had become gayer in the room, however, he could simply not forget that it was already twelve o'clock and that it was long since time to go home. So that the host couldn't somehow take it into his head to detain him, he went out of the room on the sly, found his overcoat in the front hall which he, not without regret, saw lying on the floor, shook it out, took every fluff off it, put it on his shoulders, and went down the stairway onto the street. On the street everything was still light. Some scraggy little grocery shops, those continuous clubs of servants and all sorts of people, were open, others which were closed nonetheless let out a long stream of light through the whole crack of the doorway, signifying that they were not yet devoid of society, and, probably, the serving girls or serving men were still finishing their gossip and conversations, plunging their masters into complete bewilderment as to their whereabouts. Akaky Akakievich walked along in a gay state of mind, he was even suddenly, for some unknown reason, about to dart after some lady who passed by like lightning, every part of whose body was filled with extraordinary motion. However, he stopped right away and again set out very quietly as before, even wondering himself at his gallop which came from who knows where. Soon those deserted streets stretched before him which even in the daytime aren't so gay and even less so in the evening. Now they had become still more solitary and isolated: streetlamps began to appear more seldom—less oil, evidently, was distributed here; wooden houses, fences began; not a soul anywhere; only the snow alone gleamed on the streets, and sleeping low little hovels with closed shutters sadly showed black. He approached the place where the streets intersected in an endless square with houses hardly visible on the other side, which looked like a terrible desert.

In the distance, God knows where, a light flashed in some sentry box which seemed to be standing on the edge of the world. Akaky Akakievich's gaiety here somehow significantly diminished. He stepped onto the square not without a certain involuntary fear, exactly as if his heart had a premonition

54

of something evil. He looked backwards and to all sides: just like a sea around him. "No, it's better not to look," he thought, and walked on with closed eyes, and when he opened them to find out if the end of the square were near, he suddenly saw that in front of him stood almost in front of his nose some people with mustaches, what kind exactly he could not even make out. His vision grew foggy and a pounding started in his chest. "But that's my overcoat!" said one of them in a thundering voice, grabbing it by the collar. Akaky Akakievich was about to cry "help," when another put his fist, the size of clerk's head, right up to his mouth, saying: "Just you give a shout!" Akaky Akakievich felt only how they took the overcoat off him and gave him a kick with a knee before he fell backwards onto the snow and already felt nothing more. After a few minutes he came to and got up onto his feet, but there was already no one there. He felt it was cold in the square, and he'd no overcoat, he began to shout, but his voice, it seemed, had no thought of carrying to the ends of the square. Despairing, not ceasing to shout, he set off at a run across the square straight to the sentry-box next to which stood a policeman who, leaning on his halberd, looked, it seems, with curiosity, wanting to know why the devil a person was running to him from a distance and shouting. Akaky Akakievich, having run up to him, began in a breathless voice to shout that he was asleep and not looking after anything, not seeing how they robbed a man. The policeman answered that he hadn't seen anything, that he saw how some two men stopped him in the middle of the street but thought that these were his friends; but instead of carrying on for nothing, let him drop in tomorrow to the inspector, that way the inspector would find out who took the overcoat. Akaky Akakievich ran home in total disorder, his hair which could still be found in small quantity on his temples and in back was completely disheveled, his side and chest and his entire trousers were covered with snow. The old lady, the landlady of his apartment, hearing a terrifying knock on the door, quickly leapt out of bed and with a shoe on only one foot ran to open the door, holding her nightdress to her bosom, out of modesty, with her hand; but having opened it, stepped back, seeing Akaky Akakievich in such a state. When he explained what the matter was, she threw up her hands and said that he should go straight to the commissioner and that the local inspector would trick him, make promises and start leading him a merry chase; but best of all to go straight to the commissioner, that she even knew him, because Anna, the Finn who used to work for her as a cook, had now found a job at the commissioner's as a nurse, that she often saw him himself as he drove by their house, and that he also goes to church every Sunday, prays, and at the same time looks gaily at everyone, and that, probably, by all appearances, he must be a kind man. Having heard this solution, the sad Akaky Akakievich made his way to his room, and how he spent the night there is presented for judgment to him who can the least bit imagine the position of another. Early in the morning he set out for the commissioner's; but they said he was asleep; he came at 10—they said again: he's asleep; he came at 11 o'clock—they said: but the chief isn't at home; at dinner time—but the clerks in the reception room didn't want to let him in at all and absolutely wanted to know on what business and what duty brought him and what had happened. So that finally Akaky Akakievich for once in his life decided to show character and said flatly that he needed to see the commissioner himself personally, that they wouldn't dare not to let him in, that he came from the department on government business, and that he would just lodge a complaint against them and then they'd see. The clerks didn't dare say anything against this, and one of them went to call the commissioner. The commissioner received the story of the theft of the overcoat somehow extraordinarily strangely. Instead of paying attention to the main point of the matter, he began to question Akaky Akakievich: And why was he returning so late, and hadn't he dropped in and hadn't he been in a certain disreputable house, so that Akaky Akakievich got completely embarrassed and went out, not knowing himself if the case of the overcoat had been set in proper motion or not. This whole day he wasn't in attendance (the only time in his life). The next day he appeared all pale and in his old housecoat, which had become still more lamentable. Despite the fact that there were such clerks as didn't lose the chance to laugh at Akaky Akakievich even now, the tale of the theft of the overcoat moved many. They at once decided to take up a collection for him, but they collected a mere trifle, because the clerks without this had already spent a lot subscribing to the director's portrait and to some certain book, at the suggestion of the division head who was a friend of the author—and so, the sum turned out most trifling. Only one of them, moved by sympathy, decided at least to help Akaky Akakievich with good advice, saying that he should go not to the local inspector, because it might even happen that the inspector, wanting to earn the approval of his superiors, would find the overcoat in some way or other, but the overcoat would all the same remain at the police, if he didn't present legal proof that it belonged to him; but best of all, he should consult a certain *important personage*, that the *important personage*, corresponding and communicating with the appropriate people, could make the case go more successfully. There was nothing to be done, Akaky Akakievich decided to go to the *important personage*. What was precisely and in what consisted the duty of the *important personage*, that has remained unknown to this day. One should know that the *certain important personage* had recently become an important personage, but before that time he was an unimportant personage. However, his position even now is not considered important in comparison with others still more important. But such a circle of people will always be found for whom the unimportant in the eyes of others is still important. However, he tried to reinforce his importance by many other means, namely: he ordained that the lower level clerks would meet him already on the stairway when he arrived at work, that no one would dare to come to him directly, but that everything should go in the strictest order: the collegiate registrar would report to the district secretary, the district secretary —to the titular or whatever other one he had to, and that in this way the matter would come to him. Thus in Holy Rus everything is infected by imitation, everyone emulates and simulates his superior. They even say that some titular councillor, when they made him the director of some small separate office, at once fenced himself off a special room, calling it "the audience room," and put some footmen with red collars and gold braid by the doors who would take the door by the handle and open it to every arrival, although an ordinary desk could hardly fit in the "audience room." The manners and customs of the *important personage* were sedate and majestic, but not complex. The main tenet of his system was strictness. "Strictness, strictness and—strictness," he would usually say, and at the last word would usually look the one he was speaking to very significantly in the face. Although, however, there was no reason for this whatever, because the dozen clerks who comprised the whole administrative mechanism of the office were in constant terror even without this: catching sight of him from a distance, they would leave their work and wait, standing at attention, until the director would pass through the room. His usual conversation with inferiors smacked of strictness and consisted almost entirely of three sentences: "How dare you? Do you know who you're talking to? Do you understand who is standing before you?" However, he was a kind man at heart, good to his friends, obliging; but the rank of general completely knocked the sense out of him. Having received the rank of general, he somehow got confused, lost his way and didn't know how to behave at all. If he happened to be with his equals, he was still a decent man, a very respectable man, in many respects even not a stupid man; but as soon as he happened to be in a group where there were people even one rank lower than he, there he was simply beyond everything: he would be silent, and his situation aroused pity all the more since he himself even felt that he might spend the time incomparably better. A strong desire to join some interesting conversation and circle was sometimes visible in his eyes, but the thought would stop him: wouldn't it be awfully much on his part, wouldn't it be familiar, and wouldn't he lower his importance by this? And in consequence of such deliberations he remained perpetually in one and the same silent state, only occasionally emitting some monosyllabic sounds, and in this way he acquired the title of a most boring man. To such an *important personage* appeared our Akaky Akakievich, and appeared at the most inauspicious time, quite inopportune for himself, although, however, opportune for the important personage. The important personage was in his office and was conversing very very gaily with a certain recently arrived old acquaintance and childhood friend whom he hadn't seen for several years. At this time they informed him that some Bashmachkin had come to see him. He asked abruptly:

57

"Who's he?" They answered: "Some clerk." "Ah! he can wait, now's not the time," said the important personage. Here it must be said that the important personage completely lied: it was the time, he and his friend had already long since talked over everything and had already long since been interspersing the conversation with quite long silences, only slapping each other lightly on the thigh and saying "So, that's it, Ivan Abramovich!"—"That's it, Stepan Varlamovich!" But despite all that, however, he ordered the clerk to wait, in order to show his friend, a man long since not working and living out his days at home in the country, how much time clerks spend waiting in his reception room. Finally they, having had their fill of talk and having had a still greater fill of silences, and having smoked a cigar in thoroughly restful armchairs with reclining backs, he, finally, seemingly suddenly remembered and said to the secretary who had stopped by the doors with papers for a report: "Oh yes, there's a clerk, it seems, standing out there; tell him that he may come in." Seeing Akaky Akakievich's meek appearance and his decrepit uniform, he turned to him suddenly and said: "What do you want?"—in an abrupt and hard voice which he had specially practiced previously in his room in private and in front of the mirror, still a week before receiving his present position and a general's rank. Akaky Akakievich already felt the requisite timidity in advance, was somewhat embarrassed and, as best he could, to the degree that freedom of tongue would permit him, explained with the even more frequent addition than ever of the particles "sort of," that there was, you see, an absolutely new overcoat, and now he'd been robbed in an inhuman way, and that he was appealing to him so that through his intercession he could somehow sort of correspond with Mr. Head Police Commissioner or with another someone, and find the overcoat. Such manners, for unknown reasons, seemed familiar to the general.

"What do you mean, my dear sir," he continued abruptly, "don't you know the protocol? Where have you come to? Don't you know how business is conducted? You should have submitted a petition to the office about this; it would have gone to the department head, to the head of the division, then it would have been transferred to the secretary, and the secretary would then have delivered it to me...."

"But, your Excellency," said Akaky Akakievich, trying to collect the entire small handful of presence of mind that he had in him, and feeling at the same time that he was sweating in a terrible way, "I, your Excellency, dared to trouble you because the secretaries are sort of...an undependable bunch...."

"What what what?" said the important personage. "Where did you get such nerve? Where did you get such thoughts? What rebellion has spread among young people against their chiefs and superiors!" The important personage, it seems, didn't notice that Akaky Akakievich had already passed fifty. Probably, if he could be called a young man, then perhaps only relatively, that is in relation to one who is already seventy. "Do you know who you're saying that to? Do you understand who is standing before you? Do you understand that, do you? I ask you." Here he stamped his foot, raising his voice to such a loud pitch that even a better man than Akaky Akakievich would have been terrified. Akaky Akakievich froze, staggered, his whole body shaking, and couldn't stand up at all: if the doormen hadn't at once run up to support him, he would have flopped onto the floor: they carried him out almost immobile. But the important personage was satisfied that the effect had exceeded even his expectations, and completely intoxicated by the thought that his word could even deprive a man of consciousness, stole a glance at his friend to see how he viewed it, and not without satisfaction saw that his friend was in the most indefinite state and was even for his part beginning to feel terror himself.

How he went down the stairs, how he went out onto the street, nothing of this did Akaky Akakievich remember. He felt neither his arms nor his legs. In his life he had never yet been so badly raked over the coals by a general, and by someone else's yet. He went through the storm which whistled in the streets, with his mouth agape, losing the sidewalks; the wind, according to Petersburg custom, blew on him from all four sides and from all the side streets. In an instant it blew a quinsy down his throat, and he got home not having the strength to say a single word; he swelled all up and went to bed. A proper raking over the coals is sometimes that bad! The next day it was discovered that he had a high fever. Thanks to the generous aid of the Petersburg climate, the illness progressed faster than might have been expected, and when the doctor appeared, he, having felt his pulse, found there was nothing to be done except to prescribe a poultice, if only so that the patient should not remain without the beneficent aid of medicine; he, however, immediately pronounced him a definite *kaput* in a day and a half. After which he turned to the landlady and said: "And you, my good woman, don't waste any time, order him a pine coffin at once, because an oak one would be expensive for him." Whether Akaky Akakievich heard these fateful words, and if he did hear, whether they produced a shocking effect on him, whether he regretted his miserable life—nothing of this is known, because he was delirious and feverish the whole time. Visions, one stranger than the other, came to him incessantly: now he saw Petrovich and was ordering him to make an overcoat with some kind of traps to catch the thieves which he incessantly imagined to be under his bed, and he kept calling the landlady every minute to pull one thief out even from under his blanket; now he was asking why his old housecoat was hanging before him, that he had a new overcoat; now it seemed to him that he was standing before the general listening to the proper raking over the coals and saying: "Excuse me, your Excellency"; now, finally, he was even foulmouthing, saying the most terrible words, so that the old lady, the landlady, even crossed herself, never having heard anything of the sort from him in her life, all the more since these words followed directly after the words "your Excellency." From then on he uttered absolute nonsense, so that it was impossible to understand anything; one could only see that his disordered words and thoughts revolved around one and the same overcoat. At last poor Akaky Akakievich gave up the ghost. They sealed neither his room nor his things, because, first of all, there were no heirs, and second of all, very little inheritance remained, namely: a bunch of goose quills, a quire of white government paper, three pairs of socks, two or three buttons which had come off his trousers, and the housecoat already known to the reader. Who got all this, God knows: even the narrator of this tale, I admit, wasn't interested in this. They took Akaky Akakievich down and buried him. And Petersburg remained without Akaky Akakievich as if he had never.been in it. There had vanished and disappeared a being defended by no one, dear to no one, interesting to no one, not even calling himself to the attention of a naturalist who doesn't neglect to mount an ordinary fly on a pin and examine it under a microscope—a being who had submissively borne the office jokes and gone to the grave without any extraordinary fuss, but for whom all the same, albeit before the very end of his life, there had flashed a radiant guest in the form of an overcoat, which had enlivened his poor life for an instant, and on whom disaster had then crashed down just as unbearably as it has crashed down on the tsars and the sovereigns of the world.... Several days after his death a doorman from the department was sent to his apartment with an order to appear immediately and to say the chief demands it; but the doorman had to return with nothing, reporting that Akaky couldn't come anymore, and to the query: "Why?" expressed himself with the words: "He just can't, he's dead, they buried him four days ago." In this way they learned about Akaky Akakievich's death in the department, and already the next day a new clerk sat in his place, much taller and turning out the letters not in such level handwriting, but much more slanted and sloping.

But who could imagine that this is still not all about Akaky Akakievich, that he was fated to live on noisily for several days after his death, as if in reward for a life unnoticed by anyone? But that's what happened, and our poor history unexpectedly acquires a fantastic ending. Suddenly rumors spread around Petersburg that by the Kalinkin bridge and far further a corpse in the guise of a clerk had begun to appear by night, searching for some pilfered overcoat and, on account of the purloined overcoat, pulling off of all shoulders, without regard to rank or profession, all overcoats: with cat, with beaver, with cotton; raccoon, fox, bear coats, in a word, coats of every sort of fur and hide as people have invented for covering their own. One of the department clerks saw the corpse with his own eyes and instantly recognized Akaky Akakievich; but this instilled in him, however, such fear, that he ran off at top speed and therefore couldn't get a good look, but saw only how he shook his finger at him from a distance. Complaints came incessantly from all sides that backs and shoulders, if it were only of titular, but even of the most privy councillors, were subjected to absolute chills because of the nightly pulling-off of overcoats. An order was given to the police to catch the corpse, no matter what, dead or alive, and to punish him, as an example to others, in the cruelest manner, and they even almost succeeded in this. More precisely, the policeman of some block on Kiryushkin Street was already about to seize the corpse completely by the collar on the very scene of the crime, in the act of pulling a frieze overcoat off of some retired musician who in his time had tooted the flute. Having seized him by the collar, he summoned with his shout two other comrades whom he commanded to hold him, while he burrowed just for a minute in his boot to pull a birch-bark snuffbox out of it to temporarily refresh his nose, frostbitten six times in his life; but the snuff was probably of the sort which even a corpse couldn't bear. The policeman had hardly managed, having covered his right nostril with his finger, to inhale half a handful with his left, when the corpse sneezed so violently that he completely splattered all three of them right in the eye. While they were lifting their fists to wipe them, the trail of the corpse was lost, so that they didn't even know whether he had actually been in their hands. From that time on, policemen conceived such a terror of the dead that they were even afraid to seize the living, and would only shout from a distance: "Hey you, on your way!"—and the clerk-corpse began to appear even beyond the Kalinkin bridge, causing no small terror to all timid people. But we, however, completely abandoned the *certain important personage* who, in reality, was all but the cause of the fantastic direction, incidentally, of a perfectly true story. Before everything justice demands it be said that the *certain important personage*, soon after the passing of poor Akaky Akakievich, who had been raked over the coals into a fluff, felt something akin to regret. Sympathy was not unknown to him; his heart was capable of many kind impulses despite the fact that his rank quite often prevented their discovery. As soon as the visiting friend had left his office, he even got to thinking about poor Akaky Akakievich. And from then on almost every day pale Akaky Akakievich appeared to him, who had not withstood the official raking-over the coals. The thought of Akaky distressed him to such a degree that, a week later, he even decided to send a clerk to him to find out what had happened, how he was, and whether it was in fact possible to help him with something; and when they reported to him that Akaky Akakievich had suddenly died in a fever, he was even left stunned, feeling pangs of conscience, and was out of sorts all day. Wishing to distract himself somewhat and to forget the unpleasant impression, he set off for a party to one of his friends at whose place he found a sizable gathering, and best of all, everyone there was of almost one and the same rank, so that he would be restricted by absolutely nothing. This had a surprising effect on his emotional disposition. He opened up, became pleasant in conversation, amiable, in a word, spent the evening very pleasantly. At supper he drank a couple of glasses of champagne—a means, as is well known, not ineffective in disposing one to gaiety. The champagne imparted to him an inclination for various extravagances, namely: he decided not to go home yet, but to drop in on a certain lady of his acquaintance, Karolina Ivanovna, a lady, it seems, of German extraction, with whom he had perfectly friendly relations. It is necessary to say that the important personage was already not a young person, a good spouse, a respected *pater familias*. Two sons, of whom one already served in the office, and a pretty sixteen-year-old daughter with a slightly hooked, but attractive little nose, came to kiss his hand every day, saying, "Bonjour, Papa." His wife, a woman still fresh and not at all bad, first gave him her hand to kiss and then, turning it over on the other side, kissed his hand. But the important personage, perfectly, incidentally, satisfied with domestic family tenderness, found it becoming to have a lady friend for friendly relations in another part of town. This lady friend was not a bit better or younger than his wife; but such puzzles exist in the world, and to judge them is not our affair. So, the important personage went down the stairs, got into a sled and told the coachman: "To Karolina Ivanovna's," and he, having wrapped himself quite luxuriously in a warm overcoat, remained in that pleasant state better than which you won't conceive for a Russian, that is, when you aren't thinking about anything, but meanwhile thoughts creep into your head of themselves, one more pleasant than the other, not even giving one the trouble of chasing after them and looking for them. Full of contentment, he lightly recalled all the gay moments of the evening he'd spent, all the words that had made a small circle guffaw; he even repeated many of them under his breath and found that they were all as funny as before, and therefore it's not surprising that he himself laughed wholeheartedly. Occasionally, he was bothered, however, by a gusty wind which, having suddenly sprung up from God knows where or for who knows what reason, so cut into his face, hurling clumps of snow into it, blowing out his overcoat collar like a sail, or suddenly with unnatural force throwing it onto his head and in this way necessitating perpetual fussing to extricate himself from it. Suddenly the important personage felt that someone had seized him quite firmly by the collar. Turning around, he noticed a man of short stature, in a worn uniform, and not without terror recognized Akaky Akakievich. The face of the clerk was as pale as the snow and he looked like an absolute corpse. But the terror of the important personage exceeded all bounds when he saw that the corpse's mouth twisted and, breathing the terrible smell of the grave on him, uttered these words: "Ah! So here you are at last! At last I've sort of got you by the collar! It's your overcoat I need! You didn't take any pains about mine, and raked me over to boot—now give me yours!" The poor *important personage* almost died. However much character he had in the office and in general before his inferiors, and although, looking only at his manly appearance and figure, everyone would say: "Ooh, what character!"

62

here he, like quite many who have a heroic exterior, felt such terror, that not without reason he even began to fear some kind of morbid attack. He even quickly took off his overcoat from his shoulders himself and cried to the coachman in a voice not his own: "Drive home as fast as you can!" The coachman, hearing a voice which was usually used at critical moments and would even be accompanied by something much the most effective, hid his head in his shoulders just in case, waved the whip and shot off like an arrow. In a little more than about six minutes, the important personage was already in front of the entrance to his house. Pale, panic-stricken and minus his over-coat, instead of going to Karolina Ivanovn's, he went home, dragged himself somehow to his room and spent one night in quite great confusion, so that the next day in the morning at tea his daughter said to him directly: "You're quite pale today, Papa." But Papa was silent and said not a word to anyone about what had happened to him, and where he had been, and where he had wanted to go. This event made a strong impression on him. He even began to say much less often to his subordinates: "How dare you, do you understand who is standing before you?" If he did say it, then not before first having heard what the matter was. But still more remarkable was that from that time on the appearances of the clerk-corpse entirely ceased; obviously, the general's overcoat turned out to fit him perfectly; at least, such incidents in which someone had his overcoat pulled off were no longer heard of any-where. However, many active and careful people wouldn't calm down at all and kept saying that in distant parts of town the clerk-corpse was still ap-pearing. And actually, a certain policeman in Kolomna saw with his own eyes how a ghost appeared from out of a certain house; but, being by nature somewhat feeble, so that one time an ordinary adult suckling pig rushing out of some private house had knocked him off his feet, to the enormous amusement of the coachmen standing around, from whom he demanded ten kopeks each for snuff for such mockery—so, being feeble, he didn't dare to stop him, but just walked behind him in the darkness until finally the ghost suddenly glanced around and, stopping, asked: "Whaddaya want?" and showed him such a fist as you won't find even among the living. The police-man said "Nothing," and at once turned back. The ghost, however, was much taller, wore huge mustachios, and, directing his steps, as it seemed, to the Obukhov Bridge, vanished completely in the darkness of the night.

1842

MR. PROKHARCHIN*

In Ustinya Fyodorovna's apartment, in the darkest and starkest little corner, lived Semyon Ivanovich Prokharchin, a man already middle-aged, well-meaning and non-drinking. Since Mr. Prokharchin, at his humble rank, received a salary in absolute correspondence to his business abilities, Ustinya Fyodorovna could never get more from him than five rubles monthly for the apartment. Some said that she had her own particular considerations here; but whatever there was in this, Mr. Prokharchin, as if to spite all his detractors, even became her favorite, interpreting this honor in the noble and honorable sense. It must be observed that Ustinya Fyodorovna, a thoroughly respectable and portly woman who had a particular partiality for meat and coffee and who observed fasts with difficulty, kept several boarders in her house who payed even twice as much as Semyon Ivanovich, but, not being meek and being, on the contrary, every last one "spiteful scoffers" at her woman's work and her orphaned helplessness, greatly suffered in her good opinion, so that if they hadn't paid money for their quarters, she wouldn't only not let them live but wouldn't have even wanted to see them in her apartment. Semyon Ivanovich became her favorite from the very time that a retired, or, perhaps, it would be much better to say, a certain discharged man, who was consumed by a passion for strong drink, was taken down to Volkovo cemetery. Although the consumed and discharged individual went around with an eye knocked out, in his words, for bravery, and had one leg, also somehow for bravery, broken—he nonetheless knew how to gain and use all the good will that Ustinya Fyodorovna was capable of and probably would have lived a long time more in the capacity of her most faithful sycophant and satellite, if he hadn't drunk himself to death, finally, in the most profound, the most lamentable manner. This all happened still at Peski, when Ustinya Fyodorovna kept only three boarders in all, of whom, upon moving to the new apartment where the enterprise was established on a greater scale and about a score of new lodgers was invited, Mr. Prokharchin alone survived.

Whether Mr. Prokharchin himself had his inherent defects, or whether his comrades all possessed them, matters on both sides went wrong somehow from the very beginning. Let us here observe that every last one of Ustinya Fyodorovna's new lodgers lived as brothers among themselves; some of them worked together; every first day of the month all in turn generally lost their

---

*[The name is based on the Russian word *kharchi*, "food," "board." *Prokharchit'sia* means to spend your last cent on food.]

65

salaries to each other at faro, at preference and at bixe; they liked to enjoy, as was said among them, the effervescent moments of life all together in a crowd for a jolly hour; they liked sometimes too to talk about lofty things, and although in the latter case the business rarely got by without an argument, mutual agreement in such cases was not the least destroyed, since prejudices were banished from this entire company. Particularly remarkable among the lodgers were: Mark Ivanovich, an intelligent and well-read person; then Oplevaniev the lodger; then Prepolovenko the lodger, also a modest and good man, then there was also a certain Zinovy Prokofievich, who had the imperative goal of entering high society; finally, the clerk Okeanov, who in his time had almost wrested the palm of champion and favorite from Semyon Ivanovich; then still another clerk, Sudbin; Kantarev the commoner, there were still others too. But Semyon Ivanovich was somehow not a comrade to all these people. No one, of course, wished him harm, all the more since everyone from the very first knew how to give Prokharchin his due and decided, in the words of Mark Ivanovich, that he, Prokharchin, was a good and meek person, although not worldly; trustworthy, not a flatterer, had, of course, his faults, but if he suffered sometimes, then it was not from anything other than from his own lack of imagination. As if that weren't enough: although deprived in this way of his own imagination, Mr. Prokharchin could not, for example, impress anyone particularly favorably by his figure and manners (which scoffers like to seize upon), but his figure too got by, as if nothing were the matter, at which Mark Ivanovich, being an intelligent person, formally took protection of Semyon Ivanovich and announced rather successfully and in a beautiful, flowery style, that Prokharchin was a middle-aged and respectable person and had already long ago left behind his time of elegies. And so, if Semyon Ivanovich did not know how to live with people, then it was solely because he himself was to blame for everything.

The first thing they noticed was, without a doubt, Semyon Ivanovich's miserliness and niggardliness. This they observed and took into account right away, for Semyon Ivanovich wouldn't for anything lend his teakettle to anyone to use, even if it were for the very shortest time; and what was all the more unjust in this matter was that he himself almost never drank tea, but drank, when he felt the need, some rather pleasant infusion of wildflowers and certain herbs with medicinal qualities, of which he always kept a considerable quantity. However, he also ate not at all the same way as all the other lodgers usually ate. Never, for example, would he permit himself to eat the entire dinner provided daily by Ustinya Fyodorovna for his comrades. Dinner cost fifty kopeks; Semyon Ivanovich used only twenty-five kopeks in copper and never went higher, and therefore would take either only a portion of cabbage soup with a meat pie, or only of beef; most often he ate neither soup nor beef, but would partake moderately of white bread with onion, with cottage cheese, with a salt cucumber or with other relishes, which was incomparably cheaper, and only when it got unbearable would he return again to his half dinner....

Here the biographer confesses that he would not for anything have decided to talk about such insignificant, low and even ticklish—let us say more, even insulting for some lover of elegant style—details, if in all these details were not contained one peculiarity, one controlling trait in the character of the hero of this tale; for Mr. Prokharchin was far from being so poor, as he himself sometimes maintained he was, as not even to have regular and filling victuals, but he did what was repellent, not fearing shame and people's gossip, strictly for the satisfaction of his strange whims, out of miserliness and excessive carefulness, which, however, will be much more clearly evident later on. But we will beware of boring the reader with a description of all Semyon Ivanovich's whims and will not only omit, for example, the curious and for the reader very funny description of all his outfits, but, if it weren't for the testimony of Ustinya Fyodorovna herself, we would hardly have mentioned even that all his life Semyon Ivanovich could never decide to send his linen to the laundry, or he would decide to, but so rarely, that in the intervals one could entirely forget about the presence of linen on Semyon Ivanovich. In the testimony of the landlady it appeared that "Semyon Ivanovich, the dear thing, bless his little soul, infested her corner for two score years, having no shame, for, not only for the whole duration of his earthly existence did he steadfastly and stalwartly shun socks, handkerchiefs and other similar objects," but even Ustinya Fyodorovna herself saw with her own eyes, with the help of the screen's dilapidation, that "he, the little dear, at times had nothing to cover his little white body with." Such rumors went around upon Semyon Ivanovich's death. But during his life (and here was one of the most important points of dispute) he could never endure, even despite the most pleasant comradely relations, someone sticking a curious nose into his corner without asking, even though it were with the help of the screen's dilapidation. The man was entirely intractable, taciturn and disinclined to idle talk. He didn't like any kind of advice-givers, also didn't spare upstarts and right on the spot would always reproach a scoffer or an adviser-upstart, would shame him, and the matter was closed. "You're a pup, an idler, and not an adviser, that's what; know, sir, your pocket and better count, pup, how many threads went into your foot cloths, that's what!" Semyon Ivanovich was a simple man and addressed absolutely everyone familiarly. Nor could he ever endure it when anyone, knowing his habitual sore spot, would begin out of pure mischief to insist and ask what was in his trunk.... Semyon Ivanovich had one little trunk. This trunk stood under his bed and was guarded as the apple of his eye; and although everyone knew that in it, besides old rags, two or three pairs of damaged boots and in general every chance trash and trifle, there was absolutely nothing, yet Mr. Prokharchin valued this his property quite highly, and they even heard once how he, not content with his old rather strong lock, was talking about getting another, of some special German manufacture, with various devices and with a secret spring. Once when Zinovy Prokofievich, carried away by his youthful thoughtlessness, expressed the quite indecent and coarse thought that Semyon Ivanovich was probably hiding and putting away things in his trunk in order to leave them to his descendants, everyone around was thrown into stunned amazement by the extraordinary consequences of Zinovy Prokofievich's sally. In the first place, Mr. Prokharchin couldn't even find decent expressions right away for such a bare and coarse thought. For a long time words without any meaning poured from his lips and, finally, they made out only that Semyon Ivanovich, in the first place, was reproaching Zinovy Prokofievich for a certain stingy business in the distant past; then they ascertained that Semyon Ivanovich was predicting that Zinovy Prokofievich would never enter high society, but that a tailor whom he owed for clothes would beat him, certainly beat him, because the pup had not payed him for so long, and that, finally, "you, you pup," added Semyon Ivanovich, "you, you want to get into the hussar regiments, but you just won't get in, you'll eat crow, and that's what you'll get, you pup, when the authorities hear about everything, they'll take you and make you a clerk; that's what, you hear, you pup!" Then Semyon Ivanovich calmed down, but, after lying down for about five hours, to the great and general amazement, he apparently made a decision, and suddenly again, first alone, and then turning to Zinovy Prokofievich, began to reproach and shame him anew. But again the matter didn't end with this, and in the evening when Mark Ivanovich and Prepolovenko the lodger made tea, having invited the clerk Okeanov to join them as a comrade, Semyon Ivanovich got off his bed, deliberately sat down with them, having paid his fifteen or twenty kopeks, and on the pretext of wanting to drink tea, began to go into the subject quite verbosely and to explain that a poor man is only a poor man, and nothing more, and that he, a poor man, had nothing to save up. Here Mr. Prokharchin even admitted, solely because it just now came up, that he was a poor man; only the day before yesterday he had wanted to borrow a ruble from him, that impudent man, but that now he wouldn't borrow it so that the pup wouldn't brag that that's how it is, he'd say, my salary is such that I can't even buy food; and that, finally, he, a poor man, just as you see him, himself sends five rubles every month to his sister-in-law in Tver, and that if he didn't send five rubles a month to his sister-in-law in Tver, his sister-in-law would die, and if his sister-in-law-hanger-on had died, then Semyon Ivanovich would have ordered himself new clothes long ago…. And so long and verbosely did Semyon Ivanovich speak about the poor man, about rubles and his sister-in-law, and kept repeating the same thing for the strongest effect on his audience, that, finally, he lost the thread completely, fell silent and only three days later, when no one was even thinking about teasing him anymore and everyone had forgotten about him, he added in conclusion something of the sort that when

Zinovy Prokofievich would enter the hussars, they would cut off his leg, the impudent man, in the war and would attach for him, instead of a leg, a stump, and Zinovy Prokofievich would come and say: "Give me, kind man, Semyon Ivanovich, some bread!" and Semyon Ivanovich wouldn't give him any bread and wouldn't look at the wild man Zinovy Prokofievich, and that that's how it is, he'd say; you go whistle.

All this, as one might expect, seemed quite curious and at the same time frightfully amusing. Not giving it much thought, all the landlady's tenants united for further investigations and, really out of curiosity alone, decided to invade Semyon Ivanovich in a throng and conclusively. And since Mr. Prokharchin of late, that is from the very time that he began to live among this company, had also grown exceptionally fond of investigating, questioning and wondering about everything, which, probably, he did for some secret reasons of his own, relations between both enemy camps started up without any previous preparations and without useless efforts, but as if by chance and by themselves. For the initiation of relations Semyon Ivanovich always had in reserve his peculiar, rather sly, but quite, however, intricate maneuver, in part already known to the reader: he would get off his bed, usually, around the time when tea was drunk, and if he saw that others had gathered anywhere in a bunch for brewing a beverage, he would go up to them like a modest, intelligent and affectionate person, pay his required twenty kopeks and announce that he wished to participate. Here the young folk would exchange winks and, in this way conspiring among themselves against Semyon Ivanovich, would begin an initially decent and decorous conversation. Then one of the more quick-witted of them would start, as if there were nothing amiss, to tell various news, most often about false and entirely improbable subjects. Once, for example, it was allegedly observed more than once about various of their colleagues that they were devoid of all culture and good, pleasant manners, and consequently, couldn't even be pleasing to ladies in society, and that therefore, for the eradication of this abuse, a deduction should immediately be levied on those receiving salaries, and with the collected sum they could set up the kind of hall where they could learn to dance, acquire all the attributes of gentlemanliness and good breeding, politeness, respect for their elders, strong character, kind, grateful hearts and various pleasant manners. Once, finally, they said that it was allegedly turning out that some clerks, beginning with the most ancient, in order to become educated immediately, had to take some kind of examination in all subjects and that, in this way, added the speaker, much would come to light, and certain gentlemen would be obliged to put their cards on the table—in a word, thousands of such tales and similar most absurd rumors were told. For appearances everyone would instantly believe the tale, take part in the discussion, ask questions, apply it to himself, and some, assuming a sad expression, would begin to shake their heads and look for advice everywhere, along the

69

lines of what, they would say, could they do if it happened to them? Needless to say, even a person much less good-natured and mild than Mr. Prokharchin would have been perplexed and confused by such a widely-shared rumor. Besides, by all appearances one could quite unerringly conclude that Semyon Ivanovich was exceptionally dull and dumb about any idea new and unwonted to his thoughts and that, receiving, for example, some news or other, he was always constrained to cook it over and chew it over first, to search out the meaning, to lose the thread and to get confused and, finally, possibly to overcome it, but here too in some quite personal way peculiar to him alone.... In this way various curious and hitherto unsuspected qualities were suddenly discovered in Semyon Ivanovich...gossip and chatter began, and all this as it was and with additions made its way, finally, to the office. The effect was increased by the fact that Mr. Prokharchin, who from time immemorial had almost always worn one and the same expression, suddenly, without any cause, changed his countenance: he began to wear an uneasy expression, his glances were frightened, timid and somewhat suspicious, he began to walk lightly, to shudder and listen and, as a topper to all his new qualities, now he got to like finding out the truth! His love for the truth led him, finally, to the point of venturing a couple of times to inquire even from Demid Vasilievich himself about the probability of the scores of rumors he received daily, and if we are silent here about the results of this escapade of Semyon Ivanovich's then it is for no other reason than heartfelt concern for his reputation. In this way, they found that he was a misanthrope and rejected the proprieties of society. They later found that there was much that was fantastical in him, and here also they were not at all mistaken, for more than once it was remarked that Semyon Ivanovich would sometimes forget himself entirely and, sitting in his place with an open mouth and with his pen raised in the air, as if frozen or ossified, he would resemble more the shadow of a rational being than that rational being itself. It happened not infrequently that some innocently yawning gentleman, suddenly meeting his furtive, murky and searching gaze, would start to tremble, quail, and instantly put either a smudge or some entirely unnecessary word on an important paper. The impropriety of Semyon Ivanovich's behavior embarrassed and offended truly well-bred people.... Finally, no one any longer doubted the fantastical inclination of Semyon Ivanovich's thoughts, when on one fine morning the rumor spread around the whole office that Mr. Prokharchin had even frightened Demid Vasilievich himself, for, meeting him in the corridor, he was so weird and strange that he had forced him to retreat.... Rumors of Semyon Ivanovich's action finally reached Prokharchin himself. Hearing about it, he immediately got up, carefully passed through the tables and chairs, reached the front hall, took his overcoat himself, put it on, went out—and disappeared for an indefinite period. Whether he had been scared, whether something else drew him—we do not know, but neither at home nor in the office was he to be found for some time.

We will not ascribe Semyon Ivanovich's fate directly to his fantastical inclination; however, we cannot but mention to the reader that our hero—an unworldly man, quite mild and living, up to the very time when he happened into his fellow lodgers' company, in obscure and impenetrable isolation —was distinguished by quietness and even apparent secretiveness, since the whole of his former existence at Peski he had lain on his bed behind the screens, was silent, and had no relations with anyone. Both his old roommates lived entirely the same way as he: both were also apparently secretive and also had lain behind screens for fifteen years. Happy, drowsy days and hours drew on one after the other in patriarchal stagnation, and since everything around also went its merry way, neither Semyon Ivanovich nor Ustinya Fyodorovna even remembered very well when fate had brought them together. "It may be ten years, it may be already fifteen, it may even already be a whole twenty-five," she would say at times to her new lodgers, "since he, the little dear, settled with me, God bless his little soul." And therefore it is quite natural that the hero of our tale, unused to company, was most unpleasantly surprised when, exactly a year earlier, he had found himself, respectable and modest, suddenly in the midst of a noisy and restless band of a whole score of young fellows, his new roommates and comrades.

Semyon Ivanovich's disappearance created no small disturbance in the lodgings. For one thing, he was the favorite; secondly, his passport, being in the landlady's care, turned out to be inadvertently mislaid at the time. Ustinya Fyodorovna howled, which she always resorted to on all critical occasions; for a whole two days she reproached, reviled the lodgers; she wailed that they had chased a lodger away from her like a chicken, and that "all the spiteful scoffers" had ruined him, and on the third day she chased them all out to search and catch the runaway no matter what, dead or alive. Towards evening Sudbin the clerk arrived first and announced that the trail had been found, that he had seen the ruanway at the Fleamarket and in other places, followed him, stood nearby, but hadn't dared to talk to him, but was not far from him at the fire too, when "the house on Crooked Street burned down." A half hour later Okeanov and Kantarev the commoner appeared, confirmed Sudbin word for word: they had also stood not far off, near, they had been only ten steps from him in all, but again hadn't dared to talk to him, but both had noticed that Semyon Ivanovich was going around with a mooching boozer. The remaining lodgers finally assembled and, listening attentively, decided that Prokharchin must then be not far off and wouldn't delay his arrival, but that they all knew in advance that he was going around with the mooching boozer. The mooching boozer was an utterly low, wild and fawning person, and it was clear from everything that he had somehow curried favor with Semyon Ivanovich. He had appeared exactly a week before Semyon Ivanovich's disappearance, along with his comrade Remnyov, had

71

lived a short time in the lodgings, told how he was suffering for the sake of truth, how he had formerly served in the provinces, how an inspector had come down on them, how he and his bunch had somehow been shaken down for the sake of truth, how he had appeared in Petersburg and fallen at the feet of Porfiry Grigorievich, how they had placed him, by pull, in a certain office, but that, through fate's most cruel persecution, they had fired him from there too, then how the office itself had been abolished through reorganization; but they hadn't taken him into the newly formed staff of clerks, as much for plain incapacity for business affairs as because of capacity for something else quite unrelated to business—all this together because of his love for truth and, finally, through the machinations of his enemies. Having finished the story, in the course of which Mr. Zimoveykin more than once kissed his stern and unshaven friend Remnyov, he bowed at the feet of everyone in the room in turn, not forgetting Avdotya the maid, called them all his benefactors and explained that he was an unworthy, troublesome, base, wild and stupid man, and that good people shouldn't be hard on his wretched lot and simplicity. Having asked their protection, Mr. Zimoveykin turned out to be a merry fellow, grew very happy, kissed Ustinya Fyodorovna's hand despite her modest protestations that her hand was lowly, not noble, and towards evening promised the whole group to display his talent in a certain remarkable character dance. But the next day his affair ended in a lamentable denouement. Either because the character dance turned out to have a bit too much character, or because he had somehow, in Ustinya Fyodorovna's words, "disgraced and diddled her, and furthermore she knew Yaroslav Ilich himself, and if she'd wanted, she could have long ago been the wife of a commanding officer herself," Zimoveykin was obliged to sail off to where he came from. He left, returned again, was again banished in dishonor, then wormed his way into the attention and good graces of Semyon Ivanovich, deprived him in passing of his new breeches and, finally, now appeared in the capacity of Semyon Ivanovich's toady.

As soon as the landlady learned that Semyon Ivanovich was alive and well and that there was now no need to look for his passport, she immediately ceased grieving and began to calm herself. Meanwhile some of the lodgers decided to arrange a triumphant reception for the runaway: they broke the bolt, moved the screens away from the missing man's bed, somewhat rumpled the bedclothes, took the famous trunk, put it at the foot of the bed, and on on the bed they put a sister-in-law, that is, a doll, a figure made out of the landlady's old kerchief, cap and coat, but really entirely like a sister-in-law, so that one could be completely deceived. Having finished their work, they began to wait, in order, on Semyon Ivanovich's arrival, to inform him that his sister-in-law had arrived from the provinces and had settled down in his place behind the screens, the poor dear. But they waited and waited, waited and waited.... Already while waiting Mark Ivanovich had staked and lost half a month's salary to Prepolovenko and Kantarev the lodgers; already Okeanov's whole nose had turned red and swollen in games of "nose-flicks" and "three-cards"; already Avdotya the maid had almost completely slept her fill and twice prepared to get up to get wood to light the stove, and Zinovy Prokofievich had gotten all soaked to the skin, running out to the courtyard every minute to look for Semyon Ivanovich; but no one had yet appeared—neither Semyon Ivanovich nor the mooching boozer. Finally everyone went to bed, leaving the sister-in-law behind the screens just in case; and only at four o'clock did a knock resound at the gate, but such a forceful one that it entirely compensated the expectant lodgers for all the excruciating labors they had undergone. It was he, he himself, Semyon Ivanovich, Mr. Prokharchin, but in such a condition that everyone gasped, and the thought of the sister-in-law didn't even occur to anyone. The missing man was unconscious. He was brought in, or rather, carried in, on the shoulders of a tattered night hack-driver who was all soaking and shaking. To the landlady's question, where had he, the wretched thing, gotten so drunk, the hack-driver answered: "He ain't drunk, not even hooch; I guarantee you that, but probably he's just fainted, or he's had a fit or something, or mebbe a whack's done him in." They began to examine him, for convenience leaning the culprit against the stove, and they saw that there really was no question of intoxication, and he hadn't been whacked, but there was some kind of other problem, for Semyon Ivanovich couldn't utter a word, and he seemed to twitch in a sort of convulsion, and only blinked his eyes, focusing in incomprehension now on one, now on another spectator costumed in nocturnal fashion. Then they began to ask the hack, where'd he picked him up? "From some people," he answered, "from Kolomna, who knows, gentry or not gentry, but carousing, jolly gentry; they gave him to me just like he is; they'd had a fight or something or some convulsion got him, God knows what happened; but they were jolly, nice gentry!" They took Semyon Ivanovich, raised him on a couple of pairs of stalwart shoulders and laid him down on the bed. When Semyon Ivanovich, in settling on his bed, felt the sister-in-law with his body and rested his feet on his treasured trunk, he screamed at the top of his voice, sat up almost on his heels and, all shaking and trembling, cleared and cleaned as much space on his bed as he could with his hands and body, while surveying those present with a trembling, but strangely resolute gaze, and explained, it seemed, that he would sooner die than give anyone even a hundredth part of his poor possessions....

Semyon Ivanovich lay for two or three days, solidly surrounded by screens and cut off in this way from the whole of God's world and its vain anxieties. Accordingly, the next day everyone forgot about him; meanwhile time flew by, hours gave way to hours, one day to another. A half dream, half delirium settled on the patient's heavy burning brain; but he lay peacefully, didn't groan and didn't complain; on the contrary, he grew subdued, silent and controlled, flattening himself against his bed, just as a hare falls to the ground in terror, hearing the hunter. At times a long, melancholy silence came over the apartment, a sign that all the lodgers had gone off on their business, and Semyon Ivanovich, once awake, could entertain his melancholy as much as he wanted, listening to the nearby rustling in the kitchen, where the landlady fussed about, or to the rhythmic slapping of Avdotya the maid's shoes around all the rooms when she, moaning and groaning, swept, scoured and scrubbed in all the corners for the sake of order. While hours passed in this way, drowsy, lazy, sleepy, boring, like the water, dripping loudly and rhythmically in the kitchen from the locker into the basin. Finally, the lodgers would come back, singly or in bunches, and Semyon Ivanovich could hear very conveniently how they cursed the weather, wanted to eat, how they joked, smoked, swore, forebore, played cards and clinked cups, preparing to drink tea. Semyon Ivanovich mechanically made the effort to get up and join them in his usual way for brewing a beverage but would at once fall into a sleep and dream that he had been sitting at the tea table for a long time already, participating and conversing, and that Zinovy Prokofievich had already managed, seizing the occasion, to stick into the conversation some routine about sisters-in-law and about the moral relationship to them of various good people. Here Semyon Ivanovich was about to justify himself and object, but the mightily formulaic "it has been more than once observed," which at once flew from all tongues conclusively cut off all his objections, and Semyon Ivanovich could think of nothing better than to begin anew to dream that today was the first of the month and that he was receiving his rubles at his office. Having opened his envelope on the stairs, he quickly glanced around and hurried as fast as he could to set apart an entire half of the wages he usually received, and to hide this half in his boot, then, right on the stairs and completely ignoring the fact that he was asleep in his own bed, he decided that upon arriving home, he would immediately give his landlady what he owed for his bed and board, then buy some essentials and show the proper people, as if unintentionally and accidentally, that he had been docked in pay, that he had nothing at all left and now not even anything to send to his sister-in-law, at which point he would grieve over his sister-in-law a bit, talk about her a lot the next day and the day after, and about ten days later again mention her poverty in passing, so that his comrades wouldn't forget. Thus resolved, he saw that Andrei Yefimivoch too, that small, eternally silent bald man who occupied the office three whole rooms away from where Semyon Ivanovich sat and hadn't said a word to him in twenty years, was standing right there on the stairs, also counting his rubles in silver and, shaking his head, he said to him: "Money! If you don't have it, you won't have porridge," he added grimly, going down the stairs, and already on the landing concluded, "And I, sir, have seven children." Here the bald man, probably also totally unaware that he was a vision and not at all actual and real, indicated exactly two feet six inches from the floor, and, waving his hand in a descending line, muttered that the oldest went to high school; then, with indignation glancing at Semyon Ivanovich, as if precisely Mr. Prokharchin were to blame that he had all of seven children, pulled his wretched hat down over his eyes, shook his overcoat, turned left and disappeared. Semyon Ivanovich became thoroughly terrified, and although he was entirely convinced of his innocence in regard to the unpleasant accumulation of the figure of seven under one roof, in fact it seemed to turn out precisely that none other than Semyon Ivanovich was to blame. Terrified, he set off at a run, for it seemed to him that the bald gentleman had turned around, was overtaking him and wanted to ransack him and take away all his wages because of his inescapable figure of seven, and that he firmly denied any possible relationship of any sort of sisters-in-law to Semyon Ivanovich. Mr. Prokharchin ran, ran, got out of breath...alongside him an extraordinary number of people also ran, and they all clinked their wages in the back pockets of their docktailed little frockcoats; finally, all the people bore him almost on their shoulders to the very fire at which he had been present last time along with the mooching boozer. The boozer—alias Mr. Zimoveykin— was already there, met Semyon Ivanovich, started fussing about terribly, took him into the very thick of the crowd. Just as then in reality, an indescribable crowd of people roared and hummed around them, fencing off the whole Fontanka embankment, all the side streets and alleys, between two bridges; just as then, Semyon Ivanovich was borne along together with the boozer behind some fence, where they were squeezed, as if in a pincers, inside a huge timber yard full of spectators collected from the streets, from the Fleamarket and from all the surrounding houses, taverns and pubs. Semyon Ivanovich saw everything just as he had felt it then; in the whirlwind of fever and delirium various strange faces began to flash before him. He remembered some of them. One was that same gentleman who had particularly impressed everyone, seven feet tall and with two-foot whiskers, who had stood behind Semyon Ivanovich during the fire and given him encouragement from behind, when our hero, for his part, felt something like ecstasy and stamped his little feet, as if wanting in this way to applaud the valiant work of the firemen, which he saw perfectly from his elevated position. Another was the same stalwart lad from whom our hero had gotten a shove in the form of a lift onto another fence when he was quite prepared to crawl over it, perhaps to save someone. Before him also flashed the figure of that old man with the hemorrhoidal face, in an ancient quilted belted bathrobe, who had been about to go off to the shop for crackers and snuff for his lodger just before the fire and who was now pushing his way, with a milk can and a quarter of tobacco in his hands, through the crowd to the house where burned his wife, daughter and thirty and a half rubles in the corner under the bed. But clearest of all appeared to him that poor sinful woman whom he'd dreamed of already more than once during his sickness—she appeared just as she was then—in bast shoes, with a crutch, with a wicker basket on her back, and in rags. She shouted louder than the firemen and the people, waving her crutch and her arms, about the fact that her own children had kicked her out of somewhere and that furthermore two nickles had disappeared in the process. The children and the nickles, the nickles and the children whirled around her tongue with incomprehensible profound sense-lessness, from which everyone retreated after vain efforts to understand; but the woman didn't let up, kept on shouting, howling, waving her arms, not paying, it seemed, any attention either to the fire, towards which she was borne from the street by the people, or to the whole throng around her, or to anyone else's misfortune, or even to the embers and sparks which were already about to dust all the people standing around. Finally, Mr. Prokhar-chin felt that he was beginning to be overcome by terror, for he saw clearly that all this was now somehow going on with a purpose and that he wouldn't get out of it scot-free. And in fact, just then not far from him, some peasant in a torn, unbelted smock, with singed hair and beard, got up on a wood-pile and began to incite all God's people against Semyon Ivanovich. The crowd thickened and thickened, the peasant kept shouting, and, freezing with fear, Mr. Prokharchin suddenly remembered that the peasant was the very same hack-driver whom he had cheated in the most inhuman way exactly five years ago, slipping away from him through side gates before paying and picking up his heels on the run as if he were running barefoot on a red-hot skillet. Desperate, Mr. Prokharchin wanted to speak, to scream, but his voice died. He felt that the whole enraged crowd was winding around him like a multicolored snake, crushing him, smothering him. He made an incredible effort and—awoke. Here he saw that he was on fire, that his whole corner was on fire, along with Ustinya Fyodorovna and with all her boarders, that his bed was on fire, his pillow, his blanket, his trunk and, finally, his precious mattress. Semyon Ivanovich leapt up, grabbed his mattress and ran, dragging it behind him. But in the landlady's room into which our hero had dashed just as he was, without decorum, barefoot and in his nightshirt, they seized him, pinioned him and triumphantly bore him back behind the screens, which, by the way, were not on fire at all, rather it was Semyon Ivanovich's head that was on fire, and put him to bed. In this way the tattered, unshaven and stern artist-organgrinder puts into its traveling box his Punch which has made an uproar, beaten up everyone, sold its soul to the devil and, finally, concluded its existence until the next production in the same trunk with this devil, the Negroes, Petrushka, Mademoiselle Katerina, and her fortunate lover, the district police captain.

Immediately everyone, old and young, surrounded Semyon Ivanovich, standing close around his bed and turning their expectant faces to the patient. Meanwhile he came to, but whether from shame or for another reason, suddenly began to pull his blanket over him with all his might, wanting, probably, to hide under it from the attention of his sympathizers. Finally, Mark Ivanovich broke the silence first and, like an intelligent man, began to say quite affectionately that Semyon Ivanovich needed to calm down completely, that it was shoddy and shameful to be sick, that only little children behave that way, that he should get better, and then go to work. Mark Ivanovich finished with a little joke, saying that the sick were not as yet allotted full salary payments, and since he well knew that they also held quite low ranks, in his opinion, such a title or estate didn't have great material advantages. In a word, it was obvious that they all took real interest in Semyon Ivanovich's fate and were quite compassionate. But with incomprehensible rudeness, he continued to lie on his bed, to be silent and to keep stubbornly pulling his blanket over himself more and more. Mark Ivanovich, however, wouldn't accept defeat and, grudgingly, again said something very sugary to Semyon Ivanovich, knowing that that was how to treat a sick person; but Semyon Ivanovich didn't even want to sense this; on the contrary, he muttered something through his teeth in a most distrustful manner and suddenly began to glower to the left and to the right, in a quite hostile way, wanting, it seemed, to turn all his sympathizers to dust. There was no point in stopping here: Mark Ivanovich couldn't stand it and, seeing that the man, completely offended and exasperated, had simply decided to be stubborn, declared outright and without sugary circumlocutions that it was time to get up, that it was no use lying around doing nothing, that shouting night and day about fires, sisters-in-law, boozers, locks, trunks and the devil knows what else was stupid, indecent and insulting for a man, and if Semyon Ivanovich didn't wish to sleep, then let him not disturb others and, finally, let him kindly take note of all this. The speech produced its effect, for Semyon Ivanovich, immediately turning to its orator, declared with firmness, although with a voice still weak and hoarse, that "you be quiet, you pup! You're a blabbermouth, you foulmouth! You hear, you shoe heel? Are you a prince, eh? Do you understand the business?" Hearing this, Mark Ivanovich flared up, but, observing that he was dealing with a sick man, magnanimously ceased to take offense, and, on the contrary, tried to shame him, but here too he was cut off; for Semyon Ivanovich at once observed the he would not permit himself to be jested with, even though Mark Ivanovich wrote poems. A two-minute silence followed; finally, recovering from his astonishment, Mark Ivanovich directly, clearly, quite eloquently although not without firmness, declared that Semyon Ivanovich should know that he was among decent people and that, "My dear sir, you should understand how to act with a decent personage." Mark Ivanovich could speak eloquently on occasion and liked to impress his listeners. For his part, Semyon Ivanovich spoke and acted, probably from his long habit of silence, in a more spasmodic fashion, and furthermore, when, for example, he happened to produce a long sentence,

77

as he got deeper into it, each word, it seemed, would give birth to still another word, the other word, right at its birth, to a third, the third to a fourth and so on, so that his mouth would get packed full, would begin to itch, and the packed words would finally start flying out in the most picturesque disorder. This was why Semyon Ivanovich, an intelligent man, sometimes spoke terrible nonsense. "You're lying," he answered now, "you child, you good-for-nothing! Just wait till you go begging, you'll start creeping around; you're a free-thinker, you're a skirt-chaser; take that, you poet!"

"Oh, so you're still raving, Semyon Ivanovich?"

"Ha, you hear," answered Semyon Ivanovich, "a fool raves, a boozer raves, a dog raves, but a wise man serves more sensibly. You, you hear, you don't know your business, you skirtchasing person, you scholar, you book! Just wait till you catch on fire, you won't notice that your head's burning off, so there, you heard the story?!"

"Yes,...that is, what...that is, what are you saying, Semyon Ivanovich, about a head burning off?..."

Mark Ivanovich didn't even finish, for everyone saw clearly that Semyon Ivanovich had still not sobered up and that he was raving; but the landlady couldn't resist remarking, at this point, that the house on Crooked Street had burned down because of a bald wench; that there'd been a bald wench there; that she'd lit a candle and set fire to the lumber room, but that wouldn't happen at her house, and that it'd be safe in her lodgings.

"Why, Semyon Ivanovich!" cried Zinovy Prokofievich, beside himself, interrupting the landlady, "Semyon Ivanovich, you silly, you remnant, you simpleton, are these jokes, are they joking with you now about your sister-in-law or about dancing examinations? Is that it, or what? Is that what you think?"

"Well, you listen here," answered our hero, raising himself from his bed, gathering his remaining strength, and absolutely raging at his sympathizers, "who's the joker? You're a joker, the dog's a joker, you joking person, and I, Sir, am not going to make jokes at your command; you hear, you pup, I, sir, am not your servant!"

Semyon Ivanovich wanted to say something more, but fell back weakly on his bed. The sympathizers were left bewildered, their mouths all hanging open, for they now realized what Semyon Ivanovich had gotten into, and they didn't know where to begin; suddenly the door to the kitchen squeaked, opened, and the boozer friend—alias Mr. Zimoveykin—timidly stuck in his head, carefully sniffing out the locality, as was his habit. It was just as if they had been waiting for him; everyone at once waved to him to come quickly, and Zimoveykin, extraordinarily delighted, without removing his overcoat, quickly and quite readily pushed his way through to Semyon Ivanovich's bed.

It was obvious that Zimoveykin had spent the whole night in vigil and in some kind of important exertions. The right side of his face had something stuck to it; his swollen eyelids were moist from his suppurating eyes; his frockcoat and whole attire was torn, the whole left side of his clothing was apparently spattered with something extremely foul, perhaps with filth from some puddle or other. Under his arm was someone's violin, which he was taking somewhere to sell. Apparently they weren't mistaken in calling for his help, for learning what was going on, he at once turned to the prankster Semyon Ivanovich and, with the air of a man who has the upper hand and, furthermore, knows his business, said "What are you doing, Senka? Get up! What are you doing, Senka, Wiseman Prokharchin, listen to reason! Or else I'll drag you out of bed, if you're going to carry on; stop carrying on!" Such a short but forceful speech surprised those present; everyone was still more surprised when they noticed that Semyon Ivanovich, hearing all this and seeing such a personage before him, was so dumbstruck and became so embarrassed and timid that he just barely, and then only in a whisper through his teeth, dared to mutter the inevitable protest: "You wretch, go away," he said, "you wretch, you thief! You hear, you understand? You're a bigwig, a prince, you bigwiggy person!"

"No, brother," Zimoveykin answered slowly, preserving all his presence of mind, "that's not good, you, brother-wiseman, Prokharchin, you Prokharchiny person!" continued Zimoveykin, somewhat parodying Semyon Ivanovich and looking around with satisfaction. "Don't you carry on! Calm down, Senya, calm down, or I'll report you, I'll tell everything, brother, understand?"

It seems Semyon Ivanovich understood everything, for he shuddered when he heard the conclusion of the speech, and suddenly began to look around quickly and with an utterly lost expression. Satisfied with the effect, Mr. Zimoveykin wanted to continue, but Mark Ivanovich at once checked his zeal and, waiting until Semyon Ivanovich had grown quiet, peaceful and almost completely calm, began to impress upon the uneasy man lengthily and reasonably that "to harbor such thoughts as he now had in his head was in the first place useless, in the second place not only useless but even harmful too; finally not so much harmful as even completely immoral; and the reason for this was that Semyon Ivanovich was leading everyone astray and setting a bad example." Everyone expected a sensible outcome from such a speech. Furthermore Semyon Ivanovich was now completely quiet and retorted in a moderate way. A mild argument ensued. They addressed him in a brotherly way, inquiring why was he so scared? Semyon Ivanovich answered, but allegorically. They retorted; Semyon Ivanovich retorted. Both sides retorted once more apiece, but then everyone got involved, young and old, for the discussion suddenly turned to such a marvelous and strange subject that they simply didn't know how to express it all. The argument finally led to impatience,

impatience to shouts, shouts even to tears, and Mark Ivanovich finally walked away with the foam of frenzy on his mouth, declaring that he had never before known such a mule. Oplevaniev* spat, Okeanov took fright, Zinovy Prokofievich shed tears, while Ustinya Fyodorovna positively howled, lamenting that "her lodger was leaving and had gone mad, that he would die, the dear soul, without a passport, without reporting himself, and she was an orphan, and that they would wear her out." In a word, everyone finally saw clearly that it was a good harvest, that whatever they'd sown had yielded a hundredfold, that the soil had been rich and that in their company Semyon Ivanovich had succeeded in overtaxing his wits for fair and in the most irrevocable manner. Everyone fell silent, for if they saw that Semyon Ivanovich was scared of everything, this time the sympathizers themselves were scared...

"What!" shouted Mark Ivanovich, "but what are you afraid of? Why have you gone mad? Who thinks about you, my dear sir? Do you have a right to be afraid? Who are you? What are you? A zero, sir, a round pancake, that's what! What are you yelling about? A peasant woman was run over on the street, so someone'll run you over too? Some drunkard didn't watch his pocket, so they'll cut off your coattails too? A house burned down, so your head'll burn off too, eh? Is that it, sir? Is that it, my dear fellow? Is that it?"

"You, you, you stupid!" muttered Semyon Ivanovich. "They'll eat off your nose, you'll eat it up yourself with some bread, you won't even notice..."

"If I'm a shoe heel, let me be a shoe heel," shouted Mark Ivanovich, not listening, "I'm a shoeheely person, perhaps. But I don't have to take an examination, to get married, to learn dancing; the ground, sir, won't give way under me. What is it, my dear fellow? Isn't your place big enough for you? Is the floor falling out from under you or what?"

"What then? I suppose they'll ask you? They'll close it, and it'll be gone."

"Gone. What'll they close?! Now what's the matter?"

"Just like they dumped the boozer...."

"They dumped him; but that was a boozer, and you and I are people!"

"So, we're people. But now it's there, and then it's gone...."

"Gone! Who's gone?"

"It is, the department...the de-part-ment!!!"

"But, you blessed man! After all, it's necessary, the department...."

"It's necessary, you hear that; today it's necessary, tomorrow it's necessary, and then the day after tomorrow it's somehow not necessary. You heard the story...."

---

*[The name comes from the past passive participle of the Russian verb *oplevat'*, to cover with spittle, to humiliate. The effect of "Oplevaniev spat" is equivalent to Lieutenant Scheisskopf's finally being called "that shithead" halfway through Joseph Heller's *Catch 22*.]

"But they'll give you a year's salary! A doubting Thomas, you're a doubting Thomas, you faithless person! They'd respect your seniority and give you another job...."

"Salary? But I've eaten up my salary, the thieves'll come, they'll take the money; but I have a sister-in-law, you hear? A sister-in-law! You mace...."

"Sister-in-law! You're a person who...."

"A person; I'm a person, and you, so learned, are stupid; you hear, mace, you're a macey person, that's what! And I'm not talking about your jokes; but it's the kind of place that they'll just up and abolish. And Demid, you hear, Demid Vasilievich says that the place'll be abolished...."

"Oh you and your Demid, Demid! You sinner, just...."

"Just a skip and a hop and you're out of a job; and you can go whistle."

"Either you're simply lying, or you've gone completely mad! Just tell us right out: What is it? Admit it, if that's the problem! There's nothing to be embarrassed about! Have you gone mad, my dear fellow, eh?"

"He's gone mad! He's gone out of his mind!" resounded all around, and everyone wrung their hands in despair and the landlady flung both arms around Mark Ivanovich so that he wouldn't somehow tear Semyon Ivanovich to pieces. "You heathen, you heathen soul, you wiseman!" implored Zimoveykin. "Senya, you're not a touchy person, you're attractive, amiable! You're simple, you're virtuous...you hear? It comes from your virtuousness; I'm the one who's wild and stupid, I'm a beggar; but good people haven't abandoned me; see, they respect me; I thank them and the landlady; you see, I bow to the ground to them, there; my debt, I pay my debt to you, dear landlady!" At this point Zimoveykin actually executed a bow to the earth all around, even with a certain pedantic dignity. After this Semyon Ivanovich wanted to continue to talk but this time they wouldn't let him; everyone intervened and began to implore, to reassure, to soothe him and succeeded in making Semyon Ivanovich quite ashamed, and finally in a weak voice he asked permission to explain himself.

"Well, that's fine," he said, "I'm attractive, meek, you hear, and virtuous, devoted and faithful; my last drop, you know, of blood, you hear, you pup, you bigwig...so the place is there; but I'm poor; and when they abolish it, you hear, you bigwig—be quiet, now, understand me—they'll abolish it...it's there, and then it's not there...understand? And I, brother, will have to go begging, you hear?"

"Senka!" howled Zimoveykin in a frenzy, this time drowning out the entire rising hubbub with his voice. "You're a freethinker! I'll report you right now! What are you saying? Who are you? Are you a rowdy or what, you sheep's brain! They'll fire a rowdy, a stupid man, you hear, without notice; and who are you?"

"Well, then it'll be..."

"What will?"

"Well, you go whistle!..."

"What'll be you go whistle?"

"Well he's free, I'm free; but when you keep lying around, it's...."

"What?"

"They'll say I'm a freethinker...."

"A free-think-er! Senka, you a freethinker!!"

"Wait!" shouted Mr. Prokharchin, waving his hand and interrupting the incipient clamor. "I didn't mean...understand, just understand, you sheep: I'm meek, today I'm meek, tomorrow I'm meek, and then I'm not meek, I'm surly; into the army with you, and there goes the freethinker!..."

"What are you saying?" thundered Mark Ivanovich finally, leaping from the chair he was about to sit down to rest on and running up to the bed all in a tizzy, in a frenzy, all shaking with annoyance and rage, "What are you? You're a sheep! You've neither house nor home. What are you, the only one in the world? Was the world made for you? Are you some kind of a Napoleon or what? What are you? Who are you? Are you a Napoleon, eh? Are you a Napoleon or not?! Tell me, sir, a Napoleon or not?..."

But Mr. Prlkharchin didn't answer this question. It wasn't that he was ashamed that he was a Napoleon, or that he didn't dare take such a responsibility on himself, no, he just couldn't argue anymore or say a thing.... A crisis in his illness followed. Tiny tears suddenly gushed from his gray eyes, which glittered with a feverish fire. He covered his burning head with his hands, which were bony and wasted from illness, sat up in bed and, sobbing, began to say that he was utterly poor, that he was such an unfortunate simple person, that he was stupid and ignorant, that the people should forgive him, protect, feed, and take care of him, not abandon him in misfortune, and God knows what else Semyon Ivanovich wailed. Wailing, he looked around in wild terror, as if expecting the ceiling to fall down or the floor to give way any minute. Everyone began to pity him, looking at the poor man, and everyone's heart softened. The landlady, sobbing like a peasant woman, and wailing about her orphaned state, laid the sick man in his bed herself. Mark Ivanovich, seeing the uselessness of touching on the subject of Napoleon, also immediately became jovial and also began to render aid. The others, in order to do something in their turn, proposed an infusion of raspberries, saying that it was a speedy remedy for everything and that the sick man would find it very pleasant; but Zimoveykin immediately overrode them all, adding that there was nothing better in such a case than a good dose of some kind of pungent camomile. As for Zinovy Prokofievich, having a kind heart, he sobbed and shed tears, repenting that he had frightened Semyon Ivanovich with various tall stories, and, attending to the sick man's last words that he was utterly poor and that they should feed him, ran around getting up a subscription for him, confining it to the lodgings for the time being. Everyone moaned and groaned, everyone felt sad and bitter, and meanwhile everyone was amazed at how a person could suddenly get completely frightened like that. And why had he gotten so frightened? It would be one thing if he held an important position, had a wife, had children; it would be one thing if he'd been taken to court for something or other; but the man was utter rubbish, with one trunk and a German lock he had lain behind screens for more than twenty years, kept silent, known nothing of the world or of grief, hoarded, and now the man suddenly took it into his head because of some banal, idle word or other to lose his head completely, to get completely terrified about the fact that it had suddenly gotten difficult to live in this world...but the man didn't even consider that it was difficult for everyone! "If he'd just taken that into account," Okeanov used to say afterwards, "that it's difficult for everyone, the man would have kept his head, he would have stopped fooling around and would have gotten along all right." All day they talked of nothing but Semyon Ivanovich. They kept coming up to him, inquiring about him, comforting him; but by evening he was beyond comforting. The poor man began to suffer from delirium and fever; he fell into unconsciousness, so that they almost decided to send for the doctor; the lodgers all agreed and mutually vowed to take turns watching and comforting Semyon Ivanovich all night and if anything were to happen, to wake everyone at once. For the purpose of staying awake, they sat down to a game of cards, placing the boozer friend, who had spent the day at the lodgings and had asked to spend the night, by the sick man's bed. Since the game was played on credit and was entirely devoid of interest, they soon got bored. They dropped the game, then argued about something, then began to bang and shout, finally dispersed to their corners, still angrily debating and disputing for a long time, and since everyone suddenly got angry, they lost interest in keeping watch and went to sleep. Soon it grew as quiet in the lodgings as in an empty cellar, especially since it was terribly cold. Okeanov was one of the last to go to sleep, "and I wasn't exactly asleep, and I wasn't exactly awake," as he said afterward, "but it seemed that two people were talking near me just before daybreak." Okeanov recounted that he had recognized Zimoveykin and that Zimoveykin had begun to wake up his old friend Remnyov next to him, that they had talked for a long while in a whisper, then Zimoveykin had gone out, and could be heard trying to open the door with a key in the kitchen. The key, as the landlady afterwards declared, had lain under her pillow and disappeared that night. Finally, Okeanov testified, he thought he heard them both go behind the screens to the sick man and light a candle there. He knew nothing more, he said, his eyes grew heavy; and then he woke up along with everyone else the moment everyone in the lodgings leapt out of bed at once when a shriek rang out behind the screens that would have raised the dead—many felt that the candle there had suddenly gone out at this point. A commotion arose, everyone's heart stopped; they ran helter-skelter towards the shriek, but at that instant scuffling, shouting, swearing and fighting broke out behind the screens. They lit a light and saw that Zimoveykin and Remnyov were fighting with each other, that they were both cursing and swearing at each other; but when they threw the light on them one of them shouted: "It's not me, it's this bandit!" and the other, namely Zimoveykin, shouted: "Don't touch me, I'm innocent; I'll swear on it right now!" Both had lost their human form; but in the first minute there was no time to bother about them: the sick man was no longer in his former place behind the screens. They immediately separated the combatants, dragged them apart, and saw that Mr. Prokharchin was lying under the bed, most likely having pulled his blanket and pillow down onto himself in a state of complete unconsciousness so that only the bare, ancient and greasy mattress remained on the bed (there had never been sheets on it). They dragged Semyon Ivanovich out, stretched him out on the mattress, but noticed at once that there was no point in fussing very much, because he was a complete kaput; his arms were growing rigid, and he was barely functioning. They stood over him: he still kept up a tiny tremor and his whole body shook, he made an effort to do something with his hands, he didn't say a word, but blinked his eyes exactly the same way they say the still warm and living head covered with blood blinks when it has just rebounded from the executioner's axe.

Finally everything got quieter and quieter; the pre-death trembling and spasms died down; Mr. Prokharchin stretched out his legs and went off about his business and his sins. Whether something had frightened Semyon Ivanovich or he had had some dream, as Remnyov afterwards declared, or whether there was some other problem is unknown; what matters is that even if the head clerk himself had now appeared in the apartment and personally given Semyon Ivanovich notice for freethinking, rowdiness and drunkenness, even if some mooching beggar woman bearing the title of Semyon Ivanovich's sister-in-law were now to enter through the other door, even if Semyon Ivanovich were immediately to receive a two hundred ruble reward, or the house really were to catch fire and Semyon Ivanovich's head were to start burning, he probably wouldn't have deigned to lift a finger at such news now. While the first shock was wearing off, while those present regained the gift of speech and threw themselves into commotion, speculation, doubts and shouts, while Ustinya Fyodorovna dragged Semyon Ivanovich's trunk out from under his bed, rummaging hastily under his pillow, under his mattress and even in his boots, while they subjected Remnyov and Zimoveykin to questioning, the lodger Okeanov, hitherto the most unremarkable, meek and quiet lodger, suddenly summoned all his presence of mind, and, relying on his gifts and talent, grabbed his hat and slipped out of the apartment during the hubbub. And when all the terrors of anarchy had reached their peak in the agitated and hitherto peaceful lodgings, the door opened, and suddenly, out of the blue, there appeared first a certain gentleman of noble appearance with a stern but displeased face, after him Yaroslav Ilich, after Yaroslav Ilich his subordinates and everyone else appropriate, and after all of them—the embarrassed Mr. Okeanov. The gentleman of stern but noble appearance went right up to Semyon Ivanovich, felt him, made a grimace, shrugged his shoulders and announced what was quite obvious, namely, that the deceased was already dead, adding just as an aside that the same thing had happened the other day to a certain thoroughly respectable and important gentleman who had also up and died in his sleep. The gentleman of noble but displeased demeanor then walked away from the bed, said that they had disturbed him for nothing, and went out. Yaroslav Ilich instantly took his place (at which point Remnyov and Zimoveykin were handed over to the appropriate officials), interrogated some of them, deftly took possession of the trunk which the landlady had already attempted to open, put the boots back in their place, remarking that they were full of holes and thoroughly useless, demanded the pillow back, summoned Okeanov, asked for the trunk key which had been in the mooching friend's pocket, and solemnly, in front of appropriate witnesses, opened Semyon Ivanovich's property. Everything was displayed: two rags, one pair of socks, half a handkerchief, an old hat, some buttons, old shoe soles and boot vamps—in a word, this, that and the other,* that is, rubbish, rags, odds and ends, which smelled of the trunk; the only thing that was any good was the German lock. They called Okeanov and talked to him severely; but Okeanov was ready to take an oath. They asked for the pillow, inspected it: it was dirty, but in all other respects looked just like any other pillow. They started in on the mattress, were about to pick it up, but stopped to think a minute when suddenly, quite unexpectedly, something heavy, ringing, clinked to the floor. They bent down, rummaged about and saw a paper bundle, and in the bundle was about a dozen rubles. "Aha!" said Yaroslav Ilich, pointing to a torn place in the mattress from which horsehair and stuffing were sticking out. They inspected the torn place and concluded that it had just been made with a knife, it was about a foot long; they stuck their hands in the hole and pulled out the landlady's kitchen knife, probably hastily abandoned there, which had been used to slit the mattress. Yaroslav Ilich had just pulled the knife out of the hole and again said "Aha!" when another bundle immediately fell out, and after it two fifty-kopek pieces, one quarter, then some small change and one old hefty five-ruble piece spilled out one by one. They immediately snatched all this up with their hands. Then they realized that it might not be a bad idea to cut up the mattress completely with a scissors. They asked for scissors....

Meanwhile the burned-down lard candle-end illuminated a scene an observer would have found extremely curious. About a dozen lodgers were grouped around the bed in the most picturesque costumes, all uncombed,

---

*[The original *shil'tso, myl'tso, beloe belil'tso* ("little awl, little soap, little white bleach") evokes several associations: the awl recalls the Russian proverb "you can't hide an awl in a sack," i.e., "the truth will out"; "soap" in conjunction with "white bleach" suggests the idea of whitewashing. The juxtaposition of this Russian folk flavor with the mention of the German lock creates a vivid contrast.]

unshaven, unwashed, sleepy, just as they had been when they were drifting off to sleep. Some were completely pale, some had sweat on their brows, some were seized by tremors, others by fever. The landlady, quite stupefied, stood quietly with crossed arms attendant upon the mercies of Yaroslav Ilich. From above, the heads of Avdotya the maid and the landlady's favorite cat looked down from the stove with frightened curiosity; torn and broken screens were scattered all around; the open trunk displayed its unseemly interior; the blanket and the pillow lay around covered with mattress stuffing, and, finally, a gradually increasing pile of silver and other coins glittered on the three-legged wooden table. Only Semyon Ivanovich fully preserved his equanimity, lay quietly on his bed and seemed to have no premonition of his ruin. When the scissors had been brought and Yaroslav Ilich's assistant, wanting to be helpful, shook the mattress somewhat impatiently in order to free it from under the back of its owner more easily, Semyon Ivanovich, who knew how to be courteous, first yielded a bit of space, rolling onto his side with his back to the searchers; then, at the second shake, settled face down and finally yielded still further, and since the last side slat of the bed was missing, he suddenly quite unexpectedly plunged to the floor head first, leaving visible only two bony thin blue legs which stuck up like two twigs of a charred tree. Since this was already the second time that morning that Mr. Prokharchin had inspected under his bed, he immediately arounsed suspicion, and some of the lodgers, under the guidance of Zinovy Prokofievich, crawled under it with the intention of seeing if anything were hidden there. But the searchers only knocked heads in vain, and since Yaroslav Ilich at once shouted at them and ordered them to free Semyon Ivanovich from his nasty place, two of the most reasonable of them each took a leg in both hands, dragged the unexpected capitalist into God's light and laid him across the bed. Meanwhile the hair and stuffing flew around, the silver pile kept growing—and God! what couldn't be found in it. Noble silver rubles, respectable solid one-and-a-half ruble pieces, pretty little fifty kopek pieces, plebeian little quarters, little twenty kopek pieces, even unpromising little-old-lady small fry dimes and nickels in silver—all in special wrappers, in the most methodical and consistent order. There were rarities too: two tokens of some kind, one *Napoléon d'or*, one of unknown origin but clearly a very rare coin.... Some of the ruble pieces also dated from antiquity; worn down and chopped up Elizabethan ones, German kreuzers, coins from Peter's time and from Catherine's; there were, for example, coins which were already quite rare, old fifteen kopek pieces, pierced for use as earrings, all completely worn down but with the legal quantity of dots; there was even copper, but it was all green, rusty.... They found one ten ruble note—but that was all. Finally, when the whole dissection was over and they found, upon shaking the mattress cover several times, that nothing clinked, they put all the money down on the table and set about counting it. At first glance one could have even been completely deceived and guessed there was a million there, the pile was so huge! But there wasn't a million, although it turned out to be an extraordinarily significant sum—exactly 2497 rubles and 50 kopeks, so that if Zinovy Prokofievich's subscription of the day before had been collected, there would perhaps have been exactly 2500 paper rubles in all. They took the money, put a seal on the deceased's trunk, heard out the landlady's complaints and told her when and where to submit evidence of the deceased's debt to her. They took signatures from the appropriate people; at this point the lodgers were about to let something slip about the sister-in-law; but convinced that in a certain sense the sister-in-law was a myth, that is, a product of Semyon Ivanovich's lack of imagination, for which, according to subsequent inquiries, they had more than once reproached the deceased, they abandoned the idea at once as useless, harmful and detrimental to his good name, Mr. Prokharchin; and with this the matter was closed. When the first horror subsided a bit, when they collected their wits and realized what kind of man the deceased had been, everyone quieted down and began to look at each other with some distrust. Some took Semyon Ivanovich's action extraordinarily to heart and were even apparently insulted.... So much capital! How the man had piled it up! Mark Ivanovich, not losing his presence of mind, was about to explain why Semyon Ivanovich had suddenly got frightened, but they wouldn't listen to him. Zinovy Prokofievich was very thoughtful for some reason, Okeanov got a little tipsy, the rest somehow huddled together, and the little man Kantarev, distinguished by his sparrow's nose, left the apartment towards evening, quite carefully sealing and securing all his trunks and bundles, coldly explaining to the curious that times were hard and that the rent there was beyond his means. The landlady howled without interruption, both grieving over Semyon Ivanovich and cursing him for insulting her orphaned state. They asked Mark Ivanovich why the deceased hadn't taken his money to a pawnshop. "He was simple, my dear, he didn't have the imagination for that," answered Mark Ivanovich.

"Well, you're pretty simple yourself, my dear," interjected Okeanov, "for twenty years the man hung on, was knocked down by a feather, while you were busy making soup, you didn't have the time!... Ekh, my dear!"

"Oh, my dear little one!" continued the landlady, "what did you need a pawnshop for? If he'd just brought me his little handful and said to me: take it, dear Ustinyushka, here are my worldly goods, you keep me and feed me as long as moist mother earth preserves me—then by the holy ikon, I would have fed him, given him drink, watched over him, akh, what a sinner, what a deceiver! He deceived me, cheated me, a poor orphan!..."

They again approached Semyon Ivanovich's bed. Now he lay properly in his best, although incidentally, his only, clothing, hiding his rigidified chin behind his cravat which was tied somewhat awkwardly, washed, combed but not quite fully shaved because there was no razor in the lodgings: the only one, which had belonged to Zinovy Prokofievich, had lost its edge the year before and had been profitably sold at the Fleamarket; the others went to the barber. They had not yet managed to clean up the mess. The broken screens lay as before and, exposing Semyon Ivanovich's isolation, were like an emblem of the fact that death tears away the curtain from all our secrets, intrigues, and procrastinations. The mattress stuffing, also not cleared away, lay all around in thick piles.

A poet could have quite well compared this whole suddenly frozen corner to the wrecked nest of the "thrifty" swallow all broken and torn by the storm, the nestlings and their mother killed, and their warm little bed of fluff, feathers and flocks blown all around.* However, Semyon Ivanovich looked more like an old, vain, thieving sparrow. Now he had grown quiet and seemed to have completely hidden himself, as if it were not he who was guilty, as if it were not he who had tried to hoodwink and deceive all the kind people, without shame and without conscience, in the most indecent fashion. Now he no longer heard the sobbing and crying of his orphaned and insulted landlady. On the contrary, like an experienced died-in-the-wool capitalist who wouldn't want to waste a minute in idleness even in the coffin, he seemed entirely absorbed in some speculative computations. Some deep thought appeared on his face, while his lips were pursed in such a significant expression as could never have been suspected of belonging to Semyon Ivanovich during his lifetime. It was as if he had grown more intelligent. His right eye was somehow knavishly screwed up; Semyon Ivanovich seemed to want to say something, to impart something terribly important, to explain himself, without losing time and as fast as possible, because all this business had come up and there was no time.... And it was as if he could be heard saying: "What's the matter? Stop, you hear, you stupid peasant woman! Don't whine! You, mother, go sleep it off, you hear! I'm dead; it's not necessary now; why, what for! It's nice to lie around...I, that is, you hear, I'm not talking about that; you peasant woman, bigwig, bigwiggy person, understand? I'm dead now; but, well, what if, that is, perhaps it can't be, but what if I'm not dead—you hear, I'll get up, and then what, eh?"

1846

---

*[A reference to G.R. Derzhavin's poem "The Swallow" (1792).]

POLZUNKOV*

I began to scrutinize the man. Even in his appearance there was something so peculiar that, however distracted you might be, suddenly made you
involuntarily fix your gaze on him and instantly burst into the most prolonged laughter. That is just what happened to me. It must be remarked that
this little gentleman's eyes were so mobile—or, perhaps, that he himself was
totally prey to the magnetism of each gaze directed at him to such an extent,
that he would almost instantly turn to his observer and would anxiously
analyze his gaze. Because of his perpetual twisting and turning he decidedly
resembled a weathervane. A strange business! He seemed to fear ridicule, but
he almost earned his bread by being a universal buffoon and meekly presented his head to all fillips, in the moral and even the physical sense, depend-
ing on what company he was in. Voluntary buffoons are not even pitiful. But
I at once remarked that this strange creature, this ridiculous little man, was
not at all a buffoon by profession. Something noble was still left in him. His
anxiety, his perpetual painful fear for himself, actually testified in his favor.
It seemed to me that all his desire to oblige came rather from goodness of
heart than from material interests. With pleasure he would permit people to
laugh at him at the top of their lungs and in the most indecent fashion, to his
face, but at the same time—and I swear to this—his heart ached and over-
flowed at the thought that his audience was so ignobly hardhearted that they
were capable of laughing not at a fact, but at him, at his whole being, at his
heart, head, at his appearance, at his whole flesh and blood. I am sure that he
felt the whole stupidity of his position at that moment; but his protest
would instantly die in his breast, although it would without fail be reborn
every time in the most magnanimous way. I am sure that all this happened
from nothing other than goodness of heart, and not at all from the material
disadvantages of being kicked out and not being able to borrow money from
someone: this gentleman perpetually borrowed money, that is, he begged
alms in that form, when, having made a few grimaces and enough jokes at
his own expense, he felt that in some sense he had the right to borrow. But
my God! What a loan it was! And with what an expression would he take that
loan! I could not have imagined that in such a small space as that man's
wrinkled angular face there could be room, at one and the same time, for so
many different grimaces, so many strange diverse feelings, so many utterly
killing impressions. What wasn't there on that face! Shame, false insolence,
irritation, a sudden flushing, anger, fear of failure, a plea for forgiveness for

---

*[The name comes from the verb *polzat'*, to creep or crawl.]

daring to trouble you, the sense of his own worth, the fullest sense of his own worthlessness—all this would pass across his face like lightning. He had struggled along a whole six years this way in God's world and had still not hit upon the pose to take at the interesting moment of borrowing money! It goes without saying that he could never become callous and act completely base. His heart was too sensitive, too ardent! I'll even say more: in my opinion, he was the most honorable and noble man in the world, but with a little weakness: to do something low at the least provocation, goodnaturedly and unselfishly, if only to oblige his fellow man. In a word, he was what is called a rag in the fullest sense. The most ludicrous thing of all was the fact that he dressed almost the same way as everyone else, not better, not worse, neatly, even with a certain refinement and pretensions to respectability and personal worth. This external equality and internal inequality, his anxiety for himself and at the same time his incessant self-deprecation—all this created the most striking contrast and merited laughter and pity. If he were sure in his heart (which, despite his experience, happened to him every other minute) that his listeners were the kindest people in the world who laugh only at funny statements, and not at his doomed personality, he would gladly take off his frockcoat, put it on inside out somehow and go walking around the streets in that garb to please others and entertain himself, if only to amuse his patrons and give them all pleasure. But he could never attain equality by any means. One more trait: the eccentric was proud, and sporadically, if there were no danger in it, even magnanimous. One had to see and hear how he was able, sometimes not sparing himself, and consequently with some risk, almost with heroism, to demolish one of his patrons who had unbearably infuriated him. But that was at certain moments.... In a word, he was a martyr in the full sense of the word, but the most useless and, consequently, the most comic martyr.

A general argument arose among the guests. Suddenly I saw that my eccentric had jumped up on a chair and was shouting with all his might, wanting to be given the floor.

"Listen," the host whispered to me, "he sometimes tells the most curious things...does he interest you?"

I nodded my head and squeezed into the crowd.

In fact, the sight of a respectably dressed gentleman jumping up on a chair and shouting with all his might attracted the general attention. Many who didn't know the eccentric exchanged puzzled glances, others roared with laughter.

"I know Fedosey Nikolaich! I ought to know Fedosey Nikolaich better than anyone!" shouted the eccentric from his elevation. "Gentlemen, allow me to tell you a story. I'll tell you a good one about Fedosey Nikolaich! I know a certain story—a treasure!...."

"Tell it, Osip Mikhailich, tell it."

"Tell it!!"

"Listen...."

"Listen, listen!!!"

"I'll begin; but, gentlemen, this is a peculiar story...."

"Good, good!"

"This is a comic story."

"Very good, excellent, splendid—go on!"

"This is an episode from the personal life of your most humble...."

"Then why did you bother to say it was comic!"

"And even a bit tragic!"

"Eh???!"

"In a word, this story which gives you all the pleasure of listening to me now, gentlemen, is the story in consequence of which I ended up in such *profitable* company."

"No puns!"

"This story...."

"In a word, this story—hurry up and finish the apologia—is a story which is worth something," a blond young man with whiskers added in a hoarse voice, dropping his hand into the pocket of his tailcoat and as if inadvertently pulling out his wallet instead of his handkerchief.

"This is a story, my dear sirs, after which I would like to see many of you in my place. And finally, this is a story in consequence of which I didn't get married!"

"Get married!... A wife!... Polzunkov wanted to get married!!"

"I confess, I would like to see Madame Polzunkov now!"

"Allow me to ask the name of the elusive Madame Polzunkov," piped one youth, making his way up to the storyteller.

"And so, the first chapter, gentlemen; it was exactly six years ago, in spring, March 31—notice the date, gentlemen, on the eve...."

"Of April first!" shouted a youth in curls.

"You're extraordinarily perceptive, sir. It was evening. The dusk was thickening over the provincial town of N., the moon felt like floating out... well, and everything was as it should have been. So, gentlemen, at the very last moments of dusk, on the sly, I too floated out of my little apartment, having bid farewell to my restricted late grandmother. Excuse me, gentlemen, for using such a fashionable expression which I heard the last time I was at Nikolai Nikolaich's. But my grandmother was thoroughly restricted: she was deaf, dumb, blind, stupid—you name it!... I confess, I was agitated, I was setting out on a great enterprise; my little heart beat in me like a kitten's when someone's bony paw grabs it by the scruff of the neck."

"If you please, Monsieur Polzunkov!"

"What do you want?"

"Tell it more simply; please, don't try so hard!"

"Yes sir," said Osip Mikhailich, somewhat crestfallen. "I went into

Fedosey Nikolaich's house (he owned it). Fedosey Nikolaich, as you know, is no mere civil servant, but a full department head. They announced me and immediately showed me into the study. I can see it now: a completely, almost completely dark room, and they didn't bring candles. I look, in walks Fedosey Nikolaich. So he and I remained in darkness...."

"What could have gone on between you?" asked an officer.

"And what do you suppose, sir?" asked Polzunkov, quickly turning his convulsively working face to the youth in curls.

"And so, gentlemen, at this point a strange occurrence took place. That is, there was nothing strange in it, it was what is called an everyday affair—I simply took a roll of papers out of my pocket, while he took a roll of papers out of his, only they were government...."

"Notes?"

"Notes, sir, and we exchanged."

"I'll bet there was a whiff of bribery about it," said one respectably dressed and close-cropped young gentleman.

"Bribery, sir!" chimed Polzunkov. "Ekh!

> *Let me be a liberal*
> *like the many I have seen!*

If you too, when you end up working in the provinces, don't warm your hands...at your country's hearth.... For as one man of letters has said: 'Even the smoke of the fatherland is sweet and pleasant to us!'* Our country is our mother, gentlemen, our own mother, we are her babes, so we suck her!..."

General laughter broke out.

"But, would you believe it, gentlemen, I never took bribes," said Polzunkov, mistrustfully surveying the whole assembly.

A volley of prolonged Homeric laughter drowned out Polzunkov's words.

"Really, gentlemen, it's true...."

But here he stopped, continuing to survey everyone with a strange kind of expression on his face. Perhaps—who knows—perhaps at that moment it occurred to him that he was a bit more honest than many of that whole honest company.... The serious expression on his face didn't disappear until the very end of the general merriment.

"And so," began Polzunkov when everyone had quieted down a bit, "although I never took bribes, this time I transgressed: I put a bribe in my pocket...from a bribetaker.... That is, there were certain papers in my hands

---

*[Chatsky, who says this in Griboedov's *Woe from Wit* (Act I, Scene 7), is in turn quoting Derzhavin's "Harp" (1798).]

which, had I wanted to send them to certain people, it would have gone badly for Fedosey Nikolaich."

"So he bought them?"

"He did, sir."

"Did he give a lot?"

"He gave as much as another nowadays would sell his conscience for, whole, with all the variations...if only he could get anything for it. But I felt as if tar had been poured over me when I put the money in my pocket. I really don't know how that always happens to me, gentlemen—but suddenly I'm more dead than alive, my lips twitch, my legs tremble; well, I was guilty, guilty, completely guilty, I was suddenly terribly ashamed, ready to beg Fedosey Nikolaich's forgiveness...."

"Well, what did he do, did he forgive you?"

"But I didn't ask...I'm only saying that that's how I felt then; that is, I have an ardent heart. I see he's looking me right in the eye: 'You,' he says, 'don't fear God, Osip Mikhailich.'

"Well, what was I to do? For propriety I just shrugged my shoulders, put my head to one side: 'How,' I say, 'do I not fear God, Fedosey Niko-laich?...' I just say that for propriety...myself, I'm ready to fall through the floor.

" 'Having been a friend of our family for so long, having been, I may say, a son—and who knows what heaven had in store, Osip Mikhailich! And suddenly, what, a denunciation, and just now!... What is one to think of people after that, Osip Mikhailich?'

"And what a lecture, gentlemen, what a lecture he gave me! 'No,' he says, 'you tell me what to think of people after that, Osip Mikhailich?' 'What is he to think?' I think. You know, my throat is scratching, my voice is trembling, I think of my seedy lair and grab my hat....

" 'Where are you going, Osip Mikhailich? Is it possible that on the eve of such a day.... Is it possible that even now you have forgotten; how have I sinned against you?...'

" 'Fedosey Nikolaich,' I say, 'Fedosey Nikolaich!'

"Well, you see, I melted, gentlemen, like a wet sugar cake, I melted. How could I? And the package in my pocket with the banknotes, it too seemed to scream: you ingrate, brigand, damn thief—it pulled as if it weighed two hundred pounds.... (And if only it really had weighed two hundred pounds!...)

" 'I see,' says Fedosey Nikolaich, 'I see your penitence...tomorrow, you know, you'll....'

" 'St. Mary the Egyptian's day....' *

" 'Well, don't cry,' says Fedosey Nikolaich, 'that's enough: he's sinned

---

*[St. Mary the Egyptian, a harlot, was converted and lived a penitential hermit's life in the wilderness. Presumably her day would be Marya Fedoseevna's name day.

and repented! Let's go! Perhaps I'll be able,' he says, 'to return you to the true path again.... Perhaps my humble Penates (I remember, Penates, that's exactly how he expressed it, the brigand) 'will warm' he says, 'your harden...I won't say hardened—you erring heart....'

"He took me, gentlemen, by the arm and led me to his family. A chill runs down my spine; I'm shaking! I think, what kind of expression should I make...but you need to know, gentlemen,... how to say it, here a certain ticklish little business came up!"

"Not Madame Polzunkov?"

"Marya Fedoseevna, sir, but it was not fated, it seems, for her to be this Madame that you call her, she didn't attain that honor. You see, Fedosey Nikolaich was even right in saying that I was considered almost a son in the household. At least that's how it was six months earlier when a certain retired junker, Mikhaylo Maksimich Dvigaylov by name, was still alive. Only he died, by God's will, and put off settling his business till death settled his business for him...."

"Ugh!!!"

"Well, it's nothing, there's nothing to be done, gentlemen, excuse me, a slip of the tongue—the pun's poor, and it'd be all right if only the pun were poor—but things were even worse when I was left so to speak, with zero prospects, because the retired junker—although he wouldn't let me in his house (he lived in the lap of luxury because he always had his hand in the till!)—also, perhaps not mistakenly, considered me his own son."

"Aha!"

"Yes, that's how it was! Well, they started turning up their noses at me at Fedosey Nikolaich's. I kept on noticing it, but kept on holding tight, when suddenly, to my misfortune (or maybe to my good fortune!), out of the blue, a remount officer galloped into our little town. His business really, was active, easy, cavalry style—but he ensconced himself so firmly at Fedosey Nikolaich's that, well, he landed like a mortar! In a roundabout way, according to my nasty habit, I say, 'But Fedosey Nikolaich, why insult me! I'm in some sense your son.... When will I get some fatherly...a little fatherliness....' He began, dear sir, to answer! Well, you know, when he begins to speak, he'll recite a whole epic, twelve cantos in verse, you just listen, lick your lips and throw up your hands in delight, but there's not a groat's worth of sense in it, that is, whatever sense there is you can't make out, you won't understand, you stand around like an idiot, he's fogging up the place, twisting around like an eel, wriggling out of things, it's a talent, simply a talent, such a gift that it even strikes fear into strangers! I started throwing myself all over the place: hither and thither! Dragging in love songs, bringing her candy, hatching puns, moans and groans, it aches, I say, my heart aches from amour, and all in tears, even a secret confession! Man is a stupid creature! After all, he hadn't checked with the sexton that I was thirty years old.... Well, he did. And I'd thought I'd be sneaky! But no! My affair had failed, giggles and gibes everywhere—

94

well, I got spiteful, my throat choked up completely—I sneaked out, didn't set foot in the house, thought and thought—and hit upon denunciation! Well, I acted basely, I wanted to betray a friend, I confess, there was a lot of material, such great material, a capital case! It brought one thousand five hundred in silver when I exchanged it and the denunciation for banknotes!"

"Ah! So that's what the bribe was!"

"Yes, sir, that was my little bribe; a bribe-taker had to pay it! (After all, it's not sinful, really, it's not!) Well sir, now I'll start from where I left off: he dragged me, if you will recall, into the parlor more dead than alive; they greet me: they all seem insulted, that is, not exactly insulted—so distressed that it was simply...well, crushed, completely crushed, and meanwhile such respectable importance glows on their faces, such gravity in their gazes, something so fatherly, so parental...like the prodigal son has come back to us —that's what it had come to! They sat me down to tea, but I felt as if a samovar were stuck in my chest, it's boiling inside me, while my feet are turning to ice. I shrank, I was scared! Marya Fomishna, his spouse, a court councillor's daughter (and now a collegiate councillor's wife) started talking to me familiarly from the first word: 'How did you get so thin, my boy!' she says. 'Oh, I'm just indisposed, Marya Fomishna...' I say. My voice is shaking! But she says to me out of the blue, seems she'd been waiting to get back at me, the snake: 'So, apparently your conscience,' she says, 'turned out to be better than your soul, Osip Mikhailich, my dear! Our family hospitality,' she says, 'made you squirm! My scalding tears, it seems, had their effect on you!' I swear to God, that's just what she said, with no conscience; what was it to her, the shrew! She just sat there pouring out the tea. But just go to the market, and I bet, my dear, you'd outshout all the peasant women. That's the kind she was, our councillor's wife! And then, to my misfortune, Marya Fedoseevna, the daughter, came in, with all her innocent ways, she was a bit pale, her eyes were red, apparently from tears—I like an idiot died on the spot. But it turned out later that she'd been shedding tears for the remount officer: he'd bolted for home, made tracks while he was still in one piece, because, you know, it seems (now it gets to the point) his time had come to depart, his time had run out, and not his leave either! But instead...only later did the dear parents catch on and find out the whole truth, but what can you do, they hushed up the misfortune—an addition to the household!... Well, there was nothing to be done, when I looked at her I was lost, simply lost, I stole a glance at my hat, I wanted to grab it and run off quick; it wasn't there: they'd made off with my hat...I even, I confess, wanted to go without my hat—but, I think—no, they've latched the door, friendly laughter had started up, winking and flirting, I got embarrassed, made up something, started in about love; she, my darling, sat down to the piano and sang in an injured tone about the hussar who leaned on his saber—it was the death of me! 'Well,' says Fedosey Nikolaich, 'all is forgotten, come, come...embrace me!' Just as I was, I immediately fell with my face to his waistcoat. 'My

95

benefactor, my own father!' I say, and I overflow with hot tears. My God, what happened then! He's crying, his old woman's crying, Mashenka's crying...there was also some blonde there: she's crying too...and what's more—the little kids crawled out from all corners (the Lord had blessed their little house!) and they're bawling too.... So many tears, tenderness, that is, such joy, they'd found their prodigal, just like a soldier coming home! Then they served refreshments, we played forfeits: oh, it aches! What aches?—my heart, for whom? She blushes, the darling! The old man and I drank punch—well, they exhausted and enchanted me completely.

I went home to my grandmother. Myself, my head is going round in circles; I walked the whole way chuckling, at home I paced my corner for two whole hours, woke up the old lady, told her about all my happiness. 'But did he give you the money, the brigand?' 'He did, grandma, he did, he did, my dear, he did, fortune's smiled on us, just open the door to it!' 'Well, now at least get married, now's the time to get married,' the old lady says to me, 'it seems my prayers have been heard!' I woke up Sofron. 'Sofron,' I say, 'take off my boots.' 'Well, Sofron! Congratulate me now, kiss me! I'm getting married, brother, I'm getting married, get drunk tomorrow, have a ball,' I say, 'your master's getting married!' My heart was full of rollicks and frolics!... I was about to fall asleep; no, I had to get up again, I sit and think; suddenly it flashed into my head: tomorrow's April first, a bright, playful day, what'll I do?—and I thought up something! Well, gentlemen! I got out of bed, lit the candle, sat down at the desk as I was, that is I'd completely lost control, overdone things—you know, gentlemen, when a person gets carried away! I crawled in the mud, my friends, up to my neck! That is, this is my habit: they take something from you, and you go and give them something else besides: you say, here, take this too! They strike you on the cheek, and you in your joy offer them your whole back. Then they'll start tempting you with a bun like a dog, and you'll hug them with your dumb paws with your whole heart and soul—and kiss them too! Just like now, gentlemen! You laugh and whisper, after all, I can see it! After I tell you all my private affairs, you'll start making fun of me, you'll start driving me away, and I keep talking and talking and talking! Well, who told me to! Well, who's driving me? Who's standing behind my back whispering: talk, talk, tell a story! But I talk, I tell the story, I crawl into your souls, as if you were all, for example, my own brothers, my best friends...ech!..."

The laughter beginning to rise little by little from all sides finally completely buried the voice of the storyteller who really had gone into some kind of ecstasy; he stopped, cast his eyes about the company for several minutes, and then suddenly, as if carried away by some whirlwind, waved his hand, burst out laughing himself, as if really finding his position funny, and again began telling his story:

"I hardly slept that night, gentlemen; I scribbled all night; you see, I'd

96

thought something up! Ekh, gentlemen! Just remembering it makes me so ashamed! And it would've been all right had it been at night: well, he was drunk, he made a mistake, he confused some nonsense, he made something up—but no! I woke up in the morning at the crack of dawn, I'd slept all of a couple of hours, and I was still at it! I got dressed, washed, curled, pommaded, pulled on my new frockcoat and went straight to Fedosey Nikolaich's for the holiday, keeping the paper I'd written in my hat. He opens the door to me himself with open arms, and again summons me to his parental waist-coat! I assumed a dignified air, what had happened yesterday was still in my head! I withdrew a step. 'No,' I say, 'Fedosey Nikolaich, but here, if you please, read this paper,' and I give it to him as if it were a report; and do you know what was in that report? The following: for such and such reasons the aforesaid Osip Mikhailich asks to be discharged, and under the petition I signed my full rank! That's what I thought up, gentlemen! And couldn't think up anything·cleverer! Today's April first, so I'll just pretend for the sake of a joke that I'm still insulted, that I've changed my mind overnight, changed my mind and am sulking, and am more insulted than before, and, so to speak, take that, my dear benefactors, I don't want to know either you or your daughter; I put the money in my pocket yesterday, I'm secure, so here's my request for dismissal for you. I don't want to work under such a superior as Fedosey Nikolaich! I want to transfer, and once there, look out, I'll send in a denunciation. What a scoundrel I pretended to be, I thought up the idea of scaring them! And I thought up how to scare them! Pretty good, eh, gentlemen? You see my heart had warmed to them since the day before,· so I thought because of that I'd play a little family joke, I'd tease Fedosey Nikolaich's parental heart....

"As soon as he'd taken my paper and opened it, I see his whole face has changed. 'What's this, Osip Mikhailich?' And I like an idiot: 'April Fool's! Many happy returns, Fedosey Nikolaich!' That is, just like a little boy who quietly hides behind grandma's armchair and then goes 'oof!' in her ear at the top of his lungs—I'd thought up a scare! Yes...I'm even ashamed to tell about it, gentlemen! No! I won't tell about it!"

"Yes, yes, what happened next?"

"Yes, yes, tell it! Yes, tell it!" arose from all sides.

"There arose, my good men, such a hue and cry, oohs and ahs, what a prankster I am, what a joker I am, I'd given them such a scare, well, such utter sweetness that I was ashamed, so you stand there in terror and think: how can such a sinner occupy such a holy place! 'Well, my dear fellow,' squealed the councillor's wife, 'you gave me such a fright that to this moment my legs are still trembling, I can hardly stand up! I ran off like a half-wit to Masha: Mashenka, I say, what will happen to us! Look what *your* one turned out to be like! I sinned myself, my dear, forgive an old lady like me, I made a fool of myself! Well, I thought: when he left us yesterday, he got

97

home late, began to think and maybe it seemed to him that we were deliberately buttering him up yesterday, that we wanted to distract him, and I was horrified! That's enough Mashenka, stop winking at me, Osip Mikhailovich is no stranger to us; I'm your mother, I won't say anything bad! Thank God I've been living in this world not twenty years but a whole forty-five!...'

"Well, gentlemen! I almost flopped at her feet on the spot! More tears, more kisses! We started making jokes! Fedosey Nikolaich also decided to make something up for April Fool's! He says, the Firebird has flown in with her diamond beak, and in her beak she's brought a letter! He too wanted to fool us—how we laughed! How touching it was! Foo! I'm ashamed to even tell about it.

"Well, my friends, I won't be long now! A day passed, another, a third, a week; and I'm a regular fiancé! Why not! The rings were ordered, the day appointed, only they don't want to announce it for the time being, they're waiting for the inspector. I can hardly wait for the inspector, my happiness depended on him! Let him get off our backs quick, I thought, and in the flurry and excitement Fedosey Nikolaich heaped all the work on me: the accounts, writing reports, checking the books, totalling things up—I look; the most atrocious disorder, everything gone to pot, dots and dashes everywhere! Well, I think, I'll do my best for my dear father-in-law! Meanwhile he's indisposed all the time, he takes sick, from one day to the next you see him get worse. And me, I'm thin as a matchstick, I don't sleep nights, I'm scared of dropping in my tracks! But I polished off the business beautifully! I rescued him on time! Suddenly they send a runner for me. 'Hurry,' he says, 'Fedosey Nikolaich's in a bad way!' I break my neck running—what's going on? I look, my Fedosey Nikolaich is sitting with his head bandaged in vinegar compresses, he's frowning, groaning, moaning: ooh and oh! 'My dear, my son,' he says, 'I'm dying,' he says, 'whom will I leave you with, my babes!' His wife trailed in with the children, Mashenka's in tears—well, I sniffled myself! 'Well, there's no one,' he says, 'God will be merciful! He won't make you answer for all my sins!' Then he dismissed them all, told them to lock the door behind them, and the two of us were left tête à tête. 'I have a request to make of you!' 'What is it?' 'Well,' he says, 'brother, there's no peace even on your deathbed, I'm in great need!' 'How can that be?' I immediately blushed, lost my tongue. 'Like this, brother, I had to put some of my own money into the treasury; I spare nothing, brother, for the general welfare, not even my life! Don't you go thinking anything! It saddens me that slanderers blackened my name to you.... You've made a mistake, and since then my hair has gone white from grief! The inspector's due any minute, Matveev has a deficit of seven thousand, and I'm responsible...who else! And I, brother, will have to answer for it: where was I looking? And what can I get from Matveev! He's got enough on his hands as it is; why lead the poor wretch to his slaughter! Saints, I think, what a righteous man! What a heart!

98

And he: 'Yes,' he says, 'I don't want to take my daughter's money because it's to be her dowry; that's a sacred sum! I have my own, true, I do, but I've lent it out, how can I collect it now!' Just as I was, I threw myself down on my knees in front of him. 'My benefactor,' I cry, 'I've wronged you, insulted you, slanderers wrote denunciations against you, don't torture me, take your money back!' He looks at me, tears flow from his eyes. 'That's just what I expected of you, my son, get up! I forgave you then because of my daughter's tears! Now my heart too forgives you. You've healed,' he says, 'my wounds! I bless you forever and ever!' Well, once he'd blessed me, gentlemen, I ran home lickety-split and got the money: 'Here, father, that's all of it, I've only spent fifty!' 'Well, that's all right,' he says, 'but now better dot every i; there's no time, write a note dated earlier that you're in need and are requesting fifty rubles of your salary in advance. I'll just show it to the authorities and say you were given it in advance....' Well, gentlemen! What do you think? Of course I wrote the note too!"

"Well how, well what, well how did it end?"

"As soon as I'd written the note, my dear sirs, this is how it ended. The following day, the very next day, bright and early in the morning, I get a letter with a government seal on it. I look—and what do I get? Fired. Hand in your work, it says, total up the accounts, and you can go where you please!..."

"How can that be?"

"That's just what I shouted at the top of my lungs: how can that be! Gentlemen! There was a ringing in my ears! I thought, it's for no special reason, but no, the inspector'd ridden into town. My heart sank! So, I think, it is for a reason! So just as I was, I run to Fedosey Nikolaich's: 'What's this?' I say. 'What's what?' he says. 'The dismissal, of course!' 'What dismissal?' 'And this?' 'Well, so what, it's a dismissal!' 'But what do you mean, did I ask for it?' 'What do you mean, you submitted your petition, you submitted it on April first.' (I hadn't taken the paper back!) 'Fedosey Nikolaich! I can't believe my eyes, is it you?' 'It is I, sir, what of it?' 'Oh lord my God!' 'I'm sorry, sir, sorry, very sorry that you took it into your head to leave the service so soon! A young man should work, but you, sir, have begun to be light-headed. But don't you worry about a recommendation, I'll take care of it. You always recommend yourself so well by your behavior!' 'But I was only joking then, Fedosey Nikolaich, I didn't want to, I just submitted the petition for your parental...just like that!' 'What do you mean, just like that! What kind of a joke is that, sir! One doesn't joke with such petitions! Someday they'll pack you off to Siberia for such jokes. Now farewell, I have no time, the inspector's here, duty calls; you can twiddle your thumbs, but we here have to tend to our business. But I'll give you a proper recommendation. And one more thing, I bought a house from Matveev, we're moving in a few days, so I hope that I will not have the pleasure seeing you at our housewarming.

Bon voyage!' I dashed home at full tilt: 'We're ruined, grandma!' She howled, the dear thing; and then, we look, a runner from Fedosey Nikolaich, with a note and a cage, and in the cage sits a starling; from a surfeit of feeling I'd given her a talking sparrow; and in the note was: *April Fool's*, and nothing more. There it is, gentlemen, what do you think?"

"Well, what then, what happened???"

"What could happen? Once I met Fedosey Nikolaich, I wanted to call him a scoundrel to his face...."

"Well?"

"I somehow just couldn't get it out, gentlemen!"

1848

DOSTOEVSKY AND GOGOL: TOWARDS A THEORY OF PARODY
PART ONE: STYLIZATION AND PARODY*
by Yury Tynyanov

1.

When speaking about "literary tradition" or "succession," you usually imagine a definite straight line which unites a younger representative of a well-known literary branch with an elder. However, the matter is much more complicated. There is no continuation of a straight line, there is rather a departure, a repulsion from a known point,—in short, a struggle. Representatives of another branch, of another tradition, do not even struggle; they simply bypass each other, negating each other or paying each other homage, and they are antagonistic only by the fact of their existence. Almost the whole of XIXth century Russian literature carried on precisely such a silent struggle with Pushkin, avoiding him while openly paying him homage. Tyutchev, coming out of the "older line" of Derzhavin, made no mention of this ancestor, while readily and officially praising Zhukovsky, Pushkin and Karamzin. Dostoevsky too payed homage to Pushkin. He was not even averse to naming Pushkin his forefather; blatantly ignoring the facts, already indicated by that time in literary criticism, he affirmed that "the pleiad of the 1860s" issued precisely from Pushkin.[1]

Nevertheless, Dostoevsky's contemporaries readily saw him as a direct successor to Gogol. Nekrasov speaks to Belinsky about a "new Gogol," Belinsky calls Gogol "the father of Dostoevsky," and even Ivan Aksakov, sitting in Kaluga, hears news about the "new Gogol." A change was being demanded, but the change was conceived of as a direct, "linear" succession.

Only isolated voices spoke about the struggle between Dostoevsky and Gogol. Pletnyov wrote that Dostoevsky "was chasing after Gogol" and "wanted to destroy Gogol's 'Diary of a Madman' with *The Double.*"

Finally, in the 1880s Strakhov mentioned that Dostoevsky was presenting a "correction of Gogol" from the very beginning of his career, and Rozanov directly discussed Dostoevsky's struggle with Gogol. Any literary succession is above all a struggle in which the old totality is destroyed and something new constructed from the old elements.

---

*[Originally published as a brochure by OPOYAZ ("Society for the Study of Poetic Language"), Petrograd, 1921. Only Part I is translated here; we refer interested readers to Part II, a study of Dostoevsky's *A Friend of the Family* as a parody of Gogol's *Selected Passages from Correspondence with Friends,* translated in V. Erlich, *Twentieth Century Russian Literary Criticism* (Yale, New Haven, 1975), pp. 102-116.]

2

Dostoevsky clearly takes Gogol as his point of departure, and he himself underlines this fact. In *Poor Folk,* Gogol's "The Overcoat" is mentioned by name; in "Mr. Prokharchin" the plot of "The Nose" is referred to (" 'You, you, you stupid!' muttered Semyon Ivanovich. 'They'll eat off your nose, you'll eat it up yourself with some bread, you won't even notice...' "). The Gogolian tradition is reflected unevenly in Dostoevsky's first works. *The Double* is far closer to Gogol than *Poor Folk,* and "The Landlady" is closer still to Gogol than *The Double.*

This unevenness is particularly apparent in "The Landlady," a work written after Dostoevsky had already completed *Poor Folk, The Double,* "Mr. Prokharchin," and "A Novel in Nine Letters." The characters in "The Landlady" are close to those in Gogol's "A Terrible Vengeance," and the story's style reveals an apprenticeship that has suddenly run rampant. Obvious stylistic similarities include: the hyperboles; parallelisms in which the second part of the parallel is developed in detail, acquiring as it were an independent meaning (a feature inherent in Gogol but unusual for Dostoevsky —cf. the parallel in *Dead Souls* of black tailcoats at the Governor's party and flies on the sugar lumps,[2] where the second part of the parallel is developed out of all proportion to the first, with the parallel in "The Landlady" of Ordynov's attack and the storm, where the second part is equally independent);[3] a complicated syntax, replete with Old Church Slavonicisms (such as inverted pronouns); the underlined rhythm of the sentences, which end in dactylic clausulae.

Dostoevsky has not yet determined what in Gogol is of importance for his own work; he is apparently trying out Gogol's different devices, combining them.

Hence the general resemblance of his first efforts to Gogol's works. *The Double* is close not only to "The Nose"; *Netochka Nezvanova* is close not only to "The Portrait." In the case of *Netochka Nezvanova,* certain episodes do go back to "The Portrait"[4] whereas others derive from "A Terrible Vengeance."[5] The motor images in *The Double* are close to the images in Gogol's *Dead Souls.*[6]

Dostoevsky's style so obviously repeats, varies, and combines the style of Gogol that his contemporaries were immediately struck by it. Belinsky noted his "Gogolian turn of phrase," and Grigorovich discerned "the influence of Gogol in the construction of his sentences." From the beginning Dostoevsky reflected both levels of the Gogolian style, the high and the comic. Compare, for example, Dostoevsky's repetition of a name in *The Double,*

> Mr. Golyadkin clearly saw that the time had come for a bold stroke, the time for putting his enemies to shame. Mr. Golyadkin was agitated. Mr. Golyadkin felt a kind of sudden inspiration... [Ch. IV.]

with the repetition of the phrase "an excellent man is Ivan Ivanovich" in the beginning of Gogol's "Tale of How Ivan Ivanovich Quarreled with Ivan Nikiforovich."[7] The other side of the Gogolian style is to be found in Dostoevsky's "The Landlady" and *Netochka Nezvanova.*[8] Later, Dostoevsky rejects Gogol's high style and employs the low style almost everywhere, sometimes stripping it of its comic motivation.

We find still further testimony in Dostoevsky's letters, which he regarded as literary works: "I wrote him such a letter! In a word, the model of polemics. How I dressed him down! My letters are a *chef d'oeuvre* of epistolography" (Letter of Sept. 30, 1844).

Dostoevsky's letters are crammed with Gogolian *bon mots,* names and phrases: "You're such a lazy-bones, a Fetyuk, simply a Fetyuk!" (October 8, 1845);[9] "A letter's nonsense; druggists write letters" (April 1, 1846).[10] It seems that Dostoevsky is playing in his letters with Gogol's style: "I turned in my resignation because I'd done my turn" (September 30, 1844); "Provincial laziness will ruin you in the prime of life, my good man, and there's nothing more to be said... Everywhere, I'm incredibly respected, the curiosity about me is terrific. I've become acquainted with a throng of people of the most respectable sort" (November 16, 1845); "The overcoat has its merits and its inconveniences. Merit in that it is unusually full, really double, and the color is good, most official, grey" (September 17, 1846).[11]

What we have here is stylization; it is not a question of following a style but rather of playing with it. And if one recollects how readily Dostoevsky underlines Gogol (*Poor Folk,* "Mr. Prokharchin"), how he so obviously proceeds from Gogol without concealing the fact, it becomes clear that it is more appropriate to speak about stylization than about "imitation," "influence," and so on.

There is yet another feature. In his letters and articles Dostoevsky repeatedly uses the names Khlestakov, Chichikov, Poprishchin, and he maintains Gogolian names even in his own works. The heroine of "The Landlady," just like the heroine of "A Terrible Vengeance," is Katerina; Golyadkin's lackey, just like Chichikov's, is Petrushka. The names "Pseldonimov" and "Mlekopitaev" in "A Nasty Story" and "Vidoplyasov" in "A Friend of the Family" are a usual Gogolian device, names introduced for the purpose of playing on them.[12] Dostoevsky never abandoned the pattern of Gogolian surnames (compare, say, "Ferdyshchenko," which traces back directly to Gogol's "Krutotryshchenko"). Even the name of Raskolnikov's mother, *Pulkheriya* Aleksandrovna, is perceived against the background of Gogol's *Pulkheriya* Ivanovna ["Old-World Landowners"] as a stylized name.

103

Stylization is close to parody. Both live a double life: behind the apparent structure of a work, its first level, lies a second level, that of the work which it stylizes or parodies. But in parody it is obligatory to have a disjunction of both levels, a dislocation of intent; the parody of a tragedy will be a comedy (it matters little whether this is done through an exaggeration of the tragic intent or through a corresponding substitution of comic elements), and a parody of a comedy could be a tragedy. In stylization there is no such disjunction. There is, on the contrary, a correspondence of the two levels—the stylizing level and the stylized level showing through it—one to another. Nevertheless, it is but a single step from stylization to parody; stylization that is comically motivated or emphasized becomes parody.

However, from the very beginning there was one feature of Gogol's works which incensed Dostoevsky because this feature was extremely important to him, namely Gogol's "characters," his "types." Strakhov recollected, in memoirs relating to the end of the 1850s, "I remember how Fyodor Mikhailovich made very astute observations *on the consistency of various characters* in Gogol's works, on the vitality of all his figures, of Khlestakov, Podkolyosin, Kochkaryov and so on."[13] Dostoevsky himself censured Pisemsky's *A Thousand Souls* in 1858 in the following words:

> If only he had created one *new character* which had never before appeared. We've had all this already; it appeared long ago in the works of our innovative writers, especially Gogol's.[14]

In 1871 he admired the types in Leskov's novel, *At Daggers Drawn:*

> The nihilists are distorted to the point of hopelessness, but all the same they are individual types. Look at his Vanskok! There has never been anything in Gogol more typical or truer.[15]

In the same year he wrote about Belinsky:

> His attitude towards Gogol's types was disdainful and superficial to the point of being outrageous, and he was ecstatically pleased only by Gogol's exposés.[16]

Gogol's types appear as one of the cardinal points in Dostoevsky's struggle with Gogol.

Gogol saw things in an unusual way. There are many separate instances of it: his description of Mirgorod or of Rome; Plyushkin's habitation with its celebrated heaps of junk [*Dead Souls*]; the singing doors in "Old-World Landowners"; Nozdryov's hurdy-gurdy [*Dead Souls*]. The last example also indicates another peculiarity of the way Gogol pictured things: he caught the comic nature of things. "Old-World Landowners" begins with the parallel of dilapidated little houses and their dilapidated inhabitants and further develops this parallel throughout the entire course of the story. "Nevsky Prospect" is based on the effect of a complete identification of various items of clothing and their parts with the bodily parts of the pedestrians:

> One displays a foppish frockcoat with the finest beaver, another—a lovely Grecian nose... the fourth—a pair of pretty eyes and a marvelous hat...[17]

Here the comic is achieved by the enumeration, one after the other, in the same intonation, of objects which have no connection with one another. The same device is used in the comparison of the overcoat in the tale of the same name with a "pleasant female life companion": "and that companion was none other than that same overcoat with the thick quilting, with the strong lining which wouldn't wear out." Here too the comic element lies in the disjunction between two images, the one living, the other inanimate, material. The device of material metaphors is canonical for comic description. We find it, for instance, in Heine ("the universe was painted anew... the old gentlemen put on new faces") and also in Marlinsky's tale "The Frigate Hope," where a naval officer writes about love using naval terminology. The device has great versatility, but what is emphasized here is precisely the imperfect connection or disjunction between two images.

Hence the importance of the Thing for comic description in general, and in particular for Gogol, who elevated dead nature to a unique principle of literary theory:

> He used to say that for the success of a tale and of a story in general it was enough if the author were to describe a room familiar to him and a familiar street. "Whoever has the ability to artistically convey his own apartment can later become a quite remarkable author," he used to say. (Annenkov)

Here the Thing acquires the significance of a theme.

Gogol's basic device in the portrayal of people is the mask. Above all, clothing—a dress or a suit (clothing has for Gogol especial significance in the description of external appearance)—or an exaggerated appearance may serve as a mask.

An example of a geometrical mask:

It was a face in which one couldn't observe a single angle, but on the other hand it was not marked by any light, rounded features. The forehead did not drop straight to the nose but was completely slanted, like a ski slope. The nose was a continuation of it, huge and blunt. The lips were fine, only the upper one jutted out further than the lower. There was no chin at all. A diagonal line went from the nose to the very neck. It was a triangle, the apex of which was located in the nose: a face which expressed stupidity above all else. ("The Street Lantern Guttered")[18]

More often, however, Gogol presents a mask "swimming in flesh," which such intimate nicknames as "little mug, little capon" (Chichikov to himself)[19] underscore. Furthermore, simple linguistic metaphors are realized and transformed into verbal masks. There is a gradation of the device, for instance: 1) a distiller smoking his pipe—the chimney of a distillery—a steam-boat—a cannon (in Chapter 4 of "A May Night");[20] 2) "hands" in "A Terrible Vengeance," or the monster in the first redaction of "Viy," where masks are parts; 3) "The Nose," where the metaphor is realized into a mask, resulting in the effect of a broken mask; 4) Korobochka [a character in *Dead Souls* whose name means "little box"], where a material metaphor becomes a verbal mask;[21] 5) "Akaky Akakievich," where the verbal mask has already lost its semantic connection and is anchored instead in sound, becoming a sound device, a phonetic mask.

A material mask can be broken, as in the case of "The Nose," where this process determines the general contour of the plot. A verbal mask can be doubled, e.g., Bobchinsky and Dobchinsky, Foma the Large and Foma the Small, Uncle Mityay and Uncle Minyay. The many paired names and names with inversions also relate to this doubling of a verbal mask: 1) *Ivan* Ivanovich and *Ivan* Nikiforovich, Afanasy *Ivanovich* and Pulkheriya *Ivanovna* (paired names); 2) Kifa Mokievich and Moky Kofovich (inverted names). The decisive role here is played by sound repetition, at first a purely articulatory and then a compositional device as well. Examples of this include: 1) *pulpultik, monmunya;* 2) *Lyulyu*kov, *Bubu*nitsyn, *Tentetni*kov, *Chichi*kov; 3) *Ivan Ivan*ovich, *Pifagor Pifagor*ovich (Chertokutskoy); 4) *Petr Petro*vich *Petukh;* 5) *Ivan* Ivanovich

————————,
Ivan Nikiforovich
dyadya (Uncle) *Mityay   Kifa Mokievich*
————————————,————————.
dyadya (Uncle) *Minyay, Moky Kifovich*

106

A mask can be at the same time material and ephemeral: Akaky Akaki-evich is quite easily and naturally replaced by an apparition; the mask of the Cossack in a red caftan is replaced by the mask of a sorcerer ("A Terrible Vengeance"). The movement of masks is above all ephemeral, but even so it creates the impression of action.

Hyperbole, characteristic of Gogol's images in general, is characteristic as well of his motor images. Just as he couldn't look at fast traffic on a street without immediately imagining run-over pedestrians, he created a story about a cut-off nose. A moving thing is demonic: in his stories we encounter a corpse rising from the grave;[22] dumplings flying on their own into the mouth of one character, Patsyuk;[23] the reverse flight of the horse in "A Terrible Vengeance"; Russia as a troika [*Dead Souls*]. It was enough for Gogol to know the verbal mask in order instantly to define its movement. Prince D. A. Obolensky relates how Gogol created a mask and its movement from a verbal sign:

> At a posting station I found a complaint book and read in it a rather amusing complaint of some gentleman or other. After hearing it out, Gogol asked me, "Well, what do you think, who is this man? What sort of qualities and character does the man have?" "I really don't know," I answered. "Well, I will tell you." And he began on the spot to describe to me in the most amusing and original way *first the external appearance* of this gentleman, *then he recounted his entire career in the service* to me, even going so far as to *act out* several episodes from his life. I remember that I laughed like a madman, but *he made all this up* quite seriously.

The complaint was of course signed; Gogol first transformed the surname, a verbal mask, into a material mask (the man's "appearance"), then animated the mask ("making it all up") and created a plot scheme (the man's "career in the service" and "episodes from his life").

Thus both the gesture and the plot are predetermined by the masks themselves. This is so much the case that one cannot agree more with B. M. Eikhenbaum's statement that Gogol's plots are traditional or anecdotal.[24] Even the plot of "The Nose," surprising at first glance, was not so unusual at the time of its appearance, when "nosology" was a widespread plot phenomenon. One may cite Sterne's *Tristram Shandy* and Marlinsky's *Mulla-Nur* as well as amusing articles about plastic surgery on noses in the *Son of the Fatherland* for 1820 (part 64, No. 35, pp. 95-96) and 1822 (part 75, No. 3, pp. 133-137).[25] What was effective and new in "The Nose" was apparently not the plot itself, but the unmotivated dislocation of two masks: first, "the cut-off and baked *nose*"—cf. what has already been said about the hyperbole of Gogol's motor images, as well as his "Nevsky Prospect," where Hoffmann wants to cut off Schiller's nose[26]—and secondly, "the detached, independent *Nose*"—the realization of a metaphor. This latter metaphor occurs in various degrees of realization in Gogol's letters: "Would you believe that I often get the uncontrollable desire to be transformed into *just a nose: so that there would be nothing more, neither eyes, nor hands, nothing except one huge nose,* which would have nostrils the size of big buckets, the better to draw into oneself as much more of the fragrance of the spring as possible."[27] Gogol plays on this unmotivated dislocation of the masks, toward the end of the tale laying bare the device:"No, I don't understand this at all, I absolutely don't understand!" In this dislocation, and not in the plot as such, was, for the most part, what was perceived as comic in the work.

"The Two Ivans" entirely originates from the similarity and dissimilarity of *names*. The name of Ivan Ivanovich is mentioned fourteen times in the beginning of the first chapter; the name of Ivan Nikiforovich almost as often; together, in juxtaposition, the names are mentioned sixteen times. The projection of the *dissimilarity* of the verbal masks into the material masks results in a full opposition of both:

> Ivan Ivanovich is thin and tall; Ivan Nikiforovich is a little shorter, but makes up for it in breadth. Ivan Ivanovich's head is like a radish, tail downwards; Ivan Nikiforovich's head is like a radish, tail upwards...[28]

The *similarity* of the names is projected into a *similarity* of the material masks:

> Both Ivan Ivanovich and Ivan Nikiforovich greatly dislike fleas... In spite of some dissimilarities, however, both Ivan Ivanovich and Ivan Nikiforovich are excellent people.[29]

The projection of the *dissimilarity* of the verbal masks into the plot gives rise to the quarrel between Ivan Ivanovich and Ivan Nikiforovich; the projection of their *similarity* makes them equal against the background of "boring life." In the same way the dissimilarity of the names of Uncle Mityay and Uncle Minyay [*Dead Souls*], projected into a material mask, makes them respectively tall and short, thin and fat.

Gogol's "characters" and "types" are also essentially masks, but ones that are sharply defined and don't undergo any sort of "breaks" or "development." Gogol's creativity was characterized by the principle of the leitmotif; one and the same motif runs through all the movements and actions of his heroes. The masks can be immobile, "swimming in flesh," as in the case of Plyushkin, Manilov, Sobakevich; or they can be revealed in gestures, as is

108

Chichikov's. The device of the mask was, for Gogol, a conscious device. There is an entry in his notebooks with the characteristic heading "Masks Which Are Worn by Governors": "the mask of a noble and well-bred governor"; "the military general is an upright fellow," "the Governor is a smart dealer." If we read these little sketches carefully, we discover that Gogol is writing about *types* of governors.

Masks can be either comic or tragic, corresponding to the two planes of Gogol's work: the "high" or tragic plane and the "low" or comic one. They usually go side by side, replacing one another by turns. In one of Gogol's early articles ("Boris Godunov"), where he speaks about the "two warring natures of man," the particularities of these two planes were already given, the high plane in the speech of Pollior, and the low in the conversations of the "cheerful cube" with the "coffee-colored overcoat." A difference of styles corresponds to the difference of masks: the high type is characterized by amplification, tautology, isocolon, neologisms, archaisms, etc.; the low—by irrationality, barbarisms, dialectal features, etc. Both planes differ above all in their lexicon and can be traced back to different linguistic elements, the high to Old Church Slavonic, the low to dialects.[30] The literary genres to which both planes chiefly relate pertain to different traditions: in the case of the high plane—to Gogol's letters, derivative of XVIIIth century sermons; in the case of the low plane—to his comedies.

But Gogol's main device, the system of material metaphors, of masks, has an identical application in both planes. When he turns to moralistic and religious themes, Gogol introduces his whole system of images, sometimes expanding his metaphors to the limits of allegory, as his *Selected Passages from Correspondence with Friends* (1847) demonstrates. Compare the repetition of such expressions as: "souls encumbered by clutter," "cluttered up with foreign dung," "the soul's property" (received from the "Celestial Proprietor" and which one should pay interest on or distribute to others), or: "Karamzin had a well-arranged soul"; "Europe will come to Russia in twenty years not for the purchase of hemp and tallow, but for the purchase of wisdom"; "to set up roads, bridges and various means of communication is a truly necessary matter, but to patch up our many internal roads... is a more necessary matter"; God is called the "Celestial Ruler."

In this manner Gogol introduced all the same images, only somewhat lexically varied, into the field of morals.

But the problems involved in applying the device were different. While the essence of material metaphors in the comic plane consists in the palpability of the disjunction between two images, here their purpose is just the opposite, to give a feeling of the connection between images. This was apparently what Gogol had in mind when he wrote:

How to reduce the whole world of idleness, in all its varieties, to the point of similarity with urban idleness? And how to elevate urban idleness to the point of transforming the world's idleness? To do this, *include the entire similarity* and introduce a gradual progression.

In that the strength of *material metaphors* lies precisely in the disjunction, in the dissimilarity of the terms to be linked, what was a legitimate device in the domain of art was felt to be illegitimate in moral, religious, and political spheres. Perhaps this also partly explains the impression that *Correspondence with Friends* produced even on Gogol's friends who agreed with him. Gogol himself considered the book's "means of expression" the main reason for its lack of success, and his contemporaries were inclined to explain the failure just by the "fact" that Gogol had changed his devices. In actuality, however, there is a complete correspondence between the devices of Gogol's fiction and of his moral works.

Having set his goal in *Correspondence with Friends* to "know the soul," Gogol acted in accordance with the laws of his creative work. This is clear in his request to send him a report of reactions to his *Correspondence:*

It'll be no effort for you to jot down a little bit in diary form everyday, just, for example, along the lines of: "Today I heard such and such an opinion; such and such a person gave it... I don't know his habits, but I think that he's such and such a person; in appearance he is attractive and respectable (or not respectable); he holds his arm like so; blows his nose like so," in a word, not leaving out anything the eye sees from important things to trifles. [Letter of April 15, 1847 to A. O. Rosset.]

That is, it is exactly the same as in the scene at the posting station, only the progression is slightly different: Gogol wants to infer character from gestures and appearance.

Similarly, the transformation of life was supposed to take place according to the laws of his art, especially the principle of the mutation of masks. The poetry of Yazykov or the *Odyssey* in Zhukovsky's translation would transform everything, but it would be possible even more simply to change the Russian man: just call him a peasant woman or a hamster, or say, why, look, a German says that a Russian is worthless, and in a flash of the eye he will become a completely different man.[31] There are even fragments of plot constructions in Gogol's moral teacnings. One could produce a moral revolution in the simplest, most economical way by merely travelling throughout Russia:

In the course of your voyage you can get to know them [the people] and have mutually beneficial exchanges of information, like an efficient merchant: the information you collect in one town you can sell in another at profit, enriching everyone and at the same time enriching yourself most of all.[32]

"Buying testimonies" somewhat recalls "the purchase of dead souls." Chichikov was supposed to be reborn, but his reform was to take place by Chichikovian means.

Just as the mask of the Cossack in a red caftan is transformed into the mask of a sorcerer ("A Terrible Vengeance"), so even such a character as Plyushkin *(Dead Souls)* would be transformed, miraculously and simply.

4.

Dostoevsky collided with Gogol precisely on the question of characters.

Dostoevsky began with the epistolary and memoir forms. Both forms, particularly the first, are little suited to the unfolding of a complicated plot, but from the beginning his primary concern (as I have already indicated in part) was the creation and unfolding of characters, and this task only gradually became more complicated (the unification of a complex plot with complex characters). Already in *Poor Folk* the main character, Makar Devushkin, attacks precisely this aspect of "The Overcoat": "It is simply untrue to life, because it just can't happen that such a clerk could exist" [*Poor Folk*, letter of July 8th]. Here Makar is speaking ("I didn't show my mug," wrote Dostoevsky), and the introduction of literature into the daily routine of his main characters is a successful and tested device of Dostoevsky's. But Dostoevsky, discarding the mask of a character, very definitely speaks of the same thing in the beginning of Part IV of *The Idiot*. After giving an analysis of the *types* of Podkolyosin [Gogol's "The Wedding"] and Molière's Georges Dandin, Dostoevsky speaks out against types in art:

To fill novels *only with types* or even, for the sake of interest, simply with strange or odd people, would be untrue to life, as well as *uninteresting*. In our opinion, a writer should strive to search out the interesting and instructive *nuances* even among ordinary people.[33]

In the same passage he indicates the nuances of "certain ordinary persons":

...ordinariness which does not want to remain what it is for anything and wants to become original and independent at any cost.

111

These nuances create contrasts, and Dostoevsky's characters are above all contrasting. Contrasts are revealed in the speeches of his main characters, in which the end is without fail contrasted to the beginning, and this contrast is not only in terms of an unexpected transition to another theme (an original application in Dostoevsky's dialogues of the principle of "unfulfilled expectation"), but also in terms of intonation; the heroes' speeches, beginning calmly, end up frenzied, and vice versa. Dostoevsky himself loved contrasts in his own conversation: he would conclude a serious conversation with an anecdote (A.N. Maikov) and, moreover, would build his reading on a contrast of intonations. An article in *The Historical Messenger* for 1904, "A Year of Work with a Famous Writer," describes Dostoevsky reciting Pushkin's "The Poet":

> He began to read *slowly,* with *quiet* pathos, in a *hollow, low* voice, "Until upon the poet calls/For hallowed sacrifices Apollo"; but when he reached the lines, "But the moment that the divine word / Touches his keen hearing," his voice, tense by this time, came pouring out in high, chesty sounds, and all the while he *smoothly moved his hand through the air, as though drawing* both for me and himself these waves of poetry.[34]

Strakhov also has the same to say about Dostoevsky's declamation:

> His right hand, convulsively extended downwards, apparently held itself back from an implied *gesture*; his voice was raised to the level of a shout.

The particular role of contrasting intonations was also, one would imagine, what allowed Dostoevsky to *dictate* his novels.

Hence the epistolary form, chosen by Dostoevsky from the first, is revealing: not only must each letter respond to the preceding *by contrast*, but naturally it contains in itself a contrasting succession of interrogative, exclamatory, and provocative intonations. Dostoevsky consequently carried over these properties of the epistolary form into the contrasting order of chapters and dialogues in his novels. Both the epistolary and memoir forms were traditionally characterized by weakly constructed plots. The pure epistolary form in Dostoevsky's works is given in *Poor Folk*; the pure memoir form in *Notes from the House of the Dead.* "A Novel in Nine Letters" represents an attempt to unite the epistolary form with a more developed plot; *The Insulted and Injured*—a similar attempt with regard to the memoir form.

In *Crime and Punishment* the contrast between plot and characters is already artistically organized. Dostoevsky placed into the framework of a criminal plot characters which contrast with it: the murderer, the prostitute

112

and the prosecutor of the plot scheme are replaced by a revolutionary, a saint and a wise man. The plot of *The Idiot* unfolds by contrasts and coincides with a contrasting revelation of the characters: the highest point of plot tension is coupled with the greatest revelation of the characters' essences.

But it is interesting that Dostoevsky, while dissociating himself from Gogol's "types," continued to use his verbal and material masks. I have already cited several examples; here are a few more: inverted names in "A Novel in Nine Letters"—Petr Ivanych and Ivan Petrovich; in *The Idiot*, even the device of sound repetitions,—*A*lexandra, *A*delaida, *A*ga*l*ya.

The external appearances of Svidrigaylov, Stavrogin and Lambert are emphasized masks. Perhaps this is still simply the principle of contrast: the verbal *mask* covers a contrasting *character*. The reader's first acquaintance with the Yepanchin sisters, for example, is also accomplished, as it were, by contrast. Besides the comic repetition of the letter *A* in their names, the first mention of them lays the ground for a comic impression which is afterwards completely overturned:

> *All three Yepanchin girls* were healthy young noble ladies, blooming, grown up, with magnificent shoulders, with powerful bosoms, *with arms almost as strong as a man's* and, of course, as a result of their strength and good health, *they sometimes loved to eat very well....* Besides tea, coffee, cheese, honey, butter, the special spreads which were the favorite of the General's wife herself, cutlets, and the like, they were even given to having strong hot soup.[35]

There is a complete coincidence of the verbal masks and the expression "all three girls," so that the verbal mask acquires its own environment, which is necessary for the further contrast.

Thus a device that is organic in Gogol acquires a new significance in Dostoevsky's hands through the principle of contrast. Following this paradigm, further research should clarify how Dostoevsky uses Gogol's syntactico-intonational figures. Perhaps it will be discovered that Dostoevsky placed equivalent "turns of phrase" in an order of greater contrastedness than did Gogol. Dostoevsky uses Gogol's devices, but they are not obligatory for him in themselves. This explains for us the process of Dostoevsky's parodies of Gogol: stylization, introduced to fulfill definite ends, turns into parody when these ends are lacking.

5.

Dostoevsky persistently introduces literature into his works. There is rarely a main character that does not speak about literature. This, of course, is a very convenient parodic device. It is enough for a given character to

113

express a literary opinion for it to take on a special coloring as *his* opinion; if the person is comic, then the opinion also becomes comic.

In *Netochka Nezvanova,* a play by Kukolnik, "Jacopo Sannazaro," is parodied; the hapless German, Karl Fyodorovich, reads it, after which he dances (he is an unsuccessful dancer):

> This drama dealt with the misfortune of a certain great painter, one Gennaro or Jacopo who on one page would cry: "I am unrecognized!" and on the next: "I am recognized!" or: "I am untalented!" and a few lines later: "I am talented!" And it all ended most lamentably.[36]

In *The Insulted and Injured* the old man, Ikhmenev, criticizes *Poor Folk* in what is a parody of *The Northern Bee*'s review of the book and talks a lot about Belinsky as well. In *The Possessed* one finds parodies of the verses of Ogaryov, Turgenev's article "Enough!", the letters of Granovsky, the style of Senkovsky (in polemical passages), the war memoirs of the period (in the reminiscences of General Ivolgin). But Gogol is parodied already as early as *Poor Folk*, which includes among its parodies, which play the role of episodes, a parody of "The Two Ivans":

> Do you know Ivan Prokofievich Yellowbelly? Well, the one who bit Prokofy Ivanovich on the leg? Ivan Prokofievich is a short-tempered man, but nonetheless a man of rare virtue. On the other hand, Prokofy Ivanovich is exceptionally fond of radishes with honey. And when he was still seeing Pelageya Antonovna.... But do you know Pelageya Antonovna? Well, the one who always wears her skirt inside out. [*Poor Folk*, letter of June 26th]

Compare the following from Gogol's "Two Ivans": 1) Anton Prokofievich *Pupopuz* ["Navel-Belly"]; 2) "Do you know Agafiya Fedoseevna? The one who bit off the tax assessor's ear?"; 3) "Ivan Ivanovich has a somewhat timid character; Ivan Nikiforovich has, on the other hand, trousers with such wide folds..."; 4) "He had it made before Agafiya Fedoseevna went to Kiev. Do you know Agafiya Fedoseevna?"[37]

The parody is so patent that simple juxtapositions are enough to ascertain the fact. Even the smallest details are retained: the paired names of Ivan Ivanovich and Ivan Nikiforovich are replaced by inverted names, the device of logical syntax in a nonsensical utterance is used, and the surnames are parodied.

The essence of parody lies in the mechanization of a certain device. This mechanization is perceived as such, of course, only if the device that is mechanized is well-known. Thus parody performs a double task: 1) the mechanization of a certain device; 2) the organization of new material, in the presence of which the old device is mechanized.

The mechanization of a verbal device can be produced by various means: by repeating it without having it coincide with the compositional plan; by rearranging its parts (a usual parody is the reading of a poem from the bottom up); by dislocating the meaning by punning (as in school parodies of classical poems, which traditionally add an ambiguous or suggestive refrain; cf. also the parodic refrain in Aristophanes's "The Frogs" [ll. 1208, 1216, etc.] to Euripides's verses, "he lost his little oil jar," a device that is a particular favorite in anecdotes); finally by isolating it from similar devices and unifying it with contradictory devices.

In the parody by Dostoevsky cited above, the device is not at all underscored. It is, rather, perceived as a parody only against the background of a text that totally conflicts with it stylistically.

This parody is not motivated by the epistolary style, so that it appears to be an episodic insertion. Devushkin's comments on style, however, *are* motivated by the form:

> though it's a bit intricate and at times too playful, nonetheless it's innocent, without the slightest free-thinking or liberal ideas. [*Poor Folk,* letter of June 26th.]

The parody of contemporary criticism, as well as the fact that it comes from Makar Devushkin, is equally motivated:

> But literature is a great thing, Varenka, a very great thing; I learned that from them two days ago. A profound thing! It strengthens men's hearts, educates their minds, and all sorts of other things, just as it says in that book of theirs. It's very well written! Literature is a picture, that is, in a certain sense both a picture and a mirror; passions, expression, such clever criticism, a lesson in edification, and a document too. [*ibid.*]

But in "Uncle's Dream" the parody is already unmotivated in any way:

> Marya Alexandrova Moskalyova is, of course, the leading lady in Mordasov, and of this there can be no doubt whatsoever. She conducts herself as though she didn't need anyone and, on the contrary, everyone needed her.... Such a demand is already the sign of high politics.... She knows, for example, things about some of the Mordasovians so capital and *scandaleuse* that if she were to tell them on a suitable occasion and prove them as only she can prove them, there would be a regular Lisbon earthquake in Mordasov.... She can, for instance, kill, tear to pieces, annihilate a rival with a single word.... And it is well known that such a

feature is already a quality of the very highest society.... Marya Ale-xandrovna has even been compared, in a certain respect, to Napoleon. To be sure, they said this in jest, her enemies, more for the sake of caricature than of truth.... Do you remember, what a vile *histoire* started brewing among us a year and a half ago?... How adroitly this awkward, *scandaleuse* affair was suppressed, extinguished![38]

Thus begins "Uncle's Dream" (I have only cited excerpts). All the de-vices here are Gogolian: one and the same word closing two clauses that stand side by side ("need," "needed"), hyperbole, synonyms placed at the climax of a train of thought ("kill, tear to pieces, annihilate," "suppressed, extin-guished"; cf. such phrases of Gogol's as "he reassured, refreshed him," "ob-scurely and vaguely"), the use of foreign words as a comic device ("capital and *scandaleuse* things"; cf. Gogol's phrase, "his conduct was becoming far too *scandaleuse*").[39]

Thus, nothing prevents us from taking this fragment as stylization. But towards the end of the chapter, Dostoevsky himself reveals that it is a parody by half tearing off the parodic mask (but only half tearing it off, since the revelation itself is given in the very same parodic style):

All that the benevolent reader has read so far was written by me about five months ago, entirely from excess of feeling.... I wanted to write something of the sort of a eulogy on that magnificent lady and to ex-press all of it in the form of a playful letter to a friend, on the model of the letters which used, at one time, in the old golden days that, thank God, will never return, to be published in *The Northern Bee* and in other periodical publications.[40]

The address given is false; although *The Northern Bee* contained "let-ters to a friend," they were hardly written in a Gogolian style. The epithet "playful" in reference to Gogol's style is also used here as in the parody of "The Two Ivans" (cf. p. 115 above).

Stylization thus crosses over into parody easily and unnoticeably. Who can really say how many such undiscovered (because he himself did not re-veal them) parodies there are in Dostoevsky? Is not the passage cited above about the three Yepanchin girls also a parody? Or, likewise, the beginning of *Notes from the House of the Dead*:

They (the towns) are usually quite amply provided with police officers, superintendents and minor officials of all sorts. Generally, in spite of the cold, serving in Siberia is exceptionally cosy.[41]

116

Perhaps precisely this delicate fabric of stylization-parody superimposed upon a well-developed, tragic plot constitutes the peculiarly grotesque nature of Dostoevsky's originality.

Parody exists insofar as a second level of the work parodied is visible through the surface of a work. The more narrow, definite and limited this second level is, the more all the details of the work carry a double nuance and are perceived from a double standpoint, and the stronger the parody will be.

If the second level extends as far as the general concept of "a style," parody is made one of the elements of a dialectic mutation of schools, and it becomes contiguous with stylization, as is the case in "Uncle's Dream." But what if the second level, however definite, exists but does not enter into literary consciousness and goes unnoticed, forgotten? Then, naturally, the parody is perceived on one level only, exclusively from the point of view of its organization, i.e., as is any straightforward literary work.

1921

HOW GOGOL'S "OVERCOAT" IS MADE*
by Boris Eikhenbaum

The structure of a short story depends in large part on the kind of role which the author's *personal tone* plays in its composition, i.e., on whether this tone is an organizing principle, creating more or less the illusion of a *skaz*, or whether it serves only as a formal connector of events and thus occupies an auxiliary position. The primitive short story and the adventure novel have nothing to do with the *skaz*, nor do they need it because their whole interest and their whole movement are determined by a rapid and diverse succession of events and situations. The interlacing of motifs and their motivation is the organizing principle of a primitive short story. This is also true of the comic short story: it is based on an anecdote which itself abounds in comic situations, quite apart from the *skaz* structure.

The composition becomes completely different if the plot as such, the interweaving of motifs supported by their motivation, ceases to play an organizing role, i.e., if the narrator, in one way or another, puts himself in the foreground, as though making use of the plot only to interweave separate stylistic devices. The center of gravity shifts from the plot (which is here reduced to a minimum) to the devices of the *skaz*, and the most important comic role is given to puns, which can be simply plays on words or develop into small anecdotes. Comic effects are achieved by the *manner* of the *skaz*. Therefore for the study of this kind of composition, those very "details" which are interspersed throughout the exposition prove to be so important that the structure of the story disintegrates if they are removed. In this connection two kinds of comic *skaz* may be distinguished: (1) the narrative and (2) the imitative. The first is limited to jokes, puns on meaning, and so on; the second introduces devices of verbal mimicry and gesture, inventing special comic articulations, puns based on sound, whimsical word order, etc. The first gives the impression of an even flow of speech; in the second, it is often as if an actor were hiding behind the imitative *skaz*, so that the *skaz* takes on the character of play-acting, and the composition is determined not by a simple series of jokes, but by a particular system of varied mimical articulatory gestures.

---

*Originally published in *Poètika* (Petrograd, 1919); available in B. Eikhenbaum, *O Proze* (Leningrad, 1969) with additional footnotes by the editors of that collection. This translation by Beth Paul and Muriel Nesbitt, under the supervision of Professor H. Muchnic, has been revised by the present editors.

Many of Gogol's short stories or their separate parts offer interesting material for an analysis of this kind of *skaz*. Composition for Gogol is not determined by plot—plot in his work is always scanty—rather, there is no plot, but only some comic situation (and sometimes even it is not *in itself* comic at all), serving, as it were, as an impetus or pretext for the elaboration of comic devices. Thus "The Nose" develops from a single anecdotal event; "The Wedding" and "The Inspector General" also grow out of a fixed existing situation; *Dead Souls* is put together by means of a simple accumulation of separate scenes, unified only by the travels of Chichikov. It is known that the necessity of always having something resembling a plot hampered Gogol. P.V. Annenkov writes of Gogol: "He used to say that for the success of a tale and of a story in general it was enough if the author were to describe a room familiar to him and a familiar street." In a letter to Pushkin in 1835 Gogol writes:

> Do me a favor, give me a plot of some kind, *any kind, funny or serious,* but a purely Russian anecdote.... Do me a favor, give me a plot; in spirit it [the work he has in mind] is to be a comedy in five acts and, I swear, it will be funnier than the devil!

He often asks for anecdotes; thus, in a letter to Prokopovich (1837): "Ask Jules (i.e., Annenkov) especially to write to me. He has things to write about. Surely, some kind of anecdote must have occurred in the office."

On the other hand, Gogol distinguished himself by his particular skill in reading his own works, as many of his contemporaries attest. In this connection it is possible to single out two main devices in his reading: the one—a melodic declamation full of pathos; the other—a special manner of performance, a mimical *skaz*, which nonetheless, as I.S. Turgenev pointed out, never became a simple theatrical reading of roles. I.I. Panaev's account is well known about how Gogol amazed everyone present, changing directly from conversation to play-acting, so that at first his belching and the corresponding phrases were taken to be real. Prince D.A. Obolensky recalls:

> Gogol read masterfully: not only did his every word come out distinctly, but, often changing the intonation of his speech, he varied it and compelled the listener to assimilate the most minute shadings of thought. I remember how he began in a hollow and somehow funereal voice: "Why depict poverty and more poverty...and here we are again in the wilderness, again we have stumbled upon an out-of-the-way corner." After these words Gogol suddenly raised his head, shook his hair, and continued now in a loud and solemn voice: "But what a wilderness and what a corner!" Then began the magnificent description of Tentetnikov's village which, in Gogol's reading, came out *as if it*

were written in a regular meter... I was especially struck by the unusual harmony of his speech. I saw how beautifully Gogol had taken advantage of the local names of various herbs and flowers which he collected so carefully. *Sometimes he obviously introduced some sonorous word solely for a harmonious effect.*

I.I. Panaev defines Gogol's reading in the following way:

> Gogol read inimitably. Among contemporary men of letters, Ostrovsky and Pisemsky are considered the best readers of their works: Ostrovsky reads without any dramatic effects, with the greatest simplicity, while still giving the proper shading to each character; Pisemsky reads like an actor—it is as if he acts out his play in reading... Gogol's reading was something of a mean between these two manners of reading. He read more dramatically than Ostrovsky, and with a much greater simplicity than Pisemsky.

Even dictation was transformed by Gogol into a special kind of declamation. P.V. Annenkov recounts:

> Nikolay Vasilievich, opening his notebook in front of him,... would become completely immersed in it, and would begin to dictate measuredly, solemnly, and with such feeling and fullness of expression that the chapters of the first volume of *Dead Souls* acquired a particular vividness in my memory. It resembled a peaceful, evenly flowing inspiration, such as is usually engendered by the profound contemplation of an object. N.V. would await my last word patiently and would continue the new sentence in the same voice, imbued with concentrated feeling and thought... Never yet had the pathos of dictation, I remember, reached such heights with Gogol, preserving all artistic naturalness, as in this passage (the description of Plyushkin's garden). Gogol even rose from his armchair... *and accompanied his dictation with a proud, somewhat imperious, gesture.*

All of this together indicates that the basis of the Gogolian text is the *skaz,* and that his text is made up of live spoken performances and the emotions of speech. More than that: this *skaz* has the tendency not simply to narrate, not simply to talk, but to reproduce words mimically and by means of articulation. Words and sentences are selected and ordered not according to the principle of mere logical speech, but more according to the principle of expressive speech, in which a special role is played by articulation, mimicry, sound gestures, etc. Whence the appearance in his language of the semantics of sound: the sound "envelope" of a word, its acoustic characteristic becomes meaningful in Gogol's speech independently of its logical meaning or material referent. Articulation and its acoustic effect are brought into the foreground as an expressive device. This is why Gogol loves titles, sur-names, first names, etc.—it gives scope for this kind of articulatory play. Furthermore, his speech is often accompanied by gestures (see above) and turns into a reproduction of a spoken manner which is noticeable even in its written form. The testimony of contemporaries points to these peculiarities too. D.A. Obolensky recalls:

> At a posting station I found a complaint book and read in it a rather amusing complaint of some gentleman or other. After hearing it out, Gogol asked me, "Well, what do you think, who is this man? What sort of qualities and character does the man have?" "I really don't know," I answered. "Well, I will tell you." And he began on the spot to describe to me in the most amusing and original way first the exter-nal appearance of this gentleman. Then he recounted his entire career in the service, even going so far as to act out several episodes from his life. I remember that I laughed like a madman, but he made all this up quite seriously. Thereupon he told me that at one time he had lived with N.M. Yazykov (the poet) and in the evening, upon going to bed, they used to amuse themselves with descriptions of different characters and would invent suitable names for each of them.

O.N. Smirnova also has something to report about surnames in Gogol:

> He gave an extraordinary amount of attention to the names of his characters; he looked for them everywhere; they became typical; he found them on posters (the name of the hero Chichikov in the first volume of *Dead Souls* was found on a house—formerly there were no address numbers, but only the surname of the owner), on signboards; beginning the second volumes of *Dead Souls,* he found the name of General Betrishchev in a book at a posting station and said to one of his friends that at the sight of the name the general's figure and his grey moustache appeared to him.

Gogol's special attitude to first names and surnames and his inventiveness in this sphere have already been noted by critics—for example by Prof. I. Mandelshtam:[1]

> To the period in which Gogol is still amusing himself belong, in the first place, the invention of names, obviously invented without regard to 'laughter through tears'... Pupopuz, Golopuz, Dovgochkhun, Golo-pupenko, Sverbyguz, Kizyakolupenko, Pereperchikha, Krutotry-

shchenko, Pecherytsya, Zakrutyguba, etc.[2] This manner of inventing amusing names remained, however, with Gogol later too: Yaichnitsa ["The Wedding"] and Neuvazhay-Koryto, and Belobryushkova, and Bashmachkin ["The Overcoat"],[3] the last name, in addition providing an occasion for a play on words. Sometimes he selects existing names on purpose: Akaky Akakievich, Trifily, Dula, Varakhasy, Pavsikakhy, Vakhtisy, and so on... In other instances he uses names as puns (this method has been used from time immemorial by all humorous writers. Molière amuses his audience with names such as Pourceaugnac, Diafoirus, Purgon, Macroton, Desfonandrès, Villebrequin; Rabelais, to an infinitely greater extent, uses improbable combinations of sounds which provide material for laughter just because they bear a remote resemblance to words, like Salmiguondinoys, Trinquamelle, Trouillogan, and so on).

And so plot in Gogol has only an external significance and therefore is in itself static; not without reason does "The Inspector General" end with a mute scene, in relation to which everything that went before is, as it were, only a preparation. The real dynamic, and therefore also the composition of his things, lies in the construction of the *skaz,* in the play with language. His characters are petrified poses. Above them, in the form of stage manager and real hero, rules the laughing and ever-playful spirit of the artist himself.

On the basis of these general propositions about composition and using the cited material on Gogol as support, we shall try to clarify the fundamental compositional stratum of "The Overcoat." This tale is especially interesting for this type of analysis, because in it a purely comic *skaz,* with all the devices of verbal play peculiar to Gogol, is united with a declamation full of pathos, forming, as it were, a second stratum. This second stratum was taken by our critics as the core of the narration, and the whole complex "labyrinth of links" (L. Tolstoy's expression) was reduced to one idea, traditionally repeated down to our own day, even in "research" on Gogol. Gogol might have answered such critics and scholars in the same way as L. Tolstoy answered the critics of *Anna Karenina:* "I congratulate them and can assure them boldly *qu'ils en savent plus long que moi."*

2

First let us examine separately the basic devices of the *skaz* in "The Overcoat," then let us trace the system by which they are linked.

A significant role, especially in the beginning, is played by puns of various kinds. They are constructed either on sound similarity, or on an etymological play on words, or on a hidden absurdity. The first sentence of the tale in the rough draft was equipped with a pun on sounds: "In the department of assessment and collections *(pódatey i sbórov)*—which, incidentally, is sometimes called the department of basenesses and nonsenses *(pódlostey i vzdórov).*"[4]

In the second rough redaction an addition was made to this pun introducing a further play on it:

> But may the readers not think, however, that this title was actually based on some kind of truth—not at all. Here the whole matter lies only in the etymological similarity of words. Owing to this the department of metallurgical *(górnykh)* and chemical *(solyánykh)* affairs is called the department of bitter *(górkykh)* and salty *(solyónykh)* affairs. Many things sometimes enter the minds of civil servants in the time left between work and whist.

This pun did not go into the final version. Puns of the etymological variety were particular favorites of Gogol's and for them he often invented special surnames. Thus, the surname of Akaky Akakievich was initially Tishkevich, which was not in itself conducive to puns; next Gogol wavered between two other forms—Bashmakevich (cf. Sobakevich) and Bashmakov—and finally settled on the form of Bashmachkin. The change from Tishkevich to Bashmakevich was prompted, of course, by the desire to create an occasion for puns; the selection of the form Bashmachkin can be explained both by the predilection for diminutive suffixes characteristic of the Gogolian style and the greater articulatory expressiveness (the force of enunciatory mimicry) of this form, creating its own type of sound gesture. The pun, created with the help of this surname, is complicated by comic devices, which give it the appearance of complete seriousness:

> By the very name it is already apparent that it at one time came from *bashmak,* shoe; but when, at what time and in what way it came from *bashmak,* nothing is known about this. The father and the grandfather and *even the brother-in-law* (the pun is imperceptibly carried to absurdity—a frequent device of Gogol's), and absolutely all the Bashmachkins went around in boots, only changing their soles about three times a year.

The pun is, as it were, destroyed by this sort of commentary—all the more so since details which are not at all connected with it (e.g., the soles) are introduced in passing; actually, there emerges a complex, as it were, double pun. The device of taking things to absurdity or to illogical word combinations is often found in Gogol, and moreover, it is usually masked by strictly logical syntax, thereby giving the impression that it is unintentional, for example in the words about Petrovich, who,

> despite his one eye and the *pockmarks all over his face,* engaged rather successfully in the repair of clerks' and all other sorts of trousers and tailcoats.

Here the logical absurdity is further masked by an abundance of details, distracting one's attention; the pun it not put on display, but, on the contrary, is concealed in every way, and therefore its comic force increases. One encounters purely etymological puns rather frequently:

> Various disasters strewn along the path of life not only of titular but even of privy, actual, court and all sorts of councillors, even those who *don't give anyone counsel or take it from anyone themselves.*

Such are the chief forms of Gogolian puns in "The Overcoat." Let us add to this another device, that of sound effects. Gogol's love of titles and names which have no "meaning" has been mentioned above; such "meaningless" words give scope for an original semantics of sound.[5] *Akaky Akakievich* is a definite selection of sounds; not without reason was the giving of this name accompanied by a whole anecdote, and in the rough draft Gogol makes a significant remark: "Of course it might have been possible to avoid the frequent juxtaposition of the letter k in some way, but the circumstances were such that it was quite impossible to do so."

In addition, the semantics of sound in this name are prepared for by a whole series of other names, also possessing a special expressiveness of sound and clearly selected, "contrived," for this purpose; in the rough draft this selection was somewhat different:

1) Yevvul, Mokky, Yevlogy;
2) Varakhasy, Dula, Trefily; (Varadat, Farmufy)[6]
3) Pavsikakhy, Frumenty.

In the finished form:

1) Mokkiya, Sossiya, Khozdazat;
2) Trifily, Dula, Varakhasy; (Varadat, Varukh)
3) Pavsikakhy, Vakhtisy, and Akaky

Comparing these two tables, the second gives the impression of greater selectivity for articulatory effect, of an original sound-system. The comic sound effect of these names is not contained simply in their strangeness (strangeness in itself cannot be comic), but in the selection, which prepares for the comic jarring monotony of the name Akaky, which, added to Akakievich, sounds in this form more like a *nickname,* concealing in itself the semantics of sound. The comic is further increased by the fact that the names preferred by the mother do not in the least depart from the general system. The net result is an original mimicry of articulation, a sound gesture.[7] Interesting in this connection is another passage in "The Overcoat," in which a description of Akaky Akakievich's appearance is given:

> And so, in *a certain department* served *a certain clerk,* a clerk one couldn't call very remarkable: of short stature, a little bit pocky [*ryabovat*] a little bit ruddy [*ryzhevat*], even, to look at, a little bit squinty [*podslepovat*], with a small baldspot on top, with wrinkles along both sides of his cheeks and with a complexion that is called hemorrhoidal...

The last word is so placed as to make its sound form assume a special emotionally expressive force and it is perceived as a comic sound gesture independently of meaning. It is prepared, on the one hand, by the device of rhythmic accretion, and on the other, by the concordant endings of several words which attune the ear to the perception of sound impressions *(ryabovat—ryzhevat—podslepovat)* and therefore it sounds grandiose, fantastic, beyond any relation to meaning. It is interesting that in the rough draft this sentence was much simpler:

> "and so, in this department served a clerk, not very noticeable in appearance, short, bald, pocky, ruddy, even, to look at, a little bit squinty."

In the final form this sentence is not so much a *description* of appearance, as a *reproduction* of it in a mimical articulatory gesture: the words are chosen and placed in a certain order not on the principle of the delineation of characteristic features, but on the principle of the semantics of sound. The internal vision remains untouched (nothing is more difficult, I think, than to draw Gogolian heroes); from the entire sentence one retains, more than anything else, an impression of a kind of progression of sounds, ending in the rolling, and logically almost senseless, but in its articulatory expressiveness unusually powerful word—"hemorrhoidal." Here D.A. Obolensky's observation that Gogol would sometimes "introduce a sonorous word of some kind, solely for a harmonious effect" is fully applicable. The entire sentence has the appearance of a finished whole, a kind of a system of sound gestures for the realization of which the words were selected. That is why these words, like logical units, like tokens of concepts, are almost intangible— they are distributed and collected anew according to the principle of "sound-

126

speech." This is one of the remarkable effects of Gogol's language. Some of his sentences have the effect of sound inscriptions, so much are articulation and acoustics brought to the forefront. The most commonplace word is sometimes presented by him in such a manner that its logical or material meaning fades away while sound meaning is put in its place, and a simple name takes on the appearance of a nickname:

> "he bumped into a policeman who, standing his *halberd* next to himself, was shaking some snuff out of a horn onto his calloused fist," or:
> "It could even be in the latest fashion, the collar will fasten with *silver appliquéd clasps* [*lapki pod aplike*]."

The last case is an obvious play with articulation (the repetition in *lpk-plk*).

There is no middle level of speech in Gogol—no simple psychological or material concepts logically united into ordinary sentences. The articulatory, mimical "sound-speech" alternates with a tense intonation, which shapes the sentences. His works are often constructed on this kind of alternation. In "The Overcoat" there is a vivid example of such an intonational influence, a declamatory period of rhetorical pathos:

> Even at those hours when the grey Petersburg sky completely darkens and all the clerk folk have eaten their fill and dined, each as he can, according to the salary he receives and his own whim,—when everything has already had a rest after the departmental scratching of pens, after rushing about, after their own and others' essential affairs, and after all of that which indefatigable man voluntarily assigns himself even more than is necessary...

An enormous sentence, building up the intonation to enormous tension toward the end, is resolved with unexpected simplicity:

> ... in a word, even when everyone was trying to distract himself, Akaky Akakievich wouldn't yield to any distraction.

One gets the impression of a comic disparity between the tension of syntactic intonation, beginning obscurely and mysteriously, and its semantic resolution. This impression is further increased by words which are included, as if expressly to contradict the syntactical character of the period: "little hats," "a pretty girl," "sipping tea from glasses with kopek crackers"; finally, the anecdote about Falconet's monument brought up in passing. This contradiction or disparity so acts on the words themselves that they become *strange*, enigmatic: they sound unusual, astonishing the ear, as if they were dismembered or thought up by Gogol for the first time. In "The

Overcoat" there is also a different kind of declamation—one that is sentimentally melodramatic in nature—which unexpectedly penetrates the general punning style; it is the celebrated "humane" passage which has been so fortunate in Russian criticism that from an accessory artistic device it has become the "idea" of the whole tale:

> "Leave me alone, why do you insult me?" And something strange was contained in the words and in the voice in which they were pronounced. In it resounded something so evoking of pity that one recently appointed young man... *And long after,* at the gayest moments, the short little clerk with the baldspot on top would appear to him... and in these penetrating words rang other words... *And the poor man would cover his face with his hands...,* etc.

The rough drafts do not contain this passage—it comes later and undoubtedly belongs to the second stratum, complicating the purely anecdotal style of the original drafts with elements of a declamation full of pathos.[8]

Gogol allows his characters in "The Overcoat" to speak only a little, and as always with him, their speech is molded in a special way, so that, in spite of individual differences, it is always stylized and never produces the impression of everyday speech, as does, for example, Ostrovsky's dialogue (not without reason did Gogol read differently). The speech of Akaky Akakievich belongs to the general system of Gogolian "sound-speech" and of mimical articulation. It is specially constructed and furnished with a commentary:

> One should know that Akaky Akakievich expressed himself for the most part in prepositions, adverbs, and finally, *in such particles as have absolutely no meaning whatever.*

The speech of Petrovich, as opposed to the fragmentary articulation of Akaky Akakievich, is condensed, severe, hard and it acts as a contrast; there are no ordinary nuances in it—everyday intonation is not appropriate to it; it is as "contrived" and as stylized as the speech of Akaky Akakievich. As always in Gogol (cf. "Old World Landowners," "The Two Ivans," *Dead Souls,* and his plays) these sentences stand outside of time, outside the moment—motionless and once and for all: language in which puppets might talk. Equally contrived is Gogol's own language—his *skaz.* In "The Overcoat," this *skaz* is stylized to resemble a special kind of careless, naive chatter. Seemingly "unnecessary" details leapt out involuntarily:

> ... on her right stood the godfather, a most excellent person, Ivan Ivanovich Yeroshkin, who served as head clerk in the Senate, and the godmother, the wife of a police officer, a woman of rare virtues, Arina

128

Semyonovna Belobryushkova.

Or his *skaz* takes on the character of familiar verbosity:

> One ought not to say much, of course, about this tailor, but since it is already established that the personality of every character in a story should be described completely, there's nothing to be done, let's have Petrovich too.

The comic device in this instance lies in the fact that after such a declaration the "characterization" of Petrovich consists merely of the remark that he drinks on every holiday indiscriminately. The same device is repeated concerning his wife:

> Since we have already let slip something about the wife, it will be necessary to say a couple of words about her too; but, *unfortunately,* not much was known about her, except that Petrovich had a wife, that she even wore a cap and not a kerchief; but she could not boast, it appears, of her beauty; at least, on meeting her, only soldiers of the guard would peek at her under her cap, twitching a whisker and emitting some peculiar sound.

There is one sentence in which this style of *skaz* is very sharply marked:

> Where exactly the clerk who had invited him lived, unfortunately we cannot say: our memory begins to deceive us greatly, and everything in Petersburg, all the streets and houses, have so merged and mingled in our head that it is quite difficult to *get anything out of it* in a decent state.

If one joins to this sentence all the numerous uses of "some kind of," "unfortunately very little is known," "nothing is known," "I do not remember," etc., one gets an idea of the device of the *skaz,* which lends the whole tale the illusion of its being a real history, told as fact, but not known to the narrator in every small detail. He willingly digresses from the main anecdote and introduces intervening phrases like "they say that"; thus, in the beginning, about the petition from some district police captain ("I don't remember from which town"), thus also about Bashmachkin's ancestors, about the tail of the horse of the Falconet statue, about the titular councillor who was made director, after which he partitioned off a special room for himself and called it "the audience room," etc. It is known that the story itself grew out of an "office anecdote" about a poor clerk who lost his gun, for which he had been saving money for a long time: "This anecdote was the first thought for

129

his wonderful tale 'The Overcoat,' " reports P.V. Annenkov. Its original title was "The Tale of a Clerk Who Stole Overcoats," and the general character of the *skaz* in the rough drafts is distinguished by an even greater stylization of careless chatter and familiarity: "Really, I don't remember his surname," "In its essence it was a very kindly beast," etc. In its final form, Gogol somewhat smoothed out this kind of device, garnished the story with puns and anecdotes, but then introduced declamation, complicating thereby the original compositional stratum. A grotesque resulted in which the mimicry of laughter alternates with the mimicry of sorrow, and both the one and the other have the appearance of a game, with a controlled alternation of gestures and intonations.

3

Let us now trace this alternation in order to discover the very manner of linking the separate devices. At the basis of linkage or composition lies the *skaz,* the traits of which are defined above. It has been shown that this *skaz* is not narrative but mimical and declamatory; not a narrator but a performer, almost a comedian, hides behind the printed text of "The Overcoat." What then is the "scenario" of this role, what is its outline?

The very beginning contains a collision, a break—a sharp shift in tone. The businesslike introduction ("In the department") suddenly breaks off, and the epic intonation of the narrator, which might be expected, changes to another tone, one of exaggerated irritation and sarcasm. One gets the impression of an improvisation—the original composition immediately gives way to digressions of some kind. Nothing has been said as yet, but an anecdote is already there, carelessly and hastily related ("I don't remember from which town," "the hugest volume of some romantic composition"). But after this the tone noted in the beginning apparently returns: "And so, in *a certain department* served a *certain clerk.*" However, this new return to an epic *skaz* is immediately replaced by the sentence which was discussed above, so contrived, so acoustic in nature, that nothing whatever is left of the businesslike *skaz*. Gogol steps into his role—and, having concluded this whimsical, amazing selection of words with the grandiosely resonant and almost meaningless word "hemorrhoidal," he closes this passage with a mimical gesture: "What can one do! The Petersburg climate is to blame." A personal tone, with all the devices of the Gogolian *skaz,* takes firm root in the tale and assumes the character of a grotesque gesture or grimace. This already prepares the transition to the pun on the surname and the anecdote about Akaky Akakievich's birth and christening. The businesslike sentences closing this anecdote ("In this way Akaky Akakievich *came about*... And so, that's the way all this *came about"*) produce an impression of playing with the

130

narrative form, and not without reason is there a slight pun concealed in them, giving them the appearance of awkward repetition. There ensues a stream of "mockery"—in this style the *skaz* continues right up to the sentence: "But not one word would Akaky Akakievich answer to this..." when the comic *skaz* is suddenly interrupted by a sentimentally melodramatic digression with the characteristic devices of the sentimental style. By means of this device "The Overcoat" is raised from a simple anecdote to a grotesque. The sentimental and intentionally primitive content of this excerpt (in this the grotesque coincides with melodrama) is conveyed with the aid of an intensifying intonation which has a solemn character full of pathos (the introductory "ands" and the peculiar word order: "And something strange was contained in the words... And long after... the short little clerk would appear to him... And in these penetrating words... And the poor young man would cover his face with his hands and many times later in his life he would shudder..."). There results something like the device of "theatrical illusion," when an actor seems suddenly to step out of his role and begins to talk like a human being (cf. in "The Inspector General": "Who are you laughing at? You're laughing at yourselves!" or the famous "It's a dreary world, gentlemen!" in "The Two Ivans"). It is customary to take this passage literally—an artistic device, converting a comic short story into a grotesque and preparing a "fantastic" ending, is taken as a sincere intervention of "the soul." Although such deception is "a triumph of art," in the words of Karamzin, although the naiveté of the audience may be charming, for scholarship such naiveté is not a triumph at all, because it reveals its helplessness. In this interpretation the entire structure of "The Overcoat," its whole artistic intent, is destroyed. Given the basic proposition that in a work of art not a single sentence can be in itself a simple "reflection" of the personal feelings of the author, but is always a construction and a performance, *we cannot and have no right* to see in such an excerpt anything other than a definite artistic device. The usual manner of identifying some separate judgment with the psychological content of the author's soul is not an appropriate method for scholarship. In this sense the artist's soul, like that of a man *experiencing* various moods, always remains and must remain outside the limits of his creation. A work of art is always something made, designed, invented—not merely skillful, but also artificial in the good sense of this word, and therefore *there neither is nor can there be* a place in it for the reflection of the empiricism of the soul. The skill and artificiality of Gogol's device in this fragment of "The Overcoat" are most notably revealed in the construction of its clearly melodramatic cadence, in the form of a primitively sentimental maxim, used by Gogol with the aim of confirming the grotesque:

And the poor young man would cover his face with his hands, and many times later in his life he would shudder, seeing how much inhumanity there is in man, how much fierce coarseness is hidden in refined educated breeding, and, God! even in the very man whom the world deems noble and honorable...

The melodramatic episode is used as a contrast to the comic *skaz*. The more skillful the puns, the more full of pathos and stylized, of course, in the direction of sentimental primitivism, must be the device which violates the comic game. The form of a serious meditation would not provide a contrast and would not be able to communicate a grotesque character to the whole composition at once. It is not surprising, therefore, that immediately after this episode, Gogol returns to what preceded it—now a simulated businesslike tone, now a playful, carelessly gossipy one, with plays on words, such as: "... only then would he notice that he was not in the middle of a line, but rather in the middle of the street." Having related how Akaky Akakievich would eat and how he would stop eating when "his stomach was beginning to swell," Gogol again enters into declamation, but of a somewhat different sort: "Even at those hours when..." etc. Here for the purpose of the same grotesque, a "muted," mysteriously serious intonation is used, which slowly builds up in the form of a colossal period and resolves itself with unexpected simplicity; the syntactical type of the sentence leads one to expect a balance in semantic energy between the protracted ascent ("when... when..., when") and the cadence, but this is not realized, as indeed the very selection of words and expressions intimates. The lack of correspondence between the solemnly serious intonation in itself and the semantic content is again used as a grotesque device. In place of this new "deception" of the comedian quite naturally appears a new play on words concerning councillors, with which the first act of "The Overcoat" closes: "Thus flowed the peaceful life of a man..." etc.

This pattern, noted in the first part, in which the purely anecdotal *skaz* is interwoven with a melodramatic and solemn declaration, indeed determines the entire composition of "The Overcoat" as a grotesque. The style of the grotesque demands, in the first place, that the situation or event described be contained in a world, small to the point of the fantastic, of artificial experiences (as it is in both "Old World Landowners" and in "The Two Ivans") completely cut off from the larger reality, from the real fullness of spiritual life,[9] and in the second place, that this be done not with a didactic or satirical intent, but with the aim of giving scope for *a play with reality,* for breaking up and freely displacing its elements, so that the usual correlations and connections (psychological and logical) turn out, in this *newly* constructed world, to be unreal, and each trifle can grow to colossal dimensions. Only against the background of such a style as this does the slightest gleam of real feeling acquire the appearance of something staggering. In the anecdote about the clerk Gogol valued just this fantastically limited, closed-in structure of thoughts, feelings and desires, within the narrow boundaries of which the artist is at liberty to exaggerate details and upset the usual proportions of the world. It was on this basis that the sketch of "The Overcoat" was made. Here the point is certainly not in the "insignificance" of Akaky Akakievich nor in a sermon on "humaneness" to one's lowly brother, but in the fact that, having fenced off the whole realm of the story from larger reality, Gogol can unite the incompatible, exaggerate the small and minimize the great.[10] In a word, he can play with all the norms and laws of the real life of the spirit. And so indeed he does. The spiritual world of Akaky Akakievich (if such an expression is permissible) is not *insignificant* (as was thought by our naive and sentimental historians of literature who were under Belinsky's spell), but a fantastically limited world, *his own:* "There, in this copying, he saw a certain special *varied* (!) *and pleasant world* all his own... Outside of this copying, it seemed, nothing existed for him."[11]

This world has its own laws, its own proportions. The new overcoat according to the laws of his world turns out to be a grandiose event, and Gogol provides a grotesque formula:

"he was nourished spiritually, carrying in his thoughts the eternal idea of the future overcoat."[12]

And again:

... as if he were not alone, but some pleasant female life companion had agreed to travel life's road together with him—and that companion was none other than that same overcoat with the thick quilting, with the strong lining which wouldn't wear out.

Small details move to the forefront, like Petrovich's toenail, "... thick and strong as the shell on a tortoise," or his snuffbox

with the portrait of some general, precisely which is not known, because the place where the face was had been punched out with a finger and then pasted over with a square scrap of paper.[13]

This grotesque hyperbole unfolds as before against the background of a comic *skaz* with puns, ridiculous words and expressions, anecdotes, etc.:

They didn't buy marten, because it was really expensive, but instead they chose cat, the best that could be found in the store, cat which from a distance one could always take for marten.

Or:

> What was precisely and in what consisted the duty of the *important personage,* that has remained unknown to this day. One should know that the *certain important personage* recently became an important personage, but before that time he was an unimportant personage.

Or again:

> They even say that titular councillor, when they made him the director of some small separate office, at once fenced himself off a special room, calling it "the audience room," and put some footmen with red collars and gold braid by the doors who would take the door by the handle and open it to every arrival, although an ordinary desk could hardly fit in the "audience room."

Alongside these passages there are statements "from the author" in the careless tone established in the beginning, behind which a grimace seems to be concealed:

> Or perhaps he didn't even think that—after all, it's really impossible to crawl *into a man's soul* (here also is a word play of a sort, if one bears in mind the general treatment of the figure of Akaky Akakievich) and find out everything he thinks (a play on the anecdote,—as though it were a question of reality).

The death of Akaky Akakievich is related just as grotesquely as his birth—with an alternation of comic and tragic details, with the sudden "At last poor Akaky Akakievich gave up the ghost,"[14] with the immediate transition to all sorts of trifles (the enumeration of the inheritance: "a bunch of goose quills, a quire of white government paper, three pairs of socks, two or three buttons which had come off his trousers, and the housecoat already known to the reader" and finally, with the conclusion in the ordinary style: "Who got all this, god knows: even the narrator of this tale, I admit, wasn't interested in this."

And after all this—a new melodramatic declamation, as is customary after the presentation of so sad a scene, taking us back to the "humane" passage:

> And Petersburg remained without Akaky Akakievich as if he had never been in it. There had vanished and disappeared a being defended by no one, dear to no one, interesting to no one, not even calling himself to the attention of a naturalist who doesn't neglect to mount an ordinary

fly on a pin and examine it under a microscope... etc.

The end of "The Overcoat" is an effective apotheosis of the grotesque, something like the mute scene in "The Inspector General." Naive scholars, finding the whole point of the tale in the "humane" passage, stop in perplexity before this unexpected and incomprehensible intrusion of "romanticism" into "realism." Gogol himself prompts them:

> But who could imagine that this is still not all about Akaky Akakievich, that he was fated to live on noisily for several days after his death, as if in reward for a life unnoticed by anyone? *But that's what happened,* and our poor history *unexpectedly* acquires a fantastic ending.

Actually this ending is not in the least more fantastic or "romantic" than the whole story. On the contrary, there we had the fantastic in a truly grotesque form, communicated as a play with reality; here the tale shifts to a world of more usual concepts and facts, but everything is treated in the style of a play with the fantastic. This is a new "deception," a device of the grotesque in reverse:

> the ghost suddenly glanced around and, stopping, asked: "Whaddaya want?" and showed him such a fist as you won't find even among the living. The policeman said "Nothing," and at once turned back. The ghost, however, was much taller, wore huge mustachios, and, directing his steps, as it seemed, to the Obukhov Bridge, vanished completely in the darkness of the night.

The anecdote developed in the finale leads away from the "poor history" with its melodramatic episodes. The initial, purely comic, *skaz* returns with all its devices. Together with the moustachioed ghost the entire grotesquery disappears into the darkness, dissolving in laughter. In the same way, Khlestakov vanishes in "The Inspector General," and the mute scene takes the audience back to the beginning of the play.

1919

ON GOGOL'S "THE OVERCOAT"
by Dmitri Chizhevsky*

I.

Is it necessary to write more about "The Overcoat"? We all know Gogol's tale from our school days, and if we have later happened to read books and articles about Gogol—whether they were works following the "social approach" typical of Russian literary criticism and Russian literary history or the works of "formalists"—we always find one and the same thing in reading them: "The Overcoat" is one of the steps in Gogol's development as a writer in the direction of realism. Its theme, one of the "insulted and injured," the "poor clerk," is a theme cultivated in more than a hundred Russian stories and tales, for example, in *Poor Folk,* "A Faint Heart" and other early tales of Dostoevsky, by Gogol himself in "The Diary of a Madman," the theme of Veinberg—

> He was a titular councillor,
> she—a general's daughter...

Critics usually find the central idea of "The Overcoat" in the famous "humane" passage, which comes immediately after the words of Akaky Akakievich, whom the clerks are teasing:

> "Leave me alone, why do you insult me?" And something strange was contained in the words and in the voice in which they were pronounced. In it resounded something so evoking of pity that one recently appointed young man who, by the example of the others, was on the verge of permitting himself to laugh at Akaky, suddenly stopped as if transfixed, and from that time on it was as if everything had changed for him and appeared in another form. Some preternatural force alienated him from the comrades he had become acquainted with, having taken them for decent, well-bred people. And long after, at the gayest moments, the short little clerk with the baldspot on top would appear to him with his penetrating words: "Leave me alone, why do you insult me?" and in these penetrating words rang other words: "I am your brother." And the poor young man would cover his face with his hands, and many times later in his life he would shudder, seeing how much inhumanity there is in man...

* First published in *Sovremennye zapiski,* 67(Paris, 1938), 172-95.

There is no doubt that this passage contains thoughts that are essential for Gogol. But isn't it strange that such a central passage stands at the very beginning of the tale, as though anticipating and making unnecessary all the subsequent development of events? But the tragic story of Akaky Akakievich only begins further on, a story which at first sight one could sooner call tragi-comic and in which such a discriminating connoisseur of the Russian classics as Dostoevsky saw mockery and derision of the hero, whose first human feeling is directed at... an overcoat. Did not Gogol spoil the beginning with such a continuation? Did he not weaken its effect? Did he not declare Akaky Akakievich our brother only to laugh at him spitefully later?

Such a strange disjunction in the tale's composition forces us to seek the meaning Gogol placed in it elsewhere than in the exclamation "I am your brother!"—in this thought which, with all its pathos and Christian character, smells of vulgar morality and recalls the celebrated phrase of Karamzin, "even peasants are able to feel," a phrase which we are now unable, recognizing all its justness, to read without a smile.

We will try to approach Gogol's story more closely by means of the method of "close reading," the only correct method of reading the classics, a method from which we have been weaned by newspapers, the detective novel, other "light reading," and even in school, where our own reflections on a work were made unnecessary by the explanations of textbook and teacher—yes, were we on the school bench mature enough really to understand the meaning of an artistic work?

In "close reading," in the enjoyment of Gogol's story "by bits," we notice many trifling details that seem to be insignificant features... Perhaps it is worthwhile to begin an analysis of "The Overcoat" with one of these "insignificant details." In "The Overcoat" one and the same insignificant little word is repeated extraordinarily often: *dazhe,* "even"! On the 32-40 pages which "The Overcoat" occupies in the usual editions of Gogol this little word "even" is met with neither more nor less than 73 times! Moreover, its use on several pages is particularly dense: in the space of a single page we meet it three, four, even five times! Is this an accident? Does Gogol simply repeat an unnecessary word because it happened to come to his pen?

According to everything we know about Gogol's method of work on his writings, such an explanation should seem to us hardly likely, in fact simply impossible. As is well known, Gogol endlessly polished and reworked the text of his works, reworked separate words, changing and varying them, until he achieved a final perfection, the final polish. We know from the words of S.T. Aksakov how Gogol in 1850 twice read aloud a chapter from the second part of *Dead Souls.* The Aksakovs were surprised by the second reading:

We were struck with amazement: the chapter seemed to us even better, as if it had been written anew. The corrections were to all appearances quite insignificant: there one word was removed, here added, and there transposed—and it all came out differently.

If we had doubts about the testimony of such a judge as Aksakov,—didn't he, too much carried away with Gogol as writer, man and "prophet," over-estimate him? (and, in any case, the elder Aksakov was hardly so totally captivated by Gogol as were the young Aksakovs)—there is still sufficient evidence in Gogol's published reworkings of his own works ("The Portrait," "The Inspector General," *Taras Bulba*) and in Gogol's manuscripts. These materials fully corroborate what Gogol himself said (in the same years), according to Berg, about his method of work as a writer:

At first it is necessary to jot everything down as it comes to you, even if it is bad, insipid, absolutely everything, and then forget about this notebook. Then, after a month, after two, sometimes even more (this happens by itself), take what you have written and reread it: you will see that much is not what it should be, there is much that is superfluous and something that is lacking. Make corrections and marginal notes, and again discard the notebook. At the next inspection— new marginal notes—and where there is not enough room, take a separate scrap of paper and glue it in on the side. When everything is thus covered with writing, take the notebook and copy it yourself. At this point new illuminations, cuts, additions, refinements of style will appear by themselves. Between former words new ones will jump up, words which necessarily should be there but which for some reason don't appear at first. And again put the notebook down. Travel, amuse yourself, don't do anything, or at least write something else. The hour will come, the abandoned notebook will be remembered: take it, reread it, correct it in the same way, and when it is again used up, copy it in your own hand. You will notice in doing this that, together with a strengthening of style, with finishing, refinement of sentences, your hand, as it were, also strengthens: the letters place themselves more firmly and resolutely. It is necessary to do this, in my opinion, *eight* times. For someone else, perhaps, fewer times are needed, and even more for yet another. I do it eight times. Only after the eighth copying, without fail in my own hand, does the work seem in full artistically finished, does it achieve the pearl of creation. Further corrections and revisions will perhaps spoil the matter; what artists call "overdrawing." Of course, to follow such rules constantly is impossible, difficult. I am speaking of the ideal. Another will let it go at that sooner. A man is after all a man and not a machine.

139

One could hardly suppose that a writer who worked in *this* way left, on account of simple mental inertia, an unnecessary little word in such excessive profusion in a work to which he assigned so important a role! Obviously, "even" has some meaning in this work, it "carries a certain function," or rather, several functions. This is always the case with Gogol: his artistic devices are many-sided, many-functional... Is this the role of "even" in "The Overcoat"? Let us consider it more closely.

2.

Above all, the repetition of one and the same word characterizes, in Gogol and other writers, colloquial speech or the *skaz,* as literary historians now term it. In "The Overcoat"—and one should pay attention to this— the story is narrated as if not from the person of Gogol, not by Gogol himself, but by a definite narrator whom Gogol quite carefully keeps at a certain remove, at a distance from himself. Gogol is still continuing the tradition of *Evenings on a Farm Near Dikanka* and *Mirgorod* with their narrators. He emphasizes the fact that the story is being narrated by a specific, though not more closely characterized, narrator with the help of parenthetic phrases of the sort: "nothing is known about this," "I don't remember from *which* town," "Akaky Akakievich was born, if only my memory doesn't deceive me, in the early hours of March 23rd," "it's hard to say on exactly what day," "where exactly the clerk who had invited him lived, unfortunately, we cannot say: our memory begins to deceive us greatly," "what was precisely and in what consisted the duty of the *important personage,* that has remained unknown to this day," "who got all this (Akaky Akakievich's legacy) God knows; even the narrator of this tale, I admit, wasn't interested in this," and so on. Gogol uses digressions for this very aim. For example, at the very beginning of the tale: "In the department...," the narrator breaks in: "But it's better not to say in which department," and there follow twenty (!) lines of digression, after which the story starts all over again: "And so, in a certain department served a certain clerk..." In the Ukrainian stories Gogol uses words and phrases in Ukrainian to remind the reader of the presence of a narrator. In "The Overcoat" and "The Diary of a Madman" Gogol brings his speech closest to the colloquial. In "The Diary of a Madman" this was simpler, the author had his hero keep a diary; Akaky Akakievich would hardly have been able to keep a diary! But the narrator is in some sense brought close to Akaky Akakievich. This approximation is achieved by the repetition of several unnecessary words, for instance, by substituting attributes which mean nothing for attributes which fill the nouns to which they refer with content: "a certain" ("a certain police inspector," "a certain director," and so on), "some sort of" ("some sort of relation," "some sort of town" and so on), "something or other," "some kind of," and so on. Gogol himself draws attention to the nature of his hero's speech:

> One should know that Akaky Akakievich expressed himself for the most part in prepositions, adverbs, and finally, in such particles as have absolutely no meaning whatever. And if the matter was very difficult, he even had the habit of not finishing the sentence at all, so that quite often, having begun a speech with the words: "That, really, is completely sort of...," but then there was nothing, and he himself would forget, thinking he had already said everything.

And even the Important Personage, the tale's secondary hero,

> remained eternally in one and the same silent state, only occasionally emitting some monosyllabic sounds... His usual conversation with inferiors smacked of strictness and almost entirely consisted of three sentences...

Thus, the "impoverishment" of the narrator's speech is hardly accidental. Gogol obviously could not bring this impoverishment to the level of speech of Akaky Akakievich or of the Important Personage. If the narrator were also to "express himself... in prepositions, adverbs, and finally, such particles as have absolutely no meaning whatever" or "remain eternally in one and the same silent state," then there would be no story! However, Gogol does in some measure bring his narrator's speech close to the speech of his heroes: the strange "impoverishment" of language in "The Overcoat" serves exactly this end, though it might seem to stand in contradiction to the fundamental internal laws of any artistic work, which of necessity strives for the greatest richness and splendor within the limits of the possible. Obviously, the possibilities for richness and fullness of speech are limited here by just this peculiar "tongue-tied" quality of the narrator and heroes.

In the further development of the naturalistic style in Russian literature we find examples which leave Gogol's modest rudiments far behind. Such are, for example, the speech of Makar Devushkin in *Poor Folk* and of the unknown narrator in Dostoevsky's *The Double:* on several pages the reader, having missed the author's intention, becomes quite irritated and asks himself, why pick such stutterers for narrators! Gogol surpassed himself in "The Tale of Captain Kopeykin" (from *Dead Souls*), where on eight pages such an abundance of parenthetic—and frequently senseless—words is piled up that one can only be struck by the art with which the inimitable master, Gogol, stuffed and shuffled such a quantity of *skaz* elements into so short a space. Here we come across "my dear sir" 13 times, "you can just imagine" and "you just think" 15 times, "you know" or "you see" 23 times, "such"

20 times, "some sort of" 17 times, "in a kind of a way" 12 times, "so to say" 11 times, "relatively" or "relatively speaking" 9 times, and so on. Let us recall one passage:

> All of a sudden the world, relatively speaking, unrolls before him, a veritable arena of life, as it were, such a Scheherazade fairyland, you understand. All of a sudden something like Nevsky Prospect spreads out before him, if you will picture it to yourself, or, you know, some Gorokhovaya Street, the Devil take it, or some Liteynaya. Over here some spire or other soars in the air; over there are bridges suspended in some sort of a devilish way, without any visible contact with the earth, as it were—in a word, my dear sir, the hanging gardens of Semiramis, and that's all there is to it!

Or:

> He'd be walking past some restaurant where the chef—just imagine!—is a foreigner, a Frenchman, you know, with a frank, open countenance, the linen on him of the finest holland stuff, and an apron the whiteness of which equals, in a kind of a way, the whiteness of snowy expanses, and this chef is working away at an omelet with *fines herbes,* or cutlets with truffles—in a word, some super-super-delicacy or other of such a tantalizing nature that you'd start eating your own self out of sheer appetite. Or he might happen to be going past the shops on Miliutinskaya; there, peeping out of the windows, in a manner of speaking, he'd behold such stunning smoked salmon, and little cherries at five rubles each cherry, and a colossus of a watermelon as big as your stage-coach, leaning right out of the window, so to speak, on the lookout for a fool big enough to pay a hundred rubles for it. In short, there's temptation at every step, making his mouth water, relatively speaking, as it were, yet all he keeps on hearing is the eternal "Tomorrow!"[1]

The blatant "unnecessariness" of all these verbal patterns from the point of view of the exposition of a given content is so obvious that what most clearly stand out in these examples are those characteristic features of verbal art which, in any approach to the content of a work which ignores its "form," disappear from the reader's view, namely, verbal art as a *game* and as a *craft*. But actually, as we will see, it is from just such "formal" elements, from the play with the word and from the nature of verbal art as craft ("how it is made," "how it is executed") that threads extend to the essential content of a literary work.

142

But the numerous "even's" in "The Overcoat" carry not only the above-mentioned function of stylizing the story's speech as that of a *skaz;* they are connected as well with the most essential features of Gogol's humor, of the comic in Gogol.

Gogol's humor is a unique play of oppositions, of antitheses of the sensible and the senseless, a play in which the meaningful and meaningless replace each other by turns. A phrase, word or thought seems to make sense, but suddenly turns out to be an absurdity; or vice versa, what seemed non-sense turns out to be meaningful. The use of "even" relates precisely to this play of oppositions: "even" introduces an intensification, an ascent, it signi-fies and marks a tension, an expectation, and if the ascent is not realized, if what is expected does not appear, we are disappointed, surprised, and Gogol has achieved a comic effect! Gogol often introduces instead of an intensification after "even" that "zero meaning" so characteristic of his work (nonsensical phrases are very frequent in Gogol's writings), and sometimes instead of an intensification we are struck by a slackening of tension. Thus the serious and the humorous alternate, and if the rising line is particularly underscored by pathetic intonation, then even simple speech seems to be nonsense: the rising line of speech, having begun to rise too high into pathos, suddenly breaks off and it all ends in nothing, in trifles or with the exact opposite of what the reader expected.

In such passages one often finds the word "even." Both before and after "The Overcoat." Let us take an example from *Dead Souls.* Gogol is speaking about the "enlightenment" of "the town NN":

> the others were also enlightened people—those who read Karamzin, those who read *The Moscow Record,* and *even* (!) those who read nothing at all.[2]

Or another celebrated phrase with "even" in the same role:

> (The Governor) was, however, a good-hearted fellow and *even* occa-sionally embroidered fancywork on tulle with his own hands.[3]

We come across similar passages already in Pushkin's *Eugene Onegin,* a work which undoubtedly influenced Gogol (a fact which literary historians haven't gotten around to paying attention to): the portrayal of Lensky's second, Zaretsky—

> ... a kind and simple
> bachelor paterfamilias,

> a steadfast friend, a peaceful landowner
> and *even* an honest man...
>   (VI, 4)

As though honesty were the rarest and most unusual mark of a man!

The function of "even" in "The Overcoat" is quite often the same: "even" introduces phrases and thoughts which don't stand in an expected logical connection with what precedes them, or rather, which don't have any sort of connection with the preceding at all. Examples:

> The clerk's surname was Bashmachkin. By the very name it is already apparent that it at one time came from *bashmak,* shoe; but when, at what time and in what way it came from *bashmak,* nothing is known about this. The father and the grandfather and *even* the brother-in-law, and absolutely all the Bashmachkins went around in boots, only changing the soles about three times a year.

After the first logical break, the transition to the brother-in-law, who actually has no genetic tie to Akaky Akakievich, there follows yet a second break, the transition to "soles," which have nothing at all in common with the name "Bashmachkin." A whole series of similar "even's" introducing breaks in the logical train of thought are grouped around the peculiar notions of the narrator about the relation of nature and fate to the higher levels of the Russian "Table of Ranks": the Petersburg cold causes

> the foreheads of *even* those who occupy higher posts [to] ache from the frost and tears [to] come to their eyes...

or:

> various disasters strewn along the path of life not only of titular but even of privy, actual, court and all sorts of councillors, *even* those who don't give anyone counsel or take it from anyone themselves...

(a double break: "councillor" does not signify one who gives advice or counsel). When the "ghost" starts pulling the overcoats from the shoulders of Petersburg inhabitants,

> complaints came incessantly from all sides that backs and shoulders, if it were only of titular, but *even* of the most privy councillors, were subjected to absolute chills because of the nightly pulling-off of overcoats.

144

Another phrase in the same style:

> the mistress, preparing some fish, had filled the kitchen with so much smoke that it was impossible to see *even* the very cockroaches.

Gogol "plays" in a similar way not only with "even" but with other words as well: Petrovich the tailor

> despite his one eye and the pockmarks all over his face, engaged rather successfully in the repair of clerks' and all other sorts of trousers and tailcoats, of course, when he was in a sober state and not nourishing some other notion in his head.

And here there are plenty of parallels from Gogol's other works: such an ending concludes the contrast of Ivan Ivanovich and Ivan Nikiforovich:

> Ivan Nikiforovich, *on the other hand,* wears trouser with such ample folds that if they were blown out you could put the whole courtyard with the barns and outhouses into them.[4]

Or the scene from *Taras Bulba* in which Bulba, with several friends, takes it upon himself to sound the kettledrums which convene a Cossack "Rada" (general assembly):

> At the sound of the drums, the first to arrive was the drummer, a tall man with one eye, *in spite of* however it being terribly bleary [from just having awakened].[5]

Such is the technique which Gogol uses to reduce the reader to utter· amazement! But often, and particularly in "The Overcoat," Gogol also uses the opposite method: the reader expects something usual, understandable, positive, but instead of this Gogol startles him with something fanciful, unusual, negative. Here are some examples from "The Overcoat": the names Mokkiya, Sossiya, Khozdazat are found in the Church Calendar for Akaky Akakievich, then Trifily, Duly, and Varakhisy turn up—

> "What an affliction," said the old lady, "what names they all are, I really never heard the like. At least if it were..."

We expect, after this "At least if it were," some fairly everyday names, but Gogol is merely setting us up for the startling:

> "At least if it were Varadat or Varukh, but Trifily and Varakhisy!"

145

Or:

As he climbed the stairway to Petrovich's—which, to do it justice...

here the reader expects to hear something positive about the stairway, but is doubly amazed to read—

> which, to do it justice, was all soaked with water and slops and saturated through and through with that ammoniac smell which eats at the eyes and, as is well known, is inevitably present on all the backstairs of Petersburg houses...

Gogol's play with the word "even" belongs to precisely this technique of amazing the reader.

4.

But "even" is repeated so often in the tale not merely as a technical device. "Even" is vital as well for one of the main aspects of the tale, it half opens up this aspect to us, if we are attentive enough.

We already spoke about the way in which "even" introduces an intensification, an increase, a tension which, however, Gogol goes back upon, disappointing and at the same time astounding the reader. This is a means of revealing the pettiness of the circle, of the "slice of life," depicted. What precedes "even" turns out to be pettiness, a trifle: which is to say that in this sphere of life what is insignificant, empty, what is in fact "nothing," seems meaningful and vital. It is not that easy to depict and understand "nothing"; philosophers from Hegel to Heidegger have had no small struggle with this difficulty. Gogol attempts to overcome it with his use of the word "even." The content and goals of life turn out to be insignificant, contentless; they are actually "nothing whatever."

To this sphere of the use of "even" belong those passages already cited in which Gogol gives the impression that, according to his tale's narrator, nature, fate and even the extrasensory world—a "ghost"—are oriented on the "Table of Ranks," that nature normally spares the freezing bodies, shoulders and "life paths" of clerks *of the higher ranks.*

The highest, strongest feeling of Akaky Akakievich, his passion for the new overcoat, is portrayed with the help of the same device. The clerk's feelings are presented by Gogol with a pathetic intonation, but their disclosure is rendered by insignificant, everyday trivialities. Akaky Akakievich "even" laughs or smiles, he is "even" inattentive at work, "almost" makes a slip of the pen while copying, he "even" takes notice of a pretty lady.

146

At times a fire would show in his eyes, the most daring and audacious thoughts *even* flashed through his head: shouldn't he actually put marten on the collar?

But actually, Akaky Akakievich's whole life is portrayed in the same style: his devotion on the job is such that

> If they had rewarded him in proportion to effort, he, to his own amazement, perhaps might have *even* landed among the state councillors...

His own desires, however, are still more modest:

> and *even* if the director were to be so kind as to designate, instead of a forty ruble bonus, forty-five or fifty...

Only his new life task creates something akin to character in him, makes him alive, animated:

> He became somehow livelier, *even* firmer in character, like a man who has already defined and set a goal for himself.

On the street at night for the first time, Akaky Akakievich

> walked along in a gay state of mind, he was *even* suddenly, for some unknown reason, about to dart after some lady... However, he stopped right away and again set out very quietly as before, even wondering himself at his gallop which came from who knows where.

And after the catastrophe (and one shouldn't forget that the entire catastrophe consists of the loss of an overcoat!), as Akaky Akakievich is struggling with death,

> finally, he was *even* foulmouthing, saying the most terrible words, so that the old lady, the landlady, *even* crossed herself, never having heard anything of the sort from him in her life, all the more since these words followed directly after the word "your Excellency."

Such is the highest possible stage of the "poor clerk's" protest!

But it is not only the basic line of plot development that is bespeckled with these "evens" which reveal the pettiness of the main hero's life and experiences. The secondary characters—the "Important Personage" to whom Akaky Akakievich brings his complaints against life and fate, Akaky Akakievich's colleagues, indeed the entire surroundings in which he lives, or rather,

147

"exists,"—are no better. Even Akaky Akakievich's fatal invitation to the party is prompted not by the human closeness to him of his colleagues— such closeness between people may indeed arise transitorily, but it does not arise at all in "The Overcoat"!—

> one of the clerks, some assistant, *even,* of the head clerk, probably in order to show that he wasn't a snob in the least and *even* associated with those inferior to himself, said "So be it, I will give a party instead of Akaky Akakievich and request everyone to come to my house for tea: today, as if by plan, is my name day."

The company at the assistant's was the most brilliant: in the anteroom "hung overcoats and cloaks among which some *even* had beaver collars or velvet lapels." The characterization of the "Important Personage" is built by Gogol entirely on "even" and on "breaks." The Important Personage was "in all respects *even* no fool" and "*even* himself felt" some of his shortcomings. The scene in which Akaky Akakievich is scolded by the Important Personage is full of "evens:"

> Here he stamped his foot, raising his voice to such a loud pitch that *even* a better man than Akaky Akakievich would have been terrified;

and when Akaky Akakievich is about ready to faint,

> the important personage was satisfied that the effect had exceeded *even* his expectations, and completely intoxicated by the thought that his word could *even* deprive a man of consciousness.

The Important Personage's remorse is depicted with the help of the same device: "he *even* got to thinking about poor Akaky Akakievich" and "the thought of Akaky distressed him to such a degree that a week later (!) he *even* decided to send a clerk to find out.. how he was." Having learned that Akaky Akakievich "had died suddenly in a fever," the important personage "was *even* left stunned, feeling pangs of conscience, and was out of sorts all day." After spending an agreeable evening with friends, he decides to visit a lady of his acquaintance, a certain Karolina Ivanovna, "a lady, it seems, of German extraction"; the appearance of the corpse drives him into "a dead fright"—manly and heroic in appearance, he

> felt such terror, that not without reason he *even* began to fear some kind of morbid attack. He *even* quickly took off his overcoat from his shoulders himself and cried to the coachman in a voice not his own: "Drive home as fast as you can!" The coachman, hearing a voice which

was usually used at critical moments and would *even* be accompanied by something much the most effective... shot off like an arrow.

This event made such a deep impression on the important personage that "he *even* began much less often to say to his subordinates, "How dare you? Do you understand who is standing before you?"

In the fight against the dead Akaky Akakievich the police too suffer a defeat, and their heroism is characterized with the same word, "even":

An order was given to the police to catch the corpse, no matter what, dead or alive... and they *even* almost succeeded in this.

But when the ghost was already in the hands of the police,

the policeman on duty... burrowed just for a minute in his boot to get out a snuffbox... but the snuff was probably of the sort that *even* a corpse couldn't bear;

the ghost of Akaky Akakievich sneezed so violently that "he splattered all three of them right in the eye." "From that time on the policemen had such a terror of the dead that they were *even* afraid to seize the living..." and "the clerk-corpse began to appear *even* beyond the Kalinkin Bridge."

In this aspect of "even," in the continual "breaks" of the narrative line into pettiness, into "nothingness," Gogol thus reveals the whole vain emptiness of a great love... for an overcoat. Thus, the pettiness of the entire surroundings of the "poor clerk," of Akaky Akakievich's colleagues, of the "Important Personage," who salves his conscience in the company of several friends "of the same rank," is revealed as well, and even the "heroism" of the police, wiped away by a pinch of vile snuff, amounts to "nothing."

5.

The psychological aspect of the story is heightened by the approximation of the author to the hero. It is exactly with the goal of "approximating" himself to the hero that Gogol introduces a narrator who takes everything so seriously. Such an approximation is achieved in "The Diary of a Madman" by the diary form, which allows the reader a glimpse into Poprishchin's soul. Dostoevsky achieves the same result in *Poor Folk* by having his hero write letters. In the Ukrainian tales Gogol approximates his heroes with amazing ease, even to the point of blending with them, through the mediation of his "storytellers" (Foma Grigorievich) and with the help of a mixture of two linguistic strata, the Russian literary language saturated with

Ukrainianisms. But, in some cases ("A Terrible Vengeance," *Taras Bulba*, "St. John's Eve," etc.), the internal significance of what is narrated or, in others ("Christmas Eve," "A May Night," "Old-World Landowners," etc.), the lyrical relation of the author to the "little world" *(mirok)* described by him make the author's task substantially easier. The task of approximating the hero and his internal world is much more difficult in "The Overcoat." As was already mentioned, it is much harder to depict the empty and the insignificant, to portray "nothingness," than it is to show the elevated or the sublime. To force Akaky Akakievich himself to tell the story of his adventures and experiences would be completely impossible, and it is not so simple to create a type of narrator close to Akaky Akakievich.

All the same, Gogol tries where possible in "The Overcoat" to take us into his hero's "internal world," to show us how Akaky Akakievich looks at the world. The perspective from which the world appears to Akaky Akakievich is to a significant degree revealed to us by Gogol with the help of continual repetitions of "even." "Even" points out how many things and people in the world the poor clerk sees from below. The logical sense of "even" actually consists in this: it indicates things and objects that are "high," "lofty," "significant," "inaccessible"... And so much belongs, for Akaky Akakievich and for the narrator of the story, to this higher sphere: overcoats with beaver collars and velvet lapels, state, court and other councillors, who are not subject to the action of those laws of nature and fate under whose power the "poor man" finds himself. Such is the world, as well, of the other characters in the tale: a new overcoat is a most unusual event not only for Akaky Akakievich, but also for his tailor.

The "little world" of the poor clerk appears to him as a great world precisely because it is full of objects which he looks at "from below"! Gogol wanted to make precisely this form of existence understandable to us, hence the innumerable "evens" characterizing the hero's internal orientation, his spiritual posture. The little world *is* the great world: in this contradiction is based the whole tale and all of its action. "The Overcoat" is built on oscillations between contrasting experiences. Gogol takes us into Akaky Akakievich's little world, but we are unable to remain in it, for to be reincarnated into Akaky Akakievich is not easy; therefore, our own conception of his world as a "little world" again and again destroys the illusion that we are in the "great" world experiencing a serious tragedy which decides a question of life or death for the hero. We leave Akaky Akakievich's little world, but Gogol takes us back into it again and again—to a considerable extent with the help of his "even"... The essence of the artistic structure of "The Overcoat" lies in these oscillations between evaluations of the "little," "tiny," "insignificant" (for us, for the reader) and the "huge," "great," "meaningful" (for Akaky Akakievich and for the narrator).

150

6

"The Overcoat" is one of the links in the development of the characteristic theme of the "poor clerk" in Russian literature. The better-known examples of this theme include, along with "The Overcoat," the tales of Dostoevsky already mentioned several times, *Poor Folk, The Double,* "A Faint Heart," "Mr. Prokharchin," etc.

Gogol's plot is the most successful and effective of all the plots used in such tales, calculated by literary historians to number around 200. Later, the "social point of view" ruled exclusively in tales about the "poor clerk." Belinsky understood even Gogol's tale as social protest, a protest against the situation of "poor clerks".... However, if the center of Gogol's tale were actually to consist in this, in a social protest, then wouldn't it have been much more effective to portray a fully worthwhile human being of some depth trapped in a lower grade of the civil service? We shouldn't forget that Gogol himself had, in his youth, to take time from his literary works for fruitless, petty office work.... Of course, the understanding of Gogol's tale as a moral, "ethical" protest ("I am your brother") corresponds more to his own moralistic tendencies, but is Akaky Akakievich really a successful literary type for demonstrating this idea to the reader? One would hardly need to be a particularly proud person to refuse to see in Akaky Akakievich, with his pitiful and comic tragedy, one's "brother." Mustn't Gogol have understood that the plot of "The Overcoat" and the specific nature of Akaky Akakievich's psychology would sooner lead many, so many, readers to recognize Akaky Akakievich not as a brother, but rather, at best, as some sort of distant relative? Are not other tales about the "poor clerk" much more effective, for example, Dostoevsky's *Poor Folk* or "Yakov Yakovlevich," one of the best tales on this theme, by the first biographer of Gogol, P.A. Kulish?

We are unable to pause here to show in detail that the social aspect was one of the least important for Gogol himself. The idea that every human being is "our brother" was for Gogol's Christian world view an axiom which he considered it necessary to remind the reader of, in passing, at the beginning of the tale. But actually, even in this passage, if we read it without preconceived notions, the person who acts like a "man," opposing the "inhumanity" of Akaky Akakievich's colleagues, is hardly Akaky Akakievich himself, but that "young man" for whom "everything changed"! The plot of "The Overcoat" is more vitally connected with the problem of "one's own place" so central to Gogol's world view, a problem later vulgarized in its social aspect into the pseudo-problem of the "superfluous man." (No one noticed the remarkable—ideologically and artistically—answer of Leskov to this pseudo-problem in his story "Righteous Men," where he tried to show that there are no superfluous people.) But in connection with our analysis of "The Overcoat" is given above, we shall now approach the tale's ideological content from a different point of view.

The source of "The Overcoat" is by chance known to us. It is an anecdote heard by Gogol long before the creation of the tale and related by one of Gogol's friends, Annenkov:

> Once, in Gogol's presence, someone told an office joke about some poor clerk who, by extraordinary economizing and unflagging, ceaseless work outside of his official duties, accumulated a large enough sum of money to buy a good Le Page rifle for about two hundred rubles. The first time he went out in his little boat on the Gulf of Finland to hunt, he put the precious rifle in front of him on the bow, and then, according to his own assertion, found himself in a state of oblivion; he came to his senses only upon glancing at the bow without seeing his new acquisition. The rifle had been pulled off into the water by a thick clump of rushes through which he had passed, and all his efforts to find it were unavailing. The clerk returned home, went to bed, and couldn't get up: he had come down with a fever. Only by a general subscription on the part of his comrades, who had learned of the accident and bought him a new rifle, was he restored to life, but he could never recall that terrible accident without a deathly pallor covering his face.... Everybody laughed at the anecdote, which was based on a true event, excepting Gogol, who listened thoughtfully and let his head sink onto his chest....

What did Gogol make out of this anecdote? He replaced the object of the "noble" sport of hunting, a rifle, by a prosaic object of primary necessity. Yet all the same—no doubt, intentionally—he speaks about this object of primary necessity with the language of passion, of love, with erotic language:

> ...he even entirely mastered going hungry in the evenings; but on the other hand he was nourished spiritually, carrying in his thoughts the idea of the future overcoat. From this time on it was as if his very existence had become somehow fuller, as if he had gotten married, as if some other person were with him, as if he were not alone, but some pleasant female life companion had agreed to travel life's road together with him—and that companion was none other than that same overcoat with the thick quilting, with the strong lining which wouldn't wear out.

> ...but for whom all the same, albeit before the very end of his life, there had flashed a radiant quest in the form of an overcoat, which had enlivened his poor life for an instant....

152

The reader is prepared to take such lines more as mockery directed at the poor clerk than as the expression of a real sympathy for him or as the uncovering of a consciousness of brotherhood with him. But several details in Gogol's tale become comprehensible only in terms of this "erotic" aspect. For example, the thief doesn't simply strip Akaky Akakievich of his overcoat but also says "But that's my overcoat!" Is not this night robber some sort of variation on the "strong rival" of traditional love plots? Only Akaky Akakievich's love for the overcoat awakens in him generally erotic experiences: he runs after a charming lady, looks at an erotic picture in the window of a store.... And the very appearance of the ghost in search of the overcoat (Gogol entitled the first draft of his story "The Tale of the Clerk Who Stole Overcoats," which indicates that the final pages are essential and central to the work, and not merely some sort of mischievous, unnecessary ending)— is it not a unique parody of the romantic "dead lover," who leaves the grave in search of his beloved? In this sense, the plot of "The Overcoat" is the famous plot of Bürger's "Lenore," of Zhukovsky's "Lyudmila" and "Svetlana," the theme of stanzas from *Eugene Onegin* (VII, 11 and the variants), of Pushkin's poems ("The Incantation," etc.), of Lermontov's "A Dead Man's Love." It is the theme of the all-conquering power of love, of a love which overcomes even death.

The fine—and, of course, forgotten—literary critic N.N. Strakhov focussed attention on the fact that Dostoevsky's *Poor Folk* is an original "retort," an answer to Gogol's "The Overcoat." This question has recently been beautifully illuminated by A.L. Bem. The overcoat is a meaningless, dead object, replaced in Dostoevsky's work by a live person, a girl, Varenka Dobroselova. The disinterested and timid love of the poor clerk Makar Devushkin is portrayed without a scornful glance from above, without scathing laughter, and without the slightest elements of mockery. The human honor of the "poor clerk" is restored in full!

But did Dostoevsky really understand Gogol's intention? He understood it as little as did Belinsky. As we have already stated, both the "social aspect" and the moral message ("I am your brother") are only accessory motifs in "The Overcoat." The Gogol who wrote "The Overcoat" is the very same Gogol who read the writings of the Church Fathers and the *Philokalia* [expanded in Russian as the *Dobrotoliubie*] and in whom a number of his friends saw a prophet or at least a teacher of life. It is gradually becoming clear to investigators (Zenkovsky, Gippius, Mikolaenko) what a fundamental role religious problems play in the thematics of Gogol's artistic work, and particularly the problems of "spiritual works," the feat of "spiritual combat," as presented in the writings of the Church Fathers. Gogol's letters (and not just his *Selected Passages from Correspondence with Friends*, but his actual letters—which, of course, no one reads!) are not an idle whim of "didacticism," but rather a serious, even if unsuccessful, attempt to gain a real hold

153

on human souls, an attempt at spiritual leadership. The psychological subtlety with which the writings of the Church Fathers elaborated the problems of spiritual combat, the amazing psychological insights of the *Dobrotoliubie*, could they have remained unnoticed by Gogol? Of course not! But we don't want to give here an interpretation of "The Overcoat" taking the writings of the Church Fathers as a point of departure. The immanent critical examination of "The Overcoat" itself brings us to the problems of "spiritual combat." Our observations are merely aimed at emphasizing, above all, that one must expect from Gogol's artistic works attempts to solve complex psychological questions and not a simple repetition of axioms ("I am your brother") and truisms ("even peasants"—and "poor clerks"—"can feel").

The theme of "The Overcoat" is the stirring of the human soul, its regeneration under the influence of a—granted, very peculiar—love. The possibility of the soul's stirring becomes manifest from contact with a love object, and not only with something great, elevated, or significant (an heroic exploit, one's fatherland, a live person—a friend, a loved woman, etc.), but also in meeting something everyday or prosaic. The hero's relation to the overcoat is depicted, as we have seen, with the language of eros. And a man can be ruined, led to the abyss, not only by love for something great or meaningful, but also by love for an insignificant object, if only it becomes the subject of passion, of love.

One of the central ideas of Gogol's artistic works is that each man has his own "infatuation,"* his own passion, something he is "carried away with." The theme is ancient: it is the theme of Horace, of the poetry of the European and Ukrainian Baroque, of one of the *virshi* of the Ukrainian mystic Grigoriya Skovoroda, a poem probably known to Gogol even if only from "Natalka Poltavka" by Kotlyarevsky (a writer from whom Gogol takes part of the epigraph to "The Fair at Sorochintsy"). Skovoroda was an exact contemporary and fellow-countryman of the compiler of the Slavonic *Dobrotoliubie*, Paisiya Velichkovsky (1722-1794). In one of his *virsha* (a spiritual song or devotional verse, sung at Ukrainian country fairs—in Gogol's time, as they still were sung at the beginning of the XXth century—by blind "lyricists"), Skovoroda begins by juxtaposing the gaudiness and sordidness of society's interests and amusements ("Every head has its mind, every heart has its love, every throat has its taste") to the "single-mindedness" of his own spiritual passion ("But I have only one thought in the world, but I alone will not lose my mind"), and concludes with the motley picture of the variety

---

*[The Russian word here is *zador*, usually translated as "fervor," "enthusiasm" or "passion" for something. As V. Gippius notes (*Gogol*, Leningrad, 1924, p. 232), "Gogol didn't find this expression right away; originally he used 'his own hobby,' 'his own attraction.' " We render *zador* as "infatuation" throughout, in order to differentiate it from *strast'*, "passion" in the strict sense of the word, and in keeping with the author's view of Akaky Akakievich's relationship with the overcoat as an "infatuation."]

of human "infatuations," to speak in the style of Gogol. In a passage of *Dead Souls* which V. Gippius rightly recognized as one of the ideologically most important parts of the "poem," Gogol takes us back to the humorous formulation of his fellow-countryman, Skovoroda:

> Every man has his own enthusiasm: one man's enthusiasm is turned to wolf-hounds; to another it seems that he is a great lover of music and amazingly sensitive to all the profound passages therein; a third may be a great hand at putting away a huge dinner; a fourth feels that he can play a better part in this world, even though that part be but a fraction above the one assigned to him; a fifth fellow, whose aspiration is more circumscribed, sleeps and dreams of how he might promenade on a gala occasion with some aide-de-camp, showing off before his friends, his acquaintances, and even those who aren't acquainted with him....[6]

Passions, attractions, "infatuations" are here all directed (except for the love for music, but even that is actually only a "seeming" love!) toward insignificant objects. In the beginning of "Nevsky Prospect" Gogol depicts the "display" of the daily stroll on the Nevsky:

> One displays a smart overcoat with the best beaver on it, another—a fine Greek nose, the third—superb whiskers, the fourth—a pair of pretty eyes and a marvelous hat, the fifth—a signet ring on a jaunty finger, the sixth—a foot in a bewitching shoe....[7]

This "display" is a show of the objects of "infatuation"; what we have here are not even shadows of serious interests.

But in "The Overcoat" the hero's infatuation is lower than anything we come across in Gogol's prose. Nevertheless, Akaky Akakievich does have an infatuation and he puts its object, his overcoat, on display: he shows it to his colleagues, rejoices that he can, "even in the evening," show himself off in his new overcoat. Akaky Akakievich is so passionately carried away with the object of his infatuation that he can, in a way, be included among Gogol's other—serious and humorous—heroes. He has something in common not only with Gogol's "dandies," but also with his "hoarders" and with his "unhappy lovers." The type of the dandy first appears already in Gogol's Ukrainian stories:

> In the old days in Mirgorod it used to be that only the judge and the mayor went around in cloth overcoats lined with sheepskin in the winter and the whole petty bureaucracy simply wore rawhides: now both the assessor and the judge for land disputes have prepared themselves new cloth overcoats lined with astrakhan pelts. The year before last

the clerk and the district scribe got dark blue crepe de chine at 60 kopeks a yard. The sexton made himself nankeen trousers for the summer and a vest of striped worsted. In a word, everyone's becoming a gentleman! ("Christmas Eve")[8]

But even this "infatuation" is, in the case of Akaky Akakievich, reduced to a minimum; he dreams, strictly speaking, only of a necessary bodily covering. In the process of acquiring the overcoat, Akaky Akakievich has taken the road of hoarding or acquisitiveness, thus joining the ranks of Gogol's acquisitive characters. We come across different variants of this type throughout Gogol's work, from the Ukrainian heroes (in the tradition of "buried treasure": "A Bewitched Place," "St. John's Eve") to Chartkov, Chichikov, and the "gamblers." But even here Akaky Akakievich is infinitely lower than all of his fellows: his "hoarding" is hoarding with a limited, practical goal. Akaky Akakievich perishes, strictly speaking, from love; in this respect, he is a strange variant of Gogol's tragically ruined lovers, a type to which Gogol continually returns, from Peter ("St. John's Eve") and Andrey *(Taras Bulba)* to Poprishchin and the unfortunate Piskaryov. Even Chichikov's fleeting attraction to the Governor's daughter turns out to be fatal.... In terms of this type Akaky Akakievich appears as a parody, a caricature, with his ardent love, overcoming death itself, for...an overcoat!

The meaning of this "reduction" of "passions" to the lowest possible minimum becomes clearer to us, perhaps, if we turn to Gogol's correspondence during the period when "The Overcoat" was written. One of the most important themes of Gogol's letters of 1840-42 is the question: is it possible to attach one's being to things of the "external world"? It is a question which Dostoevsky was also to pose to himself ("fixed ideas," a phrase which can be traced back to Pushkin's "Queen of Spades"). For Gogol it wasn't really even a question: he decides it categorically from the first. In a letter to Danilevsky of June 20, 1843, Gogol sharply contrasts the external to the internal life. One must have a "fixed anchor"; since all things of the world are doomed to destruction, a man should have an internal "center to fall back on, by which he could overcome even the very sufferings and grief of life." "The external life is opposed to the internal when a man, under the influence of passionate attractions, is carried away without struggle by the currents of life."

The "center" of which Gogol speaks is the *centrum securitatis* of Christian mysticism, God. Only in the Divine Being are certainty and firmness to be found. It is He who shows a man "his own place" (and every man has one) in the world; God is the "Supreme Commander" for whom we all work. The loss of connection with this center is the loss of one's own place in the world and of life's goal (its "command"). And the surrender of one's self to the external world by binding one's fate with the objects of this world is both the loss of one's center and, at the same time, the loss of one's self. "External life is outside of God, the internal life is in God," Gogol writes; therefore, knowledge of God (as it is traditionally in Christian mysticism) is self-knowledge:

> It is necessary to go deeply into oneself, to question oneself and learn which of our hidden sides are useful and necessary to the world, for there is no unnecessary link in all the world.

In his "Petersburg Tales" Gogol depicts people who are in the process of "losing themselves," or surrendering to the power of the external world. He himself says this about the artist Chartkov ("The Portrait"), who perishes from a yearning for money and fame, from a neglect of the "command" given him by God. The clerk Poprishchin ("The Diary of a Madman") and the artist Piskaryov ("Nevsky Prospect") perish from love for women. Akaky Akakievich perishes from "nothing"! His passionate attraction is directed at an insignificant, worthless object, and he has no center to fall back on whereby he might have opposed the world, or "overcome even the very sufferings and grief of life." A man's ruination is tragic and possible not only from grand passions, from passions directed towards the elevated, sublime or significant, but also from passions directed towards the insignificant and the petty. The whole of the world is rotten and carries man away with it into ruin by attaching onto him its existence, regardless of whether this wordly existence is in the form of something great or—an overcoat.

Even if we were to delineate (which Gogol, as we saw, does not) a "worldly" sphere limited to objects of "legitimate," "permissible" or even simply "intelligible" passions, of passions directed towards the "great" or simply the "large," even in this case Gogol's example in "The Overcoat" would nevertheless remain indisputable. It is probably for just this reason that Gogol chose such an extreme, paradoxical example—for us, for the "public," for the reader. In his letter to Danilevsky the question is one of grave experiences which Gogol himself takes seriously; if even in such a case Gogol considers it possible to speak about the loss of the "internal world," about a concession made to the "external world," then what is Gogol's appraisal of Akaky Akakievich! The world and the *devil* snare men not only with the great and lofty, but also with trifles, not only with ardent love for a woman, not only with a dream of unearthly happiness, not only with mountains of gold, but even with everyday trivialities, with pitiful sums saved up out of pitiful salaries, with an overcoat. If a man's entire soul becomes entangled in such details, there is no salvation for him. The plot of "The Overcoat" is an original treatment of the Gospel parable of "the widow's mite": as a mite, a penny, can be a great sacrifice, so a trifle, an overcoat, can be a great temptation (a thought from the *Dobrotoliubie*). Not only God, but the Devil as well, values such a "mite" correspondingly.

7.

The main hero of almost all Gogol's works, a hero whose name we meet in practically every work, is the *Devil*. In "The Overcoat," the Devil is apparently not mentioned. But, perhaps, only "apparently." The Devil *is* mentioned several times, but only in one passage relating to Petrovich. It is Petrovich who gives Akaky Akakievich the idea of the new overcoat by refusing to mend his "housecoat" and, by the same token, puts the plot into motion. Perhaps it is only a verbal play on the word "devil" when Gogol relates that Petrovich's wife called him a "one-eyed devil" when he was drunk: "he's glutted with rotgut, the one-eyed devil." But Petrovich was sober when Akaky Akakievich came to see him, "and therefore curt, intractable and eager to demand the *devil* knows what prices." Generally, "Petrovich was subject to the whim of suddenly asking the *devil* knows what exhorbitant price...." Perhaps it is also an accident that Petrovich is the owner of a snuffbox "with the portrait of some general, precisely which is not known, because the place where the face was had been punched out with a finger and then pasted over with a square scrap of paper." It is just this faceless general whom Akaky Akakievich sees at the moment when the question of the new overcoat is being decided. *The Devil is faceless!* Well-read in religious literature, a connoisseur and collector of folklore material, of folk songs and legends, Gogol of course knew that the devil appears faceless in the Christian and folklore traditions. And indeed, Petrovich fans the flames of passion, "the most daring and audacious thoughts" of a new overcoat, in Akaky Akakievich's soul. At Akaky Akakievich's second visit Petrovich is drunk, "but despite all this, as soon as he learned what the matter was, it was just as if the devil had given him a push. 'Impossible,' he said, 'kindly order a new one.' "

Gogol did not want merely to present Akaky Akakievich as our "brother." The main task of "The Overcoat" was rather to indicate the danger that is inherent even in details, in everyday trivialities, the danger, the ruin of passions, of "passionate attractions," regardless of their object, even if their object were as seemingly inconsequential as an overcoat. "Even" is for Gogol a means of emphasizing his basic idea: like an arrow, like an unrestrained passionate impulse, "even" takes our thought into the heights only so that it will fall more helplessly, descending back into everyday triviality. Akaky Akakievich's helpless impulse, directed at a worthless object, is "cast down" from an imaginary height ("even") by the Devil, who had actually set such a prosaically fantastic goal for this urge in the first place.

And that this urge, this "earthly" love of Akaky Akakievich, overcomes death itself means, for Gogol, the full loss of self, the loss even in life beyond the grave. Returning from the world beyond the grave to the cold streets of

Petersburg, Akaky Akakievich by the same token demonstrates that he has found no peace beyond the grave, that he is still attached with his entire soul to his *earthly* love.... The sham victory of an earthly love over death is thus in reality the victory of the "killer from time immemorial," of the evil spirit, over a human soul. The Gogolian story of the "poor clerk" is hardly funny: it is terrifying.

8.

We began our analysis with an obvious "detail," a verbal detail in "The Overcoat," the word "even." We saw how important this "detail" is for Gogol, how it is a means of stylizing the tale as colloquial speech, as a *skaz*. We saw that Gogol adapts the same "detail" as a device in the game of his humor and that humor is for Gogol a means of fighting the "pettiness," the devilish "nothingness," of this world, a fact which it is hardly necessary to repeat. We saw that this very same verbal detail is a means of approximating the hero, of understanding him psychologically, of conveying the unique view of the tale's hero "from below." We saw, finally, that this "detail" helps us to understand the idea of the work. The further development of "The Overcoat" in Russian literature (Dostoevsky is reputed to have said, "we all came out of 'The Overcoat' ") could be sketched. It would involve tracing the evolution of the *skaz*, the history of "antithetical" humor, so characteristic for Gogol, the changes in the means of the naturalistic and psychological characterization of the "insignificant" hero, and finally, the evolution of the plot of the "poor clerk" tale (the vulgarization of Gogol's psychological depth into the "social tale"). But here we can only point out these various themes.

It is appropriate to say, in passing, a few words about one point. Our analysis emphasizes the necessity and usefulness of reading and rereading the classics with attention to "details" and "trifles" (M. Gershenson's method of "close reading," A.L. Bem's "method of fine observations"). In searching only for the "content" of literary works, a method which both school and the critics, and in fact the whole tradition of Russian life, have taught us, we overlook a great deal, particularly in the very content of a work, namely, everything in the content that is based on *form* and so intimately connected with it. In the form of a literary work there are no details, precisely because there are no details in a game or in a craft, and an artistic work is simultaneously both a game and a craft. Mountains of prejudices have accumulated around the classics. In order to be freed from them, one must read these works as something entirely new and unknown, as something never before read. By the way, perhaps this is the fundamental principle for the perception of any artistic work, and not only works of verbal art, in general: to approach an artistic work as a "new man," as a newly born viewer and hearer.... It is necessary to be spiritually "born anew" in order to receive the right and possibility of access to the treasure-house of art.

1938

THE SCHOOL OF SENTIMENTAL NATURALISM
(Dostoevsky's Novel *Poor Folk* against the Background of the Literary Evolution of the 1840s)*
by Viktor Vinogradov

I. Towards a Definition of the Concept of the Natural School

In the history of literary forms, esthetic interaction creates a unification of literary works into groups that are customarily called literary schools. The concept of a school is defined not by its personnel, nor by the literary "physiognomy" of the poets included in it, but by the features of plot, architectonics and style that are shared by a homogeneous chain of chronologically contiguous works. Poetic individuality, viewed from a genetic point of view, always entails a complicated interweaving and struggle of varied artistic forms. Because of its very nature it cannot be contained within the frame of any school but rather coexists simultaneously with several schools or, in its subsequent artistic development, draws closer to one or another school. But chronologically it is always possible to identify formal esthetic sets of literary givens that are the essence of a group of literary works. Moreover, the groups of objects thus isolated by literary analysis have a focal "summit" towards which they gravitate that contains each group's constructive elements in complex, individually interpreted interweavings with other influences. Literary manifestoes often serve as the theoretical expression of a school's artistic system. This objective, supraindividual system is to some degree the basis for the work of an artist who belongs to the given school and the background against which individual peculiarities should be measured. Thus the concept of a school is determined by abstracting homogeneous, fundamental traits from a series of chronologically contiguous artistic works that gravitate toward one esthetic center.

There are several dangers involved in defining the fundamental features of a literary school and in artificially isolating the works belonging to it: that of choosing an arbitrary, subjective division as the criterion for classifying the complex of uncharacteristic features and, consequently, of impressionism in the actual grouping into schools. To avoid them one must consider the historical context of the epoch and, above all, the evidence of the artistic

---

*[Translated from V.V. Vinogradov, *Èvoliutsiia russkogo naturalizma* (Leningrad, 1929), pp. 293-390. We have omitted the first three pages of general remarks on methodology.]

perception of its contemporaries.

Contemporaries more clearly perceive the novelty of artistic combinations and discern in them the features of old traditions. Later generations, which have already quite uncritically absorbed artistic forms whose novelty was keenly sensed by their predecessors, have no clear criterion for measuring historical perspective. This is because they seek a justification of their own ripening esthetic tendencies in works of past leaders, regarding past works through the prism of artistic forms that are closer to their own time and spirit.

Therefore, in trying to establish the typical features of the Natural School, which played such a leading role in the evolution of Russian literary forms of the first half of the XIXth century, it is useful to listen to its contemporaries, whether they be its literary opponents, apologists, or impartial observers.

Apropos the Natural School in Russian literary history, it is well known only that it was connected with Gogol's name and finally took shape at the beginning of the forties. Other questions about it—its genesis, the esthetic tendencies that governed it, its devices, and the circle of works included in it —remain without clear answers.

By merely indicating that Gogol was its leader, without describing in detail the devices adopted from him and their functions, one cannot discover the fundamental traits of the Natural School. For Gogol had absorbed elements of varied, even diametrically opposed literary traditions and applied them uniquely; his work could be used to justify the most various artistic trends. Furthermore, as a result of the diversity and indefiniteness of meanings assigned to the word "nature," some contemporaries even traced the genesis of the Natural School to different sources, ignoring Gogol.

Belinsky formulated such opinions in the following words:

> Some say, and quite justly for once, that the Natural School was founded by Gogol; others, while partly agreeing with this, add that the French *école frénétique* (formed ten years ago and defunct soon thereafter) had even more of a part in the birth of the Natural School than had Gogol. ("A Survey of Russian Literature in 1847," *The Contemporary*, Vol. VII, 1848)[1]

Russian writers of the thirties and forties associated the *école frénétique* with the works of "young France": Hugo's first novels; Balzac, who in the early period of his work was carried away by the melodramas of Pixérécourt and the novels of Ducray-Duminil; Lady Radcliffe, M.G. Lewis and other representatives of the Gothic novel; Jules Janin's *L'âne mort et la femme guillotinée*; the works of Sue, Dumas and their followers. The novels of Charles Robert Maturin are also relevant here, as are the works published in Russian translation under his name (such as Thomas De Quincey's *The Confessions of an English Opium-Eater*), inasmuch as, in the words of the reviewer for *The Library for Reading* (1834, Vol. VII), he "was a precursor of the *école frénétique*."

Belinsky resolutely opposed this genealogy of the Natural School and tried to prove that Gogol's influence put an end to the trend connected with the *école frénétique* in its diverse branches. He was basically right in rejecting any direct dependence of the Natural School in its essence on "frenetic" literature, which by the time of the formation of naturalism had gone into the literary underground. But he mistakenly placed Gogol in opposition to the *école frénétique*. In rejecting devices of sentimental, romantic idealization, Gogol temporarily fell under the influence of the *école frénétique* in the early 1830s and creatively reflected its devices in his work. He even deliberately underlined them in "The Bloody Bandore-Player," as Nikitenko emphasized in the censor's prohibition of that work. Generally speaking, the Natural School and the *école frénétique* have closely connected origins.

It is impossible to establish an obvious community of basic devices between the works of the Russian Frenetic and Natural Schools because the main line of literary development issuing from the *école frénétique* led in Russian literature to "rhetorical" Gothic works that had a unique set of plots and that intensified the tragic element by using elaborate verbal formulas (they were parodied by Dostoevsky in *Poor Folk* in the form of excerpts from Ratazyaev's novels, *Italian Passions* and *Yermak and Zyuleyka*). However, such a comparison seemed ideologically possible to close contemporaries of a certain literary camp. This is explained by the fact that discussions of "debased, distorted nature," the representation of which was often discerned in the stories of the Natural School, were raised with particular sharpness when the devices of early French romanticism were transplanted onto Russian soil. Furthermore, from a distance it was possible to see a similarity with the devices of the Natural School in individual peculiarities of depiction that, it is true, were not characteristic of all "frenetic" literature and were toned down in direct Russian imitations. Because it sheds light on the poetics of one literary group that was part of the "frenetic" cycle on Russian soil, the passionate polemic aroused by the appearance of Jules Janin's *L'âne mort et la femme guillotinée* in 1831 is particularly interesting.

Janin's novel, which influenced Gogol's "Nevsky Prospect," presented a series of tales unified around the story of the transformation of a beautiful innocent into a prostitute, ending with her death. It was also an original manifesto of the new principles for depicting nature. The author, immediately declaring himself a firm opponent of sentimentalism, goes on to reveal the reverse, "natural" side of sentimental heroes:

163

What is a shepherd in essence? A ragged wretch, dying from hunger...
and a shepherdess?—a greasy hunk of meat with a ruddy face, red
hands, oily hair, stinking of cow butter and garlic. (Russian translation,
Moscow, 1831)

After rejecting pastoral scenes, Janin examines the chaos of daily city life and
describes "nature from a different point of view." "For me," he writes, "it
has become impossible to see anything in nature besides ugliness." However,
these principles, which were accepted in general form by the Natural School
as well, were developed by Janin in *L'âne mort* not only in order to strip the
sentimental veils from the vulgarity and tragic vanity of daily life, but also
to intensify the depiction of physical tortures and moral agony:

We need a nature that is horrible and gloomy. Picture an operation:
a young, healthy man lies on a wide black stone and two experienced
executioners peel off his skin, warm and bloody, as from a rabbit,
without separating a shred from the whole. That's the nature I have
chosen.

The vast group of Russian "frenetic" novelists enraptured by Marlinsky employed a type of style, rhetorically inflated and abounding in emotional tones
of horror, that corresponded to Janin's "horrible" plot schemes. But within
the boundaries of the "frenetic" cycle itself there was also a tendency to emphasize the terrifying elements of everyday existence.

Jules Janin's novel—and the translations of Hugo *(The Hunchback of
Notre Dame)*, Balzac, Xavier Saintine, M. Masson and others which followed
it—made a strong impression not only on Gogol but also on the entire Russian reading public. The journals, some with exasperation, others in a recep-
tive tone, judged the poetics of these works; the question of the choice of
poetic subjects and the means of depicting them, of "the servile copying of
naked nature," received the greatest attention.

The Northern Bee (1831, nos. 158-161) was quick to remind readers
of the thoughts of Schiller, Schlegel and other romantics on this question,
resolutely defending the devices of a "refined, ennobled representation of
nature":

It is impossible that an educated man should seek in poetry the very
same prejudices, the same low morals, the same spiritual emptiness
which so frighten one in real life. (No. 160)

But all the same, the concept of artistic reality in the "frenetic" cycle is reworked in a direction which sometimes approaches the roots of naturalism.

The ruling forms for the esthetic treatment of nature prohibited the

164

representation of the "lowly," "sordid" aspects of literary subjects. These forms sharply contradicted the typical features of the Gothic novel—grotesque hyperbole of tragic images, horror episodes alternating with scenes full of comic barbs or with a contrasting depiction of vulgarity. Subjects and themes that "lead to lowly, irrelevant presentations" were excluded from literature. Moreover, a strict censorship governing the choice of the verbal symbols themselves was established.

This problem of "naked nature" came up often during the period of keen interest in "frenetic" literature that had begun to subside by the middle of the thirties. Gogol too was confronted by it in the evolution of his work, for which the transformation of the poetics of the *école frénétique* had great significance. Russian "frenetic" literature of the thirties, particularly the group of writers closest to Jules Janin's doctrine of the "horror of the everyday," either partly merges with the Natural School or overflows into it.

It is completely understandable, against the background of these lengthy discussions about the cult of "sullied" nature in "frenetic" literature, that any emphasis on the tragically horrible, on scenes of tortures and executions, any gravitation towards "naked" nature, began to be generally regarded as a development of the principles of the *école frénétique*. Thus Polevoy, attacking the style and devices of depiction in Gogol's *Dead Souls*, wrote:

> The novels of Dickens and the frenetic novels of recent French literature are to be excluded from the realm of belles lettres. . . . After this the waxen depiction of a rotting corpse, scenes of a drunkard retching and twitching from intoxication—can these really be the subjects of art? . . . You say that the mistake of past art consisted precisely in its embellishing nature and placing life on stilts. So be it, but, picking only the dark sides of nature and life, selecting filth, dung, perversity and vice, aren't you going to another extreme, and are you presenting nature and life faithfully? . . . It was possible to complain about the virtuous heroes of the novel during the last twenty years or so, but now, when the contemporary novel depicts the refuse of humanity, when it crosses over into madness and monstrousness, with what other thought are you depicting your Chichikov besides imitation of the latest fashionable literature? (*Russian Messenger*, 1842, No. 6)

Of course, such a comparison offers little help in discovering the formal-esthetic essence of the Natural School. It defines only those pressures to search for new forms that led Gogol, for example, not only to rework the devices of the *école frénétique*, but also to use journalistic miscellanies, the vulgar anecdote, the tradition of Izmaylov and Narezhny, the amusing tales of Scarron, and other "low" genres. Moreover, it raises the more complex question of the relation of naturalism to earlier and contemporary romantic forms and shows the parallelism in the evolution of French and Russian literature. In France, according to Count de la Bart's *Investigations in the Field of Romantic Poetics and Style* (Kiev, 1908, Vol. I, p. 156), "many of the artistic convictions and principles that later lay at the basis of the poetics of the so-called naturalist school" were developed by the *école frénétique*. Likewise, in Russia, the polemical passion against classical sentimentalism in the circle of writers who were exposed to the influence of French romanticism led to the creation of the Natural School, which was based on new poetic principles. In this respect it is particularly interesting that the articles of Janin and Balzac, the leaders of the *école frénétique*, were found in a French edition that played a significant role in turning literary tastes to naturalism, *Les Français peints par eux-mêmes* (1840), or in Russian translation, "The French Described from Nature by the French Themselves" [*Frantsuzy, opisannye s natury frantsuzami zhe*].

The influence this edition had on the forms of naturalist description introduced in the forties was acknowledged by the naturalists themselves. Grigorovich wrote in his literary memoirs: "The famous Parisian edition *The French Described by Themselves* was the forefather of this kind of portrayal." It must be pointed out that precisely under the influence of this edition the tendency toward the "typical" representation of "nature" was strengthened and the word "type" gained wide currency in the Russian literary language. T. Bulgarin, who was the watchdog of the journalistic traditions of the XVIIIth and early XIXth centuries, wrote in his feuilleton "Literary Types":

It has again become fashionable in Paris to make copies from "originals," which they depict with pen, chisel and brush. But, as with the restoration of all old things, a new name was necessary, so that besides the former names—*moeurs* and *caractères*—they use the Greek word *type*, that is, prototype, a first form or original. (*Northern Bee*, 1841, No. 22)

Of course, merely indicating this passion for creating types does not clarify the concept of the Natural School, for the term "type" was used loosely with a variety of meanings, and writers of the most varied literary inclinations began to indulge in the portrayal of types. All the same, one should emphasize that this epidemic thirst for types, this desire to pick marionettes as symbols of particular classes, professions or psychological strata, sometimes even as personified passions, was a characteristic feature of the Natural School. Ivan Panaev, several of whose stories were undoubtedly written in the spirit of the Natural School in the strict sense of the term, says of himself and his colleagues that "we all create types and consider ourselves typical writers" ("Stories without Beginning or End," *The Literary Gazette*, 1844, No. 1).

But while one cannot deny the general influence of these refurbished *moeurs* and *caractères* on the Natural School, their use on Russian soil was so varied that it is equally impossible to claim that the imitation of this French genre was a distinctive feature of the Natural School. The fact is that the gravitation toward nature, toward "realistic" portrayal, was then so general that it cannot be used to elucidate the distinctive features of the Natural School. If it were, one would have to number Bulgarin in the Natural School, for he not only welcomed *The French Described from Nature by the French Themselves* but imitated it in his edition *Sketches of Russian Morals, Or the Front and Back Sides of the Human Race* and in *Mosquitoes*, which apparently derived from Alphonse Karr's "Wasps." In *Mosquitoes*, according to Grigorovich's review, the most successful type depicted was the "beggar woman" [*"Salopnitsa"*], a term introduced into the Russian lexicon by Bulgarin. But his *Mosquitoes*, according to the review of *Fatherland Notes* (1842, Vol. XXIII), "are as innocent, meek and good-natured as lambs."

Even *The Northern Bee* was sympathetic toward "nature," as is clear from its review of a Russian imitation of the French, *Us, Described from Nature by Russians* [*Nashi, spisannye s natury russkimi*]: "In our opinion, the essays in *Us* are true copies from nature, without caricature, but only in certain places are they illuminated by the light of Diogenes's lamp" (1842, No. 250). It is most interesting that Bulgarin himself (in his article on "The Russian Restoration") comically derided what he considered an insufficiently "naturalistic" representation of taverns: "It is obvious that the author wrote about Moscow taverns not from nature but from gossip" (*Northern Bee*, 1843, No. 84). Characteristically, however, Bulgarin, while generally approving the gravitation of the French towards the "gold mine" of types from the petite bourgeoisie and peasantry (a mine which "Rabelais, Scarron and Molière, and other intelligent writers of genius worked with such success"), allowed Russian writers only three "originals" for large portraits: the nobility, the merchant-shopowner class, and the peasantry.

> Particular distinguishing traits of individual persons can serve as the subject for sketches but not for large portraits. The greatest writer would be a tiresome bore if he were to take to describing in detail the way of life, the manners and occupations of some blacksmith, shopkeeper, or cabby. . . . For what is either pointed or interesting in it? . . . ("Petersburg Types," *Northern Bee*, 1841, No. 22)

This limitation related not only to the ideology of types but to thematics and stylistics as well. It is interesting to compare Bulgarin's thoughts with Belinsky's statement about the attacks on the Natural School first for "ill-intentioned caricatures of clerks," and then for the depiction of "people of low calling":

> Writers of the Natural School are now accused of a predilection for portraying people of low calling, for making peasants, house porters, and cabbies the heroes of their tales, for describing the corners and haunts of starving poverty, and often immorality of every kind. ("A Survey of Russian Literature in 1847" [cf. *Selected Philosophical Works*, p. 441].)

Thus, even though there is a superficial similarity between some literary notions shared by the representatives of the various currents in the forties, the understanding of "nature," of "artistic reality," was profoundly different in the various literary systems.

To relate Bulgarin to the Natural School in the strict sense of the term would be absurd, for he rejected "nature" as depicted by Gogol. "It is incomprehensible," he wrote about Gogol's "The Wedding," "that an intelligent man can find pleasure in making filthy statues of unheard-of creatures, and that he can be so bold as to call this nature!... Everywhere, in all of it, there is only caricature, only the distortion of nature" (*The Northern Bee*, 1842, No. 279).

The borders of the Natural School would be quite indefinite if one were to investigate the writers of this period using the formally empty criterion of their interest in "nature" and their "realistic tendencies," as has been done until now by the majority of literary historians. This is particularly clear from an analysis of the sketches which went into the series *Us, Described from Nature by Russians* (1842). It would seem that one could get some idea of the ruling devices of the Natural School on the basis of this edition. L. Brant wrote about this series in his book *An Attempt at a Bibliographical Review, or An Essay on the Last Half-Year of Our Literature from October 1841 to April 1842* (Petersburg, 1842):

> It is time to stop typing officers and clerks! Writers have grown accustomed to looking at them in a distorted mirror, presenting only caricatures and absurdities, although many of them are worthy of the brush of an artist and psychologist, instead of being plastered on some signboard over a barbershop on Gorkhovaya Street.

However, upon analyzing *Us*, the literary historian is struck by the variety of literary devices used by the collaborators to this edition. For example Bashutsky, the author of *Sketches from the Portfolio of a Student of the Natural Class* (a book that had, however, no connection whatever with the Natural School in the true sense of the term), contributed "The Watercarrier," which is characterized by devices of sentimental idealization that aroused some doubt even in *The Northern Bee*, despite the periodical's general approval:

> If all of our classes were to be described in the same spirit as "The Watercarrier" is described, that is, if from every class writers were to take one representative gifted with every virtue, then our books would be something like the Elysian fields, where only virtuous spirits roam. (*Northern Bee*, 1842, No. 1)

The Library for Reading took the occasion to joke: "Bashutsky poured a whole barrel of talent on his watercarrier when one pail would have been quite enough" (1842, No. 2). But *Fatherland Notes*, after declaring Bashutsky's sketch "bad and untrue," directly stated: "Bashutsky is hardly a creator of types or a painter from nature" (1842, No. 2). But even among the other sketches, characterized by different devices, there was no uniformity that would have permitted one to identify the core of naturalist typification. Although the "unfortunate" sketch "An Officer of the Line" was declared a pitiful caricature by hostile critics, the same critics were quite willing to see in Kvitka's "The Sorcerer" and Dahl's "Ural Cossack" "nature, Russian morals as they are, presented in lively, animated, humorous stories" (*Northern Bee*, 1842, No. 285).

Fatherland Notes gave the following opinion of the entire edition of *Us*: "*Us*, instead of becoming a mirror of contemporary Russian reality, from the first only reflected mirages" (1842, Vol. XX).

I have intentionally examined the more primitive genre in the interests of methodology. But even in other literary genres which are usually summarily assigned to the Natural School, one finds the same complex, disparate variety of devices, often even though they share, for example, French influences. However, literary old-believers, discussing "nature," loved to emphasize their independence and contrast it with the servility of the "naturalists" of the Gogolian school before French literature, though there was no basis for such polemics:

> Oh Russian mind, convince our Russian minds that it is time for us to live by our own wits and not to sing with a foreign voice! Tell them that though the French enjoy the sordid secrets of their Paris and the morals of insects and cattle [an allusion to the parody *Les animaux peints par eux-mêmes*—V.V.], *Us* can think up something besides the repulsive types of Russian Frenchmen, and our literature can do without the physiologies of Paul de Kock, and our novels without stinking Petrushkas and tavern fleas that have emigrated and leapt into our literature from abroad. (*Northern Bee*, 1848, No. 84)

169

It is apparent by now that, in order to disentangle the contradictions of the literary struggle at the beginning of the forties, the historian must approach the Natural School taking Gogol's work as his point of departure.

It is clear from the preceding that in attempting to establish the formal-esthetic essence of the Natural School it is insufficient to rely on general and, consequently, empty terminological indications of writers' gravitation toward "nature," with references to the literary genres they chose. One must identify a group of literary works of a given period which have common devices, using as one's criterion the results of an analysis of works that undoubtedly belonged to the true, i.e., Gogolian, Natural School (according to the unanimous opinion of contemporaries).

In particular, one should start with a precise knowledge of the system of devices of the works by Gogol, the commonly acknowledged head of the school, that were cultivated, reworked, and perfected in the Natural School. On the basis of this detailed dissection and comparison, it becomes possible to establish the complex of features that define the concept of the Natural School as a unique literary "system" and to determine finer "dialectal" groupings within it. But this is the task of a separate work (cf. my books *Gogol and the Natural School* [*Gogol i natural'naia shkola*] and *Studies of Gogol's Style* [*Ètiudy o stile Gogolia*].

At the same time it follows from the above sketch that to clarify the connection between the poetics of *Poor Folk* and the esthetic tendencies of the Natural School, the investigator is first obliged to isolate the principles of the Natural School that Dostoevsky developed or parodied in *Poor Folk*. Then he must describe the mixture of other elements accompanying the main line of development that are indirectly reflected in Dostoevsky's perception and reworking of literary systems.

II. Sentimentalism and the Natural School

Dostoevsky stands out in literary tradition against the background of Gogol's work. Whether critics seek to find points of attraction or repulsion, they start with Dostoevsky's deep synthetic perception of Gogol, which proved him the most sensitive of his contemporaries upon his first literary appearance. Critics unanimously assigned Dostoevsky to the Gogolian Natural School, but with reservations:

Although Dostoevsky is perhaps fated to bring the Gogolian school, that is, the Gogolian form and manner, to its *nec plus ultra*, he does not do so in the spirit of those writers who claim so energetically and harshly that it is time, at last, to give the Virtuous Man a rest. (*Finnish Messenger*, IX, 30)

170

Contemporaries immediately sensed that Dostoevsky was transferring Gogol's devices into a different sphere and even designated the frame to which the new talent adapted them: "In Dostoevsky the apotheosis of 'bourgeois virtues' flashes here and there" *(ibid.)*. In subsequent works, e.g. *The Double* and "Mr. Prokharchin," which accomplished the same artistic task, but with a different, fantastic coloring, one reviewer discerned an obscuring of the sentimental frame by the devices of the fantastic tale and called Dostoevsky "a reviver of the fantastic-sentimental sort of narrative" (Annenkov, "Remarks on Russian Literature of the Last Year," *The Contemporary*, 1849, No. 2). But this hardly excluded Dostoevsky from the ranks of the Natural School. In fact, the school of "sentimental naturalism," of which Dostoevsky was the recognized leader, was understood in the 1840s and early 1850s as one of the branches of the Gogolian trend, a branch which developed the forms of "subjective humor" in an original, if one-sided, way (cf. Apollon Grigoriev's articles). The investigator of Dostoevsky's works should try not only to discover the Gogolian elements in his poetics but also to clarify the place he occupied within the limits of the Natural School at a time when the Gogolian manner and the "poor man" motif connected with it had not yet been forced into the background by more complex artistic formulations. Above all, the investigator is faced with the question of the degree to which sentimentalism survived in the Natural School.

Gogol's battle with sentimental forms is one of the artist's great tragedies. Gogol destroyed the sentimental story with its own devices ("Old-World Landowners") or with the devices of the Gothic genre (beginning with "The Bloody Bandore-Player"); he also strove to canonize the "vulgar anecdote" (Senkovsky), which he patterned on the comic grotesque ("The Two Ivans"). Gogol characterized his own work at its height as the antithesis of sentimental poetics and the overcoming of romanticism. But the introduction of new thematics and the restructuring of the "image of the author" sharply changed the function of the sentimental romantic current which, in the "high" style of Gogol's earlier works, had stood out as rhetorical "painting" and esthetic-romantic philosophizing (cf. *Arabesques*). The dream of a synthesis of natural forms with the principles of religious-civic sentimentalism tormented and consumed Gogol. And it is not by chance that, by the very beginning of the forties, even before Dostoevsky's appearance, Gogol's "laughter" had already begun to dissolve into "tears" in the perception of his admirers. But Gogol's literary enemies had a different perspective: the increasingly sentimental, pathetic elements of Gogol's work evoked their jeers and amazement. "Our Homer," wrote Senkovsky,

> by glorifying his dear reworkings of old anecdotes, threw himself into a stormy and dangerous sea. With one hand he grabbed for the horns of goring satire, while with the other, by habit, for the vulgar and com-

pletely unliterary anecdote, renounced his good steed and without the public's affirmation proclaimed himself a comic-satiric-philosophic poet. (*Library for Reading,* LVII, 23)

Nevertheless, despite the "torrent of mockery," civic sentimentalism was on the increase in "natural" literature of the early 1840s. Gogol's "Overcoat" was taken to be a decisive step in the development of sentimental devices within the new poetics of naturalism. In Gogol's stories, plaintive notes of sentimental-pathetic declamation were contrasted with the tone of the comic-grotesque sketch. In "The Overcoat" Gogol's followers heard an appeal for the reconciliation of sentimental forms with the new devices of depiction that Gogol had taught earlier. The elements of farce and of the "vulgar anecdote," which had been used with such noisy success by the predecessors of the Natural School in the mid-1830s, gradually retreated into the literary background. Writers, taking "The Overcoat" as a point of departure, were quick to renovate the old sentimental forms with the Gogolian style. They were also influenced by the "philanthropic" trend of French literature, particularly by George Sand's work.

In order to demonstrate this development concretely, one must focus on a single theme, that of the clerk. Taking this theme, one can show how a group of literary devices that had ruled in the 1830s but were dying out by the 1840s were renovated in a new synthesis by grafting earlier, sentimental forms onto them, and how this entailed the complete transformation of old genres.

The theme of the petty clerk was the basis not only for *Poor Folk* but for the whole Natural School in general. In the middle of the 1840s Shevyryov complained that clerks "provide literature with almost the only material for vaudevilles, comedies, tales, satirical scenes, and so on. All of it almost exclusively exploits them" (*The Moscovite,* 1846, part 1, No. 2, 165-166). "The beaten track to humor in contemporary Russian life, as is well known, is the daily life of people in the civil service," wrote the *Finnish Messenger* (1845, VIII, 16).

> We want reality at all costs, and our favorite hero at present is not the poet, nor the musician, nor the artist, but the clerk, or, if you like, the lease-holder, the usurer, in general the acquisitive person, i.e., the most unpoetic being in the world. (*Finnish Messenger,* No. 1, 16-17)

Although the clerk remained the favorite hero of the naturalist story of the 1840s, the forms of the literary embodiment of this type underwent a complicated evolution. Yakov Butkov (c. 1815-50), a writer who at first tried to mix several elements of Gogol's style with the poetics of Bulgarin (cf. *The Northern Bee,* 1845, No. 243) but then completely freed himself

172

from Bulgarin's influence to become an admirer of Dostoevsky, made much of the clerk in his collection of stories, *Petersburg Heights* (i.e., attics). In reviewing this book, the critic of the *Finnish Messenger* stated:

> The complaint that it's not only the really lazy writer who attacks poor clerks has recently been repeated in all corners of the reading world. Even Lermontov wrote:
>
>> "If anywhere you come across
>> Some really Russian-sounding works,
>> They're doubtless making fun of Moscow
>> Or swearing vilely at the clerks."
>
> They've stopped laughing at Moscow but abuse clerks as before. The fool is a clerk, the deceived husband is a clerk, the scoundrel is a clerk, the rejected, mocked lover is a clerk, the bribe-taker is, to be sure, none other than—a clerk. And all sorts of scribblers mock the poor clerk as they see fit, and especially the petty, meek clerks beset by "calamity." (*Ibid.*, II, 49)

Indeed, in the 1830s the "demon of laughter" had taken possession of Russian literature. Senkovsky mocked this trend:

> Since the Ukrainian farce visited our pompous and decorous literature under the name of humor, wit and gaiety suddenly broke loose among us, and joke-making flew out at us like a volcano. And now we joke and horse around like porters in the steppes. (*Library for Reading,* 1843, LVII, 10)

And the "first swallow" of the new trend, finally hatched in the Province of Poltava, was the celebrated "Two Ivans" (*Northern Bee,* 1836, No. 11). The devices used in this story brought Gogol his greatest number of imitators and lay at the foundation of the comic story about the poor clerk's daily life. And it was through the prism of this story that Gogol's Petersburg tales ("The Diary of a Madman" and "The Nose") were perceived. Even Gogol's "The Inspector General," which was taken as a call for new ways of using the colloquial-spoken style and plot composition, was seen in the light of the "Two Ivans."

Here is the testimony of a contemporary minor writer of this epoch, Leopold Brant. Naming the hero of his short story "The Casket" Terenty Terentevich Terentevy, Brant was quick to separate himself from the crowd of admirers of Ivan Ivanovich Pererepenko (hero of the "Two Ivans") who had adopted the "modish practice of expressing a character's personality by his name and patronymic." "Since that memorable day," he writes,

> when Gogol delivered to the world his tale whose title uses these two
> unfortunate and illustrious names (i.e., Ivan Ivanovich and Ivan Niki-
> forovich), he was followed by a whole covey of imitators who want
> to make people laugh but can achieve this aim only at their own ex-
> pense, i.e., they themselves are ludicrous, boring, and insipid. At first,
> of course, Gogol's work seemed quite amusing and quite, if you like,
> witty. (He is, after all, the Teniers of our literature.) His story had
> the merits of novelty, local color, and originality, merits which, had
> Gogol begun to imitate himself one-sidedly (which many writers do,
> carried away with the sudden success of one of their works), would
> have disappeared even from his writings. How sick we are of his imi-
> tators, among whom, more's the pity, there are a few who are not
> without talent! And it would be fine to imitate the internal character
> of Gogol's creations! But no! This somehow just didn't happen with
> them. They imitate form, details, parts, style, finally, above all, the
> story's tone. This is what captivated them, and this is how they thought
> to captivate the unfortunate public, the public that in gratitude names
> them Gogol's "orchestra." ("An Evening on the Petersburg Side,"
> from the series *A Life's Reminiscences and Sketches,* 1839, part 1,
> p. 173)

The works of representatives of this genre were easily confused with imitations of Gogol's exercises in other stylistic forms, such as the Gothic and
romantic "society" genres in the spirit of the epigones Marlinsky and N.
Polevoy, whom the "naturalists" were later to call "literary lice." Beginning
with the late 1830s, writers of this type supplied worthy material for literary
parodies. We find one such writer in Dostoevsky's *Poor Folk,* Ratazyaev,
who with equal success celebrates *Italian Passions* and the love of *Yermak
and Zyuleyka* in the Gothic style (cf. the works of Khomyakov, Polevoy and
others) and paraphrases the tale of "The Two Ivans" in the "joking-descriptive" style.

But one cannot really represent "Gogol's orchestra," at least up to the
beginning of the 1840s, as a uniform row of grimacing humorists. Any attempt to characterize summarily these precursors of the Natural School is
doomed to oversimplification verging on an outright literary-historical lie.
Nevertheless, one can identify several dominant features which defined the
basic tone of the farces and anecdotes of the 1830s. The more salient peculiarities of the comic stories by Gogol's epigones include: drowning situations in a "greasy literary sauce," using "low" formulas to designate characters' poses, actions, and props; portrait-painting through accumulation of
comic detail, selecting metaphors and comparisons which surround the main

characters with bestial and material symbolism; stylizing "nonsense speech," using narrators who speak like aphasiacs, in an artifically elevated tone but with numerous slips of the tongue and concomitant disruptions of logical connections.

Here one can isolate two main types. One series of stories which had already become rarer by the 1840s was characterized by a stylistic dominant; plots were scanty and the theme set out in the title was sharply broken or the comic effects of the story line *(fabula)* were overthrown by repeated indications that it was all a dream. The architectonics of this type of story deliberately simulated a random collage of segments. The author's main efforts were directed towards the flow of the narrative *skaz,* with a forced tempo of intonational inflections and with unexpected breaks in sentences, or more rarely—towards a stylization of the tongue-tiedness of colloquial speech. Stories of this type were usually arranged in the form of excerpts mechanically joined together and having no real ending.

Such are, for example: "The Story of Who Yelpidifor Perfilevich Was and What Preparations Were Made in Chernograd for His Name Day" ("the beginning of a tale which, perhaps, will be concluded, but perhaps won't," *Literary Gazette,* 1840, Nos. 52 and 80) and the novel *The Voyages and Strange Adventures of the Bald and Noseless Bridegroom Foma Fomich Zavardynin* (1840).

The other series of stories cultivated the petty anecdote in which the esthetic center is located not in the stylistic sphere but in the comedy of things and of the body, and in the architectonics of the plot. True, this type was not clearly differentiated from the type of "joking-descriptive fragments." But in these tales the lyrically ornamented *skaz,* with its fantastic rush of colloquial-spoken intonations, was only partially inserted into a basic narrational stratum of a completely different sort (cf. the episode about the woman's cap in Dostoevsky's "A Faint Heart").[2] Other stories of this sort are written in the style of a "diary," for which the first part of Gogol's "Diary of a Madman" served as a model (e.g., Ivan Pruzhinin's "The Chronicle of an Inhabitant of Petersburg," *Literary Gazette,* 1844). In general, the comic element here was based not on the contrast of emotional, pathetic speech with the irrelevance and insignificance of the subject, not on the esthetic use of "speech disorders," but on the accumulation of comic accessories and scenes or on unique devices for the portrayal of typical physiognomies. Such are, for instance, the majority of P. Mashkov's stories, "Dreams or Tales and Stories of the Russian Nobleman Cockadoodledoo" *(Literary Kaleidoscope,* 1843), Ivan Vanenko's "Another Nose," Sementkovsky's "The Governor's Clerk" *(Literary Gazette,* 1843, No. 47), and "A Strange, Funny and Sorry Incident," a story signed "G." *(The Moscovite,* 1846).

But towards the mid-1840s a gradual differentiation and, moreover, a way of surmounting the cliché is discernible among this class of stories. The pursuit of far-fetched affectation in comic poses and actions begins to abate. The vogue for "noseless bridegrooms," "henpecked husbands," etc., and for plots bordering on farce subsides, which explains why, for instance, the authors of the story-farce "How Dangerous to Give Oneself Up to Ambitious Dreams" in the almanac *April Fool's* hide behind pseudonyms.[3] Similarly, Grigorovich admitted that after writing "The Neighbor" he was almost ashamed to sign his name to it (*Collected Works*, XII, 277). Of course, farcical elements do not entirely disappear; rather, they are inserted into the comic story (cf. the episode in Grigorovich's "The Lottery Ball" where Kuvyrkov's pants suddenly fall down). The construction of the comic story evolves along two lines: 1) the *skaz*-like anecdote, or sometimes a whole series of them woven together in a grotesque pattern which emphasizes the dissimilarity between the episode's triviality and its tragic consequences; 2) portraits built on the typical comic peculiarities of some class of clerks. The reviewer for the *Finnish Messenger* characterized the first form of the comic story as follows:

> We want to see contemporary man, whatever sort he may be, even if, along with all these strong passions and bloody fits, we have to encounter such misfortunes in the contemporary novel as the fact that Ivan Stepanovich was left without an ace in the hole and, stricken with a fit of apoplexy, for three years hasn't been able to tell whether he has a right side or not and lives only with his left, or that Gavril Kondratievich so took to the salted mushrooms at Karp Sidorovich's party that this respectable husband, after stuffing himself with them, suddenly expired, leaving a large family without a crust of bread. (*Finnish Messenger*, 1845, No. 2, 16-17).

One often finds in this cycle of stories a single feature of the hero which stands out so much that it completely determines the way comical accessories are accumulated around it. Thus one of the more mediocre "naturalists," Mashkov, in his story "Adam Adamovich Adamheim," lays bare the devices of construction of the satirical story:

> My hero is, in specific respects, a man not at all remarkable, but as a general character type he has one sharp distinguishing feature, and this feature is infinite avarice. Bah! And what could be better? I will call my hero Adam Adamovich, this will designate the greatest avarice, and in order to relate this avarice to him even more closely, I will raise it to the third power, i.e., I will add the surname Adamheim.

In the works of pale stylizers, such a story could easily develop into a series of the hero's adventures, in which case the central passion usually acted as a core around which several appropriate anecdotes were wound. Thus, Adam Adamovich is too stingy to waste money on a new hat and buys a dead man's hat from the caretaker of a cemetery; his colleagues appear to him in the form of the dead man come for his hat. A second anecdotal incident, which finally does Adam Adamovich in, is attached to the first. In answer to the pressing entreaties of a certain beneficent family, Adam Adamovich takes them out for a ride, but in such a decrepit old carriage that it falls to pieces in public. The ladies, who have fallen into the mud, threaten to steal the miser's wallet; he goes out of his mind from terror.

In the works of several writers, for example Butkov, the anecdotal nature of the story line was sometimes increased by the addition of moralizing sentiments. In such a case, the reasoner's tone entered into the tale's construction as a formulative element. But, because of the absence of a sharp stylistic demarcation between the speech of the characters and the author's *skaz,* this feature of Butkov's stories was initially seen as a result of Bulgarin's heritage. And even later, when the poetics of the Natural School had moved in the direction of *moralité,* the critics continued to blame Butkov for expounding the results of his analysis of the daily life and psychology of clerks "from his own person on the first page of the story, and then through his characters" (*Finnish Messenger,* II, 7). Novelists of this type were continually accused of filling their works with diverse "sidewalk gossip and personal incidents" (cf. Mashkov's introduction to the book *A Literary Kaleidoscope,* 1843).

In stories of the portrait genre the plot is constructed on a "biographical" basis, often closing with a comic or lyric ending. The scope of variations in such stories was extremely wide, from a series of diverse comic pictures surrounding a single typical physiognomy, to the description of a group of figures frozen in comic poses in some part of the capital, for example on Nevsky Prospect. Such are Ivan Panaev's "Mornings on Nevsky Prospect" (*Literary Gazette,* 1844, No. 1-2) or "Sketches from a Portrait Gallery" (*Ibid.,* 1840-41).

These types of naturalist stories continued even after the mid-1840s, following the development of trends determined earlier.

As late as the mid-1840s the Natural School did not depart from the principles of construction used in its early stories, and continued to be characterized as a school which "is ashamed of the sentimental and the pathetic" (*The Northern Bee,* 1845, No. 236). Its literary opponents felt that the forms of naturalism had ossified as a result of its opposition to the poetics of "embellished nature" (i.e., sentimental-romantic idealization): the cult of "sordid" details, the purely external depiction of "naked" nature, the stylization of awkward colloquial elements and the penchant for vulgarisms and the specific lexicon of professional, dialectal speech, particularly that of clerks.

The Northern Bee, in an article on Gogol's *Correspondence with Friends,* attempted to explain Gogol's success and the development of the Natural·School in terms of literary history, emphasizing in the principles of the new poetics its battle with sentimental-romantic trends, and, as before, characterized Gogolian "naturalism" as a gravitation towards farce:

> Having endured the solemn odes of Derzhavin, the epics of Kheraskov, the sentimental tales of Karamzin, the romantic-idealistic poetry of Zhukovsky, the anthological poetry of Batyushkov, the classical trage-dy of Ozerov. . . not knowing where to hide from the countless imi-tations of historical and moralistic novels. . ., not knowing how to escape the verses of young poets seduced by the noisy fame of Push-kin . . . supersaturated by the elevated, the dramatic and the senti-mental,—the public no longer wanted to sigh, cry and be pensive any longer; other amusements, similar to farce, were hardly alien; from the first tier of the theater the public was even ready to move to the rough benches of a greasy tent, where some sort of entertainer would begin to clown in front of it and make it laugh with desperate grimaces. (*Northern Bee,* 1847, No. 67)

The literary old-believers continued to think this way.

But in the midst of the Natural School itself, after the appearance of Gogol's *Dead Souls* and "The Overcoat," the search for a new synthesis intensifies. Turning to the pronouncements of the Natural School's ideo-logists and sympathizers, it is easy to catch the general drift of this aspira-tion, which had not yet been realized at the beginning of the 1840s.

> By "ideal" they now understand not an exaggeration, not a lie, not childish fantasy, but a fact of reality as it really is; but a fact that is not copied from reality, but conveyed through the poet's imagination, illuminated by the light of general (and not exclusively private and accidental) meaning, elevated to the pearl of creation, and therefore more true, more faithful to itself than the most slavish copy from reality is faithful to its original. (*Fatherland Notes,* 1843, No. 1)

Belinsky set the tone. The critical articles of the *Literary Gazette,* which published some of the most primitive examples of the anecdotal tale and of the physiological sketch, emphasized the necessity of a "lofty idea" in the description of the "slime of trivia." In an article entitled "A Survey of the Principal Works of Russian Literature in 1843," Belinsky, after a characterization of "greybeard" and "commercial" literature, wrote with condemnation:

> Most writers are occupied with trifles, sing the praises of the moon, of a maiden or champagne, and narrate with ingenuous complacency and without the slightest trace of irony inventions which are often very entertaining, but lack any sort of idea. [Cf. Belinsky, *Selected Philosophical Works*, p. 205]

Further on there are references to the already-effected breach with the romantic tradition and to the Natural School:

> Lastly, we have another literature, one that is just arising, that can barely count more than a dozen true representatives, but that is more fertile and.vital than all the others put together... Now we won't go into fits of weeping and rush out to buy *Abbadoñas*, or *Emmas*, or *The Bliss of Madness* [works by N.A. Polevoy]; we won't applaud works in which there is neither a faithful measure of reality, nor mature and powerful thoughts, but merely an unearthly maiden, or a dream floating in the ether, or love nourished on sighs and sentimental phrases... We will no longer acknowledge the vulgar reasoner who distorts our reality, edifying us with sentiments taken from the ABC's, as a moralistic-satiric writer worthy of attention. [*ibid.*, p. 206-07]

In connection with the developing tendency toward moralistic civic "philanthropy" that was sometimes the basic formulating factor of the naturalist story, and with the increasing effort to depict types as expressions of the uniqueness of certain professional and psychological classes, the criteria of evaluation changed. The *Literary Gazette*, for instance, denounces "the vaudeville wit of literary farces, satirical allegories, humorous albums" by Mashkov (The *Literary Gazette*, 1844, No. 22). Belinsky contrasts social novels and stories with the previous brand of "satirical Quixotism" ("Russian Literature in 1843," *Fatherland Notes*, 1844, No. 1). The thematics of the naturalist story become newly oriented toward sociology. Ivan Panaev— "the skillful painter of Petersburg daily life"—concludes his parody of the "literary lice" with a moral:

> The time of childish, inflated, rhetorical ecstasies and sensitive sighs has already passed, and people are appearing who, through the laughter the world sees and the tears it doesn't see, are beginning to examine the reality which surrounds them. But the dissonant and nonsensical cries of the literary lice continue to drown out the sometimes loud and mighty word of the man of conviction. (Ivan Panaev, *Works*, I, 532)

Even the *Northern Bee* dimly caught echoes of the new trends:

> At present the vogue is to hunt up and forcibly, so to speak, wring out of the most usual and simple situations some sort of imaginary, highly significant side, to closely analyze the "internal world" of a soul and heart, in other words, to make a mountain out of a molehill. (1846, No. 22)

In the course of these new quests, a new device was used in reworking the traditional theme of the petty clerk, that of emphasizing the contrast between the clerk's external insignificance and the "majesty" of the idea with which he has become obsessed. The image of an unseemly wretch who succumbs under the burden of a "great" goal, of the petty clerk with "ambition," appears already in Yakov Butkov's *Petersburg Heights*.

The content of the new principles of literary construction and the method of embodying them artistically in tales about clerks are clearer in the criticism of the *Finnish Messenger*. Reviewing *Humorous Stories of Our Time Published by Abracadabra*, the journal's critic saw fit to lecture the author, who

> ought to know that in bare stories of external adventures there is no humor as such, but rather ill-mannered mockery. In the works of Gogol and his followers the pitiful exterior is everywhere in conflict with glimmerings of the best of the internal; true humor consisted in and will consist in this principle. (1845, No. 8)

Arming itself against the established cliché of crudely comic descriptions of clerks, the *Finnish Messenger* indicated a means for overcoming this set tradition and suggested devices for a new treatment of plots taken from the world of the petty bureaucracy:

> After all, not all of them are such wretches. They really have many other aspirations, they are agitated by their own concerns, and what concerns! . . . It is necessary in portraying the clerk to remember above all that you are portraying a man; and if even a spark of love for those greater, lesser and equal to you in stature is concealed within your breast, then, believe me, you will not be so eager to laugh at the awkward figure of the clerk; you will not simply describe only the ridiculous exterior, and your portrayal will not be a dead, cold exaggeration of inadequacies. Remember Akaky Akakievich in Gogol's tale "The Overcoat"! (*Finnish Messenger,* 1846, XI, 47)

The "bulwark of naturalism," *Fatherland Notes,* gave the signal for such speeches. Commenting on Butkov's tales *(Petersburg Heights),* in which the reviewer for the *Illustration* saw the basis for Dostoevsky's depiction of nature in *Poor Folk, Fatherland Notes* singled out one of them, "The First Day of the Month," as "an unsuccessful attempt to solve the gigantic problem of humanizing, in other words, of artistically portraying, a scoundrel." Belinsky's sermon was keenly felt by the writers of the Natural School, and they sought a quick artistic solution to the questions he posed.

These deliberations by the theoreticians of naturalist poetics called for the reworking of sentimental symbolism in a naturalistic spirit, or rather, for the infusion into the naturalist comic story of "philanthropic" tendencies, which were also supposed to influence the way typical physiognomies were depicted. The new genre of the social-ideological story was developed. This task, of course, incited writers to turn to sentimental forms with the aim of renovating them. Gogol's "The Overcoat" served as a stimulus for the Natural School in this respect. "The Overcoat" was itself a destruction of the comic cliché in portraying the adventures of the titular councillor. Gogol even underscored this aim in the final draft of the story:

He was what they call a perpetual titular councillor, about which, as is well known, various writers who have the praiseworthy habit of attacking those who can't bite back have japed and jibed their fill.[4]

In line with this tendency, the grotesque pattern is complicated by the insertion of the "humane" episode; the original tone of comic "mockery" is softened, and the entire short story, the first draft of which merely contained a stream of comic details clustered around Akaky Akakievich's personality, underwent an essential alteration of its compositional plan. V.V. Rozanov's observations about the genesis of the type of Akaky Akakievich[5] characterize not a method of compositional revision common to all of Gogol's work, but rather a chronological change in Gogol's artistic aims that led him to seek a new synthesis with the very artistic forms he had earlier demolished. In view of this, one is forced to conclude that B.M. Eikhenbaum failed to evaluate the historical acuity of Gogol's artistic intention in the revised version of "The Overcoat." His article "How Gogol's 'Overcoat' is Made" contains interesting remarks on several of Gogol's stylistic devices but does not reveal the artistic structure of the tale.[6]

The new directions for poetic creation that the followers of the Natural School extracted from Gogol's tale can be most easily revealed by analyzing, however briefly, a story by Grigorovich, "The Theater Carriage" (*Literary Gazette,* 1844, No. 45). It almost seems as though the author had "The Overcoat" in front of him while he was writing this story, even though the compositional plan of Gogol's story was altered in Grigorovich's by making the "humane" episode the dramatic climax. The punning style clearly imitates Gogol ("Ivan Ivanovich let out a small bellow"... "a bald spot, which had appeared while he was still only twenty, it is unknown under what circumstances," and so on); comic details are emphasized ("A divan crammed with cobblestones," "they lowered him into the prompt-box by his coat-tails," etc.); episodes are strung together with unrestrained chatter ("we will introduce a small anecdote"). The narrative is suddenly cut in two by a touching episode in which a compassionate young singer intercedes on behalf of the prompter ("someone, the kind soul, had just suggested that they lower him by the coat-tails into the prompt-box, when suddenly a tender voice was heard amidst the laughter: 'Gentlemen, please, leave him alone! What has he done to you? I beg you to leave him alone!' "). There then follows the spiritual transformation of the prompter, drawn in sentimental colors:

> The poor man was unable to come to his senses for a long time. A strange and ineffable feeling took possession of Ivan Ivanovich. He, who in the course of twenty years had met with only mockery and reproaches, unable to find a soul who would take an interest in him— and suddenly! Oh, it is impossible to express the old prompter's agitation! He was ready to leap out of his box, to throw himself at the singer's feet, to thank her... huge tears streamed down his cheeks.

This scene results in a break in the plot. The poor prompter's fate is interwoven with the singer's; her illness causes him to go insane. The sentimental element present in the transition to the description of the prompter's madness yields to the earlier naturalist stylistic forms in the remainder of the story. The actual description of the prompter's madness is an anecdotal fantasia of visions arising from illness, with various comic reversals, and the account of the prompter's dismissal from work which follows is hardly sentimental. But even in these scenes there is an occasional sentimental note:

> The backstage society found an inexpressible pleasure in tormenting him; his fate, probably, was thus preordained, and there is nothing we can do but feel sorry for him.

Agafiya Tikhonovna's stylized chatter about the peculiarities of the prompter's madness serves as an ending, with an ironic break in it:

> This is all I could learn about Ivan Ivanovich. Perhaps I would have learned a bit more, but the conversation somehow switched to the interesting subject of the cost of firewood, beef, and the like, appur-

182

tenances indispensible in housekeeping.

This was one particular form of the sentimental-naturalist story that was emerging.

The call for a functional transformation of sentimental symbols, which, while preserving traces of their historical past and therefore recognizable as sentimental, acquired new meaning in the context of naturalism, could hardly have come as a surprise to one group of Gogol's early collaborators that was counted as part of the Natural School in the 1840s. At the head of this group were Kvitka and Grebenka. Contemporaries called them Gogol's followers, often without reservation:

> Gogol's followers, Osnovyanenko [Kvitka's *nom de plume*], Panaev and Grebyonka, caught many of the purely humorous features of provincial and Petersburg life. ("Remarks of a Petersburg Idler," *Repertoire and Pantheon,* 1844, No. 4, 452)

But in fact the relation of these writers, and particularly of Kvitka, to Gogol was extremely complex. Kvitka's literary activity proceeded in lively interaction with Gogol's work. The question of whether Kvitka's comedy "The Visitor from the Capital" influenced Gogol's "The Inspector General" is, in my opinion, most correctly answered in the affirmative. At the least it is indisputable that Gogol was acquainted with the play and its literary tradition during the period when he was working on "The Inspector General." One can see how widespread this comedy was in the literary circles of the 1830s by the fact that one of the very popular writers of that time (who was later admired by Dostoevsky as well), Weltmann, printed in the *Library for Reading* (1835) a half-comedy, half-tale entitled "Provincial Actors," in which the influence of Kvitka's comedy is even more transparent and stronger than in Gogol's "The Inspector General." Moreover, the connection of Kvitka's works with elements of the Gogolian style is obvious, if only in the novel *Pan Khalyavsky.* On the other hand, in Ukrainian literature Kvitka is considered a representative of the sentimental trend, and actually, several of Kvitka's tales are constructed on the traditional pattern of sentimental thematics (e.g., the story of the abandoned orphan in the tale "Gannusya"). Nevertheless, contemporaries related Kvitka to Gogol's school, although he touched upon Petersburg themes only slightly.

Grebyonka, who in the late 1830s and early 1840s was considered one of the most eminent representatives of the Natural School though Gogol himself ridiculed him, had a much wider plot range. True, in his works Gogol's artistic influence was superficially reconciled with the influence of Zagoskin and Marlinsky, but the Gogolian manner is present in such works as "Stories of a Piryatinets," "The Stepmother and the Young Lady," "A

Sure Cure" (in a too obvious stylization of *Evenings on a Farm Near Dikanka* and "The Diary of a Madman") and stands out distinctly in stories of another of his cycles too. Interruptions of a basically comic style by passages characterized by an elevated lyrical ascent or sentimental "loquaciousness of heart" were already usual devices for Grebenka in the early period of his literary activity; by the period prior to his death, from the mid-1840s, the sentimental element had decisively won out.

It is interesting that the marked sentimental coloration of Dostoevsky's *Poor Folk* was understood by several of his contemporaries as a deviation in the direction of that literary group. "The comic here is somehow artificial and constitutes an obvious imitation of the tone, colors, and even the language of Gogol and Kvitka," wrote the *Contemporary* (1846, v. XLI, p. 273). *The Northern Bee* seconded this interpretation, saying that Dostoevsky "in the tone of his story wanted to combine the humor of Gogol with the naive ingenuousness of the late Osnovyanenko" (1846, No. 25).

If for Kvitka, Grebenka, and a small group of other writers the deviation toward sentimentalism did not result in any essential changes in the devices of their works, then the latest writers of farce and satire, who had wanted to be "equal to the age," found themselves in a somewhat embarrassing position, unable to give a real response to the challenge of synthesizing the naturalistic and the sentimental. They got out of it by forcing first the "author" and then their clerk-heroes to spout "moral observations, advice, reasonings, and philosophical deliberations."

Feklist Paramonovich Vertikhvostov, the hero of the diverting adventures in the series *Humorous Stories of Our Time Published by Abracadabra* (actually Mashkov), in the time he doesn't spend involved in love intrigues, "thinks for whole days, having nothing better to do, about the destiny of man and of the clerk in particular." After lifting a drunken peasant out of the gutter and giving him ten rubles to set him straight, Vertikhvostov

> felt satisfied all day at having done a good deed and thought to himself how little is sometimes needed to make a man happy for the rest of his life. Why then don't rich men think about this? It seems to them that they have already done their part by tossing a sop to a beggar in order to rid themselves of the importunate fellow and don't worry about what will happen to him in the future. No! If they were for one moment to put themselves in the position of the needy person, they would provide for entire families for their whole lives, often with just a little help. ("Happiness from a Dog," January 1846, p. 26; cf. Makar Devushkin's deliberations along similar lines.)

The adventures of Feklist Paramonovich follow the usual route of the sentimental novel, and the author himself often comments on the devices of sentimental construction: "My readers, I think, noticed in the first chapter of the adventures of Feklist Paramonovich that he is by habit somewhat sentimental" ("The Commissioner of Private Commissions," p. 11).

The story of Agrafena Petrovna, a tale from this cycle of Mashkov's humorous stories, provides interesting material for a characterization of the devices used by writers of Mashkov's type, especially since its plot shares a common origin with the history of Varenka Dobroselova. Agrafena Petrovna is a seduced orphan in whose fate Vertikhvostov took a part. "I was completely happy until my sixteenth year," she writes. But her father soon ruined himself financially: "My unhappy father visibly melted like wax. Often, turning his dimmed eyes to me, he would dissolve into tears. I read in these troubled looks all the grief of the horrible future awaiting me." The father dies and a relative takes the orphan into her charge. "This beneficent act of a woman who had until that time persecuted me with jeering and contempt greatly touched me." But the relative turns out to be a procuress and, after lulling Agrafena to sleep, hands her over to a rich man named Slavin.

Feklist Paramonovich enters in the role of the unfortunate orphan's comforter. He "kissed her little hands, showered her with all sorts of tender words, promised to take care of her as if she were his own sister." Then there follows a sharp break in tone:

> How we are carried away by the feeling of sympathy when the object of it happens to be a pretty woman. He dared to imprint a fiery kiss on her coral lips, a kiss from which all his nerves started trembling as from an electrical shock. Then she returned him the kiss. Women know how to be grateful. That is their weakness. Little by little the kisses became more and more frequent, more and more passionate. And the unworthy Slavin was entirely forgotten. And it serves him right!
>
> Such are the goings on in Kolomna. Foreigners think that we are incapable of feeling. You are quite wrong, dear sirs!

Thus, in the work of a writer like Mashkov who is more experienced in composing literary farces, earlier devices are mechanically adapted to the new artistic demands that had been drafted in the mid-1840s by the theoreticians of the Natural School in relation to the traditional themes of the poor clerk. As a result the portrayal of the hero is patchy, influenced as it is by two conflicting styles.

This return to sentimental forms was not simply a refuge for the Natural School from the farce and the crudely comic stories of the mid-1830s and early 1840s. It was conditioned by extremely complex causes; one of the main ones was a desire to overcome the comic canon of Gogol's

185

"epigones." The quest for new literary forms led to the new ideational "load" of the story, to the insertion of philosophical, social, and other "extra-literary" material into artistic works. Finding support in the personal initiative of a leading writer ("The Overcoat") and in the parallel "philanthropic" trends of French literature, the deviation in the direction of "civic," social, and philosophical sentimentalism provoked a revival of a set of sentimental plot schemes, devices of depiction, images, stylistic accessories, and symbolism. All this acquired new functional content upon entering into a complex synthesis with the poetics of existing literary currents. As a result, individual artists created completely unique forms of sentimental-comic stories, "bourgeois" naturalist novels, family novels, and so on. This movement swept up F. Dostoevsky, Grigorovich, Turgenev, Nekrasov, M. Dostoevsky, Kudryavtsev, L. Tolstoy, and a series of other more minor writers and aroused their interest in Russian and foreign forms of sentimentalism from the XVIIIth and early XIXth centuries. The diverse aspects of this "civic sentimentalism" of the 1840s require careful study, for this new trend split the Natural School into several branches and, in its evolution, eliminated the Natural School entirely to give rise to new literary groupings.

And in this growth of sentimental trends, Dostoevsky's *Poor Folk* played a unique role.

III. *Poor Folk:* Plot and Architectonics

1.

Poor Folk takes the traditional form of the sentimental bourgeois novel: a correspondence between lovers which includes a diary expounding the *Vorgeschichte* of one of them and has a tragic ending. In this genre as practised by past literary schools it was the hero who kept the "diary," so that, understandably, the heroine was the center of action. The sentimental style ("loquaciousness of heart") was most clearly developed in the letters of the heroine, characterized by sharp emotional oscillations which accompanied the flow of the novel and around which reminiscences about the past were arranged. A typical example of this can be found in "The Diary of Faldoni" from Léonard's novel *Teresa and Faldoni, or the Letters of Two Lovers Who Lived in Lyons* (Russian translation, 1816). In *Poor Folk,* on the contrary, in keeping with the poetics of the Natural School, in which there was a ban on sentimental love and beautiful heroines, and in which, in any case, the heroine was allotted only a secondary role, the "diary" is given over to Varenka Dobroselova for different purposes. She is necessary in the novel mainly as an *addressee,* who provides replies which provoke changes in the emotional background of Devushkin's letters and propel him into one or another action. It goes without saying that the central figure in *Poor Folk* could only have been the traditional hero of the Natural School, the titular councillor, who is seen in a new light as the result of being placed for the first time in the framework of the bourgeois novel. Dostoevsky's contemporaries all noted this distribution of roles. For instance, Nikitenko wrote: "The girl in the novel is entirely sacrificed to its basic idea, so that hardly anything feminine is left in her. She is well-built, and correctly, but you feel that she is built out of stone."

The novel's general sentimental design determines even the names of the main characters. Devushkin [from *devushka,* 'young girl, maiden'] is a "virginal, benevolent old man," with the corresponding first name *Makar,* from which, according to his own admission, "they made a proverb."[7] Dobroselova [from *dobroe,* 'good' and *selo* 'village'] has the first name *Varenka,* which goes back to the titles of sentimental novels of the beginning of the XIXth century (such as Ducray-Duminil's *Katenka, or the Child of Misfortune*). But the names of the main characters in *Poor Folk* are interesting not only as an indication of a sentimental tone complicated by humor (*Devushkin* is at the same time Makar). With sharp and intentional emphasis, these names also symbolized a literary displacement of old sentimental themes and heroes, which, like *Teresa* and *Faldoni,* were supposed to serve the heroes and general tendencies of naturalist poetics. It is not by chance that Teresa and Faldoni, whose names "were for our most beloved writers the crowning ornament of their compositions,"[8] are made into servants carrying out Makar Devushkin's errands.

In order to provide comic motivation for Devushkin's sentimental frame of mind, the "circle" of his past reading is revealed (letter of July 1st): next to Zhukovsky's "The Cranes of Ibicus"[9] there is a reference to the "nonsensical" novel of "dear" Ducray-Duminil, *The Little Bell-Ringer* (Russian translation, 1820, *The Boy Who Played Various Tunes on Little Bells*). Similarly, Devushkin's "moral" deliberations on man, obligatory for the "bourgeois" sentimental novel, are justified by his statement that he read "an intelligent composition," a university course of the 1830s on moral philosophy: *A Picture of Man, An Experiment in Moral Reading on Subjects of Self-Knowledge For All Educated Classes by A. Galich* (Saint Petersburg, 1834). This "intelligent composition" dedicated to man's enlightenment had the aim not only of "contributing to the progress of general science or philosophy," but also of "furnishing instructive reading to enquiring youths, to business men, artists, literary men, and finally, to those of that respected age which is no longer able to find nourishment in novels, dramas, and the pages of periodicals, but which appreciates the pleasant only in the form of the useful" (Foreword).

Devushkin's reading of Pushkin's "The Stationmaster" and Gogol's

"The Overcoat" has a quite special significance. One should define the function of Devushkin's "reviews" of these works only in terms of an analysis of the plot construction of *Poor Folk*. But first it is necessary to clarify Dostoevsky's *motives for choosing precisely this form of the sentimental novel.*

What attracted Dostoevsky above all was the characteristic demand in works of the Natural School for a scant, uncomplicated story line—"Life is simple..."—with a wealth of accessory details. By the time Dostoevsky wrote *Poor Folk* this demand had to be reconciled with the psychological use of the naturalistic background for an internal characterization of a "microscopic personality." A lack of "external content" is indissolubly connected with the epistolary form of the sentimental novel. All of Dostoevsky's contemporaries knew this, as they also knew that the choice of this genre presupposed particular artistic interests—in the detailed presentation of surroundings and daily life *(Kleinmalerei),* in the psychological analysis of "microscopic joys and sorrows," and in producing new forms of poetic style. Even *The Northern Bee* wrote about this: "Letters are a form of narration that demands an unusual talent by which the lack of eternal content might be redeemed (cf. Rousseau's *La Nouvelle Héloïse,* George Sand's *Jacques*)." Meanwhile, "involvement in the twists and turns of a personality" *(Moscow City Register,* 1847, No. 51) constituted the subject of Dostoevsky's particular artistic concerns. The critics noted this tendency: "microscopic joys and sorrows, petty sufferings, which had already long ago become standard stuff for narrators, are taken by the pens of Mr. Dostoevsky and Mr. Butkov to the greatest extremes" *(Moscow City Register,* 1847, No. 116). Dostoevsky himself understood his relation to preceding literary traditions in this respect quite differently and, of course, more correctly:

> The old schools are vanishing; the new ones don't write, they scribble. All talent dissipates in one wide stroke, which reveals a monstrous unfinished idea and the muscular effort of the stroke, and the whole business dissipates into insignificance. (Letter to M. M. Dostoevsky, March 24, 1845.)

The analytical finishing of details, not only of the external surroundings but also of psychological vibrations, the filigreed delicacy Dostoevsky so prided himself on, fits most conveniently into the framework of the sentimental epistolary novel. In this form, freed from the complications of the story line, petty events accumulate and are colored by the main characters' quickly changing emotions and "moral" deliberations. In *Poor Folk* it was particularly important that the "poor people" themselves speak about themselves, about their own and others' lives. They themselves reveal, as it were, the thematics of their own literary embodiment.

2.

The concentration on style and the resolution of a definite artistic problem are extremely significant in Dostoevsky's first novel. It is just this which determines the unique position Dostoevsky occupied; it is here one finds the roots of his transformations of the literary system of naturalism which resulted in an original synthesis of artistic forms that was strikingly novel. Not by chance was Dostoevsky agitated when he saw how this side of his novel was misunderstood:

> They don't understand how it is possible to write in such a style. They have become accustomed to seeing the author's mug in everything; I didn't show mine. And it doesn't even occur to them that Devushkin is speaking, and not I, and that Devushkin cannot speak in any other way. They find the novel longwinded, but there is not a superfluous word in it. (Letter to M.M. Dostoevsky, February 1, 1846)

By this declaration Dostoevsky was emphasizing the fact that one could speak about the stylistic innovation of *Poor Folk* only in terms of Makar Devushkin's style. And actually, it is quite easy to show that the image of Varenka Dobroselova and her style—which was transferred from the heroines of the bourgeois novel to the diary of a sentimental pensionnaire (cf. Nadenka's style in Grebenka's novella *The Forester*) and which struck contemporary critics as too "well-formed," "cold," "reminiscent of a student's exercise on an assigned theme"—entered *Poor Folk* from the arsenal of sentimental poetics in an almost ready-made form.

In order to appreciate the greatness of Dostoevsky's artistic achievement in organizing the verbal mannerisms of the petty clerk *against the background of a new treatment of this figure,* one must first see the blind alley the "naturalists" found themselves in after answering the call of the theoreticians of their poetics "to humanize microscopic personalities." The verbal mosaic based on colloquial speech that Gogol had created with such exceptional skill, which had struck his contemporaries most strongly of all and had incited imitation, was not suited for "touching" spiritual effusions, for the expression of an elevated "loquaciousness of heart." It could serve only as an illustration of comical poses that some spurious narrator rendered in the pettiest detail by means of their "vulgar" names or of artificially elevated descriptions. Sometimes Gogol's "cobweb" of speech performs a specific function: it esthetically transforms slips of the tongue and the anomalies of everyday word usage, which has become automatized. Sometimes

189

he introduces narrow, "family" jargon by means of artistic imitation of the tone of a "well-meaning acquaintance." In all these and other aspects Gogol's verbal mosaic did not at all presuppose any *action* behind it, so that its full effect was esthetically perceived only as a "mockery" of speech.

In the 1840s, when new principles for sketching the figure of the clerk had been set forth and a wide use of awkward conversational speech elements—exclusively for comic effect—could only destroy the general tone of a short story, the clerk heroes of the naturalist tale took pains to be more silent or to speak in the language of the authors themselves. We find examples of this in the works of Butkov and Grebenka. At this point Dostoevsky takes upon himself the most difficult task: that of working out a style for the "humanized" clerk. For the first time the petty clerk was allowed to speak at such length and with such tonal vibrations. The *Moscovite* noted this:

> Makar Devushkin is a copying clerk, although, judging by the style of his letters and his many very true reflections which reveal an observant mind, one could conclude that he is not devoid of abilities the way Akaky Akakievich is. (1846, part 1, p. 167)

The new psychological motivation transformed the established "naturalist" forms of clerk speech. Moreover, the reformer took the same model as his point of departure that all the other naturalists had taken: Devushkin's speech was "based on the style of characters introduced by Gogol," as S.P. Shevyryov observed (the *Moscovite*, 1846, No. 2). The colloquial, oral basis of Devushkin's letters, which has its formal genesis in the speech of Gogolian heroes, was obvious to the majority of the critics of *Poor Folk* as well (cf. the *Moscow Scientific and Literary Symposium*, 1847, p. 27; Strakhov's review in *Fatherland Notes*, v. 170, p. 551).

At the same time the critics also understood that Devushkin's style caused Dostoevsky particular artistic pains and efforts. Konstantin Aksakov wrote:

> We are sure that Devushkin spoke, could speak exactly as he does in the tale; but at the same time we are sure that he never wrote like that... only a writer who places the character described outside himself, having created and caught him with artistic force, can write like that. (*Moscow Scientific and Literary Symposium*, 1847, p. 27)

Aksakov thus posed the problem of the "image of the author" in the language structure of Devushkin's letters sharply and emphatically. Nikitenko wrote that "this language is very artificial" and continued by observing how the process of reworking old forms in Devushkin's language was sometimes accompanied by the insertion of expressions and phrases into the general structure of the clerk's style that destroyed its "artificial simplicity" ("I *simply do not exist*"... "Listen, how they begin to *controvert*" . . . *"One puts on* new boots, for instance, *with such delight"* . . . "He ran out *in an unheard-of frenzy"*).

Annenkov noted the same inconsistency even more clearly at a later date. He stated that in Dostoevsky's first works the "image of the narrator" served only as an occasion for stylistic play and for the elaboration of new devices of plot architectonics:

> The reader is constantly occupied not with the narrator, but with the author's manner and his devices, with his given style, which actually, to the detriment of the tale's internal content, constantly intrudes on one's opinion, on one's appreciation. (*The Contemporary*, 1849, No. 2, p. 6)

In this connection the "moralistic" ending of Dostoevsky's "An Honest Thief" is particularly illuminating. There the chosen form of the stylized speech of an "experienced man" proved unsuitable for the consecutive development of the oxymoronic word-combination *honest thief*, and the author had to emerge openly from behind the narrator. Since the oxymoron was based on the demand of the Natural School "to humanize the scoundrel," the man of experience had to conscientiously fulfill this task as narrator. And at the story's conclusion, with the help of the author looking out from behind him, he even delivers a sentimental "moral" ("if it is really necessary to have one here") on the following theme:

> *the depraved man,* despite his depraved life, all the same did not ruin the whole man in himself... *he dies not from a shameful deed but from anguish,* because he has ruined *all that is best in him, in the name of which he is still called a man,* for nothing... My Yemelya, had he remained among the living, would not be a man but, to give an example, a trifle. And so he died from anguish and from conscience, so as to prove to all the world that whatever he was, he was still a man. ("Stories of a Man of Experience," *Fatherland Notes*, LVII, 1848, p. 305)[10]

Annenkov explained this inconsistency of stylistic coloration very nicely:

> The tailor resembles a rhetor more than a simple-minded narrator; behind him there constantly appears the author himself, who uses him as an instrument for a kind of narrative *tour de force*. ("Notes on Russian Literature of the Last Year," *The Contemporary*, Jan. 1849)

New stylistic devices, as one of the dominant tendencies of Dostoevsky's work in the first period, were connected with the creation of new forms of ideology and were perceived as such by the more sensitive of his contemporaries.

That this was Dostoevsky's aspiration is attested not only by his personal avowals. Even Devushkin constantly declares that the aim of his literary activities is the formation of a *style*. At first he complains: "There's no style, Varenka, there's no style whatever, if only there were some sort of style" (letter of April 12th). But gradually, with the development of his interest in literature, Devushkin's style "takes on form"; both the lexical stock and the syntactic organization of his letters become more complex and varied. Even such symbols as a "blood-thirsty tiger" appear in Devushkin's style under the influence of the writer Ratazyaev. And Varenka urges him to work on his style. After having been transformed into a "composer of literature and a poet," Makar Devushkin states outright:

> I begin to describe all of this to you, in part in order to unburden my heart, but more in order to show you a model of the good style of my compositions. (Letter of September 5th)

In his critical article on *Poor Folk* Nikitenko noted that Makar Devushkin's style shows him to be not merely a copier of papers, but "a true writer" as well (*Library for Reading,* v. 75, p. 34).

The sharp effects of the novel's artistic structure are based on the fact that Devushkin follows the poetics of the Natural School in his compositions, changing only the emotional coloring of details that relate to "poor folk." Thus the choice of the epistolary form of the sentimental "bourgeois" novel permitted the "titual councillor" himself to become a man of letters. However, this idea will be more deeply and fully explored after an analysis of the plot and composition of *Poor Folk*.

3.

In the "bourgeois" novel such as *Teresa and Faldoni,* which is presented in the form of a sentimental correspondence, there is usually an interlacing of two plot lines. These unfold tragically against the background of the general emotional states of the heroes and of their mutual attraction, broken off either by external obstacles or death. The necessity of using letters alone, which are monologues of a sort, compels the author to separate the spheres of action of each of the heroes. Otherwise the letters would not move the given story line along but would only contain reminiscences about the past. Besides which, if the heroes were spatially connected and shared a common sphere of action, the correspondence itself would lose its psychological motivation. On the other hand, the external separation of the two levels of action that is a precondition for the epistolary genre emphasizes all the more clearly the heroes' emotional involvement. Therefore, the question of the two plot lines should be connected to the basic problem of the "syntagmatics" of the plot morphemes in the novel's dynamic flow. Solving the problem of "syntagmatics" should also provide an explanation of the internal sequence of emotional breaks in the alternation of the letters.

Thus we can identify three problems of plot composition in *Poor Folk:* 1) the morphological constituents of the plot skeleton of Varenka Dobroselova's letters, the genesis of their parts, the devices used in transforming them into an organic whole, and the teleology of this process; II) the plot outline of Makar Devushkin's letters, its connections with the plot theories of the Natural School, and its dynamic development in the novel; III) the plot architectonics of the novel as a whole, i.e., the devices used in interweaving the two plot lines, their points of conjunction and disjunction.

I.   The story of Varenka Dobroselova is basically built on the traditional plot skeleton of the sentimental novel. We find it, for example, in a novel by one of the writers Makar Devushkin knows, *Katenka, or the Child of Misfortune,* subtitled "a true happening," (Russian translation, 1820) by François-Guillaume Ducray-Duminil (1761-1819). Cécile du Ranville loses both her father and mother. Even before their deaths the du Ranville family had been ruined and was forced to move to the city. As a result of the base intrigue of a certain Madame de Linvalle, who posed as the cousin of a deceased friend of Cécile's father, the poor girl is given a sleeping potion and deprived of her honor. The guilty party, Saint Ange, later marries her.

This story scheme was very popular in the 1840s. For example, A. Villamov, in "Meetings on Nevsky Prospect" (*Finnish Messenger,* VII, 1845), tells the story of a poor orphan, Karolina, who after the ruin and death of her parents puts her trust in a certain benefactress, Mrs. B. This "benefactress" sells her to a sham relative, an unpleasant fifty-year-old man with a repulsive physiognomy. However, the fallen girl is rescued by a certain Mr. V. and her honor is restored; she becomes a governess and finally, as the happy wife of a court councillor, bumps into the man who saved her on Nevsky Prospect.

A quite similar situation is woven into M. Voskresensky's story "A Moscow Teresa and Faldoni" (*Literary Gazette,* 1843, No. 7-8). An orphan named Klavdinka lives with a woman who has taken an interest in her. This woman, Olimpiada Dmitrievna Kostochkina, sells her to a Baron Nigel. But by chance the door to Klavdinka's bedroom is locked and the criminal plan fails.

The scheme of Varenka's tragedy, which goes back in its fundamental features to a set of thematically unified motifs, is compliated by the insertion of the student Pokrovsky's story. The touching episodes—the awakening of Varenka's love for the poor teacher—were easily combined with the story of an orphan, since they have common sentimental origins. Dostoevsky's originality in this case consisted in motivating the relationship between Varenka and Pokrovsky by introducing hints that Pokrovsky's mother was an early victim of Anna Fyodorovna and, thus, Varenka's predecessor. These hints are part of the novel's background, though the events alluded to occur somewhere outside the actual framework of the novel. The existence of this completed, if veiled, tragedy frees Dostoevsky from the necessity of developing Varenka's story to its biographical conclusion. Furthermore, it allows him to play on the reader's dim presentiments and contrasting expectations, based on the parallelism between the veiled story of Pokrovsky's mother and the developing story of Varenka, in such a way as to prepare for the final emphasis on the tragedy of *Devushkin alone*. Moreover, it is interesting that Dostoevsky creates a shadow following Varenka's path, her cousin Sasha. The function of this character, besides creating an accessory, emotionally contrasting semantic level, was to sharpen Varenka's "childishness" in the period of her happiness ("Big girl though I was, I was in on all of Sasha's pranks") and then to intensify the tragic element of Varenka's ruin ("Horror! and she will be ruined, the poor girl!") and the vileness of Anna Fyodorovna ("She corrupted your cousin and ruined you").

The use of this *triad* to depict the image of the poor and ruined girl is a characteristic feature of the novel's plot construction that demonstrates Dostoevsky's originality in reworking a traditionally sentimental plot scheme. And in order to construct the type of Makar Devushkin, it is essential that Varenka's image be shaded with two accessory variations on it. The image of Makar Devushkin also has two accompanying incomplete copies in the persons of Gorshkov and Pokrovsky. This device of grouping images together focuses attention more sharply on the main characters. Ducray-Duminil formulated this demand of the sentimental novel as follows:

> In works designed for pleasant entertainment one must concentrate the reader's attention on a single action and on one or two characters. For the reader, keeping sight of and being compelled at each step to be astonished by the nobility of their actions and the loftiness of their sensibilities, quickly becomes involved in their stories, their misfortunes and the reversals of their fortunes. (From the foreword to *Julie, or the History of a Human Heart,* 1803)

Besides concentrating the attention on the main characters, the triad of variants in Dostoevsky fulfills other, more complicated plot functions. Thus, a "literary relative" of Devushkin, the old man Pokrovsky, turns up in Varenka's diary. This type, a descendant of Balzac's *Father Goriot,* demanded

194

the corresponding devices of artistic embodiment and stylistic finish. Sketching the external history of this type with Balzacian strokes, Dostoevsky could not avoid complicating the general sentimental tone of Varenka's story with completely different emotional impressions. Varenka tells her story with a long-established rule of sentimentalism in mind:

> Scenes of frenzy, revenge, and despair—the triumphs of the ordinary novel—have little place in this sort of composition. But since it is impossible to leave them out completely, as they unfortunately relate to the history of the human heart, one should at least present them in profile or at a certain remove, so that they make less of an impression. (Ducray-Duminil, *ibid.*)

The psychological image of the Balzacian hero entailed sharper, contrasting devices of portrayal. Dostoevsky could merely adapt them to the general manner of Varenka's tale.

Thus Dostoevsky was trying to effect an extraordinarily original synthesis. The historical significance of this task becomes clearer if one adds that Dostoevsky placed the image of Pokrovsky (as one would indeed expect) in the stylistic setting of naturalist poetics. It is hardly by chance that only his dress constantly attracts Varenka's attention, and his external appearance is described statically, with an emphasis on comic details that serve as objective signs of the character's image rather than as emotional reflections of it in the narrator's "psyche." In order to see the distance that separated the two artistic schools whose synthesis Varenka was called upon to effect, it is enough to juxtapose the description of Pokrovsky's son's appearance:

> He was of *such strange appearance, walked so awkwardly, greeted one so awkwardly and spoke so weirdly that at first I couldn't even look at him without laughing...*

with the devices used in portraying the old man:

> A *shabby* little old man, *badly dressed, small, grey-haired...* he had a way of *shrinking into himself, of making faces;* he had such strange ways and *tics* that *one could, almost without error, conclude that he was not in his right mind...* He always had *a hat full of holes, with a torn brim...* The old man *would preen himself, straighten his waistcoat, tie, frockcoat... He would turn red as a crab... He would wink his left eye at us so comically...* A tear was about to roll from his pale cheek *onto his red nose...*

One must also keep in mind the stylistic handicap that finally overcame the sentimental orphan in her account of Pokrovsky: she had to describe how the old man "expressed himself comically," to reproduce the forms of his verbal expression, and not simply paraphrase his speech. This entailed including in the framework of a sentimental novella the foreign element of defective, colloquial language that displays Varenka's skill in imitating Makar Devushkin's style, e.g.:

"Listen," [Pokrovsky] began shyly, in a low voice, "listen, Varvara Alekseevna! You know what?"... "So look, do you see?—both you'll have something to give him and I'll have something to give him; we'll both of us have something to give him."

Thus Varenka's diary clearly deviates from the canons of sentimentalism, sacrificing its precepts in the name of naturalist poetics.

After including the naturalist story of Pokrovsky in her tale, Varenka completes it with the scene of the funeral, where the father's despair is not only not shown in profile but, on the contrary, is intensified by enumerating all the details. Of course, the fragmentation in depicting the scene of the "crazy" old man chasing after the coffin hardly harmonized with the general forms of Varenka's sentimental style:

The *tails* of his *dilapidated* frockcoat *flapped* in the wind *like a pair of wings. Books stuck out of all his pockets; in his arms* there was some *huge book, which he clutched desperately.* The passersby took off their hats and crossed themselves. *Others stopped* and *stared* at the poor *old man. Every moment* books *fell from his pockets into the mud. People stopped him, pointing out a book he had dropped;* he would pick it up and *rush off again in pursuit* of the coffin. At the corner of the street, some old beggar woman *tagged along* with him to follow the coffin.[11]

Nikitenko astutely noted that the image of the old man Pokrovsky and the artistic devices the author used to formulate it ended up in unaccustomed surroundings:

The scene of the funeral, the poor man's chase after his son's coffin, already departs somewhat from the conventions of natural depiction which the author himself masters to such a high degree. It is somewhat artificial and exaggerated, as is the father's childish fear of his son. (*Library for Reading,* LXXV, "Criticism," p. 34)

Varenka's diary, designed to solve a most complicated artistic problem, is the summit of her creative achievement. In the further course of the novel Varenka dwells entirely in the past. She passively retires under the sway of elegaic thoughts or "moralistic" concerns for Devushkin, now and then frightening him with the specter of her departure (becoming a governess). This undercurrent of parting in Varenka's letters is intensified by contrasting breaks. After the episode with the first "adventurer" (letter of July 28th) is settled, Varenka writes the excited, joyful letter of August 2nd ("Somehow, I feel unusually cheerful today"), but then follows her desperate wail (August 4th) about the "most horrible unpleasantnesses" connected with the appearance of a new suitor, a "disgusting" old man. The tragic element further intensifies; naturally, reminiscences about the past increase. It is interesting that the principle of the triad is once again the organizing factor. The appearance of two rejected "clients" prepares by contrast for Bykov's return.

Such is the plot scheme of Varenka Dobroselova's letters and its genesis. The way this plot outline is used is defined by the novel's dynamics, by the devices for the intersection of Varenka's diary and letters with Devushkin's letters, as well as by their emotional and ideational parallelism.

II.   The plot outline that Makar Devushkin follows in relating his episodic adventures includes the favorite situations of the naturalist story, though Dostoevsky changes them somewhat, especially at the end of the novel. Annenkov characterized the basic motifs that Dostoevsky canonized as follows:

> Most of [his] tales...open with the description of rented lodgings, that difficult condition of Petersburg life, and then go into an enumeration of the lodgers, beginning with the house porter. Cold rain, wet snow, the inventory of the hero's property, and finally, the account of his misfortunes—these are practically all the resources at the writer's disposal. (*The Contemporary*, 1849, No. 2. p. 10)

It was Dostoevsky who introduced the description of the hero's fellow-lodgers into this scheme (cf., besides *Poor Folk*, the construction of "Mr. Prokharchin"). The influence of Balzac's novels, e.g. *Father Goriot*, on this Dostoevskian device of plot and composition is clear. This method of portraying a hero against the background of the crowd of his fellow-lodgers was taken from F.M. Dostoevsky by his brother, Mikhail Dostoevsky, and by Yakov Butkov (cf., e.g., the novella "A Dark Man," *Fatherland Notes*, vol. 7). An ironic characterization of this device, which shows that it had already degenerated into a cliché, can be found in *The Contemporary* for 1850:

> There are tales and novels that are written as though following a well-known recipe. To put together such a tale the writer usually sits down on a couch and strikes up a conversation with himself.... Question:

would you like, dear friend, to write a tale? Answer: Not a bad idea, though not much. Deduction: Still it'd be better to write it, because then you'll want to even less. Question: Tell me, did you ever happen to rent an apartment—large, small, with light green, or yellow, or dirty walls, in a brick house, in a corner, or at a dacha? Answer: Yes, I have, and I remember all the details. Deduction: There's a setting for you, ready-made. Question: And didn't there happen to be any funny old men, pretty little girls, skinflints, or idlers among the lodgers? Answer: How could it be otherwise? So there are your main characters. Question: Well, and the main thing: didn't some sort of drama unfold among these lodgers, if only, for example, something to do with puppy love, jealousy, the opposition of an angry landlady? And what sort of things did the lodgers do? What sort of things did the pretty girl think about? Answer: To tell the truth, there wasn't really any drama, but in life, everything's a drama. Microscopic joys, failures, and sufferings are no worse than other sufferings, failures, and joys. Of course there's a drama, there's everything we need, and the tale's as good as written. (V. II, p. 29 f.)

Thus in the "school of the young Dostoevsky," Dostoevsky's plots and stylistic forms degenerated with unusual speed into schematic clichés.

Makar Devushkin's correspondence also opens with the description of his new apartment and fellow-lodgers, a description that is interrupted at the very beginning, for the sake of contrast, by reminiscences about his tranquil life "in the old apartment." Then Devushkin singles out from the throng of lodgers, besides the servants, Teresa and Faldoni (whose particular function we mentioned above), "a clerk in the literary department," Ratazyaev, and Gorshkov. It was easy to describe the growth of the "poor man's" interest in literature through Devushkin's association with Ratazyaev, excerpts of whose works are effectively marked as parodic material by Devushkin's ecstatic acclaim. Against this background Devushkin's letters stand out as original literary exercises. Devushkin's critical remarks about Pushkin's "The Stationmaster" and Gogol's "The Overcoat" assume a particular significance in characterizing his own "exercises," since these stories are models of the two genres whose synthesis the "composer of literature" Devushkin tries to effect. What strikes Devushkin most forcibly in Pushkin's tale is the narrator's personal tone and the direct simplicity of the style: "As though I'd written it myself; it's exactly, more or less, *my own heart*..." (letter of July 1st). Devushkin takes "The Stationmaster" for a "sentimental-naturalist" story: "Yes, it's natural! You just read it: it's natural! It's living!" It is as if Devushkin, the hero of a sentimental-naturalist "novel in letters," were emphasizing in his appraisal of Pushkin's work that he himself will write about "our poor clerk" in the same tone of sincere compassion and using the same descriptive devices as Pushkin: "After all, perhaps he's just like Samson Vyrin, only he has a different name, Gorshkov"; "he's the same kind of goodhearted wretch...." "And it's a simple business, my God; and how! Really, I'd have written it exactly like that; why wouldn't I have written it like that?" And Devushkin wants to give a sentimental tinge not just to Gorshkov, but to himself as well. More than that: he is not averse to borrowing even "autobiographical" episodes from Pushkin—"the same could happen to me." And it is against this background that one unconsciously perceives the episode in which an officer, an unworthy "adventurer" who is after Varenka, "sort of pushes" Devushkin down a flight of stairs (letter of July 28th). "The Stationmaster" also sheds light on the end of Devushkin's story with his "lamb gone astray" and on his ways of consoling himself in grief. It would be a gross error to characterize Devushkin's pronouncements on literature as Dostoevsky's personal confession. It is, after all, "Devushkin speaking"; Dostoevsky himself, by his own avowal, didn't show his "mug." "The image of the author" is not revealed directly, but rather as a form of organizing Devushkin's image, as a "superimposition" on him. The sharp effect of Devushkin's literary deliberations is based on this displacement of styles, on the fact that "the poor clerk," "the eternal titular councillor," himself assumes the role of a man of letters—and, what's more, he does so in the framework of a sentimental novel. This resulted in unique comic contrasts, the nature of which become clearer upon examining Devushkin's reflections about Gogol's "The Overcoat." Devushkin saw a "caricature" of himself in this tale and was indignant at its thematics, at its author's descriptive devices, and at the development of its plot scheme. And among his own "compositions" Makar Devushkin actually writes a tale on a theme parallel to that of "The Overcoat"—"Boots"—with a diametrically opposed resolution.

The motif of boots is introduced when Gogol's tale is under discussion:

> Of course one does sometimes get something new—and is so pleased, one can't sleep, one is so pleased; one puts on new boots, for instance, with such delight; that is true, I have felt it, because it is pleasant to see one's foot in a fine smart boot—that's truly described! (Letter of July 8th)

This motif recurs several times in Devushkin's correspondence (letters of June 26th, August 1st, 4th, and 5th) and is even directly juxtaposed to the theme of an overcoat: "Why, will someone who reads it order me an overcoat because of it?—Will he buy me new boots?" (letter of July 8th).[12] In line with Devushkin's wish, the boot theme is developed differently and is resolved sentimentally: "Virtue triumphs, and Fyodor Fyodorovich (that is, what's the matter with me!—the General...),"[13] having learned of the virtues

199

of Devushkin, "hurriedly takes out his wallet" and "thrusts a hundred-ruble note into [his] hand" (letter of September 9th). It is interesting that Dostoevsky's contemporaries saw a contrasting parallelism with "The Overcoat" in this scene and in the psychological treatment of Fyodor Fyodorovich:

> Makar Devushkin takes offense not only for the poor man, he takes offense for His Excellency as well. One must add that Dostoevsky shows His Excellency to be a most noble and excellent man. (*Moscow Scientific and Literary Symposium*, 1847, p. 33)

Furthermore, criticism hostile to Dostoevsky poked fun at Devushkin's attachment to the boot theme:

> Let us note that Devushkin incessantly discusses the woeful state of his footwear, of his boots, in the majority of his letters. It is his *idée fixe*. He simply can't stop talking about his boots. He keeps fiddling and fussing over his boots, so that the whole novel is written *à propos de bottes*. At one point [letter of September 5th] Devushkin even says: "Darling, every one of us, my dear, is a bit of a shoemaker." (*The Northern Bee*, 1846, No. 22)

Thus Makar Devushkin, like the "lover" in the sentimental novel, cultivates a tone of personal sympathy, of deep authorial involvement. This is why he does not want to accept the "humane episode" in "The Overcoat," despite its rhetorical form, without moralistic and sentimentally civic judgments on the part of the author, and without the "author's" evaluation of Akaky Akakievich's "personality":[14]

> Well, it would be all right if he made up for it a little at the end, if he had softened it a bit, *if he had put in*, for instance, *after that part where they sprinkle papers on his head, that for all that he was conscientious, a good citizen, that he did not deserve such treatment* from his fellow clerks. (Letter of July 8th)

And, to counteract "The Overcoat," Makar Devushkin writes his tale, "Boots," in a different tone.

The comic effects hidden in this contrasting juxtaposition, which was based on the displacement of styles from the author to the "titular councillor," are quite striking when Makar Devushkin, after taking it upon himself to rehabilitate the new devices for portraying the "titular councillor,"[15] begins to expound the principles of the theoreticians of naturalism, in particular their civic preaching, in his own style. Here features of the "image of the author" begin to enter quite obviously into the structure of *Poor Folk* as a new "casing." This image is based on *the relationship* between the image of Makar Devushkin and the world of "literary reality" that appears in his letters.

But what was most striking of all was that Makar Devushkin was himself following the poetics of naturalism in the plots of his tales and in the devices he used for the artistic embodiment of nature, merely infusing it with a sentimental aura; and even then, hardly in every case, but only in speaking about "poor folk."[16] Actually, Makar Devushkin writes everything for which he reproached the author of "The Overcoat" about himself, only he gives it a different emotional coloration. Thus, he protests against "indecent caricaturists" who

> look to see whether one puts one's whole foot down on the pavement or walks on tiptoe; they notice that such and such a clerk, of such and such a department, a titular councillor, has his bare toes sticking out of his boot, that he has holes at his elbows—and then they sit down at home and describe it all, and publish such rubbish.... (Letter of August 1st)

But then, a paragraph later, he himself writes that his "elbows are seeing daylight through [his] sleeves, and [his] buttons are hanging on threads." Describing his trip to the moneylender, he notes: "Just at Voskresensky Bridge the sole came off my boot, so I really don't know what I walked upon."

In a word, the whole material "stuffing," the recording of details, the descriptive devices (not to mention the vocabulary and phraseology) that were characteristic for novelists of the Natural School appear in Devushkin's letters as well.[17] From this point of view it is extremely interesting to note how Devushkin makes original stylistic transpositions and revisions in the spirit of the Natural School when he repeats the thematics of Pushkin's "The Stationmaster" in his own words: "I read that he *became a drunk, the sinner*" (in Pushkin, *became a drunk* is the brewer's wife's expression); "he cries piteously, wiping his eyes with his *dirty* coattails" (in Pushkin, he "*picturesquely* wiped his tears with his coattails"), etc.

This "naturalist" coloration of Devushkin's letters stands out in bold relief when our "composer of literature" begins to write "satirically." The devices of portraiture in his style include unsystematically accumulated epithets, in which negative internal and external features alternate and which tend to emphasize the comic aspects of dress and external appearance. Devushkin's descriptions of Faldoni and Teresa are a case in point: "He's red-haired, kind of a pig, one-eyed, snub-nosed, a churl"; "You know what she is like, as thin as a plucked, dried-up chicken" (letter of April 12th). The portrait of Yemelyan Ivanovich's stingy moneylender resembles Gogol's description of the miser Plyushkin: "gray-haired, with such thievish little eyes, in a greasy dressing-gown belted with a cord" (letter of August 5th). The peasant woman whom Devushkin stumbles over just inside the money-lender's doorway reminds one of Agafiya Fedoseevna in Gogol's "Two Ivans": "The stupid woman shrieked and screamed...and started howling like the Devil" (letter of August 5th).

One hardly needs to add parallels from stories of the Natural School: anyone who wants further proof should simply read Gogol. The passages I have mentioned suffice to clarify the plot and compositional scheme of Devushkin's letters. The question of Devushkin's style is one of the most interesting problems in Russian literary history and demands a separate investigation. But even without it, it is clear what things an investigator of the plot should examine: Makar Devushkin's infatuation with the actress (letter of July 7th), the episode where he tries unsuccessfully to get a loan (letter of August 5th), in short, the whole clerk milieu that makes up Devushkin's background and all the poses of its heroes, all of which were incorporated into the "compositions" of the "poor man" from the works of his literary admirers, the naturalists.

Thus Makar Devushkin, like Varenka, tries to effect a synthesis of "naturalist" and sentimental forms, only he achieves this more profoundly, originally and, most important, more contemporarily. In his letters, sentimental effusions overlie a naturalist background, and what is basically sentimental moralism is given a "philanthropic," socialist commentary in the spirit of naturalism's ideologists (such as Belinsky). Makar Devushkin, vaunting his clerkish style, which was based on Gogolian models, sanctions the new trends of the Natural School in the name of all "titular councillors" and "poor folk" in general, fractures its outlived forms, and parodies the "literary lice." In so doing, he becomes one of the most progressive and talented heralds and creators of new artistic forms.

Varenka's case is just the opposite: the traditional themes and stylistic accomplishments of sentimentalism constitute the core of her letters.[18] They serve as a mass of unrecognizable material, a background. The naturalist (Gogolian) devices which are poured into them inconspicuously dissolve one moment and sharply stand out the next, filling in several isolated fragments and only externally coming into contact with this general background, like oil on water.

So far we have outlined the general tendencies of plot composition in Makar Devushkin's and Varenka's letters, their relation to one another against the background of the interaction of sentimental and "naturalist" devices, and the profound difference in the nature of the synthesis effected by each.

At the same time it becomes clear from this general survey that Dostoevsky had a deep (prophetic) intuition which allowed him to find the seeds of the future development of literary forms in the still undefined judgments of the contemporary literary world. And, having comprehended his historical mission, he nurtured the outmoded forms of "naturalism" that had already been fated to extinction, renovating them with striking mastery and artistic strength.

III.   Dostoevsky renovated sentimentalism and created fresh forms for the Natural School which were based on a new treatment of Gogol's style.

The artistic synthesis that Dostoevsky achieved in his first novel was not merely an answer to the dim presentiments of the writers who shared his literary sympathies[19] and a poetic realization of the theoretical aspirations of "naturalist" criticism which were made clearer to the ideologists themselves by *Poor Folk*; the novel's esthetic finish and the harmonious coherence of its parts made it "eternal."

Therefore, if only for a modest approximation of the esthetic perception of the novel's integral structure, it is indispensable to take a look at the way in which Makar's and Varenka's letters are coupled and interwoven. It was precisely through this interweaving that Dostoevsky effected a synthesis which made Devushkin's literary attempts and the poor orphan's letters part of a new, unified artistic work. And here Dostoevsky does not hide behind his heroes' backs; he shows himself as the "storyteller" who "unearths every sort of hidden secret" (the epigraph from V.F. Odoevsky). The novel's tragedy appears as a result of this synthesis of two lines of monologue. The structural problem of the "image of the author" is the task of a separate work. The questions before us at the moment concern the plot architectonics of this "dialogue" in letters.

Landscape is important in the architectonics of the novel, sometimes only to set the mood. The role it plays in the progression of the letters reveals the dynamics of the artistic "action" and gives the oscillations of emotional "tensions and resolutions" an aesthetic consistency. The landscape in *Poor Folk* is either described directly or is invisible and guessed only from the dates of the letters. *From the joyous spring morning with "tender daydreams"* through unjustifiable spring hopes—"I was so delighted with the spring, like a fool, that I went out in a thin overcoat" (letter of April 8th)—the visible landscape of Devushkin's letters changes to summer "rain and mud": "And at that time the rain, mud, and depression was terrible..." (letter of August 5th). And then *against the background of autumn "fogs"* (September 5th) *and mud—with the temporary clearing of the weather* on the occasion of Devushkin's receiving help from His Excellency—"And the weather is so wonderful today, Varenka, so fine" (letter of September 11th)—the tragic break between Devushkin and Varenka is completed *in the autumn rain*.

It is characteristic that in Varenka's letters there is not a full harmonious correspondence to the picture of nature that Makar Devushkin draws in his letters. Varenka has no *spring*. More than that: it is she who destroys the spring joy of her "protector." In her diary and in her letters to Devushkin,

Varenka depicts only *summer and autumn*. In the beginning of her diary Varenka's happy childhood is described against the background of a *summer landscape* ("A thick, green, shady, branchy grove") that is colored by the romantic style ("As if someone were calling you thither, as if someone were beckoning you thither"). And so on up to the end of *autumn*: the autumnal but clear landscape at the hour of parting is contrasted to the filthy Petersburg autumn, the "clear, dry, frosty autumn morning" in Petersburg when Varenka begins a new life at Anna Fyodorovna's after the death of her father. Varenka's diary breaks off in the *"depth of autumn,"* in days "sad and melancholy, like the poor failing life of the dying man [Pokrovsky]," with the image of Pokrovsky's father at the funeral, "his head drenched by the rain and the wind, the sleet lashing his face." Such is the progression of the landscape in her notes about the past.

The pictures of nature in Varenka's letters about the present begin with the description of the *summer "greenery" of the islands.* This is the landscape of "evening calm," of the faint peace returning to Varenka's life. And the main actor against this background is Makar Devushkin: the landscape is illuminated not so much by Varenka's emotions in themselves as much as by Makar Devushkin's relation to them. "Whether it was a bush, an avenue, a piece of water—you were there standing before me showing its beauties and peeping into my eyes as though you were displaying your possessions to me" (letter of June 11th).

In this way Varenka's image is as if isolated from the landscape's dynamics, and only Devushkin's changing emotions run parallel to it; sometimes Varenka's melancholy recollections and presentiments are directly violated to give a more contrastive shading to Devushkin's emotions. And it is not by chance that a reference to the "fresh, clear, brilliant" *autumn* morning is made once more in Varenka's letters as an occasion for associations about the happy fall days of her "golden childhood" (the pictures of the lake, the woods—from various points of view), in contrast with the "dim," "dark" present. Consequently, the landscape of Varenka's letters *does not in itself move the action forward*.

This peculiarity in the nature of Varenka's depiction of the landscape stands out more clearly if one remembers that Dostoevsky eliminated the description of the summer groves at the beginning of her diary when he revised *Poor Folk*, whereas he preserved the autumn pictures of her golden childhood in the letter of September 3rd.

In this way the image of Varenka is found only *in the aura of autumnal nature*.

Naturally, the emotional impressions created by the intensification of the tragedy from spring to fall—with rays of hope contrasting to the background of the landscape—are concentrated around the image of Devushkin. This results in the fact that Varenka's relation to the landscape, which changes in the course of time, is perceived through metaphors Devushkin creates for her, rather than through her own feelings.

Devushkin's comparison of Varenka to a "little bird" in his letters moves along the line of these temporal transitions. *On the morning of his spring ecstasies* Makar writes to Varenka: "You flew out of your room exactly like a spring bird" (letter of April 8th). But Devushkin's presentiments begin from August 4th, when he writes to Varenka: "You'll fly away like a bird from its nest, to escape these owls, these birds of prey that were trying to peck at it."

This is one of the threads unifying the novel's architectonics. But the original way its parts are connected becomes clear only upon examining the emotional and semantic connections apparent in the letters' alternation. In the same way, noting their dates helps to identify the accentual, peak passages.

The novel opens with the inspired speech of a happy lover. After a series of enthusiastic exclamations, there is a break filled with tender reminiscences. The narrative tone, ornamented with sentimental lyricism, establishes the frame in which the first letter is placed: the conventional symbolism of two lovers communicating by signs (with a comical turn—"there is no need of letters!") and sentimental spring gifts ("a couple of pots of balsam and geranium"). It begins with a "report," which consists, however, simply of a paraphrase of some "verses" about spring and tender dreams. Then, in an associative jump, a transition is made to the beginning of a naturalist story, Devushkin's description of his apartment. Replying that evening, Varenka ridicules Devushkin's "morning of chancellery love." Her whole letter is a contrasting response to the expressive form and emotional content of the letter she has received. The core of several allusions to the tragic past and to the possibility of revealing it in the letters ("It is dreadful to look back, too. There everything is such sorrow.") is completely overshadowed[20] by emotional "point by point" replies to Devushkin's "report." This contrast is revealed even in the official salutation: "Dear Sir, Makar Alekseevich!" Thus Varenka's letter is, as it were, directed at destroying the position in which the semantics of the first letter places Devushkin. Her agonizing expectation of the unknown future, her anguish and boredom (despite the superficial parallelism of the construction, "I too got up this morning feeling gay"), is set against the rapture and selfless contentment of the "lover." This device of dramatic contrast defines the dynamics of the correspondence.

Devushkin's gloomy answer places the novel's heroes in new positions. Falling into harmony with the melancholy conclusion of Varenka's letter ("It seems it's an unlucky day!"—"Yes, dear friend, yes, my own, it seems it was a sad day for poor luckless me!"), and picking up the tone of the same official salutation ("Dear Madam, Varvara Alekseevna!"; cf. in the first letter, "My precious Varvara Alekseevna!"), Devushkin absolutely disavows the romantic "verses" and the sentimental, enamored tone of his first letter: "I ought not in my old age, with a tuft of gray hair on my head, to have launched out into Cupids and equivoques...I am...vexed that I wrote to you in such a flowery, stupid way." And further on, by the selection of details ("I did not walk but *dragged myself* home"..."I suppose *I got chilled to my spine*"..."*in old age, with only a tuft of gray hair on my head*") and by a contrasting opposition of naked nature to the previous romantic transfiguration of it *("I fancied all that in my foolishness")*, Makar Devushkin dispels the emotional impressions made by the first letter. He now presents himself, with a sort of paternal friendliness, as Varenka's "relation" and protector, her "*disinterested* friend." And to cast light on this image, so unlike the earlier romantic role, Devushkin makes use of an association by contrast between his new and old apartment and proceeds to describe his past personal life—this time in an "uncomplicated" style. In her letter of April 9th, Varenka gives the final sanction, so to speak, to Devushkin's role as respected *"friend and benefactor,"*[21] along with a mention of his defending her from "evil people, from their persecution and hatred." This letter has a seemingly submissive closing ("I have the honor to remain, your most devoted and *obedient servant*") which is developed in the novel as having the opposite meaning.

In this way the heroes' break from the cliché roles of the sentimental bourgeois novel is effected: Makar Devushkin, as the protector of a helpless orphan, is given the right to move the action forward; Varenka, with modest allusions, merely prepares the introduction of her notes about the past and begins, from April 9th, to complain of her illness.

Then, in his letter of April 12th, Makar Devushkin freely gives himself over to "naturalist" writing: he humorously dethrones the old "lovers who lived in Lyons," Teresa and Faldoni, and introduces the tale of Gorshkov, establishing the circle to which he will apply sentimental forms and motivating them ideologically *("the thought of those poor people!")*.

Devushkin's despondent refrain about Varenka's illness shrouds the beginning and end of the letter, and his spring raptures are buried once and for all: "Oh, these Petersburg springs, these winds and rain mixed with snow—they'll be the death of me, Varenka!"

By this point Devushkin's role in the novel is defined and the conditions of his home life are established. Therefore, *the material for the spring letters is exhausted.* Naturally, attention shifts to the parallel disclosure of Varenka's image. For the moment it is given only in the contradictory emotional aura of an "empty-headed," unfortunate person who is given to mocking and in vague allusions to the tragic past.

At this point Varenka's illness is introduced, causing an interruption of the letters (at first, only from April 12th to 25th), so that *the action during this period is sensed precisely through the absence of letters.* In the postscript to his letter of May 20th, Devushkin makes the action explicit: "As it was, my angel, I scarcely left you at all while you were ill, while you were unconscious." Two letters are included from the period of Varenka's illness: her letter of April 25th and Devushkin's of May 20th. In the former, the main characters of Varenka's drama are named, thus preparing the reader for its later development. The latter, written at the end of Varenka's illness, presents the condition of her sickness and the troubles Devushkin has gone to on her behalf, hinting at his expenditures as a source of future conflicts, and at the same time touches on Varenka's literary tastes. These two letters prepare the reader for the introduction of Varenka's diary, which is motivated by her desire "to do something nice that will please" Devushkin "in return for all the care and trouble" he has taken.

Varenka divides her "Diary" into two chapters: "Childhood" and "Youth." The first part depicts in contrasting tones Varenka's life as a child (till the age of fourteen) in the country and in Petersburg *against the background of her father's story.*[22] The beginning is placed in emotional opposition to the end: "My childhood was the happiest time of my life"—"it was an oppressive time"; "the early summer morning" in the village—the autumn morning in Petersburg when Varenka and her mother moved to Anna Fyodorovna's.

The second chapter of Varenka's diary, parallel to the first, should naturally have ended with *the death of her mother.* It is characterized by the same general type of sentence construction with a contrasting break in the middle whereby the whole acquires a tonality that rises, then falls, and then rises again. But a "naturalist story" about the old man Pokrovsky is introduced into this part of the diary, and the deviation toward "naturalism" is apparent as well in several external characteristics of its architectonics. The beginning of this part, their moving into a new apartment, gives Varenka the opportunity of characterizing, one by one, the lodgers at Anna Fyodorovna's and her relations with them. The sharpening of interest in the poor student motivates "a few words about the most strange, most curious and most pathetic person," a visitor to Anna Fyodorovna's house. But since *Varenka* is placed within the limits imposed by the plot, she is able to tell "the story of this poor old man" only *in the words of the student Pokrovsky,* i.e. against the background of *his* "childhood and youth." This is the *Vorgeschichte* of the heroes. Immediately after this, returning to the autobiographical framework, Varenka concentrates entirely on the Pokrovskys. The son is the pivotal point of the sentimental tale of the touching birth of a first, maidenly love for a poor teacher, whereas the father is the hero of a comic story that breaks off tragically, preparing the reader for the tragic outcome of the story of the other "poor people," Gorshkov and Devushkin.

Thus, *"Mother" is put in the background:* her illness is merely the occasion for Varenka's intimacy with the "poor" student. This constitutes the sharp difference between the tale of Varenka's "youth" and the story of her "childhood." As a consequence, the tragic summit of the entire "Diary" —the death and funeral of Pokrovsky—precedes the death of "Mother." A more detailed analysis of Varenka's diary could easily lead one to conclude that on the basis of the parallelism (true, complicated by insertions) in the distribution of emotional accents throughout the chapters, its composition as a whole repeats in more elevated tones the same "melodic" picture one finds in the separate chapters.

Varenka's past and present is explained by her "Diary": the "lovers" recede irreversibly into the past. *Spring ends....*

Varenka's letter of June 11th opens the "summer." This letter and Devushkin's answer of June 12th are, so to speak, an *"overture."* The dates of the letters establish *a delimitation of two periods in the summer correspondence.* The first period breaks off on July 8th. The next letter is separated by a twenty-day interval (July 27th) and signifies a decisive emotional shift in the novel's entire development—*a tragic turning point toward the autumn of parting.* This parting is also prepared by clear compositional indications, i.e. a preceding break in the correspondence and an "overture" by Varenka (her letter of September 3rd).

Parallel to the beginning of *Poor Folk*, which depicts the coming of spring, *the summer correspondence likewise opens with a description of the "greenery" of the islands* (Varenka's letter of June 11th). The general emotional basis of the following letters, the "evening calm" in the fate of the poor people, is already determined by the landscape. And since this landscape fulfilled another specific function for Varenka, bringing her back from the past into life in the present, Makar Devushkin—in a parallel to Varenka's *expectation* of verses in his description of the spring landscape—now reminds her of these verses: "Well, I expected, my dear soul, that you would write me a description of our yesterday's expedition in real poetry" (letter of June 12th). And he adds a crafty allusion: "I have no talent for it. Even if I smudge a dozen papers nothing ever comes out...*I've already tried.*" Along with the description of the landscape, Varenka also outlines in her first summer letter a theme that Devushkin then begins to develop, namely *the theme of Makar Devushkin's "kind heart."* Responding to Varenka, Devushkin indicates the plane on which this motif should be developed. He sets about to rehabilitate the "rat," the petty copying clerk, whom "they have almost made a swear word—they attacked my boots, my uniform, my hair; nothing was to their taste, everything has to be done over."

Thus it becomes clear from this overture that, against the background of the "calm" which has set in, Devushkin will engage in propaganda for new devices in portraying the "rat-clerk." And here the expectation is established that this problem will be translated into the sphere of literary quests and judgments. But this shift is not realized immediately. In her letter of June 20th Varenka again recalls, as it were, the concrete situation of the novel

(*"Though you are only a distant relation* you will protect me with your name") and, moreover, explains that there will not be a continuation of her diary. Devushkin likewise confirms the impression of familial calm ("Why, it's as if the Lord had blessed me with a little home and family of my own!" —letter of June 21st) and prepares the reader for his literary passions ("There's a meeting today: *we are going to read literature. So you see how we are getting on now, my dear,—you see!*"). Immediately following this, in his letter of June 22nd, Devushkin depicts a scene evoking *compassion*, and not the usual laughter, from the history of the "rat-clerk" Gorshkov, as though prefacing his account of new descriptive principles with a concrete illustration. In this respect it is interesting to note the original use of "sordid" details in a new emotional light: "The father was sitting *in a greasy old tailcoat* on a *broken* chair. The tears were flowing from his eyes, but perhaps not from grief, *but just the usual thing, his eyes were inflamed.*" Moreover, the very choice of the motif (the death of the child) predisposes the reader to Devushkin's impressions of Pushkin's "The Stationmaster." Devushkin's transition to the sphere of literary men, as a "composer of literature," even if with a comic overtone, is sufficiently motivated by faint emotional allusions which arise and grow into a still indefinite presentiment that Devushkin has some sort of connection to literature. And Varenka's letter of June 25th, betraying the "acme" of his esthetic sense ("I am sending you back *your book. It's a wretched, worthless little book!*"), intensifies the comic tone that accompanies the birth of Devushkin's literary sympathies. And the parody of the "literary lice" is realized against this background:

> Now, Ratazyaev has promised to give me something really literary to read.... This Ratazyaev *gets the point, he's a connoisseur!*; he writes himself, ough, how he writes! *His pen is so bold and there's loads of style....*

Devushkin is drawn to literature with his entire soul.

After all of Devushkin's reasoning, his critical evaluations, his dreams of a literary career, the path is cleared for him to preach his "poetics" and realize his synthesis of literary forms. But, so as not to obscure the framework of the "bourgeois" novel completely with these "literary pursuits" of the new "poet," Varenka frightens Devushkin with the specter of her departure to "live with strangers" (the episode in her letter of June 27th alluding to a possible "good position as a governess in a family"), at the same time that she sends him Pushkin's "The Stationmaster" and Gogol's "The Overcoat," i.e. the novels whose synthesis Devushkin will realize in the tale of his life.

In his letter of July 1st Devushkin dispels Varenka's "whimsy" without any emotional anxiety; on the contrary, he even emphasizes their summer prosperity ("You are snug and fine among us—*just as if you'd found shelter in a little nest*") and continutes to be occupied with literary questions.

Pushkin's story incites Makar Devushkin not only to sanction the forms realized in it and to hint at a future likeness of his fate to that of "Samson Vyrin, the poor fellow," but also to project its contents into his own *present* in the form of his advice to Varenka: "Reread that little book of yours again, *reread it attentively; it will do you a lot of good*" (cf. "For God's sake, get all those willful ideas out of your head...don't listen to nonsensical advice and gossip").

Devushkin's literary opinions of Gogol's "The Overcoat" are introduced gradually by the same compositional devices that prepared the reader for Devushkin's perception and evaluation of "The Stationmaster." In contrast, an episode completely Gogolian in tone and style written the night before (July 7th) precedes them. This episode, about the young Makar Devushkin's passion for an "actress-canary" is prepared for by Varenka's letter of July 6th about a proposed excursion to the theater. And a new contrast is realized in the evaluation of "The Overcoat": recognizing a "caricature" of himself in the image of Akaky Akakievich, Makar Devushkin indignantly rejects the thought "that such a clerk could exist."

Thus, Devushkin's artistic position and the further conception of the novel are determined against the background of summer "calm."

After Varenka's letter of July 27th, the novel takes a crucial turn toward a tragic ending and, moreover, a redistribution of roles occurs: Varenka now acts *as the benefactress of the fallen Devushkin.*

The break in the letters makes it possible to use the compositional device of the riddle: again, as at the novel's beginning, the reader finds himself in the very thick of things, in the midst of tragic events which the sharp changes in situation, motivated by the chronological interval,[23] only gradually clear up. A strained, emotionally elevated tone is present from the first lines of the letter, evoking even more disturbing expectations. Such a sudden change in the tempo and direction of the action ("Your latest doings and letters have frightened, shocked me..."–letter of July 27th) demands a clue. Gradually the fog clears. Already in Varenka's letter of July 27th Devushkin's desperate situation and his drunken adventures are revealed from what Fedora tells Varenka. But slight hints are also given about an "affair with some officers."

Moreover, in this letter Varenka points out to Devushkin a new sphere for description, new material for the letters: "What will *your superiors* say when they learn the true cause of your absence?" Until this time the only material from the circle of clerks, transferring the action into *the world of the chancellery*, was an incidental mention of Yevstafy Ivanovich, a colleague of Devushkin's. Now the "repulsive vice" is qualified as *a crime against "work and the service."* Makar Devushkin begins "in an uneven style" to *depict himself in civil life against the background of his colleagues and the clerk milieu in general* (letter of July 28th). Irrelevant episodes are included from this sphere to illustrate incidents involving one's personal life and "reputation" ("how Aksenty Osipovich presumed on the person of Pyotr Petrovich"), and Makar Devushkin himself, in connection with his troubles over borrowing money, transfers the center of action from his apartment to the office. This displacement of the sphere of description is sensed as a development of the principles for depicting the "poor man" that Devushkin had already outlined in his analysis of Gogol's "The Overcoat" (cf. the letter of August 1st about the poor man's "ambition" and about "scribblers"). Moreover, the episode with the officers is perceived as already prepared by allusions in Devushkin's discussion of "The Stationmaster." The development of Devushkin's and Varenka's relations parallels the introduction of this new succession of images. And the people who earlier surrounded Devushkin, his fellow lodgers, now enter the picture in a contrasting light, against a changed emotional background.

From August 2nd, "the hoard of all sorts of misfortunes" seems to begin to disperse. The emotional tone of the letters changes. Varenka is sure that "everything will be all right" ("I feel somehow particularly cheerful today"). True, a muted warning penetrates even this letter, disposing one to dark forebodings, but it is masked by being given merely as Fedora's suspicion ("She suspects that Anna Fyodorovna had some hand in all my latest unpleasantnesses"). In connection with this, the emotional ascent is passed on to Devushkin's letters ("I hasten to tell you, my little life, I have fresh hopes of something"—letter of August 3rd). And new episodes from office life (the attempt, following Yemelyan Ivanovich's advice, to get a loan from Pyotr Petrovich) that derive from Gogolian models are inserted into this frame of hope. But towards the end of the letter the tone of expectation of joyful changes gives way to feelings of uncertainty and despondency, with an enumeration of all the "misfortunes" threatening Devushkin ("Misfortune" *unexpectedly comes from the other side*. The sharp outburst of despair, the call for help, the whole series of emotional cries of supplication that set off Varenka's story about a new "adventurer" (letter of August 4th) create extraordinarily sharp effects precisely because of their dissonance with the preceding major chords. And this emotional dissonance grows: Makar Devushkin adds his own lamentations to Varenka's wailing ("Such terrible calamities destroy my spirit!... And they'll be [the death of me], they will, I swear they will.... *You know I am ready to die sooner than not help you!*"). His fears and torments become all the more intense in his attempts to take care of their material needs enumerated in the same passage.

The tragic tone here reaches its peak, since "ruination," Varenka's departure, threatens Devushkin—even in the event that he manages to get a loan.

This accentual peak, a letter full of wrenching emotional vacillations, naturally demanded, above all, a contrast. And it is given in Varenka's letter of August 5th. Here, besides a call for calm and courage, the effect of Devushkin's desperate cries is destroyed by reproaches for his lack of prudence and by an accusation of *unwarranted kindness of heart*. This absolute emotional descent, sensed even more vividly alongside the indication that the loan didn't come through, motivates Devushkin's transition *to a comic narrative style* in the "detailed" story of "how, in essence, it all happened today" (letter of August 5th). And only in the letter's refrain do plaintive notes resume: "Ah, my dear, *my golden days are gone for good....*" In keeping with this, Devushkin's postscript reveals the "artificiality," the falsity of the "joking" tone he uses in describing his visit to the moneylender: "I meant to describe my troubles half in jest, Varenka, only it's plain that it doesn't come off with me, this joking. *I wanted to please you.*" Sadness lies hidden beneath the comic tone.

Thus, there is no complete resolution of the collision. A disturbing expectation is also aroused by the interval that separates this letter from the following one of August 11th, which again begins with wailing: *"I am lost, we are both lost...."*

However, the "real" cause of these woeful cries turns out to be not a new misfortune of Varenka's, which the reader had come to expect, but *the disclosure of the secret of the correspondence*, Devushkin's loss of self-respect. This letter, which is placed in an emotional frame of despair ("I am lost!–I am ruined!"), sets up the awful expectation of a new "fall" by Devushkin. After Varenka's deliberately laconic communication about burning her hand and thus losing the ability to work, a communication that is accompanied by a reference to her *last* thirty kopeks (letter of August 13th), Devushkin's fall seems inevitable. And Varenka, amidst the fervent, persuasive enthusiasm of her letter of August 14th, in the middle of reproaches and admonitions, *raises the curtain to reveal the drunken Devushkin*, who goes into the *embarrassedly philosophical monologue of a man who has not yet sobered up* (letter of August 19th).

In conclusion, Makar Devushkin, having finally come to his senses, makes an apology and reveals the psychological reality behind his fall: it is the consequence of a loss of self-respect. The end of the letter is a "moral" discussion, which, moreover, closes the whole cycle of "falls" described in this part of the novel, on the theme that "All the same I am a man, in heart and mind I am a man" (letter of August 21st).

Thus, this whole group of letters (from July 27th to September 3rd), marked off by Dostoevsky himself as an independent chapter of the novel, presents an unusually convoluted line of emotional transitions. This line begins from a dramatic peak (letter of July 27th), then, through a narrative descent complicated by Devushkin's confused *moralités*, goes over to cheerful expectations (letters of August 2nd and 3rd). Suddenly and sharply, it again rises to a tragic height (letter of August 4th), reaches a climax in Devushkin's letter of August 4th, is sharply broken by Varenka (letter of August 5th), and then passes through Devushkin's sad narration mixed with joking. Finally, once again in an unexpected jump, it rises upward, here reflecting complex emotional nuances in a zigzag, and is then untangled by Devushkin in his repentant confession.

Moreover, this chapter represents the realization of a new form of the "naturalist" story about the clerks' daily life, complicated by philanthropic tendencies, a story Devushkin dreamed about upon his first acquaintance with literary trends.

And, finally, the tense ascent of the emotional tone, indicating the crucial point at which the novel turns toward its tragic denouement, distinguishes this chapter as the apex of everything preceding it.

The novel's last chapter opens with long monologues by Varenka and Devushkin. The joyful *fall landscape* of Varenka's golden childhood *(the overture)* illuminates by contrast her "gloomy forebodings," her expectation of the end: *"How will it end, how will it all end?* You know, I have a sort of conviction, a feeling of certainty, that *I shall die this autumn..."* (letter of September 4th).

In Devushkin's letter of September 5th, against the background of the "damp, dark evening" Petersburg landscape, amid contrasts of poverty and luxury, to the cacaphony of the barrel-organ, amidst children, hungry "beggars," one hears *the social protest of the "poor man,"* a protest colored by Devushkin's personal grief over his inability "to give decent support" to his "orphan," "the defenseless Varenka." But this letter is resolved by contrast in the story of how Makar Devushkin did in fact give "decent support" to the unfortunate Gorshkov. His vague allusions naturally give the impression that there is some hope. And the following letter of September 9th, full of "dreadful spiritual distress, dreadful agitation," raises Devushkin to the heights of good fortune, depicting the happy denouement of all his misfortunes, and seemingly showing the nearness of a joyful denouement to the entire novel. This tone of limitless satisfaction, though in more moderate colors, is supported by Varenka's letter of September 10th and washes over Devushkin's whole letter of September 11th like a wave. The latter depicts Devushkin's reconciliation with all his "ill-wishers" and his bold dreams of paying back the "debt" to His Excellency; it contrasts the happy present to the "sorrowful" past ("But there, no matter, it's *past!*") against a background of cheerful, "youthful" memories and of humble repentance for "free thinking."

Varenka's following letter (September 15th) is in sharp, emotional, dramatic dissonance to Devushkin's. It presents him with ghosts of the past and frightens him with the shadow of Bykov, the most dangerous "adventurer."

The tragic tone also intensifies in Devushkin's neighboring letter of

September 15th. For the moment the tone is not connected to gloomy thoughts evoked by the specter of Varenka's departure, but rather is conveyed through the objective description of a detached episode, Gorshkov's death after winning his lawsuit. This episode is projected by Devushkin onto his own fate: "It's sad to think that one really does not know the day or the hour.... *One dies so easily, for no reason at all...*"

And Devushkin's next letter (September 19th) postpones, as it were, the tragic denouement of Bykov's appearance. Aimed at convincing Varenka of the happy carefreeness of their future *life together* ("now there will be extra money"), it contains only a covert warning.

But Varenka's letter of September 23rd, written after a three-day interval, decides the tragic outcome of the novel. The dramatic line rises sharply, even though the dialogue is contructed by means of interweaving contrasting expressive forms. The dry, businesslike tone of the commissions with which Varenka's notes are now filled still more sharply emphasizes the emotional tension, first, of Devushkin's perplexed and sad attempts to dissuade her and then, of his disorderly and delirious but restrained accounts.

The unusual richness of intonational vibrations accompanied by broken transitions in Devushkin's letter written on the eve of Varenka's marriage prepares for the tragic crescendo of funeral lamentations with which the novel breaks off at the highest point of its dramatic ascent. Moreover, with these final chords Makar Devushkin is again presented as a *forsaken lover*, i.e. he confirms the role that he at first tried to reject. Of course, the striking power of emotional tension, the delicate net of verbal vibrations, the fantastic complexity of the architectonic design of *Poor Folk* can only be fully appreciated upon integrating the analyses of plot, style, and composition. I have attempted to note only the general contours of such an analysis and tried to show that answers to two problems are harmoniously combined in *Poor Folk*: the first concerns the means of renovating naturalist poetics using the forms of sentimentalism and the thematics of socialism, and devices for transcending the comic cliché in depicting the "titular councillor"; the second concerns the "timeless value" of true artistic constructions, even though they be created as a lively response to contemporary issues.

Conclusion

The conclusions which can be drawn from the proposed analysis of *Poor Folk* against the background of the evolution of "naturalist" poetics may be formulated as follows:

1. One must reject the extension of the name "Natural School" to cover all genres of the 1830s and 1840s that gravitated toward the artistic reproduction of "reality." This term should rather be connected only with the group of works of the 1840s which carry the indelible imprint of the

214

influence of their models, i.e. Gogol's works, and which often include Gogolian devices in a complicated reworking and in an original synthesis with side influences.

2. Connected indissolubly with its predecessors, Gogol's "orchestra" of the 1830s, and having absorbed many of them into its ranks, the "Natural School" repudiated in the mid-1840s the series of outlived clichés of "Gogolianism." Its fundamental nucleus, *the school of F.M. Dostoevsky*, proclaimed the necessity of synthesizing "naturalist" forms with "bourgeois" sentimentalism, the necessity of rendering them more complex through the positive thematics of socialist humanism.

3. The return to sentimental forms was not a "fight with Gogol" in the consciousness of contemporaries; on the contrary, they saw it as a realization of Gogol's precepts, especially those they found in "The Overcoat."

4. Dostoevsky's *Poor Folk* was the first artistic realization of the tendencies noted by the ideologists of naturalism towards a rapprochement between Gogolian and sentimental forms (particularly in the interpretation of revived sentimentalism presented by "philanthropic" French literature).

5. The extraordinary originality of *Poor Folk* is based on its variety of devices of synthesis and the boldness with which Dostoevsky destroyed both the canon of sentimentalism and the clichés of naturalism.

6. The vivid originality of these artistic reforms is intensified by the fact that the "humanized" titular councillor Makar Devushkin, infected by utopian socialist ideas, is himself made a man of letters who tests the potential of his style for solving the most complex questions of the poetics of naturalism.

7. Having answered the most complicated questions of the poetics of the 1840s and having channeled the movement of wide literary currents into civic sentimentalism and sentimental naturalism, *Poor Folk*—as a result of the unusual, subtle architectonics of the letters and the complexity and completeness of the stylistic-compositional design—surpassed the historical conventionality of its thematics and the limitedness of the meanings its contemporaries assigned to it.

1923-1924

TOWARDS A MORPHOLOGY OF THE "NATURALIST" STYLE*
By V.V. Vinogradov

> Someone was grimacing before
> me, hidden behind this whole
> fantastic crowd, and pulling some
> sort of strings, mainsprings, and
> these puppets were moving, and
> he kept on laughing and laughing...

> *"St. Petersburg Visions in Verse
> and Prose"*

I
[The Contemporary Setting of *The Double*]

The "Petersburg poem"[1] *The Double*, which Dostoevsky himself always valued highly for its ideational content, had no success with the public upon its appearance and even undermined the author's reputation of a budding genius.[2] The critics, in justifying their cold, sometimes even ironically inimical attitude toward the novel, pointed out its formal weaknesses. However, the architectonics of *The Double*, the stylistic problems it tackles and the devices it uses for realizing them were not elucidated either by the reviewers at the time of its appearance or by subsequent investigators of Dostoevsky's work. Following Apollon Grigoriev, they sought and found in the "Petersburg poem" shreds of various works by Hoffmann,[3] or analyzed the "Poprishchin-like" psychology of Golyadkin, a genetic point of view that proved to be particularly seductive. Golyadkin's adventures were perceived until recently against the background of the socio-psychological interpretation of Gogol's Poprishchin,[4] and the juxtaposition of *The Double* with "The Diary of a Madman" has become a commonplace of Dostoevsky scholarship. Yet one should note that even Belinsky, from whom these opinions on *The Double* as an artistic reworking of "The Diary" ultimately derive, had

---

*[Originally published in *F.M. Dostoevskii: Stat'i i materialy*, vol. 1, ed. A.S. Dolinin (Moscow-Leningrad, 1922); translated from V.V. Vinogradov's *Èvoliutsiia russkogo naturalizma: Gogol' i Dostoevskii* (Leningrad, 1929), "K morfologii natural'nogo stilia (Opyt lingvisticheskogo analiza Peterburgskoi poèmy 'Dvoinik')," section I (pp. 206-217) and VII (pp. 280-290). We have translated only the first and last sections of Vinogradov's study, supplying subtitles, since the remainder of the article, concerned as it is with nuances of language, is virtually untranslatable.]

simply noted the common character of certain stylistic devices in the two works—"the masking, by means of humor, of a deeply tragic coloring and tone."[5] He had, moreover, firmly rejected any close literary kinship between the "types" of Poprishchin and Golyadkin. And, indeed, the majority of contemporary reviewers of *The Double* were struck by the coincidence of specific scenes, situations, and figures in Dostoevsky's second novel with *other* works by Gogol. For example, S.P. Shevyryov wrote: "In the beginning one is continuously encountering acquaintances from Gogol: now Chichikov, now the Nose, now Petrushka, now the turkey-cock in the shape of a samovar, now Selifan" (*The Muscovite*, 1846, Part I, No. 2, p. 172).[6]

Actually, the similarity of the main figures in *The Double* and "The Diary of a Madman" (Poprishchin—Golyadkin) could hardly have struck or surprised the contemporary reader. The "somewhat squinty and rather bald figure" of the wretched petty clerk with "ambition," an image canonized by Gogol, had already become quite traditional by Dostoevsky's time. P.V. Annenkov stated that "this type has ossified in our literature" (*The Contemporary*, 1849, Vol. XIII, p. 10). Yakov Butkov and a whole series of other writers of the Natural School had experimented with different stylistic types and varied combinations of plot schemes, using the "Petersburg summits" (i.e. attics) as the scene of the action, and had taken as their hero the standard type of the petty clerk "with ambition" who ends up going mad. (Besides Gogol's "Diary of a Madman," for example: in the *Northern Bee* February 15, 1834, "Three Pages from a Madhouse"; in the *Literary Supplements* to *The Russian Invalid* of 1835 (No. 54), "Pages from the Notes of a Madman" by E.G.; in Yakov Butkov's *Petersburg Heights,* the stories "One Hundred Rubles" and "The First of the Month"). Rather, contemporaries saw in *The Double* a completely new treatment of a traditional plot. Gogol's "Diary of a Madman" began to be viewed as the direct model for *The Double* only later, after a chronological distance had obscured the literary landscape of Dostoevsky's time.

The distinction between these two works in artistic intention and stylistic implementation is indisputable. Their similarity is limited merely to partial coincidences of the story line. One finds elaborated in both "The Diary of a Madman" and *The Double* a variant of the motif of the unhappy love of a titular councillor for the daughter of a general (or almost a general —in *The Double* it is the daughter of the Director, Klara Olsufievna), who prefers a brilliant young man from high society (the Kamerjunker Teplov in "The Diary"—Vladimir Semyonovich in *The Double*) to the clerk. "The crafty intrigues of the enemy" are lead in both story lines by the Division Head (the "Division Head" in "The Diary"—Andrey Filippovich in *The Double*). However, the elements of this traditional scheme were used by Gogol and Dostoevsky in completely different ways.

In Gogol's story the love intrigue is inserted into the framework of

Poprishchin's diary. The diary, in the strict sense, can include only the "works and days" of Poprishchin himself, and therefore the plot elaboration of relationships and intimate events in the Director's house has to be put in the form of the correspondence between the dogs, stolen from them by the author of the diary. The central device here—that of depicting things from the dogs' point of view, which is ironically juxtaposed to the human point of view in Poprishchin's remarks ("Give me a person! I want to see a person; I demand food of the kind that would nourish and delight my soul..."), thus generating a series of unexpected comic effects—creates an effective variety of styles. Poprishchin's madness motivates the inclusion of the correspondence of Madgie and Fidèle in the diary ("I confess, recently I've begun to hear and see such things as no one has seen or heard before"), and the sharp break in the story's basic design and the sudden changes in style follow from this motivation. The fact is that Gogol's rendering of the motif of an *idée fixe* presupposed the application of one of his favorite devices, the realization of a verbal metamorphosis: in this instance—the transformation of the madman into the object of his fixation (in "The Diary of a Madman"—into the King of Spain, in "The Order of Vladimir of the Third Class"—into the order of Vladimir of the Third Class).[7] The style changes in accordance with the crossing of the basic story with this new motif. There is a gradual transition to a mosaic-like coupling of phrases, logically unconnected, sometimes mechanically linked on the basis of common features of separate words, with interruptions full of pathos, imitating megalomania, and with sharp breaks in the lyrical *clausulae*. The figure of the madman served here to justify innovations in language.

There was no such pasting together of two different plot structures in *The Double*, and this novel was the realization of a quite different compositional plan.[8]

Apollon Grigoriev, who with particular persistence emphasized the tie between Dostoevsky's early works and Gogol's "Diary of a Madman," found the connection to lie not in plot dynamics, but in the relation of the "image of the author," the artistic "I," to the "literary reality" represented. He maintained that the Natural School, headed by Dostoevsky, "took from Gogol only that morbid tone of humor which is found throughout 'The Diary of a Madman' and 'The Overcoat,' and, after removing any aspiration toward an ideal, set about reproducing it in innumerable, though always dismal and monotonous, 'variations' " ("Russian Belles-Lettres in 1852").[9] Tracing the disintegration of Gogol's system into two schools—of *documentary* and *sentimental* naturalism,—Apollon Grigoriev characterized the relation of *The Double* to the tradition of the "The Diary" in the following way:

> Regard Akaky Akakievich from a sentimental point of view, become
> filled not with a universal human, decent sympathy for him, but

with an exclusive, morbid empathy,—in a word, go against the eternal wisdom of nature, weep about the fact that ugliness is ugliness, that what is funny is funny, that what is a pity is merely a pity;—raise to the level of a right the demands of the hero of "The Diary of a Madman" —and you will have Makar Alekseevich Devushkin, Mr. Golyadkin, Mr. Prokharchin, all these heroes of the stinking, dark haunts [of the Petersburg poor] ...[10]

Thus, the dependence of *The Double* on "The Diary" is here established on the basis of the norms for constructing the "fictional universe" of the work, and not of the pattern of its plot composition, or of a direct succession of literary types.

Even the part of *The Double*'s plot scheme that coincides with "The Diary" became lost in its different thematics. If, for the Natural School before Dostoevsky, literary madness, used in plots based in the world of the petty clerk, had been merely a tool for the denouement (as in Butkov's works, partly in Gogol's "The Order of Vladimir of the Third Class," and in the story by a minor writer, P. Mashkov, "Adam Adamovich Adamheim"), or had served as the motivation for new stylistic devices as in "The Diary," then Dostoevsky made Golyadkin's madness into a *naturalist theme* in *The Double.* Depiction of "madness for madness' sake" was how one contemporary, P. Annenkov, formulated the intention of *The Double*'s plot, and its novelty repelled other contemporaries as well: "An unpleasant and boring nightmare," "a tale boring to the point of exhaustion," "a breach of decency intolerable to the circle of educated readers," etc. "*The Double* is the history of a madness analyzed, it is true, to the extreme, but nonetheless repulsive as a corpse"(*The Finnish Messenger*, Vol. IX, p. 30).

The old romantic motif of madness had been overturned against a new stylistic and compositional background,[11] and a new plot arose.

In *The Double* Dostoevsky applied a device of plot construction characteristic of his poetics. It consisted in the stylistic transposition of well-known literary constructions, often even those of an artistic school which he rejected. What resulted was the unique two-leveledness of his plot semantics, where the silhouettes of old forms, whimsically transformed, show through the new devices of composition employed. The "fictional universe" that arose from the verbal fabric of the work was as if superimposed on the rejected literary world, which distinctly showed through the new plot structure. In essence this is not merely an individual peculiarity of Dostoevsky's manner as a writer: it is one of the principles of literary struggle, of literary reformation. A parodic tendency is not obligatory here. There is no stylization at all. There is, rather, a sort of "metaphorization" of an integral verbal composition or of its parts. The thematics of the plot are perceived as a double literary entity. Such a background level of the plot semantics (or more accurately, several such levels), underlying the directly revealed system of meanings, can be found in *The Double* once the work is placed in the context of the literary history of its epoch. The plot of *The Double* can be understood at this level as a naturalist transformation of the romantic "doubles" of Russian Hoffmannism. It is easy, for purposes of illustration, to point to the literary connection of *The Double* with a short story of the type of Evgeny Grebenka's "The Double" (1836, from the series *Stories of a Piryatinets*). The roots of the plot and style of Grebenka's story extend in various directions, but a part of them undoubtedly closely approximates the tradition of Nikolay Polevoy's *The Bliss of Madness* (cf. the authorial reflections in Grebenka's story: "Did not the soul of the poor man seek in the soul of the landowner's daughter its other half? What do you think, my philosopher gentlemen? Couldn't it be so?").

The narrator in Grebenka's story, now declaiming with elevated pathos and indulging in sentimental effusions, now rendering comic descriptions with chatty familiarity, tells about his meeting with a madman, Andrey, in the style of Gogol:

"Enlarge...a gopher to about five and a quarter feet, dress it in rags, stand it on its hind legs—and you would have a faithful portrait of the man who turned up in our courtyard...." The madman is being persecuted by his "double." The story of the sick man's life interests the narrator, and his companion acquaints him with it.

Andrey had been a renowned Cossack, the hero of the district. He falls in love with Ulyassya.

And truly Ulyassya was worthy of attention: her seventeenth spring had only just shaped her luxurious forms.... But I don't want to, will not begin to describe sculptural charm: a lot has been written and said about that without my help. Besides, can one say: I like a girl because she has black curls, a slim waist and a little foot? No; you can praise a horse that way, you can praise a hunting dog, but not the most beautiful half of God's beautiful creation—man....

Andrey languishes, seeks an opportunity to have a look at the landowner's daughter, sits opposite her father's house trying to penetrate the window with his gaze. Comes the day of a family celebration in the landowner's (Foma Fomich's) house: "But was everyone there happy?... Our world is so constructed that extremes are unavoidable in it.... Extremes disappear into contradictions: sobs turn into guffaws, prolonged laughter produces tears. But at Foma Fomich's there was a huge feast...." Andrey observes the noblemen's amusements from the courtyard: he yearns for Ulyassya.... There is dancing. "A skinny clerk in a blue frock coat with a huge cornelian seal on a long chain was capering about with her, his legs, exactly like two exclamation points, bent and broke at various angles...."

Andrey is indignant at the conduct of the clerk, who, "grinning, like a fool in front of a pie, comes up to Ulyassya, takes her in his arms—and off they whirl!" Andrey curses the insolent good-for-nothing not only mentally but out loud as well. Ulyassya's father hears his shout and asks the Cossack: "What are you looking over here like a sheep for?"

"A hundred thousand dozen barrels of devils take you, good-for-nothing," mutters Andrey, not seeing Foma Fomich and not hearing his words.

The nobleman orders his men to chase "that drunkard Andrey" out of the courtyard.

The nobleman's sharp voice brings the enamored Andrey to himself and the poor man's heart contracts spasmodically....

> The menials, showering him with blows and abuse, dragged him out of the courtyard.... He walked mechanically, like an animal, not understanding what they were doing to him; his whole life seemed to pass before his eyes which sought Foma Fomich's house; there a waltz still resounded, an old German beat out the rhythm, Ulyassya flashed by the window in the clerk's embrace. And how awfully all of nature looked at Andrey! The nobleman's house guffawed like an old dragoon, rolling from side to side; the garden smiled significantly; the brook grinned maliciously; even the lopsided pigeon-house, it too made grimaces.... And the people!... They celebrated. But how terrifying they were; their faces fell, their eyes darkened, their mouths distorted furiously, their breasts were bared; there it was black as pitch, there boiled an entire hell full of blood; they mockingly wink at Andrey: they come near him; they touch his heart with their cold fingers....

Andrey stops loving Andrey: "He imagined himself as two individuals, would converse with someone, calling him Andrey, and would say that he would have gotten married soon but that Andrey had prevented him...."

The "double" everywhere bars the way of the insane hero. And Ulyassya "gets married and—becomes a landed lady."

One could hardly deny the reflection in Dostoevsky's *The Double* of that evolutionary chain, one link of which is formed by Grebenka's story.

Moreover, one can easily understand why Dostoevsky did not cast the story, following Gogol, in the form of Golyadkin's diary or notes. It was not in harmony with the artistic task before him: a diary could not so precisely, in such a short time-span (four days), have provided such a thorough description of the hero's smallest actions, preserving Dostoevsky's usual speed of plot development, in depicting the curious adventures of Mr. Golyadkin. For this reason Dostoevsky chose a "detached observer" as a "decoy" narrator whose style conditions both the compositional scheme and the means

222

of depiction, as almost always in Dostoevsky's works.

II
[The Compositional Principles of *The Double*]

A narrational *skaz* which mainly records motions completed in time is best suited to chronological plot development. This perhaps partly explains the fact that *The Double* is constructed in the form of a sequential narrative of the events of four days. The short time span in which the intrigue is developed followed naturally from the unique peculiarities of a style which notes every motion, regardless of repetition. (Cf. a story by Alexander Palm, a representative of the "school of the young Dostoevsky," which reflects the devices of *The Double*: "One Day in a Humdrum Life," *Moscow City Register*, 1847, No. 110-118.)

Corresponding to this chronological principle, the poem is broken down into four parts, each of which is a narrative about the events of a single day. The first three such parts (Ch. I-V, VI-VII; VIII-XI)[12] have an almost identical beginning (Golyadkin's awakening); however, in the beginning of the last part, a description of a nightmare precedes the exposition of the day's events, since by this time the borderline between dream and reality, between delirious visions and real life, has already disappeared for the hero.

At the beginning of the "poem" the narrator acts as a completely detached, but very attentive, observer, who notes with interest the details of Golyadkin's surroundings, his conversations and actions. He regards Golyadkin quite objectively: "His sleepy, squinty and rather bald figure," according to the narrator's admission, "called *absolutely* no one's particular attention to itself" [Ch. I]. The significance of many of Golyadkin's actions remains unclear to the observer, and he limits himself to modest conjectures ("Evidently the livery had been hired for some special occasion," etc. [Ch. I]). The artistic "reality" of Golyadkin's life flows on as if independent of the narrator's relation to it; for him it is a foreign, somewhat puzzling existence. Ironic notes and occasional puns vary the epic trend of the narrative.

Then—skillfully and unnoticeably—Golyadkin himself reveals the best way of remaining unnoticed, of stealing away from people who, like Andrey Filippovich, arouse his "fear" and "anguish": "Shall I pretend that it's not me, that *it's someone else strikingly like me....* Precisely, it isn't me, it isn't me, and that's all there is to it" [Ch. I]. In this way the idea of the "double" hazily comes to the surface.

The action moves quickly and directly. "Suddenly," impelled by an inspiration of some sort, "he turns back to Liteynaya Street." "The fact was that Mr. Golyadkin suddenly needed, *probably for his own peace of mind,* to communicate *something of the greatest importance to his doctor,* Krestyan Ivanovich Rutenspitz" [Ch. I].

223

Then follows Golyadkin's meeting with his doctor, a scene full of obscure but significant hints. Although the scene is borrowed from Gogol, Dostoevsky adapted it to the demands of his plot ("madness for madness' sake"). Indeed, Golyadkin's meeting with his doctor acquires so major a role that it not only sets the plot in motion but also provides the novel's resolution in the epilogue. This apparent break in the direct line of actions directed toward Golyadkin's participation in Klara Olsufievna's "celebration" is completely understandable: in the scene at the doctor's the pattern of the story line according to which the mentally deranged Golyadkin is acting, is brought into the open. This underlying story line is the *battle* with the "deadly enemies" who "have sworn to ruin" [Ch. II] Golyadkin and have sought out an "imposter" for this purpose.

In the light of these clarifications, Golyadkin's actions are seen as preparations for a possible battle, which continue after an obligatory break. (Cf. the stylistic device used throughout *The Double* of presenting a single movement in triune form: an initial action, a retreat, and a return to the action.) Finally, Golyadkin is ejected from the "celebration": this is a call to arms, a public humiliation.

In this plot scheme the love intrigue serves merely as a motivation for the animosity of Golyadkin's enemies toward him. It remains for the most part dormant, outside of the actual limits of the narration, and enters in relief only when the plot is set in motion, at which point the alignment of the forces of the hero and his enemies is clarified, and in the denouement, when, in the midst of the sentimental situation of the hero's "reconciliation with people and with fate," a situation which contrasts with the main action, the sentence passed on Mr. Golyadkin, "perfidiously deceived" by his enemies, resounds "sternly and terribly" [Ch. XIII].

Chapter IV, where the hero appears in the midst of his enemies, is the beginning, in the strict sense, of the "poem" celebrating a heroic battle. It serves to justify the transition to a lyrical comic *skaz* of mock solemnity. Golyadkin's appearance at the ball is depicted by means of a favorite stylistic device of Dostoevsky's which also influences the way the compositional parts of the novel are joined together. This is the device of describing one movement in triune form, as a progression of three movements: the attempt at some action, the retreat, and the final accomplishment of the action. But before taking action at the ball, Golyadkin bides his time, for the moment merely surveying the general course of events in the role of a "detached observer."

In this way the roles of the narrator and Golyadkin coincide: stepping back into the position of a "detached observer," Golyadkin, so to speak, shields himself with the narrator. Correspondingly, there is a shift from the objective narrational *skaz* to what is virtually a transcription of Golyadkin's cumbersome speech ("He was also there, ladies and gentlemen—not *at the ball,* that

224

is, but almost at the ball" [Ch. 4]). When Golyadkin again returns to his role as "main actor," the narration resumes its former objectivity.

Golyadkin's "bold stroke" ("Mr. Golyadkin clearly perceived that the time for a bold stroke, the time for the humiliation of his enemies was at hand" [Ch. IV]) and his defeat are portrayed in a continuous counterpoint, an effective interplay, of the two types of narration, the lyrical comic *skaz* of mock solemnity and the businesslike narrative style which unexpectedly interrupts and replaces it. During Golyadkin's "flight" from his enemies, against the background of a landscape coinciding with the basic action ("Mr. Golyadkin fled...seeking safety from his enemies.... The snow and rain...suddenly and with one accord attacked Mr. Golyadkin—crushed as he was with misfortunes already—giving no quarter or respite...as if expressly conferring and concurring with his enemies..." [Ch. V]), the "impostor," "prepared" by his enemies, makes his appearance.

Golyadkin comes to recognize his "double" in a series of meetings through a progressive accumulation of signs indicating their terrible likeness. Thus, the idea which had occurred to Golyadkin at the beginning of the day —"It's not me, but someone else strikingly like me"—is contrastingly realized that night.

It is quite understandable that further in the narrative the enemies quit the scene, leaving Golyadkin and the "impostor" alone. But, although they appear only sporadically, they incessantly hover invisibly above the scene and direct the actions of the "impostor" from the wings.

The mutual relations of the two Golyadkins, Senior and Junior, are depicted with the usual devices of the fantastic short story of the grotesque sort, whimsically interweaving the phantasmagoria of tragic apparitions with comic scenes of commonplace vulgarity. According to the observations of Grossman and Rodzevich, which require revision in the light of the corresponding Russian tradition which existed prior to Dostoevsky, "here Hoffmann bursts through at every step," not only in the common motif of the split peronality, but also in stylistic juxtapositions which are designed to eliminate the thin borderline between the fantastic world in which the tragic battle is taking place and the comic details of the stylized reality surrounding it.

Several means are used toward this end in the narrative of the second day [Ch. VI]. First, there is a firm denial of suppositions that the hero is raving, that he has suffered a momentary derangement of the imagination, or that it was all "a dream" (cf. Gogol's "The Nose"), and grounds are offered for the reality of the events of the previous day by references to the "fierce diabolical malice of his enemies" and to his "bitter experience of life" [Ch. VI]. Secondly, by way of contrast to Golyadkin's "horror" at seeing his double in the office, the chance coincidence of two identical Golyadkins is given a "rational," everyday explanation in a conversation with

225

a "kind" comforter, the clerk Anton Antonovich [Ch VI]. Finally, there is the general shift of the narrator, who is transformed from an impartial "detached observer" into an ardent advocate of Golyadkin,[13] "strikingly like" him in his perception of events. In connection with this last device, the businesslike narrative *skaz* is replaced by the lyrically-tinged elements of the "high" style. The relationship between Golyadkin and the "double" during the second day is determined by a principle which is revealed at the very beginning of that day's narrative: "I won't protest and will completely submit" [Ch. VI]. Golyadkin's attempt to win over the "impostor," its seemingly happy outcome, and the agreement reached during the "friendly evening party"—"We'll fox 'em together. We'll start an intrigue of our own" [Ch. VII] —are in keeping with his policy of pacification.

One should note that the "double's" entrance on the scene is always accompanied by assertions of his real existence ("No, it's no illusion" [Ch. VI] ; cf. the same statement about the letter [Ch. IX]).

The narrative of the third day is contrastingly juxtaposed to the exposition which preceded it: "It was now no longer a question of some kind of passive defense—there was something decisive, something of an offensive in the air..." [Ch. VIII]. The "eternal friendship" turns out to have been a snare, "the first move" in the impostor's intrigue. And now the "impostor," supported by Golyadkin's enemies ("all these people," "all in cahoots with one another" [Ch. VIII]), assumes the role of a crafty seducer of people. The doubts about the real existence of the "double" that had crept into Golyadkin's soul— "It's probably been some sort of an illusion—either something different happened from what actually did—or it was I who went, and somehow I took myself for someone else" [Ch. VIII]— are dispersed by the "reality" of the "twin's" opportune entrance.

Golyadkin's unsuccessful attempt to expose the impostor—"Imposture and shamelessness, my good sir, don't lead to good, they lead to the gallows. Grishka Otrepiev was the only one, sir, to gain by imposture—after deceiving a blind people, and then not for long" [Ch. VIII] —is depicted in a counterpoint of contrasting styles, imitating the battle between resoluteness and sensible caution.

The impostor evades pursuit. "Everything, even Nature herself, seemed to be up in arms against Mr. Golyadkin" [Ch. IX]. This motivates one of the novel's most characteristic stylistic-compositional devices: the return to an initial resolution—in this case, "I'll triumph through meekness" [Ch. IX] [14]— from which there were temporary deviations. Golyadkin makes concessions: he agrees to recognize the "impostor" as a twin created by Providence and petted by "beneficent officialdom." But the diplomatic correspondence about the terms of peace, in which the exact "bounds" occupied by each of the "completely alike" Golyadkins are fixed (to avoid "substitutions" of the sort that occurred in the restaurant [Ch. IX]), only leads to a breaking-off of relations.

In the narrative of the last, decisive day of battle, the parallelism with the preceding parts of the "poem" is deliberately destroyed: at its beginning [Ch. X] there is the description of Golyadkin's nightmare, which brings him to the realization that "even his waking hours were hardly any happier." The sinister atmosphere intensifies with the mention of a seeming "anomaly in the course of the heavenly luminary" and with the sudden discovery of the "strategic diversion" of the "niggardly German woman" who is in the service of his enemies.

The battle opens with the presentation of an ultimatum to the "impostor" ("It's either you or me. There isn't room for both of us" [Ch. X]) and Golyadkin's reconnaissance operations (he sends a clerk to the German woman's: "You inquire, brother, find out whether something's being cooked up there on my account—what action he's taking" [Ch. X]. [15]

Finally, Golyadkin himself penetrates enemy territory. Infuriated by the "sallies" of the "double," he decides to appeal for help to a benevolent superior, on the way unsuccessfully "accosting Andrey Filippovich, who was very much surprised by such an unexpected assault," and finally turning to Anton Antonovich ("Back me up, Anton Antonovich, intercede on my behalf, Anton Antonovich" [Ch. X]), with the same lack of success. The pursuit of the enemy, which had been interrupted by the deceptive truce, also ends in failure—and this returns Golyadkin to the beginning—to Izmaylov Bridge, to the home of Olsufy Ivanovich. In depicting all these peripeteia of the "battle," the real relations of things are completely dissolved in the delirious visions of Mr. Golyadkin.

This is achieved by the stylistic device described above, by which the narrational *skaz* is abundantly larded with quotations from Golyadkin's thoughts and speech. As a consequence of this device, the narrator seems to merge with the hero and tells only about actions and events which are passing through Golyadkin's consciousness (cf. the constant formula introducing a "new circumstance": "Having come to his senses, our hero noticed..."), depicting them as they seem to Golyadkin himself ("so it seemed, at least, to our hero"—"so it seemed to Mr. Golyadkin").

From the whole course of the exposition it is clear that the battle has to finish with Golyadkin's defeat and ruin. But the "tragic" outcome of the battle is presented against the background of an original parody of the standard denouement of sentimental love novellas, the unsuccessful abduction of the loved one who is cloistered as a result (cf. the parody of this motif of abduction in the novel *The Voyages and Strange Adventures of the Bald and Noseless Bridegroom Foma Fomich Zavardynin*, when the sentimental lady, Irina Alekseevna, says of her husband: "To me he was a lover, a real Romeo, straight from the stage...he abducted me...in terrible weather...chilled to the spine, the poor dear..."). Golyadkin's speeches accompanying the would-be abduction are strewn with allusions to a whole series of novels by "vile German poets and novelists" [Ch. XIII] and to the French and Russian love novellas, including, by the way, Pushkin's "Count Nulin" (Klara Olsufievna had studied at the same boarding school of the emigrée Falbala as the heroine of Pushkin's poem, Natalie Pavlovna, and had there adopted the same habits).

But, as one would expect, the abduction in *The Double* is resolved not by the cloistering of the "fiancée" but by Golyadkin's confinement in a madhouse, or as his doctor refers to it, "a lodging, viz firevood, light and service" [Ch. XIII].

Thus, the compositional plan of *The Double*, which is predetermined to a significant extent by its stylistic devices, also sharply distinguishes this "poem" from Gogol's "Diary of a Madman," to which literary history has hitherto traced its origin.

In examining the system of stylistic devices used in *The Double* attentively, one easily notes a feature characteristic of all of Dostoevsky's early works: the absolute dominance of the speech of the "poor clerk," which serves as the framework within which Dostoevsky conducts his experiments in all other stylistic forms. Under the influence of the determining significance of precisely this stylistic form, Dostoevsky, having rejected the framework of a diary by Golyadkin himself, had to subtly turn the narrator into Golyadkin's "double." With this transformation, lyric sentimental notes entered the narrational *skaz*. And, indeed, contemporaries saw in *The Double* the birth of a "particular fantastic sort of sentimental novel."

1921-1922

228

"THE NOSE" AND *THE DOUBLE**
by A.L. Bem

> "I could tell you much about how...he, with his own typical atomistic analysis, perceived the character of Gogol's works."
> —*From a letter of Dr. Yanovsky to A.G. Dostoevsky*

> "My God! My God! Why such misfortune?"
> —*Gogol, "The Nose"*

> "My God! My God!... Give me strength in the inexhaustible depths of my woes...."
> —*Dostoevsky,* The Double

There is no need to prove the fact that the Gogolian manner, and in particular the tale "The Nose," influenced Dostoevsky's *The Double: A Petersburg Poem*, since it is obvious.

There have already been so many convincing comparisons of the two works in the critical literature, beginning with S. Shevyryov's vivid statement about *The Double*, "...here one is constantly encountering acquaintances from Gogol: now Chichikov, now the Nose, now Petrushka, now the turkey-cock in the shape of a samovar, now Selifan,"[1] and ending with V. Vinogradov's most recent comprehensive work on *The Double*,[2] that it is unnecessary to deal with this topic again from the usual point of view of influence.

In this work, I would like to pick up the topic of Gogol's influence on Dostoevsky where my predecessors left off.

The fact of influence, or even, as I shall attempt to demonstrate later, of more than influence, is undeniable. It is so undeniable and obvious that as early as the first appearance of *The Double* it produced total bewilderment. K.S. Aksakov, for example, responded to Dostoevsky's newly-published "poem" as follows:

---

*[Originally published in *Slavia*, VII, No. 1 (1928), pp. 63-86 and as a separate brochure under the title *K voprosu o vliianii Gogolia na Dostoevskogo* (Prague, 1928). Later included in Bem's *U istokov tvorchestva Dostoevskogo*, Vol. III of *O Dostoevskom*, ed. A. Bem (Prague, 1936), pp. 139-63, with some corrections, which have been included in this English translation by Peter B. Stetson.]

In this tale we see not the influence of Gogol, but an imitation of him. But one should not copy creative works, one should produce one's own, which are not simply imitations. But since Mr. Dostoevsky copies only Gogol's devices, the surface movement of his work, only its exterior, without understanding, as is obvious, that all of this is fine in Gogol's work because it is spontaneous and alive, because it flows from inner causes, and when someone chasing after likenesses seizes only the bare exterior, only the devices, without catching the spirit and life embodied therein, it will turn out unbearably lifeless, dry, and boring. This is what Dostoevsky does in this long and unbelievably tiresome tale. In it, Dostoevsky constantly mimics Gogol, frequently imitating him to such an extent that what results is no longer imitation, but appropriation. *We do not even understand how this tale could have appeared. All Russia knows Gogol, knows him almost by heart; and here, in front of everyone, Mr. Dostoevsky rearranges and repeats outright whole sentences from Gogol.* Naturally, these are just mere sentences, deprived of their vitality; they are only a bare imitation of the exterior of Gogol's great works. The entire tale consists only of this; there is neither sense, nor imitation, nor ideas, nothing. From the rags of the once-beautiful clothing of a true artist Mr. Dostoevsky has sewn himself a garment and brazenly shows himself to the reading public. (*Moscow Literary and Scientific Symposium* for 1947, pp. 33-34)

Without passing judgment on *The Double,* we are still asking, ninety years after its publication, the same perplexing question, "How could this tale have appeared?" Surely Dostoevsky must have understood that by imitating Gogol so blatantly he was condemning his own work to failure in advance? Surely he must have realized that, after Gogol, his tale was either total nonsense, as K. Aksakov believed, or else a challenge to the entire Russian reading public?

Even by simply juxtaposing various parts of "The Nose" and *The Double*, which has already been done to a certain extent in the critical literature, it becomes apparent just how right Aksakov was when he asserted that Dostoevsky, in his "poem" (as he called *The Double*, following Gogol's subtitle to *Dead Souls*), "frequently imitates him to such an extent that what results is no longer imitation, but appropriation." I will use these juxtapositions of parts of the two works and supplement them with my own observations.

The second chapter of "The Nose," which is compositionally entirely independent, and whose plot, as we shall see, is obviously related to the opening of *The Double*, begins as follows:

The collegiate assessor Kovalyov woke up rather early and went "Brrr" with his lips, which he always did when he woke up, although he himself could not explain for what reason. Kovalyov *stretched, and ordered the small mirror* standing on the table *to be brought to him. He wanted to look at the pimple* which had popped up on his nose the evening before, but to his great amazement, he saw that instead of a nose, there was an entirely smooth space!

Dostoevsky begins his "poem" with an obvious imitation of Gogol's style:

It was a little before eight o'clock in the morning when the titular councillor Yakov Petrovich Golyadkin awakened after a long sleep, yawned, *stretched* and finally opened his eyes completely.... Having leapt out of bed, he at once *ran to a small round mirror* which stood on his bureau.... [Golyadkin] remained entirely satisfied with everything he saw in the mirror. "Wouldn't it be something," said Mr. Golyadkin under his breath, "wouldn't it be something if I were not up to the mark, if, for example, something weren't right—if some strange pimple had popped up there, or if some other unpleasantness had happened; however, so far it's not bad; so far everything's going well." [Ch. I]

Not only the common features of style, which can be explained by the general orientation on the Gogolian manner traditional in tales about "the little man," but also the similarity of the situations and details betrays a definite connection between these two approaches to stories about doubles/impostors. In these two works, the meetings of the heroes with the impostors are also very close stylistically and compositionally.

Gogol describes Kovalyov's meeting with the Nose as follows:

Suddenly he stopped by the doors of a house *as if rooted to the spot*; before his eyes an inexplicable phenomenon occurred: a carriage stopped in front of the entrance; the doors opened; bending over, a gentleman in a uniform jumped out and ran up the stairs. *What was the horror and at the same time astonishment of Kovalyov when he realized that this was his own nose!* At this unusual spectacle it seemed to him that everything whirled before his eyes; he felt that he could hardly stay on his feet; but he, all trembling as if in a fever, decided at any cost to wait until the nose returned to his carriage.

Already in the description of Golyadkin's meeting with the stranger, before he recognizes him as his double, Dostoevsky uses similar stylistic devices in describing his hero's horror.[3] However, I will quote only the scene of

Golyadkin's recognition of the stranger as his double:

> All Mr. Golyadkin's presentiments were completely realized.... *He gasped for breath, his head started to whirl.* The stranger sat before him, also in a hat and coat, on his bed, smiling slightly, and, squinting a little, nodded his head in a friendly way. Mr. Golyadkin wanted to scream, but couldn't—to protest in some way, but he hadn't the strength. *His hair stood on end and he sat down on the spot, numb with horror.* ... Mr. Golyadkin had recognized his nocturnal friend beyond the shadow of a doubt. His nocturnal friend *was none other than he himself* —*Mr. Golyadkin himself*, another Mr. Golyadkin, but exactly the same as he himself—in a word, what is called a double in all respects.... [Ch. V]

The heroes' sense of improbability and of the impossibility of the double's materialization is transmitted in *The Double* with the same closeness to Gogol.[4] " *'Only no, it can't be,..'* " says Major Kovalyov in Gogol's story. " 'It's incredible that a nose should disappear; *incredible by any means. This, probably, is either a dream or simply a daydream;* perhaps somehow by mistake I drank the vodka I rub my beard with after shaving instead of water. Ivan, that fool, didn't take it away and I, probably, picked it up.' In order really to convince himself that he wasn't drunk, *the major pinched himself* so painfully that he shrieked. *This pain completely convinced him that he was acting and living in a waking state.*"

In Dostoevsky this feeling of uncertainty, of the absurdity of events, is twice conveyed in a quite similar style: "*All this was so strange, incomprehensible, wild, seemed so impossible*, that it was really difficult to give credence to the whole business; *Mr. Golyadkin himself was even ready to admit that these were all delirious ravings,* a sudden derangement of the imagination, loss of mind..." [Ch. VI] .

And in another place in the same sixth chapter: " 'What is it, *a dream or not*,' he thought: 'is it real or is it a continuation of yesterday's.... *Am I asleep, am I dreaming?' Mr. Golyadkin tried pinching himself*, even tried pinching someone else.... *'No, it's not a dream and that's all there is to it....*' "

These juxtapositions are probably sufficient to confirm the indisputable stylistic similarity of "The Nose" and *The Double*. V.V. Vinogradov, carefully examining the style of *The Double*, came to the interesting conclusion that "in *The Double* Dostoevsky too openly combines various devices of Gogol's in his own stylistic formulations."[5]

To be sure, Dostoevsky actually does irritate the reader with his blatant way of dealing with Gogol's works. Without a moment's hesitation he takes the names of some of his characters from Gogol, such as, for instance, Petrushka and the German woman, Karolina Ivanovna (from "The Overcoat");

he brings in the names of minor characters which make one think involuntarily, once again, of Gogol's: a few which come to mind are "the Basavryukovs" (*Evenings on a Farm near Dikanka*), and "Princess Chevchekhanova" suggesting "the state councillor's wife Chekhtaryova"; he introduces entire episodes that parody the most memorable passages in Gogol's works, like the beginning of Chapter IV—the ball at the home of Klara Olsufyevna—which is written entirely in the style of one part of "The Tale of How Ivan Ivanovich Quarrelled with Ivan Nikiforovich." In Chapter VII an imitation of the famous "humane" passage in Gogol's "The Overcoat" suddenly and unjustifiably intrudes:

> There was something abject, downtrodden and fearful in all his gestures, so that at this moment he was, if one may use the simile, rather like a man who, having no clothes of his own, has donned someone else's, and can feel the sleeves riding up and the waist nearly round the back of his neck, and is all the time pulling down the miserably short waistcoat; he edges away, tries hard to hide, looks at every face to see if people are ashamed on his account or laughing at him, strains his ears to find out if they're discussing his affairs; *the man goes red; the man gets confused; his pride suffers.*

Who can read this and not recall Gogol's "Leave me alone! Why are you insulting me?"

I shall omit comparisons of plot, even with "Diary of a Madman," which suggested themselves as soon as *The Double* appeared in print, since they would lead me far astray of my topic.[6] I will merely point out a few more of the less striking similarities, which are sometimes more significant and indicative than those resemblances which could be ascribed to the similarity of the general plot structures.

When he first discovered that his nose was missing, Major Kovalyov decided to confirm this unlikely occurrence, and

> ...*went into a pastry shop* expressly *in order to look in the mirror.* Fortunately there was no one in the pastry shop; *little boys were sweeping the rooms and arranging the chairs*; some *with sleepy eyes* were bringing out *hot meat pies* on trays; *yesterday's coffee-spattered newspapers* were scattered around on the tables and chairs. "Well, thank God no one's here," he said, "now I can have a look." *He shyly approached the mirror and took a look.* "The devil take it, what rubbish!" he said, spitting. "At least if there was something in place of a nose, but nothing!..."

Later, after the nose's happy return to its rightful place, Major Kovalyov goes into the pastry shop a second time:

> Kovalyov hurried to dress right away, took a cab and drove straight *to the pastry shop*. Entering, he called out still from a distance: *"Boy, a cup of chocolate!"* and himself the same minute turned to the mirror: there's the nose.

Restaurants and coffeehouses appear several times in the course of Dostoevsky's tale, and nearly every detail mentioned by Gogol is used to describe them. After walking through the shops in Gostiny Dvor (which also is found in "The Nose"), Golyadkin goes to "a well-known *restaurant* on Nevsky Prospect," for a bite to eat; here he "quietly *settled down with a certain meager national newspaper*." "After reading a couple of lines he rose, *looked at himself in the mirror*, righted his dress and smoothed his hair..." [Ch. III]. The meat pies mentioned by Gogol in his description of the pastry shop were used by Dostoevsky in the scene of Golyadkin's encounter with the double in the *"restaurant"* where Golyadkin is charged for the ten "fish *pasties"* [Ch. IX] eaten by the double. During Golyadkin's meeting with his double in the *"coffeehouse"* [Ch. XI], other details from Gogol's description of the pastry-shop are used.

> The *coffeehouse* the two Mr. Golyadkins entered stood secluded from the main streets, and *was* at that moment *quite deserted*.... Mr. Golyadkin and his unworthy enemy passed through into a second room, where a *pasty-faced urchin with close-cropped hair* was fiddling around by the stove with a bundle of firewood, making an effort to bring some life back into a dead fire. At Golyadkin junior's request, *chocolate was served.*

Dostoevsky also included *The Northern Bee*, in which the clerk in the newspaper office recommended the incident with the nose be published "...as a rare phenomenon of nature...for the edification of youth...or simply for general curiosity." In his room, the exhilarated Golyadkin casually mentions to the double "an anecdote he had read recently in *The Northern Bee*" [Ch. VII].

Obviously, Dostoevsky did not at all attempt to conceal the similarity between his poem and Gogol's "The Nose" from the reader, but rather he emphasized it by the general Gogolian background of his novel.

Is it possible to suppose that the young Dostoevsky simply displayed complete incompetence in this work, and that he, as Aksakov claimed, merely mimics the externals of Gogol, without justifying his "poem" with any content?

I think that at the present time, when we have before us all of Dostoevsky's writings, it is not hard to show that *The Double* is an essential and ideationally crucial link in his life's work. If this were not the case, Dostoevsky would not have given the ideational aspect of this early work such a high evaluation in *The Diary of a Writer* (1877), many years after the publication of *The Double*. "This tale didn't work out for me at all," he wrote, *"but the idea was rather inspired, and I never dealt with anything in my writing more serious than this idea."*[7] We now know, although still only in the most general terms, how *The Double* is connected with such high points in Dostoevsky's work as "Notes from the Underground,"[8] *The Possessed,* and *The Brothers Karamazov.* It is significant that V. Pereverzev is able to associate the idea of the double with all of the author's works. In the most recent criticism, the ideational meaning of this early tale appears more and more frequently as a source of many of the central artistic notions of the future author of *The Brothers Karamazov.*[9] Consider, for example, the significance of *The Double* for the well-known scene of Ivan Karamazov's nightmare. A.S. Dolinin sees the ultimate development of the idea of *The Double* in this scene with the devil. He states that "the 'idea' which Dostoevsky had been unsuccessful in realizing in *The Double*, but which he had cherished throughout his life, found its consummate artistic expression" in this scene.[10] After this it is hardly possible to assert that Dostoevsky did not incorporate any ideational content into *The Double*. But if this is the case, then why did he connect this ideational content with Gogol's "The Nose," and why in such a provocative manner? This is precisely the question which I would like to answer in the present article.

I make the assumption that Dostoevsky's *The Double* was produced under the direct influence of Gogol's "The Nose," that some aspect of the ideational content of Gogol's tale offended Dostoevsky and elicited a sharp literary refutation on his part. In this case, because of its very nature, the work must be examined as a unique parody with a different ideational-literary content.[11]

In such an analysis the question of influence is shifted from the customary plane and requires a somewhat different methodological approach. We should not be satisfied with searches for more and more new juxtapositions of the two works, but rather with the discovery of gradations and contrasts in those situations which are externally similar. After all, in an artistic polemic or, more accurately, in a polemic between artistic works, one can closely approximate the form of the work with which one is polemicizing even while sharply diverging in content. By failing to understand this, one could be irritated by what is artistically justified, which is just what happened with the contemporary critics of Dostoevsky's second novel.

Therefore we must first of all establish a foundation for our point of view on Dostoevsky's *The Double* as a literary refutation of Gogol.

Let's retrace our steps a little, however, and go back to questions of a formal nature.

Dostoevsky begins his poem with the awakening of Yakov Petrovich Golyadkin. We have already noted that this scene repeats to a certain extent the awakening of Major Kovalyov in Gogol's "The Nose." It is as if Dostoevsky were here intentionally both comparing and contrasting the two heroes at the same time. Not by chance is the beginning of *The Double* compared to the *second* chapter of Gogol's tale. With the discernment of an artist Dostoevsky here catches something which literary history was to realize only considerably later. Compositionally, besides the author's introduction and conclusion, "The Nose" consists of two independent parts: the first elaborates a plot about a nose which has somehow become detached and baked in a loaf of bread, and has its own hero, the barber Ivan Yakovlevich; the second is "the nose's own story," with a plot about an impostor/double.[12] Only "the nose's own story" could have interested Dostoevsky, and he begins his narrative from the moment of its hero's awakening. Then follow the coinciding events. Both heroes wake up and, before anything else, turn to the mirror.[13] Major Kovalyov "wanted to take a look at *the pimple* which had popped up on his nose the evening before." Mr. Golyadkin feared more than anything else that which Major Kovalyov had sought on his own nose. " 'Wouldn't it be something,..' said Mr. Golyadkin under his breath, 'wouldn't it be something if I were not up to the mark, if, for example, something weren't right—*if some strange pimple had popped up there*, or if some other unpleasantness had happened' "[Ch. I]. Dostoevsky does not repeat that "pimple" fortuitously. Precisely this sort of detail underlines the formal closeness of the point of departure of the two works. But then, after coming very close to the story of the nose, Dostoevsky abruptly changes the direction of his poem's plot.

Instead of the missing "Nose," Dostoevsky introduces the "Double." True, Dostoevsky does not lose sight of the "nose" altogether; it crops up again and again in his tale, as if to remind us of its close relation to the "Double." Dostoevsky's work is full of expressions like these: "...every little whippersnapper...looks down his *nose* at a gentleman"; "there are people who don't like...*poking their noses in* where they're not asked"; "The hem of the stranger's coat *struck his nose*"; "they practically *bumped noses*"; "He thrust out the tip of his *nose*"; "As if someone had pricked his *nose* with a pin."

I am told that one cannot base anything on such trifles since, after all, the word "nose" is not particularly uncommon in everyday speech. Nevertheless, this objection can no longer have any force. After the work of Freud, we know what kind of a role trifles can play in psychological existence, and therefore we must not ignore trifles in a literary work as well. B.M. Eikhenbaum is correct when he emphasizes the significance of trifles in the analysis of a short story whose organizing principle is not in the tale, but in the telling, which reflects the personal tone of the author. "The center of gravity," states B.M. Eikhenbaum, "shifts from the plot (which is here reduced to a minimum) to the devices of the *skaz*, and the most important comic role is given to puns, which can be simple plays on words or develop into small anecdotes. Comic effects are achieved by the *manner* of the *skaz*. Therefore, for the study of this type of composition, those very 'details' which are interspersed throughout the exposition prove to be so important that the structure of the story disintegrates if they are removed" [see above, p. 119].

To those who are prepared to see this type of repetition as a coincidence, I suggest that they find another excerpt from Dostoevsky, of the same size, in which the word "nose" appears as frequently. It is extremely significant that in reworking *The Double* Dostoevsky removed a number of passages where the word "nose" appeared. It is necessary to emphasize that among the discarded parts we find not only common expressions like "to put someone's nose out of joint," and "they stood nose to nose," but also some that are extremely relevant for an understanding of the basic connection with Gogol's "The Nose." Such phrases as these ring almost of paranoia for the fate of one's nose: *"Everyone protects his own nose"; "it's not always good to stick your nose out too far"; "you shouldn't stick your nose out too far; so to speak, you've got to take good care of your nose now, because it can only bring misfortune to stick your nose out too far...."* The following quote also points out the obsessional associations connected with the nose: *" 'Here we stand nose-to-nose,'* our hero thought. *'What would happen if our noses grew permanently together?'* Just then he recalled the fairy tale which told about the *sausage that attached itself to the nose of the old man's greedy wife."*[14]

But no matter how tempting the "story of the nose itself" was for Dostoevsky, as is evident from these quotations, he turned emphatically away from it.

Apparently Dostoevsky realized the impossibility of producing a *skaz* in the spirit of Gogol. The grotesque short story, which produces no consciousness of internal tension and has no "idea," evoked in Dostoevsky a feeling of deep dissatisfaction, the more so since he keenly appreciated that horror which lay at the basis of Major Kovalyov's story. For him, the fantastic tale of the disappearance of the nose grew into the tragedy of the hero's personality. Dostoevsky, with his unique sense of the tragic—not of the comic—detected in Gogol's "The Nose" the elements of a genuine human tragedy. But in order to liberate these elements from the spiritual paraphernalia of the grotesque short story, he had first to discard its unusual hero, "the nose," which had appeared in Gogol on the basis of a long oral and written tradition.[15]

Rejecting a Gogolian treatment of the plot, Dostoevsky nevertheless retained in his poem a number of *plot situations* which betray the essential closeness of the two conceptions.

Thus, for example, the episode with the doctor, which Gogol had given a purely comic significance, became an important element of the plot. It tells us a great deal about Dosoevsky that the doctor of all people should grow into almost a tragic symbol of the unfortunate Golyadkin's dire fate.

The closeness and even the direct dependence of the scene at Dr. Krestyan Ivanovich Rutenspitz's on the episode with the doctor in Gogol becomes clear through a simple juxtaposition of their descriptions:

> [Major Kovalyov] called Ivan and sent him for the doctor who rented the best apartment in the same house on the ground floor. This doctor was *a fine figure of a man,* had beautiful *pitch-black sidewhiskers, a fresh, healthy wife,* ate fresh apples in the morning and kept his mouth in a state of unusual cleanliness, rinsing it every morning for almost three quarters of an hour and brushing his teeth with five different sorts of brushes.

Dostoevsky describes Krestyan Ivanovich as follows:

> The doctor of medicine and surgery, Krestyan Ivanovich Rutenspitz, a *quite healthy,* although already middle-aged, man, *blessed with thick gray eyebrows and sidewhiskers,* an expressive, flashing glance, by the sole means of which, apparently, he banished all illnesses, and, finally, a significant medal, sat that morning in his office, in his comfortable armchair, drank coffee *brought to him by his wife with her own hands,* smoked a cigar and from time to time wrote prescriptions for his patients....[16] [Ch. II]

In his usual fashion, Dostoevsky takes insignificant episodes which for some reason or other have made an impression on his creative fancy and gives them the importance of major components of his plot. This is what happened with the character of the servant, Ivan, whom Gogol had only mentioned in passing, and who had no real significance in "The Nose." "Coming into the foyer, [Major Kovalyov] saw...on the dirty leather divan his servant Ivan, who, lying on his back, was spitting at the ceiling and kept landing rather successfully on the same place. *The indifference of the man enraged him*; he hit him on the forehead with his hat, saying: 'You pig, you're always doing stupid things.' " It is significant that in *The Double,* Dostoevsky used not so much the comic side of this character, as much as the contrast he provides in comparison with his master. Dostoevsky altered this character in a way which intensified the tragic impression of his tale. Petrushka's "indifference" to Golyadkin's tragedy, which was unfolding right before his eyes, and finally, his leaving at the culmination of this tragedy—this is what Dostoevsky saw in the servant whom Gogol had barely mentioned. Senselessness and randomness are replaced here by meaningfulness and necessity. He opposes Gogol's intent with his own; the grotesque short story is elevated to a tragic poem.

The scene where Major Kovalyov seeks the protection of the authorities is also used by Dostoevsky in a novel fashion. We know that Major Kovalyov's first thought upon meeting the Nose was that he should complain to the chief of police:

> "Oh, the Devil take it!" said Kovalyov. "Hey, coachman, take me straight to the chief of police."
>
> Kovalyov got into the droshky and merely shouted to the coachman, "Full speed ahead!"
>
> "Is the chief of police in?" he cried, entering the hall.
>
> "Not at all," answered the doorman, "he just left."
>
> "How do you like that!"
>
> "Yes," added the doorman, "not even so long ago, but he left. If you had come just a minute earlier, then, perhaps you would have found him at home."

This scene is reminiscent of Golyadkin's arrival at his Excellency's:

> "Is his Excellency at home?" asked Mr. Golyadkin, thus addressing himself to the servant who had opened the door to him.
>
> "What do you want?" asked the servant, examining Mr. Golyadkin from head to foot.
>
> "I, my friend, that is...Golyadkin, the clerk, titular councillor Golyadkin. Say, to explain this and that...."
>
> "Wait, you can't...." [Ch. XII]

However, the outward similarity conceals both a different development of the same situation (the hostility of the servant, his Excellency's presence and his reception of Golyadkin) and a deeper treatment of the motif of "seeking the protection of the authorities."

Golyadkin persistently seeks the *protection of the authorities* throughout the whole story. He cannot understand why none of the officials has "unmasked this rogue and imposter"; for him authority is somehow connected with his father and even with the Higher Being, God: "I have...made it known as my view," he complains to Anton Antonovich Setochkin, "that these two entirely identical beings were created by Divine Providence, and that our beneficent authorities, seeing the hand of Divine Providence, gave the twins refuge"; "I look upon our benevolent superior as a father," he says

239

continually. His imagined words to his Excellency sound almost like a prayer:

"No, this is what I'll do: I'll go, throw myself at his feet, if I can, and make humble entreaties. Such and such, I'll say; I put my fate into your hands, into the hands of my superiors; protect me, I'll say, your Excellency, show me your support; this and that and such and such a thing is an unlawful act, I'll say; don't ruin me, I look upon you as a father, don't forsake me...rescue my pride, honor, and good name... and deliver me from a depraved villain.... You, my benevolent superior, I regard as a father, I'll say, and I put my fate in your hands and I'll make no objections, I trust in you, and I myself withdraw from the affair. That's how it is, I'll say!" [Ch. XII]

From all this, it is apparent that Dostoevsky gave the episode with the authorities substantial significance in the development of the idea of his tale. It is possible only to hint at it here.

The idea of "authority" played an essential role for Dostoevsky in his understanding of *The Double*. This is confirmed by the extremely valuable notes to *The Double* in two of Dostoevsky's notebooks dating from the period when Dostoevsky wanted to rework the novel. In the first, dated approximately 1861, Golyadkin ponders the problem of one's relationship to "authority" several times. Here, among other things, is the following note, "Mr. Golyadkin Jr. explains to Sr.: that I, you see, regard the benevolent authorities as a father and there's something chivalric in this. The juridical and patriarchial relationship to authority and the fact that the government itself wants [to be regarded] *as a father*. Here is the anatomy of all Russian relationships to authority." In another place in the same notebook he writes: "If the authorities relate [to a man] on a purely legal basis, [what results] is only [his] gross subservience and obedience to authority. But if they act as a father, you have familiality, you have the submission of one's whole self and all those close to one, instead of an authoritarian relationship. The principle of the child's relationship to the father. *A child's innocent babble, and this is more pleasing to authority.* This is Jr.'s theory. Jr. is the incarnation of baseness."[17] These notes show that even in the 1860s, when he was again thinking out the "idea" of *The Double* which he so valued, much was connected for Dostoevsky with the problem of "authority." It is easy to see that there are obvious hints of the Slavophile theory of the "paternal" origin of power in these later notes.[18]

The tendency of the dreamer-hero or of the rebel to rely on a higher authority after a disaster or catastrophe enters into Dostoevsky's usual set of ideas. Here this escape from internal crisis is given still in the most general and unclear terms. Golyadkin frantically seeks the support of the highest authority, but cannot find it. He is already on the verge of rebelling against the authorities, but is himself afraid of his own "free-thinking." He has yet to go through that rebellion, so that later he might transcend the bounds of his own "I" to find support in genuine faith. This is how Dostoevsky's idea sketches itself out to me.

In Gogol's tale the *concept of "guilt"* has only an incidental significance: it connects the diverse subject material into a unified whole. Someone must be guilty for "the nose's" disappearance, and Major Kovalyov expresses the opinion "that the guilt of this should belong to none other than the field officer's wife Podtochina, who wished him to marry her daughter...." In this early story Dostoevsky already poses the question of "guilt" at a completely different level. To Golyadkin it is also obvious who is guilty for all these evildoings: "In the den of that odious German woman [i.e., Karolina Ivanovna] — that's where the evil genius is hidden now!" [Ch. X]. It seems beyond doubt to me that one should seek the source of Golyadkin's tragedy precisely here, in the rather mysterious relations betweeen Karolina Ivanovna and Golyadkin. In the novel itself, there are only hints at the fact Golyadkin has wronged his former landlady in some way, but these hints remain unexplained to the end. In subsequent notes of 1861 to *The Double*, Dostoevsky reveals the significance of these hints somewhat more fully. There is, for examply, the following remarkable note about "the German woman": "NB. A poor, very poor lame German woman who lets rooms, who had helped Golyadkin at one time, and whom Jr. spied on, whose existence Sr. is afraid to admit. His [Sr.'s] affairs with her told pathetically to Jr. He deceives and betrays her."[19] Dostoevsky here lets us know that this "affair" with the German woman, whose existence Golyadkin is so "afraid" to admit, even to himself, contains the very essence of the tragedy that is unfolding before us.

Thus, *Golyadkin's tragedy is a tragedy of conscience, the tragedy of a "little man" with a nonetheless tragic fate, who realizes his own overwhelming guilt.*[20]

One detail of the conversation between Golyadkin and Petrushka has an obvious connection with the idea of "guilt" in Dostoevsky, the importance of which, in my opinion, is rather vital for an understanding of the idea of *The Double*. It is the passage where the drunken Petrushka declares to his master, "I'm going to nice people.... *Nice people...don't live falsely and never come in pairs....*" These words stun Golyadkin; his "hands and feet turned to ice. He couldn't breathe." In order to intensify the significance of these words, Dostoevsky has Petrushka repeat them a second time. " 'Yes,' continued Petrushka, *'they never come in pairs, they aren't an insult to God and honest men....' *"[21] From the mouth of the drunken Petrushka comes a condemnation of Golyadkin, a declaration that all of his misfortunes are connected with some sort of guilt before "honest men." Dostoevsky could have found the suggestion for this passage in Gogol in the words of the district police superintendant, who greatly offends Major Kovalyov by telling him that *"they don't pull the nose off a respectable man."*

In connection with the appearance of the culprit in the person of Podtochina, Gogol resorts to the device of correspondence between his characters. Major Kovalyov writes a letter to the field officer's wife Podtochina in which he expresses the conviction that the nose's "sudden separation from its place, its escape and masquerade...is nothing more than the consequence of sorcery effected by you or by those who practice similar noble pursuits."[22] Podtochina replies with a letter based upon word play. The letter convinces Kovalyov of this person's innocence.

In his poem, Dostoevsky used this device of correspondence to an enormous extent. Instead of an exchange of letters between only two characters, Golyadkin enters into correspondence with the double, with Vakhrameev (who appears in the story as the defender and representative of the interests of the German woman, Karolina Ivanovna), and finally, he receives the fateful letter from Klara Olsufievna. In the original edition, the correspondence played an even more essential role in the tale's composition. Once again, in Dostoevsky's work the letters do not serve to produce comic effects or plays on words but, retaining the general style of Gogol's letters, underline the tragic side of events. Above all, this is no real correspondence, but rather the ravings of Golyadkin's diseased imagination. The letters suddenly disappear—"Yesterday's letter to Vakhrameev was gone" or "the letter, to his surprise, wasn't in his pocket"– because in reality Golyadkin neither wrote nor received them.

Klara Olsufievna's letter is full of the horror of this imminent madness.

We are having another ball, and the handsome lieutenant is coming. I shall leave and we shall fly.

Besides, there are other official posts where one may still be of service to one's country. Remember at all events, my friend, that innocence is the strength of innocence.

Farewell. Be waiting with a carriage at the entrance. I shall rush to your protecting embrace at exactly 2 a.m.

> Yours till the grave,
> Klara Olsufievna [Ch. XII]

In the original text the delirious character of this letter was expressed even more clearly. The same passage read as follows:

We are giving a ball. I shall leave, and we shall fly, fly...*and we shall live in a cottage by the shore of the Khvalynskoe Sea.*

Besides, there are other places to be of some sort of service: *as a chief clerk in the regional government....*

By the way, this passage, which was removed by Dostoevsky when he abridged the tale for publication in a separate volume of his works, explains the origin of Golyadkin's mental rebuke of Klara Olsufievna: " 'Be outside the windows at such and such a time in a carriage,' she says, 'and sing a tender Spanish ballad. I'll be waiting. I know you love me, and we'll run away together and *live in a cottage*,' " or in another passage, when he is sitting on a log behind the woodpile in Klara Olsufievna's yard:

> "As to living in a cottage, my dear lady, as you say, no one does nowadays, no one... *'Work as a chief clerk, and live in a cottage by the sea,'* you say. In the first place, my dear lady, there are no chief clerks by the sea; and in the second, the post of a chief clerk is something you and I won't get." [Ch. XIII]

Thus, here too the same literary device serves different artistic purposes for Gogol and Dostoevsky. But for us, those passages of "The Nose" which appear to hint at the possible deepening of the plot which served as its basis have an even greater significance. And this is because, in our opinion, precisely these hints showed Dostoevsky what a promising theme Gogol had let escape him. For Dostoevsky, Gogol's approach to the theme of the nose as an anecdote which provided an opportunity for a literary fantasy was fundamentally unacceptable. I believe that Dostoevsky was dissatisfied with the double meaning of the very anecdote which was at the heart of Gogol's story.[23] But the plot itself, as Gogol used it, contains other possibilities and almost unmistakable guidelines for the development of the plot in the direction of a tragic poem.

Above all, as I mentioned above, Dostoevsky had to rid himself of the unappealing hero of Gogol's tale—the Nose. There was no place for him in Dostoevsky's poem. But Gogol himself had already indicated the manner in which he could be disposed of. *The idea of the "double"* was suggested plainly by Gogol in his tale. Consider the conversation between Major Kovalyov and the clerk in the newspaper office where Kovalyov had brought his advertisement about the disappearance of his nose. The clerk, refusing to accept such an "absurd" advertisement, refers to an incident with "a poodle." He had been brought an advertisement which "consisted in the fact that a poodle with a black coat had run away. You'd think, what could be the harm in that? But it turned out to be a libel: that poodle was a treasurer, I don't remember of what department." To this Major Kovalyov replies angrily, "But after all I'm not asking you to advertise about a poodle, but about my own nose: *that is, almost the same thing as about myself.*"

One need only comprehend a little differently the "absurd" incident with Kovalyov to feel more than merely the comic side of its absurdity, to evoke not the image of the Nose, detached and traveling around Petersburg in a carriage, but the image of a "double" pursuing the hero of an enigmatic story. After all, the "Nose" was almost the same as Kovalyov himself; one need only throw out that "almost" and subsititute "double" for "Nose." I am not asserting that the subject of *The Double* came directly from Gogol in precisely this way, especially since there were enough personal psychological motives and a large enough selection of literary precedents to explain its appearance.[24] I find it important simply to point out that "The Nose," which, in my opinion, was the starting point for Dostoevsky's literary development of the theme of the double, already contained the possibility of replacing its ambiguous hero with the figure of the "double," once its plot was perceived in a new light.[25] I am even inclined to believe that it is possible to point out the intermediate link connecting the two concepts. And here we come to one of the crucial themes of Dostoevsky's poem. *This is the theme of "imposture."*

Gogol had mentioned the theme of imposture in "The Nose" only in passing. Collegiate assessor Kovalyov *"never called himself simply a collegiate assessor, but always a major,"* and this desired advancement in rank was reflected in the person of his detached Nose, which, after all, was "almost the same thing as he himself," by its appropriation of his utmost ambition: "From his plumed hat one could conclude that *he held the rank of state councillor.*" Here we run across a valuable detail: the attainment by the "Nose," who had disappeared illegally, of that which the hero himself had only timidly dreamed of. The "Nose" is not only the personification of part of his "I," but also the usurper of the subconscious motivations of that "I." Against the will of that "I," the Nose reveals and clarifies what should have remained hidden in the depths of the subconscious. The motif of imposture, which is only mentioned by Gogol in passing, becomes one of the most disturbing themes of Dostoevsky's "poem." This focus on the theme of "imposture" makes the figure of Dostoevsky's "double" unique in world literature.

In Gogol's tale Major Kovalyov attempts to put the impostor in his place. "He turned around," Gogol states, "in order to say straight out to the gentleman in the uniform *that he was only posing as a state councillor, that he was a swindler and a scoundrel and that he was nothing more than merely his own nose....*" Dostoevsky takes this motif to extremes. Golyadkin Sr. is shocked and upset by the "imposture" of his double more than by anything else. For him he is *"a scoundrel and a depraved man"* primarily because he has put on "a mask,"[26] because he is supplanting the real Golyadkin. He is deeply shocked that nature and the authorities put up with such an outrageous and public "imposture." An array of disturbing protests is directed against this "imposture" by Golyadkin: *"Imposture and shamelessness,* sir, *get you nowhere in our day and age. Imposture and shamelessness,* my good sir, *don't lead to good, they lead to the gallows.* Grishka Otrepiev was the only one, sir, *to gain by imposture*—after deceiving a blind people, and then not for long" [Ch. VIII] ; *"I am amazed that no one here should have unmasked this rogue and impostor..."* [Ch. X] ; *"Imposture won't get you anywhere here. An impostor, sir, is good for nothing, and no use to his country"* [Ch. XII] ; " 'Such and such a thing,' I said, your Excellency, *'but imposture will get you nowhere in our day and age'* " [Ch. XII] .

It is significant that in the original edition this motif of imposture is even more sharply expressed. In a letter to Vakhrameev, later left out by Dostoevsky, this statement appeared: "To this well-known unprincipled, and at the same time unfortunate person, who is now playing the pitiable and, moreover, dangerous role of a *fraud and impostor,* I want you to say that, first of all, 1) *imposture and especially shamelessness and insolence have never brought anyone to anything good and virtuous;* and 2) that *Grishka Otrepievs are impossible* in this day and age...."

A letter to Golyadkin Jr. had previously contained these words: "I don't know, or, more accurately, don't really remember where you came from, but as a Christian I warn you that *impersonation here, in this country and in this day and age won't get you anywhere* and that we are not living in the wilds. And therefore I ask you for the sake of your own well-being *to cast off your mask,* step aside, and make way for truly honorable people with good intentions. Otherwise, I will be prepared to take even the most extreme measures, and then *the mask will come off by itself* and certain things will be brought to light." This same motif, an obsessive one in Golyadkin's consciousness, surfaces in Vakhrameev's return letter, in which he replies to Golyadkin's letter to him: "Finally, you write, sir, as if in self-justification that *imposture will get you nowhere in our active, industrial age,* and, as you justly maintain, that *a Grishka Otrepiev cannot appear again."* Finally, there is a passage in Klara Olsufievna's letter which clearly shows that Golyadkin's protest against imposture played a primary role in the "omitted idea": "The moral idea of 'a place of one's own' is also good, and the historical idea, that *Otrepievs are impossible in this day and age."*

I will not here attempt to solve the problem of the connection between the theme of imposture and the general idea of *The Double.*[27] I want only to stress that it had been hinted at but ignored by Gogol, and picked up by Dostoevsky. He must have felt an internal protest against the placid neglect of the psychological problem of imposture, which contained so many tragic possibilities. We know that Dostoevsky returned to this theme later, both in *The Possessed* and in *The Brothers Karamazov.*[28]

L.P. Grossman has advanced the hypothesis that Dostoevsky excluded the majority of references to imposture from his final edition of *The Double* precisely because at the time he was rewriting it, new uses of the theme were occurring to him. "It is possible," L.P. Grossman says, "that during this final rewriting, that is in the middle of the 1860s, Dostoevsky was already thinking of reworking the theme of imposture, and therefore, unsatisfied with the first sketches of one of his favorite ideas, decided to delete all of these passages from his early tale. In this case *The Possessed* and *The Brothers Karamazov* represent new attempts to revitalize this old plan. In the figures of Stavrogin, whom Lebyadkin actually brands 'Grishka Otrepiev,' an impostor, and so on, in the relationships between Stavrogin and Verkhovensky, between Ivan Karamazov and Smerdyakov, between Ivan and the Devil, Dostoevsky gives us these glimpses of 'a completely rewritten *The Double.*' "[29]

It seems to me that Dostoevsky's reason for excluding these references to imposture in rewriting his novel was different. When *The Double* was written, it took on the form of a unique artistic protest against Gogol's "The Nose." Gogol "wasted an idea," he didn't feel horror at the thought of the possibility of the embodiment in another person of everything that is hidden in the depths of one's "I," of everything that one is afraid to admit even into one's own consciousness and that breaks through only in dreams or during mental illness. Dostoevsky particularly emphasizes just this point, making it the *idée fixe* of the mentally deranged Golyadkin.

Many years after writing *The Double*, when he undertook the rewriting, this original connection with "The Nose" had disappeared. The unnecessary repetition of the idea of imposture damaged the artistic unity of the work, and Dostoevsky calmly omitted those passages. After all, the same thing happened, as we have already seen, with those places where the word "nose" had appeared. If in the first edition these repetitions served to underline the similarities and the contrast between the two works, then during the rewriting this consideration no longer had importance for Dostoevsky.

And the other idea which had bothered Golyadkin, which he calls *"the moral idea of 'a place of one's own,'"* had also been suggested by Gogol in passing. At his first meeting with the Nose in the Kazan Cathedral, Major Kovalyov expresses his bewilderment and displeasure: "I'm surprised, my dear sir, it seems to me...*you should know your place*. And suddenly I find you, and where?—in church. You must agree...." In Dostoevsky this concept of "a place of one's own," mentioned casually by Gogol, suddenly becomes extremely significant. He deepens it and connects it with the problem of imposture. In Dostoevsky's formulation the two concepts complement one another. At the base of imposture lies the psychological trait of dissatisfaction with "one's own place," the conviction of one's own right to occupy the highest position in the hierarchy of human relationships. One must be daring, one must overcome false prejudices, one must simply assert one's rights. But this daring implies ousting someone else, removing any obstacles in attaining one's goal.[30] The basic idea of *Crime and Punishment* is already indicated here in a somewhat veiled form.

In the letter to Vakhrameev this idea of "a place of one's own" finds vivid expression. "In conclusion, I beg you, dear sir, to convey to these persons that their strange pretensions, and their ignoble and chimerical *desire to oust others from the places that they occupy by their very existence in this world, and to supplant them, are deserving of consternation, contempt, compassion, and furthermore, the madhouse;* that furthermore, attitudes such as these are strictly forbidden by law, and in my opinion, quite justly so, *for everyone must be content with his own place.* There are limits to everything, and if this is a joke, it is an unseemly one, I will say more—it is utterly immoral, for I venture to assure you, my dear sir, that *my own ideas, amplified above, about keeping one's place are purely moral"* [Ch. IX] .

But it is possible to carry within oneself that same flame of dissatisfaction without crossing the bounds established by fate and the limits of one's existence. Then this dissatisfaction is expressed as an "internal imposture," as a way of rewarding oneself in fantasies of another existence. Thus, the problem of imposture approaches that of "dreaming." "The dreamer" is in reality the same impostor, but he doesn't cross the established bounds. This is the first mention of the *problem of the underground.*

The underground hero considers himself justified in drawing a magic circle around his "I," into which no one has the right—nor the audacity— to penetrate. Sinner or saint, innocent or guilty, my "I," locked in that circle, is neither responsible nor accountable to anyone. The formula of the underground man, still timid in his ideology, is contained in the Nose's phrase: "I'm on my own."

Golyadkin Sr. continually attempts to hide from the outside world, from the misfortunes piling on his unfortunate head, behind this sacramental formula: *"I keep to myself, and so far as I can see am not dependent on anyone"*; *"I'm here on my own account.* This is my private life"; *"But here I'm on my own,..* that's all, I don't bother anyone else, and being innocent, I scorn my enemies." Golyadkin states the matter just as if he were reciting a charm. And this charm, which plays such a substantial role in *The Double,* Dostoevsky could once again have taken from Gogol's "The Nose." In answer to Kovalyov's statement "Why, you are my own nose," the Nose replies with the same verbal formula, "You are mistaken, sir. I'm on my own."[31] But we see how deep a meaning Dostoevsky puts into these words and how they are connected with the basic problems of his work. This verbal formula is used in *The Double* to round out the novel's ideational content, which has enormous relevance in the general system of Dostoevsky's ideas.

It is scarcely possible to consider these correlations between the details of these two works accidental, especially against the general background of Gogol's style. It is hard to imagine that Dostoevsky himself didn't feel how closely his *The Double* resembled Gogol's tale "The Nose." In this case, then, why did he connect an entire circle of highly personal artistic ideas with someone else's form and style? I cannot explain this other than *as an attempt to juxtapose his own* The Double *to Gogol's "The Nose."* And I think he emphasized this juxtaposition even more sharply by retaining in his work so many obvious traces of Gogol's "The Nose." The presence of influence here is indisputable, but it is an influence of repulsion, not of attraction. *And in this case we are justified in seeing Dostoevsky's* The Double *as a unique literary rebuttal of Gogol's tale "The Nose."*

1927/1934

THE HERO'S MONOLOGIC DISCOURSE AND NARRATIONAL DISCOURSE IN DOSTOEVSKY'S EARLY NOVELS*
by Mikhail Bakhtin

Dostoevsky began with the epistolary form, a type of discourse in which the speech of the letter-writer refracts the anticipated speech of the recipient. Apropos of *Poor Folk*, he writes to his brother:

> They [the public and the critics—M.B.] have become accustomed to seeing the author's mug in everything; I didn't show mine. And it doesn't even occur to them that Devushkin is speaking, and not I, and that Devushkin cannot speak in any other way. They find the novel long-winded, but there is not a superfluous word in it. (Letter of February 1, 1846)

In this novel the main characters, Makar Devushkin and Varenka Dobroselova, do the speaking; the author merely distributes their words: his intentions are refracted in the words of the hero and the heroine. The epistolary form is a variant of the *Ich-Erzählung* (first-person narrative). Discourse in this genre is oriented on the anticipated reactions of an auditor *(double-voiced discourse)*, and in the majority of cases it acts as the compositional surrogate of the author's voice, which is absent here (*the uni-directional variant* of double-voiced discourse).[1] We shall see that the author's conception is very subtly and carefully refracted in the words of the hero-narrators, although the entire work is filled with both obvious and hidden parodies, with both obvious and hidden (authorial) polemics.

But for the present we are interested in examining Makar Devushkin's speech only as the monologic utterance of a hero, and not as the speech of a narrator in an *Ich-Erzählung*, a function which it in fact performs here, since there are no other speakers besides the heroes. The speech of any narrator, employed by the author for the realization of his artistic plan, itself belongs to some specific type of discourse, apart from that type which is determined by its function as narration. Of what type is Devushkin's monologic utterance?

The epistolary form in and of itself does not predetermine the type of discourse which will be found in it. In general this form allows for broad

---

*Chapter Five, Section Two of Bakhtin's *Problems of Dostoevsky's Poetics,* tr. R. W. Rotsel (Ann Arbor: Ardis, 1973), revised by the present editors.

verbal possibilities, but it is most suited to the *active type* of double-voiced discourse, which reflects *the speech act of another person*. A characteristic feature of the letter form is the writer's acute awareness of his interlocutor, the addressee to whom it is directed. The letter, like a line of dialogue, is addressed to a specific person, and it takes into account his possible reactions, his possible reply. It can do this more, or less, intensively. In Dostoevsky's work this attention to the absent interlocutor has an extremely intensive character.

In his first work Dostoevsky develops a style of speech, characteristic of his entire oeuvre, which is determined by the intense anticipation of the other person's speech act. The significance of this style in his subsequent work is enormous: the most important confessional self-revelations of his heroes are permeated by a hypersensitivity to the anticipated speech acts of others about them and to others' reactions to their own words about themselves. Not only the tone and style, but also the internal conceptual structure of these self-revelations is determined by the anticipation of another person's speech, from the reservations and loopholes which stem from Golyadkin's easily-offended nature to the ethical and metaphysical loopholes of Ivan Karamazov. The "servile" variant of this style began to develop in *Poor Folk* —speech which seems to cringe with timidity and shame at the awareness of another's possible response, yet contains a stifled cry of defiance.

This self-conscious awareness is manifested above all in the halting speech and the reservations which interrupt it that are characteristic of this style.

> I live in the kitchen, or, more correctly speaking, here next to the kitchen is a little room (and I would like to point out that our kitchen is clean and bright, a very good one), a little nook, a humble little corner ...that is, to put it even better, the kitchen is large, with three windows, and along one wall there is a partition, so it is as if there were another room, a supernumerary one; it is all roomy and convenient, and there is a window, and it is all—in a word, it is convenient. Well, so, this is my little corner. Well now, my dear, don't think that there is anything strange here, some mysterious significance—Aha, he lives in the kitchen!—that is, you see, I do live in this room behind the partition, but that doesn't matter; I keep to myself, away from the others, I live in a small way, I live quietly. I have a bed, a table, a chest of drawers, a couple of chairs, an ikon on the wall. True, there are better apartments, perhaps even much better ones, but then convenience is the main thing; I live like this for convenience's sake, and don't go thinking that it is for any other reason. (Letter of April 8th)

After almost every word Devushkin takes a sideward glance at his absent interlocutor, he is afraid that she will think he is complaining, he tries in advance to destroy the impression which the news that he lives in the kitchen will create, he does not want to distress his interlocutor, etc. The repetition of words results from his desire to intensify their accent or to give them a new nuance in light of his interlocutor's possible reaction.

In the excerpt which we have quoted, the speech act reflected is the potential speech of the addressee, Varenka Dobroselova. In the majority of instances Makar Devushkin's speech about himself is determined by the reflected speech of the "other person, the stranger." Here is how he defines this stranger. He asks Varenka Dobroselova:

> And what will you do out there among strangers? Don't you know yet what a stranger is?... No, you've asked me a question, so I'll tell you what a stranger is. I know him, my dear, I know him well; I've had to eat his bread. He is mean, Varenka, mean, he is so mean, your poor little heart won't be able to stand the way he torments it with his reproaches and rebukes and his evil glance. (Letter of July 1st)

The poor, but "ambitious" man, such as Makar Devushkin, in keeping with Dostoevsky's intention, constantly feels other people's "evil glance" directed toward him, a glance which is either reproachful or—perhaps even worse in his eyes—mocking (for the heroes of the prouder type the worst glance of all is the compassionate one). Devushkin's speech cringes under this glance. He, like the hero from the underground, is constantly listening in on other people's speech about him.

> The poor man, he is demanding: he looks at God's world differently, and he looks askance at every passerby, he casts a troubled gaze about him and he listens closely to every word—aren't they talking about him? (Letter of August 1st)

Makar Devushkin's sideward glance at the speech of the other who is socially foreign to him determines not only the style and tone of his speech, but also his very manner of thinking and experiencing, of seeing and understanding himself and the little world which surrounds him. In Dostoevsky's artistic world there is always a profound organic bond between the superficial elements of a character's manner of speech, his way of expressing himself, and the ultimate foundations of his Weltanschauung. A person's every act reveals him in his totality. The orientation of one person to another person's speech and consciousness is, in essence, the basic theme of all of Dostoevsky's works. The hero's attitude toward himself is inseparably bound up with his attitude towards the other and with the attitude of the other towards him.

251

His consciousness of self is constantly perceived against the background of the other's consciousness of him—"I for myself" against the background of "I for the other." For this reason the hero's speech about himself takes shape under the continuous influence of the other's speech about him.

This theme develops in various forms in various works, with varying content and on various spiritual levels. In *Poor Folk* the poor man's self-awareness unfolds against the background of a socially foreign consciousness of him. His self-affirmation has the sound of a continuous hidden polemic or hidden dialogue with the other, the stranger, on the subject of himself. In Dostoevsky's first works this is expressed rather simply and directly—the dialogue has not yet been internalized, become part of the very atoms of thought and experience, so to speak. The heroes' world is still small, and they have not yet become ideologists. Their very social servility makes their inner sideward glance and inner polemic direct and clear-cut, without the complex internal loopholes which grow into the whole ideological constructions that we see in Dostoevsky's final works. But the profoundly dialogic and polemic nature of self-awareness and self-affirmation are already revealed here with complete clarity.

> The other day in a private conversation Yevstafy Ivanovich said that the most important civic virtue is the ability to make a lot of money. He was joking (I know he was joking), it was a moral lesson that one shouldn't be a burden to anyone else, but I'm not a burden to anyone! I have my own piece of bread; true, it is a modest piece of bread, sometimes it's even stale, but it is mine, I win it with my own labor and use it lawfully and blamelessly. But what can one do? I know myself that my copying is not much of a job, but, still, I am proud of it: I work, I spill my sweat. Well, and really, so what if I just copy! Is it a sin to copy, or something? "He just copies!..." What is so dishonorable about that? I realize now that I am needed, that I am indispensible, and that I shouldn't let their nonsense disturb me. Well, so I'm a rat, if they find some resemblance! But that rat is necessary, that rat accomplishes something, they're all supported by that rat, and that rat will get its reward—that's the kind of rat it is! But enough on this subject, my dear; I didn't want to talk about that, I just got a little carried away. All the same, it is nice to do oneself justice now and then. (Letter of June 12th)

Makar Devushkin's self-awareness is revealed in an even sharper polemic when he recognizes himself in Gogol's "The Overcoat"; he perceives it as the other's speech about him personally, and he seeks to destroy polemically that speech as being inapplicable to him.

But let us now take a closer look at the structure of this "speech with

252

a sideward glance."

Already in the first excerpt we quoted, where Devushkin anxiously informs Varenka Dobroselova of his new room, we notice the peculiar verbal counterpoint determining the syntactic and accentual structure of his speech. The other's replies as it were wedge their way into his speech, and although they are in reality not there, their influence brings about a radical accentual and syntactic reorganization of that speech. This other line of dialogue is not actually present, but casts a shadow on his speech, and that shadow is real. But sometimes the other's reply, in addition to its influence on the accentual and syntactic structure, leaves behind a word or two, and sometimes a whole sentence, in Makar Devushkin's speech:

> Well now, my dear, don't think that there is anything strange here, some mysterious significance—Aha, he lives in the *kitchen*!—that is, you see, I do live in this room behind the partition, but that doesn't matter.... (Letter of April 8th)

The word "kitchen" bursts into Devushkin's speech from out of the other's possible speech as it is anticipated by him. This word is presented with the other's accent, which Devushkin polemically exaggerates somewhat. He does not accept this accent, although he cannot help recognizing its power, and he tries to evade it by means of all sorts of reservations, partial concessions and extenuations, which distort the structure of his speech. The smooth surface of his speech is furrowed by ripples fanning out from the other's word, which has taken root in that speech. Except for this word, which obviously belongs to the other's speech and carries the accent of that speech, the majority of words in the quoted passage are chosen by the speaker from two points of view simultaneously: as he himself understands them and wants others to understand them, and as others might in fact understand them. Here the other's accent is merely noted, but it already gives rise to reservations or hesitations in his speech.

The embedding of words and especially of accents from the other's speech in Makar Devushkin's speech is even more marked and obvious in the second of the passages which we have quoted. Here the word containing the other's polemically exaggerated accent is even enclosed in quotation marks: "He just copies!..." In the immediately preceding lines the word "copy" is repeated three times. In each of these three instances the other's potential accent is present in the word "copy," but it is suppressed by Devushkin's own accent; however, it becomes constantly stronger, until it finally breaks through and takes on the form of the direct speech of the other. Thus we are presented here with the gradations of the gradual intensification of the other's accent: "I know myself that my *copying* is not much of a job...[a reservation follows—M.B.]. Well, and really, so what if I just *copy*! Is it a sin

253

to _copy_ or something? 'He just COPIES!..' " We have indicated the other's accent, which gradually grows stronger and finally completely dominates the word enclosed in quotation marks. Even so, in this last, obviously foreign word Devushkin's own voice is present, too, as he polemically exaggerates the other's accent. To the degree that the other's accent is intensified, Devushkin's counter-accent is also intensified.

We can thus descriptively define all the phenomena which we have discussed: the hero's self-awareness was penetrated by the other's consciousness of him, and the other's speech about him was injected into what the hero had to say about himself; the other's consciousness of him and the other's speech about him give rise to specific phenomena which determine the development of the theme of Devushkin's self-awareness, its breaking points, loopholes and protests, on the one hand, and the hero's speech with its accentual counterpoint, syntactic breaking points, repetitions, reservations and prolixity, on the other.

Or we can give another definition and explanation of the same phenomena: let us imagine that two lines of very intense dialogue—a speech and a counter-speech—instead of following one after the other and proceeding from two different mouths, are superimposed one on the other and merge into a _single_ utterance coming from a single mouth. These lines of dialogue move in opposite directions and collide with one another; therefore their overlapping and merging into a single utterance produce a tense counterpoint. The collision of entire, integral lines of dialogue is transformed within a new utterance (which results from the merging of those lines) into a sharp counterpoint of voices which are contradictory in every detail and atom. The dialogic collision has been internalized into the subtlest structural elements of speech (and correspondingly—of consciousness).

The passage which we have quoted could be roughly paraphrased in the following crude dialogue between Makar Devushkin and the other, the "stranger":

> Stranger: One must know how to make a lot of money. One shouldn't be a burden to anyone. But you are a burden to others.
>
> Makar Devushkin: I'm not a burden to anyone. I've got my own piece of bread.
>
> S.: But what a piece it is! Today it's there, and tomorrow it's gone. And most likely a stale piece, at that!
>
> M.D.: True, it is a modest piece of bread, sometimes it's even stale, but it is mine. I win it with my own labor and use it lawfully and blamelessly.
>
> S.: But what kind of labor! All you do is copy. You're not capable of anything else.
>
> M.D.: Well, what can one do! I know myself that my copying is

not much of a job, but, still, I am proud of it!

     S.: Oh, there's something to be proud of, all right! Copying! It's disgraceful!

     M.D.: Well, and really, so what if I just copy!...etc.

It is as if this statement of Devushkin's about himself resulted from the overlapping and merging of the lines of this dialogue into a single voice.

Of course this imagined dialogue is terribly primitive, just as the content of Devushkin's consciousness is still primitive. For he is, in the final analysis, an Akaky Akakievich who is enlightened by a self-awareness and who has acquired speech and elaborated a "style." But on the other hand, as a result of its primitiveness and crudeness, the formal structure of his self-awareness and self-expression is extremely clear-cut and apparent. That is why we are examining it in such detail. All of the essential self-revelations of Dostoevsky's later heroes could also be turned into dialogues, since they all, as it were, arose out of two merged lines of dialogue, but in them the counterpoint of voices goes so deep, into such subtle elements of thought and speech, that to turn them into an obvious and crude dialogue, as we have just done with Devushkin's self-revelation, is, of course, completely impossible.

The phenomena which we have examined, produced by the speech of the other within the hero's speech, are in *Poor Folk* presented in the stylistic accoutrements of the speech of a Petersburg petty clerk. The structural characteristics of "speech with a sideward glance," of speech which is internally dialogic and conceals a hidden polemic, are refracted here in the strictly and skillfully sustained sociotypical verbal manner of Devushkin.[2] For this reason all of these phenomena of language—reservations, repetitions, diminutives, diverse particles and interjections—could not appear in the same form in the mouths of other heroes of Dostoevsky, who belong to different social worlds. The same phenomena appear in a different sociotypical and individually characteristic form of speech. But their essence remains the same: the crossing and intersection in every element of a character's consciousness and speech of two consciousnesses, two points of view, two evaluations—the intra-atomic counterpoint of two voices.

Golyadkin's speech is constructed within the same sociotypical verbal milieu, but it has a different individually characteristic manner. The peculiar nature of consciousness and speech which we have examined above is found in *The Double* in a more exteme and clear-cut form than in any other of Dostoevsky's works. The tendencies which were already contained in the character of Makar Devushkin are here developed with extraordinary boldness and consistency to their conceptual limits on the basis of the same deliberately primitive, simple and crude material.

Dostoevsky himself, in a letter to his brother written while he was working on *The Double*, gave a parodic stylization of Golyadkin's speech and conceptual system. As is the case in any parodic stylization, the basic characteristics and tendencies of Golyadkin's speech are plainly and crudely made visible here.

> *Yakov Petrovich Golyadkin* holds his own completely. He's a terrible scoundrel and there's no approaching him; he refuses to move forward, pretending that, you see, he's not ready yet, that for the present he's on his own, he's all right, nothing is the matter, but that if it comes to that, then he can do that, too, why not, what's to prevent it? He's just like everyone else, he's nothing special, just like everyone else. What's it to him! He's a scoundrel, a terrible scoundrel! He'll never agree to end his career before the middle of November. He's already just spoken with his Excellency, and he just may (and why shouldn't he) announce his retirement. (Letter to M.M. Dostoevsky, Oct. 8, 1845)

As we shall see, *The Double* itself is narrated in this same style, parodying the hero. But we shall turn to the narration later.

The influence of the other's speech on Golyadkin's speech is completely obvious. We immediately feel that his speech, like Devushkin's, relates not just to itself and its referential object. However, Golyadkin's interrelationship with the speech and the consciousness of the other is somewhat different from Devushkin's. Therefore the phenomena in Golyadkin's style which result from the other's speech are also of a different sort.

Golyadkin's speech above all seeks to simulate total independence from the other's speech: "He's on his own, he's all right." This simulation of independence and indifference also leads to endless repetitions, reservations and prolixity, but here directed to himself, and not outside himself to the other: he tries to convince, reassure and comfort himself, playing the role of the other in relation to himself. Golyadkin's self-comforting dialogues with himself are the most widespread phenomenon in *The Double*. Along with the simulation of indifference goes another attitude to the other's speech: the desire to hide from it, to avoid calling attention to oneself, to get lost in the crowd, to become inconspicuous: "He's just like everyone else, he's nothing special, just like everyone else." But he is actually trying to convince not himself, but the other, of this. Finally, the third attitude to the other's speech involves Golyadkin's yielding to it, subordinating himself to it, and submissively adopting it, as if he himself were of the same opinion and sincerely agreed with it: "If it comes to that, then he can do that, too, why not, what's to prevent it?"

These are the three general lines in Golyadkin's orientation, and they are complicated by other secondary, but rather important, ones. Each of these three lines in and of itself gives rise to very complex phenomena in Golyadkin's consciousness and in his speech.

We shall concentrate above all on his simulation of independence and composure.

As we have said, the pages of *The Double* are full of the hero's dialogues with himself. One might say that Golyadkin's entire inner life develops dialogically. We quote two examples of such dialogues:

"But, still, will it be right?" continued our hero, alighting from the coach near the entrance to a certain five-storied house on the Liteynaya, beside which he had ordered his carriage to halt. "Will it be right? Will it be proper? Will it be appropriate? But really why all the fuss," he continued as he climbed the steps, catching his breath and checking the thumping of his heart, which was in the habit of thumping on other people's stairways. "Why the fuss? I'm on my own business, there's nothing reprehensible here at all.... I would be silly to hide myself. I'll just pretend that nothing's the matter, that I just happened by.... He'll see that everything's as it should be." [Ch. I]

The second example of interior dialogue is much more complex and pointed. It takes place after the appearance of Golyadkin's double, i.e. after the second voice has become objectified for him within his own field of vision.

Mr. Golyadkin's delight thus expressed itself, though at the same time something was still tickling in his head, not exactly melancholy, but now and then it tugged so at his heart that he was almost inconsolable. "Still and all, we'll wait until morning before rejoicing. But really, why all the fuss? Well, we'll think it over, we'll see. Well, let's think it over, my young friend, let's think it over. Well, in the first place, he's a person just like you, exactly the same. Well, what does it matter? Should I cry about it or something, just because he's a person like that? What's it to me? It doesn't involve me; I'll go my merry way, and that'll be all there is to it! That's the way he wants it, and that's all there is to it! Let him do his job! Well, it's a miracle and an oddity, they say that there are Siamese twins.... Well, but why do they have to be Siamese? Let's assume that they are twins, but great men have sometimes been odd-looking, too. It's even known from history that the famous Suvorov crowed like a rooster.... Well, yes, that was for political reasons; and great generals...but what are generals, anyway? I'm on my own, that's all there is to it, I don't need anybody, and in my innocence I have nothing but contempt for the enemy. I'm not an intriguer, and I'm proud of it. I'm pure, I'm straightforward, orderly, pleasant, and gentle...." [Ch. VI]

The first question to arise is that of the function in Golyadkin's life of this dialogue with himself. The answer can be briefly formulated thus: *the dialogue allows him to substitute his own voice for the voice of the other.*

The function of Golyadkin's second voice as a substitute is felt everywhere. Without understanding this it is impossible to understand his interior dialogues. Golyadkin addresses himself as if addressing another person ("my young friend"), he praises himself as only another person could, he verbally caresses himself with tender familiarity: "Yakov Petrovich, my dear fellow, you little Golyadka,[3] you—you have just the right name!" and he reassures and comforts himself with the authoritative tone of an older, more confident person. But this second voice of Golyadkin's, confident and calmly self-satisfied, cannot possibly merge with his first voice, the uncertain, timid one; the dialogue cannot turn into the integral and confident monologue of a single Golyadkin. Moreover, that second voice is to such a degree unable to merge with the first one and feels so threateningly independent, that teasing, mocking, treacherous tones begin to appear in place of comforting, reassuring ones. With amazing tact and art, in a way almost imperceptible to the reader, Dostoevsky transfers Golyadkin's second voice from his interior dialogue to the narration itself: it takes on the sound of the voice of the narrator. But we shall speak of the narration a bit later.

Golyadkin's second voice must make up for the fact that he receives too little recognition from other people. Golyadkin wants to get by without such recognition, to get by on his own, so to speak. But this "on his own" inevitably takes on the form "you and I, my friend Golyadkin," i.e. it takes on the form of a dialogue. In fact Golyadkin lives only in the other, he lives by his reflection in the other: "will it be proper," "will it be appropriate?" And this question is always answered from the possible, conjectured point of view of the other: Golyadkin *will pretend* that nothing is the matter, that he just happened by, and the other will see "that everything's as it should be." Everything depends on the reaction of the other, on his speech and his answer. The confidence of Golyadkin's second voice cannot completely possess him and actually take the place of an actual other person. The other's speech is the most important thing for him.

> Although Mr. Golyadkin said all of these things [about his independence—M.B.] as clearly and confidently as could be, weighing and calculating every word for the surest effect, he was now looking uneasily, very uneasily, most uneasily at Krestyan Ivanovich. He was all eyes, and he timidly awaited Krestyan Ivanovich's answer with annoying, melancholy impatience. [Ch. II]

In the second quoted excerpt of interior dialogue the function of the second voice as a substitute is completely obvious. But in addition, a third voice appears here, the direct voice of the other, which interrupts the second, the merely substitute voice. Thus we have here phenomena which are completely analogous to those which we analyzed in Devushkin's speech—the other's words and words which partly belong to the other, with the corresponding accentual counterpoint:

> Well, it's a miracle and an oddity, they say that there are Siamese twins.... Well, but why do they have to be Siamese? Let's assume that they are twins, but great men have sometimes been odd-looking, too. It's even known from history that the great Suvorov crowed like a rooster.... Well, yes, that was for political reasons; and great generals... but what are generals? [Ch. VI]

Everywhere, but especially in those place where ellipses appear, the anticipated reactions of others wedge themselves in. This passage, too, could be elaborated in the form of a dialogue, but here the dialogue is much more complex. While in Devushkin's speech a single, integral voice polemicized with the "other," here there are two voices: one is confident, too confident, and the other is too timid, it gives in to everything, capitulating totally.[4]

Goyadkin's second voice—the one which serves as a substitute for that of another person, his first voice—the one which hides itself from the other's speech ("I'm like everyone else, I'm all right"), then gives in to it ("but if that's the case, then I'm prepared"), and finally the voice of the other which sounds constantly within him, are interrelated in such a complex way that they provide sufficient material for the entire intrigue and permit the whole novel to be constructed on them alone. The actual event, namely the unsuccessful courtship of Klara Olsufievna, and all the attendant circumstances are in fact not represented in the novel: they serve merely as the stimulus which sets the inner voices in motion, they merely intensify and make immediate the inner conflict which is the real object of representation in the novel.

Except for Golyadkin and his double, none of the characters takes any actual part whatever in the plot, which unfolds totally within the bounds of Golyadkin's self-awareness; the other characters merely provide the raw material, the fuel, as it were, necessary for the intense work of that self-awareness. The external, intentionally obscure plot (everything of importance has taken place before the novel begins) also serves as the barely discernible skeleton of Golyadkin's inner plot. The novel relates how Golyadkin wanted to get along without the consciousness of the other and without recognition by the other, how he wanted to avoid the other and to assert his own self, and what resulted therefrom. Dostoevsky intended *The Double* to be a "confession"[5] (not in the personal sense, of course), i.e. the representation of an event which occurs within the bounds of the character's self-awareness.

The Double is the *first dramatized confession* among Dostoevsky's works.

Thus at the basis of the plot lies Golyadkin's attempt, in view of the total non-recognition of his personality on the part of others, to find himself a substitute for the other. Golyadkin plays at being an independent person; his consciousness plays at being confident and self-sufficient. The new, violent collision with the other during the party when Golyadkin is publicly devastated intensifies the split in his personality. Golyadkin's second voice over-exerts itself in a desperate simulation of self-sufficiency, in order to save face. Golyadkin's second voice cannot merge with him; on the contrary, the treacherous tones of ridicule grow louder and louder in it. It provokes and teases Golyadkin, it casts off his mask. The double appears. The inner conflict is dramatized; Golyadkin's intrigue with the double begins.

The double speaks in the words of Golyadkin himself, bringing in no new words or tones. At first he pretends to be a cringing, capitulating Golyadkin. When Golyadkin brings the double home with him, the latter looks and behaves like the first, uncertain voice in Golyadkin's interior dialogue ("will it be appropriate, will it be proper," etc.):

> The guest [the doube—M.B.] was, obviously, extemely embarrassed, he was very timid, he submissively followed his host's every movement, he tried to catch his glances in order, so it seemed, to divine his thoughts from them. All of his gestures expressed something abased, downtrodden and terrified, so that, if the comparison will be permitted, in that moment he bore a fair resemblance to a person who, for lack of his own clothes, has put on someone else's: the sleeves crawl up his arms and the waist comes almost up to his neck, and he is constantly either straightening the tiny vest, shuffling sideways and getting out of the way, trying to hide somewhere, or glancing at people's faces and listening carefully to hear if they are talking about him or laughing at him or are ashamed for him—the fellow grows red, the fellow is flustered, and his pride suffers.... [Ch. VII]

This is a characterization of the cringing, self-effacing Golyadkin. The double also speaks in the tones and style of Golyadkin's first voice. The part of the second—the confident and tenderly reassuring—voice in relation to the double is played by Golyadkin himself, who this time as it were merges completely with this voice:

> "You and I, Yakov Petrovich, shall live like a fish with water, like blood brothers; we, my friend, shall be crafty, we together shall be crafty; we shall think up intrigues to spite them, to spite them we shall think up intrigues. And don't you trust any of them. Because I know you, Yakov Petrovich, and I understand your character: you'll

go and tell everything, you're a truthful soul! You must keep away from all of them, old boy."[6] [Ch. VII]

But subsequently the roles change: the treacherous double takes over the tone of Golyadkin's second voice, parodically exaggerating its tender familiarity. Already at their next meeting at the office the double takes on this tone and sustains it to the end of the novel; now and then he himself emphasizes the identity of his expressions with the words of Golyadkin (i.e. the ones Golyadkin said during their first conversation). During one of their meetings at the office the double, familiarly poking Golyadkin, "with the most venomous and broadly suggestive smile, said to him: 'Oh no you don't Yakov Petrovich, old boy, oh no you don't! You and I'll be crafty, Yakov Petrovich, we'll be crafty' " [Ch. VIII]. Or a little later, before their face-to-face confrontation in the café:

"Well, so then, as you say, my good fellow," said Mr. Golyadkin Jr., getting out of the droshky and shamelessly patting our hero on the shoulder, "you're such a buddy; for you, Yakov Petrovich, I'd go through thick and thin (as you, Yakov Petrovich, once justly saw fit to remark). He is a rascal, though, he'll do to you whatever comes into his head!" [Ch. XI]

This transferral of words from one mouth to another, in which their tone and ultimate meaning is changed, while their content remains the same, is one of Dostoevsky's basic devices. He causes his heroes to recognize themselves, their idea, their own speech, their orientation, and their gesture in another person, in whom all of these manifestations take on a different integral and ultimate meaning and a different sound, the sound of parody or ridicule.[7]

As we have said, almost all of Dostoevsky's major heroes have a partial double in another person or even in several other people (Stavrogin and Ivan Karamazov). In his last work Dostoevsky again returned to the device of fully embodying the second voice, though on a more profound and subtle basis. In its externally formal plan Ivan Karamazov's dialogue with the devil is analogous to the interior dialogues which Golyadkin carries on with himself and with his double; despite the dissimilarity in situation and in ideological content, in both instances essentially the same artistic problem is being solved.

Thus Golyadkin's intrigue with his double develops as a dramatized crisis of self-awareness, as a dramatized confession. The action does not go beyond the bounds of his self-awareness since the characters are merely detached elements of that self-awareness. The actors are the three voices into which Golyadkin's voice and consciousness have dissociated: his "I for

261

myself," which cannot do without the existence of the other and the other's recognition; his fictitious "I for the other" (reflection in the other), i.e. Golyadkin's second substitute-voice; and finally, the voice of the other which does not recognize Golyadkin, and which at the same time has no real existence outside him, since there are no other characters of equal stature in the work. (Other equal consciousnesses appear only in the big novels.) The result is a peculiar mystery play or, more precisely, a morality play, in which the actors are not whole people, but rather the spiritual forces battling within them, a morality play, however, devoid of any formalism or abstract allegoricalness.

But who tells the story in *The Double*? What is the position of the narrator and what is his voice like?

In the narration too we do not find a single element which goes beyond the bounds of Golyadkin's self-awareness, a single word or a single tone which could not be part of his interior dialogue with himself or of his dialogue with his double. The narrator picks up Golyadkin's words and thoughts, the words of his *second voice,* intensifies the teasing, mocking tones present in them, and in these tones depicts Golyadkin's every act, gesture and movement. We have already mentioned that Golyadkin's second voice, by means of imperceptible transitions, merges with the voice of the narrator; the impression is created that *the narration is dialogically addressed to Golyadkin himself,* it rings in his ears as the taunting voice of another person, the voice of his double, although formally the narration is addressed to the reader.

This is how the narrator describes Golyadkin's behavior at the most fateful moment in his adventures, when he tries to crash the ball given by Olsufy Ivanovich:

We should better turn our attention to Mr. Golyadkin, the true and only hero of this our most veracious story.

At the moment he is, to put it mildly, in a very strange situation. He, ladies and gentlemen, is also here, that is he is not at the ball, but he is almost at the ball; he, ladies and gentlemen, is all right; he may be on his own, but at this moment he is on a somewhat less than straight and narrow path; he is now—it seems strange even to say it—he is now standing in a passageway on the back stairs of Olsufy Ivanovich's house. But it's all right that he is standing here, it is nothing special. He is, ladies and gentlemen, standing in a corner, jammed into a little space, if not a very warm one, at least very dark, hiding partly begind a huge cabinet and some old screens, in the middle of all sorts of rubbish, trash and junk, waiting for the proper time, and at the moment just observing the general course of events in the capacity of a detached observer. He is, ladies and gentlemen, just observing now; but, ladies and gentlemen, he, too, could make an entrance...why shouldn't he make an entrance? He only has to step out, and he will make his entrance, and make it very adroitly, at that. [Ch. IV]

In the structure of this narration we observe the counterpoint of two voices, the same kind of merging of two lines of dialogue that we observed already in Makar Devushkin's utterances. But here the roles have been changed; here it is as if the other's line of dialogue has swallowed up the hero's. The narration glitters with Golyadkin's own words: "He's all right," "He's on his own," etc. But the narrator gives these words an intonation of ridicule, ridicule and in part reproach, directed at Golyadkin himself and constructed in such a form as to touch his sore spots and provoke him. This mocking narration imperceptibly infiltrates the speech of Golyadkin himself. The question "why shouldn't he make an entrance?" belongs to Golyadkin himself, but it is spoken in the teasing, egging-on intonation of the narrator. But this intonation, too, is not in essence foreign to Golyadkin's own consciousness. All of these things could ring in his own head, as his second voice. Actually, the author could insert quotation marks at any point without changing the tone, the voice or the construction of the sentence.

Somewhat further on he does precisely that:

So, ladies and gentlemen, he is waiting quietly, now, and has been doing so for exactly two-and-one-half hours. And why shouldn't he wait? Villèle himself waited. "But what does Villèle have to do with it?" though Mr. Golyadkin. "There's no Villèle here! But what should I do now...should I up and make my appearance? Ach, you nobody, you." [Ch. IV]

But why not insert quotation marks two sentences earlier, before the words "And why shouldn't," or still earlier, changing "So, ladies and gentlemen, he..." to "Golyadkin, old boy," or some other form of Golyadkin addressing himself? The quotations marks are, of course, not inserted at random. They are inserted in such a way as to make the transition particularly subtle and imperceptible. Villèle's name appears in the narrator's last sentence and in the hero's first. Golyadkin's words seem to continue the narration without interruption and to answer it in an interior dialogue. "Villèle himself waited." " 'But what does Villèle have to do with it?' " These are in fact lines from Golyadkin's interior dialogue with himself which have become separated, one going into the narration and the other remaining with Golyadkin. This is the reverse of the phenomenon which we observed earlier: the merging in counterpoint of two voices. But the result is the same: a double-voiced construction in counterpoint with all the accompanying phenomena. And the arena of action is the same: a single self-awareness. The difference is that this consciousness is ruled by the speech of the other which

263

has taken up residence in it.

We shall quote another example with the same kind of vascillating border between the narration and the hero's speech. Golyadkin has made up his mind and at last entered the hall where the ball is going on; he appears before Klara Olsufievna:

> Without the slightest doubt, without batting an eye, he would at this moment have been most happy to fall through a hole in the earth; but what's done is done.... What could he do? "If it doesn't work out—stand firm; if it does—hold on. Mr. Golyadkin was, naturally, no intriguer, nor a master at polishing the parquet with his boots...." So it happened. In addition, the Jesuits somehow had a hand in the affair.... Mr. Golyadkin was, however, in no mood for them! [Ch. IV]

This passage is interesting because it contains no direct speech belonging to Mr. Golyadkin, and therefore there is no basis for the quotation marks. The portion of the narration included here in quotation marks was apparently mistakenly set off by the editor. Dostoevsky probably set off only the proverb, "If it doesn't work out, stand firm; if it does, hold on." The following sentence is given in the third person, although it obviously belongs to Golyadkin himself. Further on, the pauses indicated by ellipses also belong to Golyadkin's inner speech. According to their accents, the sentences preceding and following these ellipses are related to one another as lines in an interior dialogue. The two adjacent sentences concerning the Jesuits are quite analogous to the above-quoted sentences about Villèle, which were set off by quotation marks.

Finally, one more excerpt in which, perhaps, the opposite mistake has crept in—quotation marks have been omitted where, grammatically, they should have been inserted. Golyadkin, having been ejected from the ball, runs home in a snowstorm and meets a passerby who later turns out to be his double:

> Not that he was afraid that he was a dangerous person, but then, perhaps.... "Who knows who this fellow is, out so late," flashed through Mr. Golyadkin's mind. "Maybe he's just out late like I am, but then maybe he's not here for no reason, maybe he has a purpose, to cross my path and bump into me." [Ch. V]

Here the ellipsis serves as a divider between the narration and Golyadkin's direct inner speech, which is given in the first person *("my path," "bump into me")*. But the two are so closely merged here that one really does not want to put in the quotation marks. This sentence must be read as a sentence which contains a single voice, although this voice is internally dialogized. The transition from the narration to the hero's speech is executed with amazing success: we feel, as it were, a wave of a single current of speech which carries us, with no dams or barriers, from the narration into the hero's soul, and from it back into the narration; we feel that we are, in essence, moving within the circle of a single consciousness.

It would be possible to cite many more examples proving that the narration is a direct continuation and development of Golyadkin's second voice and that it is dialogically addressed to the hero, but the examples which we have cited are sufficient. Thus the entire work is constructed as an interior dialogue of three voices within the bounds of a single dissociated consciousness. Every essential element of the work lies in the point of intersection of these three voices and of their sharp, agonizing counterpoint. To make use of our image, we can say that, while this is not yet polyphony, it is no longer homophony. One and the same word, idea, phenomenon passes through three voices, and has a different sound in each of them. One and the same complex of words, tones and inner orientations passes through Golyadkin's own speech, through the narrator's speech, and through the speech of the double; these three voices are situated face to face and speak not about one another, but with one another. The three voices sing the same song, but not in unison—each has its own part.

But these three voices have not yet become completely independent, real voices, they are not yet three full-fledged consciousnesses. That takes place only in Dostoevsky's big novels. In *The Double*, monologic discourse, which relates only to itself and its referential object, is not present. Every word is dialogically dissociated, every word contains a counterpoint of voices, but the genuine dialogue of unmerged consciousnesses which appears later in the big novels is here not yet present. The rudiments of counterpoint are already here: it is hinted at in the very structure of discourse. The analyses we have made are, as it were, already contrapuntal analyses (figuratively speaking, of course). But this counterpoint has not yet gone beyond the bounds of monological material.

The provoking, mocking voice of the narrator and the voice of the double ring relentlessly in Golyadkin's ears. The narrator shouts his very own words and thoughts in his ear, but in a different, a hopelessly foreign, hopelessly censorious and mocking tone. This second voice is present in every one of Dostoevsky's heroes, but as we have said, in his last novel it again takes on the form of independent existence. The devil shouts Ivan Karamazov's own words in his ear in a mocking commentary on his decision to confess in court, repeating his intimate thoughts in a foreign tone. We shall not discuss Ivan's actual dialogue with the devil, since we will concern ourselves with the principles of the genuine dialogue later on. But we shall quote the story which Ivan excitedly relates to Alyosha immediately after his dialogue with the devil. Its structure is analogous to the structure of *The Double* as we have analyzed it. The same principle of the combination of voices is present here, though here everything is deeper and more complex. In this story Ivan passes his own personal thoughts and decisions through two voices simultaneously, he communicates them in two different tonalities. In the quoted excerpt we shall omit Alyosha's replies, since his real voice does not yet fit into our scheme. For the moment we are interested only in the intra-atomic counterpoint of voices and their combination only within the bounds of a single dissociated consciousness (i.e. a microdialogue).

> "He teased me! And cleverly, you know, cleverly: 'Conscience! What is conscience? I create it myself. Why do I torment myself? Out of habit. Out of a universal human habit seven thousand years old. When we get out of the habit, we will be gods.' That's what he said, that's what he said!...
>
> "Yes, but he is evil. He laughed at me. He was insolent, Alyosha," said Ivan with an offended shudder. "And he slandered me, he slandered me in many ways. He lied about me to my face. 'Oh, you are going to perform an heroic deed of virtue, you are going to announce that you killed your father, that you incited that lackey to kill your father....'
>
> "That's what he says, he, and he knows it. 'You are going to perform an heroic deed of virtue, but you do not believe in virtue—that is what torments and enrages you, that is why you are so vindictive.' He told me these things about myself, and he knows what he is talking about....
>
> "No, he knows how to torture, he is cruel," continued Ivan, not listening. "I always had the feeling I knew why he was coming. 'Let us assume that you went out of pride, but still there was the hope that they would find Smerdyakov out and send him to prison, exonerate Mitya, and only *morally* condemn you (he laughed here, do you hear?), and others would praise you. But then Smerdyakov died, hanged himself—well, now who is going to take your word alone in court? but still you are going, you are going, you will go anyway, you have resolved to go. But why are you going now?' This is terrible, Alyosha, I can't endure such questions!" [*The Brothers Karamazov*, Part IV, Bk. 11, Ch. 10]

All the loopholes of Ivan's thoughts, all his sideward glances at the other's speech and consciousness, all his attempts to avoid the other's speech and to replace it in his soul with his own self-affirmation, all the reservations of his conscience which create a counterpoint in his every thought, his every word and experience, all these things are brought to a focus and intensified here in the full statements of the devil. The difference between Ivan's words

266

and the devil's replies is not one of content, but merely of tone, of accent. But this change of accent alters their entire ultimate meaning. The devil as it were transfers to the main clause that which in Ivan's sentence was merely a subordinate clause and which was pronounced in a low voice with no independent accent; he in turn transforms the content of the main clause into an unaccented subordinate clause. The devil turns Ivan's reservation regarding the main motif of his decision into the main motif, while the main motif becomes a mere reservation. The result is a profoundly tense and extremely eventful combination of voices, but one which at the same time is not based on any opposition whatever in content or theme.

But, of course, this complete dialogization of Ivan's self-awareness is, as is always the case in Dostoevsky's work, prepared gradually. The other's speech stealthily, little by little, penetrates the speech and consciousness of the hero: now in the form of a pause where none would occur in monologically secure speech, now in the form of an accent which is foreign to the speaker and thus breaks up his sentence, now in the form of the abnormally raised, exaggerated or hysterical tone of the speaker, etc. The process of the gradual dialogic dissociation of Ivan's consciousness begins with his first words and his whole inner orientation in Zosima's cell, and is drawn out through his conversations with Alyosha, with his father, and especially with Smerdyakov (before his departure for Chermashnya), and, finally, through his three meetings with Smerdyakov after the murder; this process is more profound and ideologically complex than in the case of Golyadkin, but structurally the two are completely analogous.

The phenomenon of a foreign voice whispering the hero's own words in his ear (with a rearranged accent) and the resulting inimitable combination of vari-directional words and voices within a single word or a single speech and the intersection of two consciousnesses within a single consciousness are present—in one form or another, to one degree or another, in one ideological direction or another—in each of Dostoevsky's works. This contrapuntal combination of vari-directional voices within the bounds of a single consciousness also serves for him as the basis, the soil, on which he introduces other actual voices. But we shall turn our attention to this question later on. At this point we would like to quote a passage from Dostoevsky in which he presents with astounding artistic power a musical image of the interrelation of voices which we have analyzed. This page from *A Raw Youth* is all the more interesting since, except for this passage, Dostoevsky almost nowhere in his works discusses music.

Trishatov is telling the raw youth of his love for music and elaborates for him a plan for an opera:

"Listen, do you love music? I love it terribly. I'll play you something when I come to visit you. I play the piano very well, and I studied for a very long time. I studied seriously. If I were to write an opera, I would, you know, take the plot from *Faust*. I like the theme very much. I am constantly creating the scene in the cathedral, just imagining it in my head. A gothic cathedral, the interior, choirs, hymns, Gretchen enters and, you know—medieval choirs, so that you can hear the fifteenth century. Gretchen is in anguish, first a recitative, a soft, but terrible, agonizing one, and the choirs thunder somberly, severely, without sympathy:

Dies irae, dies illa!

And suddenly—the voice of the devil, the song of the devil. He is invisible, just his song, alongside the hymns, together with the hymns, almost coinciding with them, but still completely different from them—this would have to be done somehow. The song is long, indefatigable—this is the tenor. It begins softly, tenderly: 'Do you remember, Gretchen, how. you, still innocent, still a baby, would come with your mother to this cathedral and babble prayers from an old book?' But the song becomes ever stronger, more passionate and impetuous; the notes get higher: there are tears, hopeless, undying agony in them, and, finally, despair: 'There is no forgiveness, Gretchen, there is no forgiveness for you here!' Gretchen wants to pray, but only shrieks burst from her breast—you know, when the breast is convulsed from weeping—and Satan's song goes on, piercing deeper and deeper into the soul, like a spear, even higher, and suddenly it is nearly broken off by a cry: 'It is the end, accursed one!' Gretchen falls on her knees, wrings her hands—and then comes her prayer, something very short, a semi-recitative, but naive, completely unpolished, something utterly medieval, four lines, just four lines in all—there are a few such notes in Stradella—and with the final note—she swoons! Confusion. People lift her up and carry her—and then suddenly a thundering chorus. It is like a clap of voices, an inspired, triumphant, overwhelming chorus, something like our Dori-no-si-ma-chin-mi—so that everything rattles on its foundations, and then it all turns into a rapturous, exultant exclamation: Hosanna!—Like the cry of the entire universe, and she is carried away, carried, and then the curtain falls. [Part III, Ch. 5, iii]

A part of this musical plan, in the form of literary works, was, indisputably, realized by Dostoevsky, and realized more than once, using diverse material.[8]

But let us return to Golyadkin—we have not yet finished with him; more precisely, we have not yet finished with the speech of the narrator. In his article "Towards a Morphology of the Naturalist Style" V. Vinogradov gives a definition of the narration in *The Double* which is analogous to ours, though it proceeds from a completely different point of view—namely from

268

the point of view of linguistic stylistics.

Here is Vinogradov's basic assertion:

> The introduction of the interjections and expressions of Golyadkin's speech into the narrational *skaz* achieves an effect whereby it seems at times that Golyadkin himself, hidden behind the mask of the narrator, is relating his own adventures. In *The Double* the convergence of Mr. Golyadkin's colloquial speech with the narrational *skaz* of the story-teller is also intensified because Golyadkin's style remains unchanged in "indirect" speech, thus seeming to belong to the author. And since Golyadkin says one and the same thing not only with his language, but with his glance, his appearance, his gestures and movements as well, it is easy to understand why almost all descriptions which underscore some "perpetual custom" of Mr. Golyadkin's swarm with un-set-off quotations from his speeches.

Citing a series of examples of the coincidence of the narrator's speech with that of Golyadkin,[9] Vinogradov continues:

> There are many more examples, but those that we have quoted, which illustrate this combination of Mr. Golyadkin's self-definitions and the little verbal brush strokes of a detached observer, sufficiently emphasize the idea that the "Petersburg poem," at least in many parts, takes on the form of Golyadkin's story as told by his "double," that is, "by a person with his language and notions." The reason for the failure of *The Double* lay precisely in the use of this innovative device.[10]

Vinogradov's analysis is sound and astute and his conclusions are correct, but of course he remains within the bounds of the method he has adopted, and the most important and essential points simply do not fit within these bounds.

It seems to us that V. Vinogradov was not able to perceive the real uniqueness of *The Double*'s syntax, since its syntactic system is determined not by the *skaz* in and of itself and not by the clerk's colloquial dialect or by the official bureaucratic jargon, but above all by the collision and the counterpoint of various accents within the bounds of a single syntactic whole, i.e. precisely by the fact that this whole, while being one, encompasses the accents of two voices. Furthermore, he does not comprehend or point out the fact that the narration is *dialogically addressed* to Golyadkin, which is made manifest by very clear external features, for example by the fact that the first sentence of Golyadkin's speech is very often an obvious reply to a preceding sentence in the narration. Finally, he does not understand the basic bond between the narration and Golyadkin's interior dialogue: the narration, after all, does not reproduce the general pattern of Golyadkin's speech, but rather, picks up only the speech of his second voice.

In general, it is impossible to approach the real artistic purpose of style while remaining within the bounds of linguistic stylistics. No one formal linguistic definition of a word can cover its artistic functions in a work. The true style-determining factors remain outside the field of vision of linguistic stylistics.

There is in the style of the narration in *The Double* yet another essential feature which Vinogradov correctly noted, but did not explain. "Motor images," he says, "predominate in the narrational *skaz*, and its primary stylistic device is the registration of movements, regardless of their repetitiveness."[11]

Indeed, the narration registers with the most tedious exactness all the hero's minutest movements, not sparing endless repetitions. It is as if the narrator were riveted to his hero and cannot back far enough away from him to give a summarizing, integrated image of his deeds and actions. Such a generalizing, integrated image would lie outside the hero's own field of vision, and in general such an image assumes the existence of some firm external position. The narrator is not in possession of such a position, he does not have the required perspective for an artistic summation of the hero's image and his acts as a whole.[12]

This peculiarity of the narration in *The Double* is retained, with certain modifications, throughout the course of all of Dostoevsky's subsequent creative work. Narration in Dostoevsky is always narration without perspective. To use a term from art criticism, we might say that in Dostoevsky there exists no "perspectival representation" of the hero and the event. The narrator finds himself in immediate proximity to the hero and to the event which is taking place, and he represents them from this maximally close, aperspectival point of view. True, Dostoevsky's chroniclers write their notes after the events have come to an end, i.e. from an apparent temporal perspective. The narrator of *The Possessed*, for example, quite often says, "now that all of this is over with," "now, as we recall all of this," etc., but in fact he constructs his narration without any significant perspective whatever.

On the other hand, in contrast to the narration in *The Double*, Dostoevsky's later narrations do not at all register the hero's minute movements, are not in the least long-winded, and are completely devoid of all repetition. The narration in Dostoevsky's later period is brief, dry, and even somewhat abstract (especially when it gives information about events that have already taken place). But the brevity and dryness of the narration in the later works, "sometimes equalling *Gil Blas*," stems not from perspective, but, on the contrary, from the lack of perspective. This deliberate lack of perspective is predetermined by Dostoevsky's entire artistic intention, for, as we know, a firm, finalized image of the hero and the event is excluded in advance from that

270

intention.

But let us return once again to the narration in *The Double*. Along with its relationship to the speech of the hero, which we have already examined, we note yet another parodic tendency in it. Elements of literary parody are present in the narration of *The Double*, just as they are present in Devushkin's letters.

Already in *Poor Folk* the author made use of his hero's voice to refract his own parodic intentions. He achieved this by various means: the parodies were either motivated by the subject matter and simply introduced into Devushkin's letters (the excerpts from the works of Ratazyaev: the parody on the high society novel, on the historical novel of the time, and, finally, on the Natural School), or the parodic strokes were presented in the very structure of the novel (Teresa and Faldoni, for example). Finally, the author introduces into the novel the polemic with Gogol, which is refracted directly in the hero's voice; it is a parodically tinted voice (Devushkin's reading of "The Overcoat" and his outraged reaction to it. The following episode, involving the general who helps the hero, contains an implied juxtaposition to the episode with the "important personage" in Gogol's "The Overcoat").[13]

In *The Double* a parodic stylization of the "high style" in *Dead Souls* is refracted in the voice of the narrator, and, in general, parodic and semi-parodic allusions to various of Gogol's works are scattered throughout *The Double*. It should be mentioned that these parodic tones in the narration are directly intertwined with the narrator's mimicry of Golyadkin.

As a result of the introduction of the parodic and polemic element into the narration it becomes more multi-voiced and contrapuntal and has less relation to itself and its referential object. On the other hand, literary parody intensifies the element of literary conventionality within the narrator's speech, thus depriving it still more of its independence and finalizing power in relation to the hero. In Dostoevsky's subsequent works as well the element of literary conventionality and its exposure in one form or another always served to increase the full significance and independence of the hero's position. In this sense literary conventionality, in keeping with Dostoevsky's intention, did not only not reduce the ideational content and significance of his novel, but, on the contrary, could only increase it (as was, by the way, the case with Jean Paul and even with Sterne). The destruction in Dostoevsky's works of the ordinary monologic orientation led him to completely exclude certain elements of that monologic orientation from his structure, and to carefully neutralize others. One of the means of that neutralization was literary conventionality, i.e. the introduction of conventional discourse into the narration or into the principles of structure: stylized or parodic discourse.

The phenomenon of dialogically addressing the narration to the hero was still present, of course, in Dostoevsky's subsequent works, but it was modified and became more complex and profound. It is no longer the narrator's every word that is addressed to the hero, but rather the narration as a whole, its whole orientation. Speech within the narration is in the majority of cases dry and lustreless; "documentary style" is the best definition for it. But the basic function of this documentation is to expose and provoke; it is addressed to the hero, speaking as if to him and not about him, speaking with its entire mass, not with its individual elements. True, even in Dostoevsky's last novels certain heroes were presented in the light of a style which directly parodied and taunted them and which sounded like an exaggerated line taken from their interior dialogue. The narrator in *The Possessed*, for example, is so constructed in relation to Stepan Trofimovich, but only in relation to him. Isolated notes of this taunting style are scattered throughout the other novels, too. They are present in *The Brothers Karamazov*. But in general they are considerably weakened. Dostoevsky's basic tendency in his later period was to make his style and tone dry and precise, to neutralize it. But wherever dry, documentary, neutralized narration is exchanged for sharply accented tones colored with value judgements, those tones are in every case addressed to the hero and are born of the speeches in his potential interior dialogue with himself.

1929/1963

NOTES

Introduction

1. See, e.g., Charles Passage's studies, *Dostoevski the Adapter* and *The Russian Hoffmannists.*

2. Iurii Tynianov, "On Literary Evolution," in *Readings in Russian Poetics: Formalist and Structuralist Views,* eds. L. Matejka and K. Pomorska (Cambridge: M.I.T. Press, 1971), p. 76.

3. A. Slonimskii, *Tekhnika komicheskogo u Gogolia* (Petrograd, 1923); cf. the English translation, "The Technique of the Comic in Gogol," in *Gogol from the Twentieth Century,* ed. by R. A. Maguire (Princeton: Princeton University, 1974), pp. 324-73.

4. Dmitry Chizhevsky's essay on the same story by Gogol is included here by way of contrast to Eikhenbaum's. While emphasizing with Eikhenbaum the fundamental role that formal elements play in determining the "message" of a work, Chizhevsky is more interested in the generalizations that can be drawn from an analysis of this story for Gogol's world view and in the way it fits into the total pattern of the writer's creative output.

5. Tynianov, *op. cit.,* p. 68.

6. Iurii Tynianov, "Literaturnyi fakt" (1924), in his book *Arkhaisty i novatory* (Leningrad, 1929), p. 15.

7. For the best recent work examining the numerous theoretical questions underlying this discussion, see Claudio Guillen's *Literature as System: Essays toward the Theory of Literary History* (Princeton: Princeton University, 1971), especially the essays "Literature as System" and "On the Object of Literary Change."

8. V. Vinogradov, *Evoliutsiia russkogo naturalizma* (Leningrad, 1929), pp. 291, 292. These quotes are from the short preface to his study, which has been eliminated in our translation because of its obscurity.

9. "Language of literature" is used here to indicate the coherent system of literary components available to the writer; it is not synonymous with the "literary language." Cf. Iu. M. Lotman, *Struktura khudozhestvennogo teksta* (Moscow, 1970), p. 29.

10. Vinogradov's statements here are taken from another essay in *The Evolution..,* "On Literary Cyclization" (pp. 104, 106, 107), which follows the approach of "The School of Sentimental Naturalism" but in a discussion of literary "cycles" rather than "schools."

11. Victor Erlich, *Russian Formalism: History—Doctrine* (The Hague: Mouton, 1965), p. 268. Ch. XIV, entitled "Literary Dynamics," contains a complete discussion of several aspects of the Formalists' approach to literary history and evolution that had to be simplified here for reasons of space.

12. Iurii Tynianov, "On Literary Evolution," in *Readings..,* p. 67.

13. Roman Jakobson and Iurii Tynianov had posed the question of the "correlation between the literary series and other historical series" in their 1928 theses "Problems in the Study of Literature and Language" (cf. *Readings..,* pp. 79-81), thus anticipating Bakhtin and his followers. See I. R. Titunik, "The Formal Method and the Sociological Method (M.M.Bakhtin, P. N. Medvedev, V. N. Voloshinov) in Russian Theory and Study of Literature," in V. N. Voloshinov, *Marxism and the Philosophy of Language,* (New York: Seminar, 1973), pp. 175-200; V.V. Ivanov, "The Significance of M.M.

Bakhtin's Ideas on Sign, Utterance and Dialogue for Modern Semiotics," *Soviet Studies in Literature,* XI, 2-3 (1975), pp. 186-243.

14. See B. Eikhenbaum's "Pushkin's Path to Prose," in *The Complection of Russian Literature*, ed. A. Field (New York: Atheneum, 1971), pp. 30-41, or better, in its complete Russian version (*O proze*, Leningrad, 1969, pp. 214-30).

15. J.T. Baer's book *Vladimir Ivanovich Dal' as a Belletrist* (Mouton: The Hague, 1972) contains a great deal of information valuable for a student of this period.

16. *Ibid.*, p. 38.

17. *Lermontov* (Leningrad, 1924), p. 128.

18. Dostoevsky, among others, was later to return to Pushkin's prose in formulating the narrative style of the realistic novel. See Ch. X of D.S. Mirsky's *Pushkin* (Dutton, N.Y., 1963).

19. See D. Iakubovich's article in the collection *Pushkin v mirovoi literature* (Leningrad, 1926), pp. 160-187; V.V. Vinogradov, *Ètiudy o stile Gogolia* (Leningrad, 1926).

20. See J. M. Holquist, "The Devil in Mufti: The *Märchenwelt* in Gogol's Short Stories," *PMLA*, LXXXII (Oct. 1967).

21. See Boris Eikhenbaum, "The Illusion of 'Skaz' " (tr. Martin P. Rice), in *Russian Literature Triquarterly*, 12 (Spring 1975), pp. 233-36; V.V. Vinogradov, "The Problem of 'Skaz' in Stylistics," *op. cit.*, pp. 237-50; Martin P. Rice, "On 'Skaz,' " *op. cit.*, pp. 409-24.

22. "How the Character Akaky Akakiyevich Originated," in *Essays in Russian Literature,* ed. S.E. Roberts (Athens: Ohio University, 1968), p. 379.

23. On the *école frénétique*, see the books by R.W. Hartland and M. Praz (especially pp. 120-31) and the recent article by P. Kalinine, cited in our bibliography.

24. See V. Vinogradov, "O literaturnoi tsiklizatsii," in his *Evoliutsiia russkogo naturalizma* (Leningrad, 1929), pp. 89-126.

25. In his book *Gogol et Pétersbourg* (Stockholm, 1954), Nils Åke Nilsson convincingly argues for the influence of the feuilletons of Victor-Joseph Jouy and of the early Balzac on "Nevsky Prospect."

26. A. Belyi, *Masterstvo Gogolia* (Moscow, 1934), p. 186.

27. On Odoevsky, see R. Matlaw's introduction to *Russian Nights* (N.Y.: Dutton, 1965) and the chapter in Charles Passage's *The Russian Hoffmannists* (Mouton: The Hague, 1963).

28. See J. Mersereau's *Baron Delvig's "Northern Flowers" 1825-1832* (Carbondale: Southern Illinois University, 1967), which gives one a good picture of the various currents in Russian literature during this period.

29. See I. Zolotussky, " 'Diary of a Madman' and the 'Severnaya Pchela,' " *Soviet Literature* (1975), No. 10 (331), pp. 38-54, and M. Holquist, *Dostoevsky and the Novel* (Princeton, 1977), p. 24 f.

30. V. Erlich, *Gogol* (New Haven: Yale, 1969), p. 93.

31. Herbert Bowman, "The Nose," *Slavonic and East European Review*, XXXI (1952), p. 209.

32. V. Vinogradov, "Naturalisticheskii grotesk: siuzhet i kompozitsiia povesti Gogolia 'Nos,' " in his book *Èvoliutsiia russkogo naturalizma* (Leningrad, 1929), p. 35.

33. Cf. Nabokov's list in his discussion of Gogol's artistic "anatomy," in which "the belly is the belle of his stories, the nose is their beau," *Nikolai Gogol* (New York: New Directions, 1944), pp. 3-5.

34. Cf. V. Erlich, *op. cit.*, p. 86.

35. See Iurii Mann's article, "Èvoliutsiia gogolevskoi fantastiki," in the collection *K istorii russkogo romantizma* (Moscow, 1973), pp. 219-58.

36. Letter of June 15, 1880, to Iu. F. Abaza, *Pis'ma*, IV (Moscow, 1959), p. 178.

37. *Ibid.*

38. *A History of Russian Literature,* ed. F.J. Whitfield (New York: Alfred Knopf, 1949), p. 152.

39. F.M. Dostoevskii, "Peterburgskie snovideniia v stikhakh i proze," *Polnoe sobranie khudozhestvennykh sochinenii,* V. XIII (Stat'i za 1845-1878 gody), ed. B. Tomashevskii and K. Khalabaev (Moscow-Leningrad, 1930), p. 157.

40. *Ibid.,* p. 156. Translated in K. Mochulsky, *Dostoevsky, His Life and Work,* tr. Michael Minihan (Princeton, 1967), pp. 27-29, and in D. Fanger, *Dostoevsky and Romantic Realism* (Cambridge, 1967), p. 150, which discusses "Petersburg Visions" at length.

41. A.L. Bem, "Pervye shagi Dostoevskogo," *Slavia,* XII (1933), pp. 134-61.

42. Cf. A. Tseitlin, *Povest' o bednom chinovnike Dostoevskogo* (Moscow, 1923).

43. Cf. Iurii Mann, "Filosofiia i poètika natural'noi shkoly," *Prolemy tipologii russkogo realizma* (Moscow, 1969), p. 279 ff.

44. V. Maikov, *Sochineniia v dvukh tomakh,* V. I, p. 57, quoted in Iu. Mann, *op. cit.,* p. 283.

45. Cf. V.L. Komarovich, "Iunost' Dostoevskogo," in *O Dostoevskom, stat'i,* ed. D. Fanger (Providence, 1966) for a detailed discussion of Dostoevsky's relationship to Belinsky and Utopian Socialism; on Belinsky see *Belinsky, Chernyshevsky and Dobrolyubov: Selected Criticism,* ed. R.E. Matlaw (New York: Dutton, 1962).

46. Cf. C. Passage, *The Russian Hoffmannists* (The Hague, 1963).

47. Cf. Elliott Mossman, "Dostoevskii's Early Works: The More than Rational Distortion," *Slavic and East European Journal,* X, 3 (Fall 1966), pp. 268-78.

48. V. Terras, *The Young Dostoevsky* (The Hague, 1969), p. 26.

49. Cf. G.M. Fridlender, *Realizm Dostoevskogo* (Moscow, 1964), pp. 54-62.

50. Quoted in Iu. Mann, *op. cit.,* p. 304.

51. See Bem, p. 240 below.

52. Cf. M.S. Al'tman, "Gogolevskie traditsii v tvorchestve Dostoevskogo," *Slavia,* 1961, V. XXX, 3, pp. 443-461.

53. *Op. cit.,* p. 27.

54. M. Bakhtin, *Problemy poètiki Dostoevskogo* (Moscow, 1963).

55. Cf. S. Bocharov, "Pushkin i Gogol'," *Problemy tipologii russkogo realizma,* ed. N.L. Stepanov and U.R. Fokt (Moscow, 1969), pp. 210-40.

56. Cf. V. Maikov, "Nechto o russkoi literature v 1846 godu," *Otechestvennye zapiski,* N. 1 (1847), p. 5.

57. Cf. Inokentii Annenskii, *Kniga otrazhenii* (St. Petersburg, 1906), pp. 50-51. Annenskii suggests that Dostoevsky created the character of Prokharchin as the simplest form of human existence to render the idea of the "terror of life" more intense.

58. Cf. V.A. Tunimanov, "Nekotorye osobennosti povestvovaniia v 'Gospodine Prokharchine' F.M. Dostoevskogo," in *Poètika i stilistika russkoi literatury* (Leningrad, 1971), pp. 203-12.

59. "Peterburgskie ugly," originally published in Nekrasov's collection, *Fiziologiia Peterburga,* Part I (St. Petersburg, 1845), in *Russkie ocherki* (Moscow, 1956), V. 1, pp. 281-300.

60. A. Bem, "Skupoi rytsar' v tvorchestve Dostoevskogo," in *O Dostoevskom,* V. III (Prague, 1936).

61. *Op. cit.,* p. 291.

62. Cf. A.L. Bem, "Dramatizatsiia breda," *O Dostoevskom* (Prague, 1929), V. I, pp. 77-124.

63. Cf. V.V. Vinogradov, *O iazyke khudozhestvennoi literatury* (Moscow, 1959), pp. 477-93.

64. Cf. *Dostoevsky's Occasional Writings,* sel. & tr. D. Magarshak (New York:

Random House, 1963), pp. 35-37.

65. Cf. V.G. Belinsky, *Selected Philosophical Works* (Moscow: Foreign Languages Publishing House, 1956), p. 508.

66. M.S. Al'tman, "Iz arsenala imen i prototipov literaturnykh geroev Dostoevskogo," in *Dostoevskii i ego vremia*, ed. V.G. Bazanov and G.M. Fridlender (Leningrad, 1971), pp. 196-216.

Tynyanov / Dostoevsky and Gogol: Towards a Theory of Parody

1. "Anna Karenina as a Fact of Special Significance," *The Diary of a Writer* (for 1877), [tr. Boris Brasol (New York: Scribner's, 1949), V. II, p. 784].

2. [*Dead Souls*, tr. Bernard Guerney (New York: Heritage, 1944), pp. 9-10; cf. Vladimir Nabokov's translation and commentary in his *Nikolai Gogol* (New York: New Directions, 1944), p. 79.]

3. ["The Landlady," Ch. 1, in *The Short Stories of Dostoevsky*, tr. Constance Garnett (New York: Dial, 1946), p. 69.]

4. Cf. this passage from Ch. VII with the leitmotif of "The Portrait": "All at once it seemed to me that the eyes in the portrait looked away in embarrassment from my probing, questioning gaze, that they were trying to avoid it, that there was hypocrisy and deceit in those eyes; it seemed to me that I had guessed the truth...." [*Netochka Nezvanova*, tr. Ann Dunnigan (Englewood Cliffs: Prentice-Hall, 1970), p. 171].

5. Pyotr Aleksandrovich looking in the mirror: "It...seemed to me that he was rearranging his face.... No sooner had he looked into the mirror than his face completely changed. The smile disappeared as at a word of command.... An intent look was gloomily hidden behind his spectacles...." [*ibid.*, pp. 177-78]. Cf. the transformation of the Sorcerer in "A Terrible Vengeance." [*The Collected Tales and Plays of Nikolai Gogol*, ed. Leonard Kent (New York: Random House, 1964), pp. 136-37].

6. Cf. the gestures of Golyadkin Junior in Ch. VIII of *The Double* with Chichikov's in the second chapter of *Dead Souls*, Part Two: "Golyadkin kicked up his short little legs and darted to and fro..."; Chichikov "bowed with adroitness...and bounced back with the buoyancy of a little rubber ball" (*Dead Souls*, p. 350). Cf. also the following from the beginning of *The Double* with "The Nose": "Wouldn't it be something... wouldn't it be something if...I weren't up to the mark, if, for example, something weren't right,—if some strange *pimple* had popped up there, or if *some other sort of unpleasantness had occurred*" [Ch. I].

7. See I. Mandel'shtam, *O kharaktere gogolevskogo stilia* (St. Petersburg-Helsingfors, 1902), p. 161.

8. "My soul did not recognize yours, even though it was radiant in the proximity of its beautiful sister," and so on. [Cf. *Netochka Nezvanova*, p. 162.]

9. [The expression "a Fetyuk, simply a Fetyuk" is a favorite of the character Nozdryov in *Dead Souls*. It derives from the characteristic pose of a dandy, with his hands on his hips, which resembles the Cyrillic letter *feta* (ф).]

10. [A direct quote from the character Poprishchin in "Diary of a Madman"; see above, p. 17.]

11. [A play on a sentence in "The Overcoat"; see above, p. 52.]

12. ["Pseldonimov" echoes the Russian word for "pseudonym," "Mlekopitaev," that for "mammal"; the characters are portrayed accordingly and Dostoevsky plays on the derivations and the general strangeness of both names and their juxtaposition. See "An Unpleasant Predicament," *The Short Stories of Dostoevsky*, tr. Constance Garnett, pp. 412, 447-49 and *passim*. "Vidoplyasov" derives from "appearance" and "dance"; Dostoevsky develops a situation out of this character's desire to change his strange name,

and the punning is extended to the point of absurdity. See "The Friend of the Family," Part I, ch. XI, *The Short Novels of Dostoevsky,* tr. Constance Garnett (New York: Dial, 1945), pp. 733-37.]

13. N.N. Strakhov, *Biografiia, pis'ma i zametki iz zapisnoi knizhki F.M. Dostoevskogo* (St. Petersburg, 1883, p. 176). [The italics are Tynyanov's throughout.]

14. *Ibid.*, p. 114.

15. *Ibid.*, p. 244.

16. *Ibid.*, p. 313.

17. [*The Collected Tales*, p. 425.]

18. [A short unpublished fragment written by Gogol in 1831-1833 which relates to his "Petersburg Tales," especially "The Portrait."]

19. [Cf. *Dead Souls*, Guerney trans., p. 425.]

20. Compare the further development: "And *the stubby frame of the distiller* shook anew from loud laughter." [See *The Collected Tales*, p. 61-62.]

21. "Zemlyanika" [a character in "The Inspector General" whose name means "strawberry"] and "Yaichnitsa" [in "The Wedding," literally "omelet"] exemplify a more complex development of the device. Here the names attached to the characters do not coincide with them either in terms of semantics or as types of verbal masks; this results in a much greater and unexpected comical effect. In these names what is important is their formal semantic aspect. [Cf. *The Collected Tales*, pp. 690, 695-96.]

22. ["A Terrible Vengeance."]

23. [In "Christmas Eve"; cf. *The Collected Tales*, p. 114.]

24. [Cf. Eikhenbaum, p. 120 below.]

25. See V.V. Vinogradov, "Naturalisticheskii grotesk: siuzhet i kompozitsiia povesti Gogolia 'Nos,' " in *Evoliutsiia russkogo naturalizma* (Moscow, 1929), pp. 7-88.

26. [*The Collected Tales*, p. 445.]

27. [Letter to Balabina from Rome, April, 1838, *Pol. sob. soch.*, V. 11, p. 144.]

28. [*The Collected Tales*, p. 378.]

29. [*Ibid.*, p. 379.]

30. Dialectal features in Gogol's language are hardly limited just to Ukrainian and South Russian particularities; in Gogol's notebooks one comes across words of the Simbirsk province, which he copied down from the Yazykovs, as well as "words of the Vladimir Province" and "words of a man from Volzhekhod." There are also many technical words relating to fishing, hunting, agriculture, etc. Gogol shows an interest in family argot: for instance, the word "Pikot," the family nickname of Praskoviya Mikhailovna Yazykov, is noted down. One comes across foreign words with parodic semantic displacements: *moshinal'nyi chelovek* ["a lousy man," from French *moche*] becomes *moshennik* ["swindler, rogue"] ; *proletarii* ["proletarian"] is "derived" from *proletat'* ["to fly through or past": Gogol uses this pun in *Dead Souls*–cf. Guerney, p. 444], anticipating the language of Leskov. In *Dead Souls* one finds North Russian words (*shanishki, razmychet,* etc.). One should notice the fact that Gogol *writes the words down* in his notebook quite exactly but often makes mistakes in their semantics; thus he confuses *podvalka* and *podvoloka*, words with similar sounds but with different meanings, and so on. Apparently he is less interested in semantics than in phonetics.

The introduction of dialectal features, which in *Dead Souls* is weakly motivated, was a conscious artistic device of Gogol's, picked up and developed by writers who followed him. The choice of dialecticisms and technical terms (cf. in particular the names of dogs: *murugie* ["rusty-hued"], *chistopsovye* and *gustopsovye* ["smooth" and "shaggy-coated"], [*Dead Souls*, p. 80]) reveals the articulatory principle.

31. [A paraphrase of general arguments in the *Correspondence*; see *Selected Passages from Correspondence with Friends*, tr. Jesse Zeldin (Nashville: Vanderbilt, 1969), p. 141.]

32. [*Ibid*., p. 121.]

33. [*The Idiot*, tr. Magarshack (Baltimore: Penguin, 1955), p. 500.]

34. ["The Poet" is translated in Walter Arndt's collection *Pushkin Threefold* (New York: Dutton, 1972), p. 217.]

35. [*The Idiot,* pp. 62-63.]

36. [*Netochka Nezvanovna*, p. 43.]

37. [Cf. *The Collected Tales*, p. 378, 375, 379, 375 respectively.]

38. [*The Short Novels of Dostoevsky,* pp. 225-26.]

39. [About Nozdryov's behavior at the Governor's ball: *Dead Souls*, p. 203.]

40. [*The Short Novels of Dostoevsky*, p. 228.]

41. [*Notes from the House of the Dead*, tr. Constance Garnett (New York: Dell, 1959), p. 27.]

Eikhenbaum / How Gogol's "Overcoat" Is Made

1. *O kharaktere gogolevskogo stilia. Glava iz istorii russkogo literaturnogo iazyka* (St. Petersburg-Helsingfors, 1902), pp. 251-52. The book is interesting in its observations, but disorderly from the standpoint of methodology.

2. [Approximate translations are: "Navel-Belly," "Naked Belly," "Long Sneeze," "Naked Navel," "Scratch-Ass," "Peat-Dung Picker," "Over-Pepperer," "Abrupt Roarer," "Miss Mushroom," "Curl-Lip."]

3. ["Omelet," "Don't Respect the Feeding-Trough," "White-Belly," "Shoe."]

4. [Cf. V. Rozanov, "How the Character Akaky Akakiyevich Originated," in *Essays in Russian Literature*, tr. and ed. S.E. Roberts (Athens: Ohio University, 1968). The first draft, entitled "The Story of a Clerk Who Stole Overcoats," is given in Rozanov's essay, pp. 372-75.]

5. Cf. Pul'pul'tik and Mon'munia in "The Carriage."

6. The names which the mother prefers.

7. This device of Gogol's is repeated by his imitators, as in the early tale of P.I. Mel'nikov-Pechersky, "The Story of Who Yelpifidor Perfilievich was..." (1840). See A. Zmorovich, "O iazyke i stile proizvedenii P.I. Mel'nikova (Andreia Pecherskogo)," *Russkii filologicheskii vestnik*, No. 1-2 (1916), pp. 178 ff.

8. V. Rozanov speaks about this passage, explaining it as "the artist's sorrow for the law of his creative work, his lament for an amazing picture, which he could not draw differently..., and having drawn it in this way he admires it, but at the same time he hates and despises it" [The article "How the Character Akaky Akakiyevich Originated" (1894), *op. cit.* p. 380.] And again: "And then, as if interrupting this torrent of mockery, and striking the hand irresistibly depicting it, there is added in the side margin a sort of postscript, which was later pasted into the text: '... But not one word would Akaky Akakievich answer to this...,' etc." Leaving aside the question of the philosophical and psychological meaning of this passage, we look on it in the given instance only as an artistic device and evaluate it from the standpoint of composition, as the embedding of a declamatory style in the system of a comic *skaz*.

9. "I sometimes like to descend for a moment *into the sphere of that extraordinarily secluded life in which not a single desire flits beyond the palisade* surrounding the small courtyard..." ("Old World Landowners" [*Collected Tales*, p. 207]). Already in "Shponka" Gogol suggests the devices of his grotesque. Mirgorod is a fantastic grotesque town, completely fenced off from the whole world.

10. "But such is the strange order of things that insignificant causes give rise to great events while, on the other hand, the consequences of great enterprises are often quite insignificant" ("Old World Landowners" [*Collected Tales*, p. 219]).

278

11. "The life of their modest owners is so quiet, that for a moment you are lost to the world of reality and you imagine that the passions, desires, and restless promptings of the evil spirit that trouble the world do not exist at all and that you have only seen them in some dazzling, glittering dream" (Old World Landowners" [*Collected Tales*, pp. 207-08]).

12. In the rough draft, not as yet developed into a grotesque, it was different: "carrying continually in his thoughts the future overcoat."

13. Naive people will say that this is "realism," "daily life," and so on. To argue with them is useless, but let them consider the fact that much information is given about the toenail and the snuffbox, but about Petrovich himself we know only that he drank on all the holidays, and about his wife, that she *existed* and that she even wore a cap. This is an obvious device of grotesque composition—to set forth minutiae in exaggerated detail, but put things which would seem to deserve greater attention in the background.

14. In the general context even this ordinary expression sounds unusual, strange, and has the appearance almost of a pun—a constant occurrence in Gogol's language.

Chizhevsky / On Gogol's "The Overcoat"

1. [*Dead Souls*, Guerney trans., pp. 245 and 249-50.]
2. [*Dead Souls*, p. 182.]
3. [*Dead Souls*, p. 8.]
4. [*Collected Tales*, p. 379.]
5. [*Collected Tales*, p. 252.]
6. [*Dead Souls*, p. 23. "Enthusiasm" is Guerney's rendering of *zador*.]
7. [*The Collected Tales*, p. 245.]
8. [*The Collected Tales*, p. 95.]

Vinogradov / The School of Sentimental Naturalism

1. [Translated in V.G. Belinsky, *Selected Philosophical Works* (Moscow: Foreign Languages, 1956), p. 462.]

2. [Cf. *The Short Stories of Dostoevsky*, pp. 178-80.]

3. ["How Dangerous...," published in 1846, was the collective work of N.A. Nekrasov, D.V. Grigorovich, and F.M. Dostoevsky. A mixture of comic verses, farcical dialogue and the "physiological" sketch, it takes up the clerk theme with none of the humanism that marks *Poor Folk*, though traces of Dostoevsky's psychological approach and such themes as the clerk with "ambition" are apparent. The almanac *April Fool's* and this "dramatic farce" in particular were the object of the conservatives' scornful criticism: Kukolnik described it as "a new sort of book...*for lackeys*"; Bulgarin railed, "And they call this literature!"]

4. Cf. the first draft of this passage: "He was what is known as a perpetual titular councillor—a rank about which, as is well known, various writers have japed whose works (still being read in the country to this day) still amuse naive readers who like to read a little from boredom or to while away the time." This merely reflects an ironic allusion to the tradition of Bulgarin (e.g., his portrayal of the titular councillors of Chukhin). Hence, it is more accurate to propose that Gogol wrote the first drafts of "The Overcoat" in the mid-1830s (cf. Vinogradov, *Gogol' i natural'naia shkola*, pp. 7-9). [The editors of Gogol's *Collected Works* have established 1839 as the date of the first drafts of "The Overcoat"; see Vol. II (Leningrad, 1938), pp. 675-77.]

5. ["How the Character Akaky Akakiyevich Originated," in *Essays in Russian*

Literature—The Conservative View, ed. and tr. S.E. Roberts (Athens: Ohio University, 1968), pp. 369-83.]

6. Several parallel passages in Part Two of *Dead Souls* that conclude Chichikov's story at General Betrishchev's illuminate the compositional function of the "humane" passage in "The Overcoat."

7. [Most likely it was the common Russian proverb, *Na bednogo Makara vse shishki valiatsia*, literally "it is upon poor Makar that all the cones fall," for which Smirnitsky's *Russian-English Dictionary* has the equivalent, "an unlucky man would be drowned in a teacup." Roman Jakobson mentions several such bywords, proverbs, and spoonerisms relating to the "ill-fated fellow" Makar in his *Selected Writings, IV*: "Slavic Epic Studies" (The Hague: Mouton, 1966), p. 638.]

8. From the foreword to the Russian translation (1816) of Léonard's novel cited above. Cf. the translator's conclusion: "One could boldly say that Teresa, after la Nouvelle Héloïse and Werther, occupies first place in the library and heart of the sensitive reader."

9. [A ballad by F. Schiller (1797) translated by V.A. Zhukovsky (1813).]

10. [Dostoevsky eliminated this moralistic conclusion when working on the final version of the story for the 1860 edition of his collected works.]

11. Cf. the following passage from Gogol's "Nevsky Prospect": "I always feel annoyed at the sight of a magnificent catafalque with a velvet pall, but my annoyance is mingled with sadness when I see a drayman dragging the red, uncovered coffin of some poor fellow and only some old beggar woman who has met it at the crossways trailing after it, having nothing else to do." [*Collected Tales*, p. 441-42.]

12. Cf. in another passage: "As far as I am concerned, I don't mind going about without an overcoat and without boots in a crackling frost" (letter of August 5th).

13. [This slip of the tongue on Devushkin's part was eliminated from the text first published in Nekrasov's *Petersburg Miscellany* (1845) when Dostoevsky edited the novel for its appearance in book form.]

14. Dostoevsky was criticized for this by Imiarek in the *Moscow Scientific and Literary Symposium for 1847*.

15. Cf. the discussion of the "rat-clerk" and of himself as a "good man" (letter of June 12th).

16. Cf. the characterization of "the poor man" (letter of August 1st) and the repeated mentions of "ambition."

17. Cf., for instance, the judgment of the clerk's social significance by means of a projection from their "handwriting": "my handwriting is fairly legible and attractive..." (letter of July 8th); "he is a good clerk and his handwriting is pure copperplate" (letter of August 3rd).

18. *The Finnish Messenger* (Vol. IX) made the following interesting observation: "The idea of Gogol's 'Nevsky Prospect' was present in the creation of Varenka, only taken in the opposite sense. Let it not be said that we are stretching a point in finding this resemblance...." This similarity by contrast is conditioned by Dostoevsky's return to the sentimental models that Gogol wanted to overcome and render more complex in "Nevsky Prospect." Actually, the sentimental tradition presented the theme of the fallen woman using completely different types from those of Jules Janin's school, with which Gogol was associated in "Nevsky Prospect." For example, in Ducray-Duminil's *Julie or the History of the Human Heart* (v. II, p. 24) we read: "Fallen girls ready to do manual labor would obey, thank and respect as a god a man who would give them peace, food, and clothing without any bad intentions attached."

19. Cf. the quick adoption of Dostoevsky's artistic devices by a group of writers that included M. Dostoevsky, Iakov Butkov, Pleshcheev, Saltykov-Shchedrin, and Aleksandr Palm.

20. Cf. Devushkin's request: "Answer me as fully as possible, my angel." Varenka carelessly returns it: "Yes! I almost forgot: you must write me all about your life and your surroundings as fully as possible."

21. And the final end to his sentimental, amorous tone: "I thought that *you meant to make fun of yourself in your letter.*"

22. The connection of Varenka's "childhood" with the fate of her father is emphasized by a repetition occurring in the opening and before the epilogue, where it refers to her transition to "youth": "I was only fourteen when my father died..." "I had then just turned fourteen."

23. With an allusion to some letters not included in the structure of the novel.

Vinogradov / Towards a Morphology of the "Naturalist" Style

1. [In calling his novel a "poem" (*poèma*—any epic composition like Homer's *Odyssey*), Dostoevsky is responding to Gogol's subtitle to *Dead Souls: A Poem.*]

2. See the essay by R.I. Avanesov "Dostoevskii v rabote nad 'Dvoinikom,' " in *Tvorcheskaia istoriia*, ed. N.K. Piksanov (Moscow, 1927).

3. Cf., e.g., I.I. Zamotin, *Dostoevskii v russkoi kritike* (Warsaw, 1913), Part I, p. 27 ff.; Prof. Kirpichnikov, *Dostoevskii i Pisemskii*; Leonid Grossman, "Gofman, Balzak i Dostoevskii," *Sofiia*, V (1914), pp. 91-93 ff.; S.I. Rodzevich, "K istorii russkogo romantizma," *Russkii filologicheskii vestnik* (1917), No. 1-2, pp. 223-230. Cf. also Leonid Grossman, *Biblioteka Dostoevskogo* (Odessa, 1919), pp. 109-110.

4. Cf. Pereverzev, *Tvorchestvo Dostoevskogo* (Moscow, 1912).

5. V. Belinskii, *Otechestvennye zapiski*, XLV, Part V., p. 8.

6. Cf. K.S. Aksakov's comment: "In *The Double* Dostoevsky constantly imitates Gogol, often copies him to such an extent that the result is no longer imitation but appropriation . . . in front of everyone Dostoevsky modifies and repeats outright whole sentences from Gogol" (*Moscow Literary and Scholarly Symposium for 1847*, p. 34).

7. The *idée fixe* which tormented Poprishchin was prompted by contemporary journalistic literature, in which "the Spanish affair" began to occupy a primary place from the second half of October, 1833 (e.g., *The Northern Bee* for October 19th, 24th, and particularly, 28th). Cf., likewise, in the work of Hoffmann, the episode with Nettelmann in "Fragment from the Lives of three Friends"; see A. Stender-Petersen, "Gogol und die deutsche Romantik," *Euphorion*, XXIV, No. 3.

8. Notwithstanding the opinion of L.P. Grossman, I find no similarity in plot between Dostoevsky's *The Double* and Lermontov's "Fragment of an Unfinished Tale" [Lermontov's last prose work, better known as "Shtoss" (1841); see the translation of D. Lowe, *Russian Literature Triquarterly*, No. 3 (Spring 1972), pp. 69-80], although the general devices used in the latter to represent Petersburg and its dreamers are antecedents of the "Dostoevskian manner."

9. *Polnoe sobranie sochinenii*, ed. V. Spiridonov, Vol. I (St. Petersburg, 1918), p. 151.

10. "Russian Literature in 1851," *ibid.*, p. 128.

11. The motif of madness is necessarily connected with the romantic poetics of the 1820s-1830s. It played a complicated role in the Hoffmannist tradition. During the late 1820s the journals were eager to print facts and stories about madmen. For examples, see V. Gippius's *Gogol'* (Leningrad, 1929), pp. 91-92. Cf. the theme of madness in the French *littérature frénétique* of the 1830s.

12. I am examining the composition of the *second* redaction. In the first, the level of the heroic epic poem about the battle with "the imposter Grishka Otrepiev," which served as the background for Golyadkin's actions, stood out more clearly. See: "Zabytye i neizdannye stranitsy Dostoevskogo" in Leonid Grossman's edition of Dostoevsky's

Collected Works, Vol. 22, p. 10. Cf. likewise Avanesov's article, "Dostoevskii v rabote nad 'Dvoinikom.'"

13. The narrator takes it upon himself to point out the validity of Golyadkin's "terror": "He felt as if he was being slowly roasted alive, *and not without reason*" [Ch. VI].

14. Cf. other analogous formulae earlier in the book [Ch. VI].

15. It is interesting that the theme of the impostor, of Grishka Otrepiev, the "False Demetrius," was already a favorite in the literature of the 1830s. One finds, for example, the following, from *The Library for Reading* of 1836 (No. 7-8, p. 33), in a review of the "novels and tales" of Vas. Narezhny: "The hero of his tragedy is one who was depicted before and after Narezhny by Sumarokov, Pogodin, Khomiakov, Bulgarin, Pushkin,—in a word, it is Otrepiev, the impostor."

Bem / *"The Nose" and* The Double

1. *The Muscovite*, 1846, part I, no. 2, pp. 172-73.

2. *Èvoliutsiia russkogo naturalizma* (Leningrad, 1929), pp. 206-90. [Cf. our partial English translation above.]

3. Cf. *"Suddenly he stopped as if rooted to the spot.... He shuddered and opened his eyes...he looked and uttered a cry of amazement and horror. It was the same familiar pedestrian..."* [Ch. V].

4. See also A. Slonimskii, *Tekhnika komicheskogo u Gogolia* (Petersburg, 1923), pp. 33-34. [In English, *Gogol from the Twentieth Century*, ed. R.A. Maguire (1974).]

5. Vinogradov, *op. cit*, p. 243. Cf. Andrei Belyi's comment: *"The Double* reminds one of a patchwork quilt sewn out of the movements of Gogol's plots, gestures and style" (*Masterstvo Gogolia*, Moscow, 1934, p. 285).

6. On the influence of "The Diary of a Madman" on *The Double*, see: Kirpichnikov, *N.V. Gogol': ocherki* (Moscow, 1903), p. 332; V. Pereverzev, *Tvorchestvo Dostoevskogo* (Moscow, 1922), p. 35; and Vinogradov, *op. cit.*, pp. 211-14 [See above pp. 217-220].

7. *The Diary of a Writer* (for 1877) [tr. Boris Brasol (New York: Scribner's, 1949, V. II, p. 883)]. See also Dostoevsky's letter of October 1, 1859, to his brother.

8. On *The Double* and "Notes from the Underground," see Dr. Prohaska, *F.M. Dostojevski. Studia o sveslavenskom covjeku* (Zagreb, 1921), pp. 186, 190.

9. See D. Chizhevskii, "K probleme dvoinika," in *O Dostoevskom*, I, ed. A. Bem (Prague, 1929), pp. 9-38. [English translation: "The Theme of the Double in Dostoevsky," in *Dostoevsky: A Collection of Critical Essays*, ed. R. Wellek (Englewood Cliffs, N.J., 1962), pp. 112-129.]

10. A.S. Dolinin, "Zarozhdenie glavnoi idei Velikogo Inkvisitora," in *Dostoevskii: odnodnevnaia gazeta russkogo bibliograficheskogo obshchestva* (Petrograd, Oct. 30, 1921), p. 16. See also Prohaska, *op. cit.*, p. 56.

11. M. Bakhtin also notices parodic elements in *The Double*. In his words, "a parodic stylization of the 'high style' of *Dead Souls* is refracted in the voice of *The Double*'s narrator; and, in general, parodic and semi-parodic echoes of various of Gogol's works are scattered throughout *The Double*." [See below, p. 271.] On the essence of parody, see Tynianov's "Dostoevski i Gogol': K teorii parodii" [see above, p. 104]. Bakhtin makes essential points about the significance of the parodic elements in a work and its influence on a writer in his book on Dostoevsky [see M. Bakhtin, *Problems of Dostoevsky's Poetics*, tr. R.W. Rotsel (Ann Arbor: Ardis, 1973; cf. also p. 249 ff. below, an excerpt from Chapter V. of Bakhtin's book].

12. See V. Vinogradov's article on "The Nose," "Naturalisticheskii grotesk...," in his *Èvoliutsiia russkogo naturalizma* (Leningrad, 1929), p. 47.

13. The "mirror," which plays an important role in both works, is closely tied in world literature to the theme of the double. Its appearance in Gogol and Dostoevsky could have been conditioned both by this literary tradition and by the actual psychological basis of the phenomenon of split personality. For more detail on the latter, see: Otto Rank, *The Double: A Psychoanalytic Study* [tr. H. Tucker (Chapel Hill: Univ. of North Carolina, 1971)]; and G. Roheim, *Spiegelzauber* (Leipzig, 1919). In his article on "The Theme of the Double," D. Chizhevsky notes the significance of the "mirror" and observes that "the state of being in a 'trance' as a result of contemplating brightly reflecting objects is one of the favorite devices of E.T.A. Hoffmann, a writer whom Dostoevsky greatly admired." In another passage of Gogol's tale, Kovalyov "dropped into a pastry shop expressly in order to look in the mirror." The "mirror" reappears in *The Double* in Ch. IX (the meeting with the double in a restaurant) and in Ch. XII (at his Excellency's).

14. I am citing *Pol. sob. soch. Dostoevskogo*, ed. L.P. Grossman, Vol. XXII: *Zabytye i neizdannye stranitsy* (Petrograd, 1918), pp. 21, 30, 26, 18, 26 (twice), 31. [Or see Dostoevskii, *Pol. sob. soch.* (Moscow, 1971), Vol. I, variants.]

15. "The basis of 'The Nose' was a current anecdote which combined popular talk and puns about noses, their disappearances and appearances, which were further elaborated among educated readers at the beginning of the nineteenth century by allusions from literary works." V. Vinogradov, "Naturalisticheskii grotesk...," *op. cit.,* p. 7.

16. Noted in Vinogradov, *op. cit.*, p. 242 and Belyi, *op. cit.*, p. 286. The double repetition of "Hm" with which the Doctor in Gogol's story answers Kovalyov becomes the favorite reply of the doctor in Dostoevsky's novel.

17. [Cf. *The Unpublished Dostoevsky*, ed. Carl Proffer (Ardis, 1973), pp. 14-15. The translation of this particular passage given there differs from our understanding of the original.]

18. See: P.I. Avanesov, "Dostoevskii v rabote nad 'Dvoinikom,' " pp. 161-69; D. Chizhevskii, "Goljadkin-Stavrogin bei Dostoevskij," *Zeitschrift für Slavische Philologie*, VII (1930), No. 3-4, pp. 358-62.

19. See Avanesov, *op. cit.*, p. 165.

20. On the significance of "guilt" for the psychology of split personality, cf. O. Rank, *op. cit.*, p. 76: "The most prominent symptom of the forms which the double takes is a powerful consciousness of guilt which forces the hero no longer to accept the responsibility for certain actions of his ego, but to place it upon another ego, a double, who is either personified by the devil himself or is created by making a diabolical pact."

21. Among the passages that Dostoevsky deleted is the following, which is relevant here: "Finally even Petrushka, though in a drunken state...announced yesterday that other people don't live in pairs, but live honorably" (from Ch. X of the first edition).

22. Golyadkin calls Karolina Ivanovna a "witch": "It's the German woman's work. It's she, the witch, who's the spark that's setting the forest on fire" [Ch. X].

23. Prof. I.D. Ermakov's essay on "The Nose" in his *Ocherki po analizu tvorchestva N.V. Gogolia* (Moscow, 1924), pp. 167-216, written in the spirit of naive Freudianism, brings out the sexual symbolism of Gogol's tale in an extremely primitive way. But it is hardly possible to deny the double meaning of the nose as presented in folklore and literature. [Available in English in *Gogol from the Twentieth Century*, ed. Robert A. Maguire (Princeton, 1974).]

24. The question of the connection of *The Double* with Dostoevsky's personality and the very problem of the double are worthy of a separate examination. The following works offer material for such an approach: I. Annenskii, " 'Vin'etka na seroi bumage' k 'Dvoiniku' Dostoevskogo," in his *Kniga otrazhenii* (St. Petersburg, 1906); T.K. Rozental', "Stradanie i tvorchestvo Dostoevskogo. Psikhogeneticheskoe issledovanie," *Voprosy izucheniia i vospitaniia lichnosti*, 1919, No. 1, pp. 88-107); O. Rank, *op. cit.*; N.E. Osipov, "*Dvoinik,* 'Peterburgskaia poèma' F. M. Dostoevskogo: Zametki psikhiatra," in *O*

Dostoevskom, I, ed. A. Bem (Prague, 1928), pp. 39-64; D.I. Chizhevskii, "K probleme dvoinika."

25. In substituting the "Double-Golyadkin Jr." for Gogol's grotesque hero, the "Nose," Dostoevsky is again employing a device he used earlier in *Poor Folk,* where Varenka Dobroselova replaces Gogol's inanimate overcoat.

26. Major Kovalyov also accuses the Nose of "masquerading."

27. See D. Chizhevsky, *op. cit.,* p. 115.

28. The problem of imposture goes back not just to Gogol, but also, to a great extent, to Pushkin, in whose works imposture plays such a significant role. See D. Darskii, *Malen'kie tragedii Pushkina,* pp. 14-15.

29. *Pol. sob. soch.,* ed. L. Grossman, XXII, p. 10.

30. See D. Chizhevskii, *op. cit.,* p. 116.

31. This phrase of Gogol's "I'm on my own" *(Ia sam po sebe)* was perceived by contemporaries as a formula. For example, in a letter to Herzen, Belinsky wrote: "Like the Nose in Gogol's tale of the same name, you can say of yourself: 'I'm on my own!' " (See his letter of April 6, 1846.)

Bakhtin / The Hero's Monologic Discourse and Narrational Discourse in Dostoevsky's Early Novels

1. [To show how these terms fit into the larger context of Bakhtin's system, we include the following chart from the preceding section of his *Problems of Dostoevsky's Poetics* (translated as "Discourse Typology in Prose" in *Readings in Russian Poetics,* eds. L. Matejka and K. Pomorska [Cambridge, M.I.T., 1971], p. 191-92):

I. *Direct unmediated discourse, focused solely on its referential object, as expression of the speaker's ultimate conceptual authority.*

II. *Objectified discourse (the speech of a person represented).*

1. With a predominance of sociotypical determinations.	Various degrees of objectification.
2. With a predominance of individually characteristic determinations.	

III. *Discourse with emphasis on another speech act (double-voiced discourse).*

1. Uni-directional variants.	With reduced objectification, these var-
a. Stylization	iants approach a fusion of voices, i.e. ap-
b. Narrator's narration.	proach the first type of discourse.
c. Unobjectified speech of a character who carries out the author's intentions (in part).	
d. *Ich-Erzählung.*	
2. Vari-directional variants.	With reduced objectification of the other
a. Parody with all its shadings.	intention, these variants become inter-
b. Parodic narration.	nally dialogized to some degree and ap-
c. Parodic *Ich-Erzählung.*	proach a division into two speech acts
d. Speech of a character who is parodically represented.	(two voices) of the first type.
e. Any reportage of someone else's speech with an altered accent.	
3. Active type (another speech act reflected).	The other speech act exerts an influence from within; the forms of relationship
a. Hidden, internal polemic.	between the two voices may vary widely,

b. Polemically colored autobiography and confession.

c. Any speech with an awareness of another's speech ("speech with a sideward glance").

d. The single line of dialogue.

e. Hidden dialogue.]

as may the degree of the deforming influence of the other speech act.

2. In his book *O iazyke khudozhestvennoi literatury* (Moscow, 1959, pp. 477-92), V. Vinogradov gives a brilliant analysis of Makar Devushkin's speech as that of a specific *social character*.

3. [From *goliada*, "beggar, tramp," which in turn comes from *golyi*, "naked, bare."]

4. The rudiments of interior dialogue were, it is true, present already in Devushkin.

5. While at work on *Netochka Nezvanova* Dostoevsky writes to his brother: "But soon you shall read *Netochka Nezvanova*. It will be a confession, like *Golyadkin*, only of a different tone and kind." (Letter to M.M. Dostoevsky of Jan.-Feb., 1847.)

6. Not long before Golyadkin had said to himself: "That's just like you!... You're so happy, you'll start singing in a minute! You're a truthful soul!"

7. In *Crime and Punishment*, for example, Svidrigaylov (Raskolnikov's partial double) repeats literally Raskolnikov's most intimate words, which he had said to Sonya, and he repeats them with a meaningful wink. We quote this passage in its entirety:

"Ach! You're a distrustful person!" laughed Svidrigaylov. "Didn't I say that I don't need this money? Well, simply for humanitarian reasons, can't you believe it? After all, she was not a "louse" (he poked his finger toward the corner where the dead woman lay), like some old usuress. Well, you'll agree, well, 'Should Luzhin really go on living and doing awful things, or should she die?' And if I don't help, then 'Polechka, for example, will go down the same path....' "

He said this with a look of *winking*, jolly roguishness, without taking his eyes off Raskolnikov. Raskolnikov grew pale and went cold at hearing the very expressions he had used in his conversation with Sonya. [Part V, Ch. 5]

8. In Thomas Mann's novel *Doctor Faustus*, a great deal was suggested by Dostoevsky, including precisely Dostoevsky's *polyphony*. I shall quote an excerpt from the description of one of the works of the composer Adrian Leverkühn which is very close to Trishatov's "musical idea":

Adrian Leverkuhn is always great at *making things that are alike different*.... So it is here—but nowhere [is his art] so profound, mysterious and great as it is here. Every word that evokes the idea of "the Beyond," of metamorphosis in a mystical sense, i.e. of transubstantiation—transformation, transfiguration—is to be hailed here as being exact. The horror which came before is, to be sure, transposed to a completely different pitch in the indescribable children's chorus, in fact it is totally reorchestrated and rerhythmatized, but *there is not a single note in the searing, sussurant tones of the spheres and the angels which could not be found to be in strict correspondence to the hellish laughter.* (Thomas Mann, *Doctor Faustus*, tr. H.T. Lowe-Porter [N.Y.: Knopf, 1948], pp. 378-79, amended by the present editors.)

285

9. Belinsky was the first to note this characteristic of *The Double*'s narration, but he offered no explanation for it. [Belinsky's remarks about *The Double* were made in his review published in *Fatherland Notes* for 1846 (Vol. XLV, No. 3, sec. V), of *A Petersburg Miscellany,* the collection edited by Nekrasov which contained Dostoevsky's *Poor Folk*. More than half of Belinsky's review was devoted to Dostoevsky, whose importance he recognized immediately, and among his comments on *The Double* one finds the observation which Bakhtin mentions and the phrase which Vinogradov quotes: "The author himself relates the adventures of his hero, but entirely with his (the hero's—eds.) language and with his notions: on the one hand, this reveals the abundance of humor in (the author's—eds.) talent, his infinitely powerful ability to contemplate the phenomena of life objectively, the ability, so to speak, to get inside the skin of another being completely foreign to him; but, on the other hand, this same feature has obscured many of the novel's events...."]

10. V. Vinogradov, "K morfologii natural'nogo stilia...," in his *Èvoliutsiia russkogo naturalizma* (Leningrad, 1929), pp. 267, 265.

11. *Ibid.*, p. 279.

12. This perspective is lacking even for the generalizing "authorial" construction of the hero's indirect speech.

13. V. Vinogradov's article "The School of Sentimental Naturalism" [see our translation above—eds.] contains valuable remarks from the standpoint of literary history about literary parody and polemic in *Poor Folk* .

Al'tman, M.S. "Gogolevskie traditsii v tvorchestve Dostoevskogo," *Slavia*, XXX (1961), pp. 443-61.

Al'tman, M.S. "Iz arsenala imen i prototipov literaturnykh geroev Dostoevskogo," in *Dostoevskii i ego vremia*, ed. V.G. Bazanov and G.M. Fridlender. Leningrad, 1971. Pp. 196-216.

Annenskii, I.F. *Knigi otrazhenii*. St. Petersburg, 1906-1909. 2 vols.

Avanesov, R. "Dostoevskii v rabote nad *Dvoinikom*," in *Tvorcheskaia istoriia: issledovaniia po russkoi literature*, ed. N.K. Piksanov. Moscow, 1927. Pp. 154-91.

Baer, Joachim T. *Vladimir Ivanovich Dal' as a Belletrist*. The Hague: Mouton, 1972.

Bakhtin, M. "Discourse Typology in Prose," in *Readings in Russian Poetics*, ed. Matejka and Pomorska. Cambridge: MIT, 1971. Pp. 176-96.

Bakhtin, M. *Problemy poètiki Dostoevskogo*. Moscow, 1963. English translation *Problems of Dostoevsky's Poetics*, by R.W. Rotsel. Ardis, 1973

Beebe, M. and Newton, C., comps. "Dostoevsky in English: A Selected Checklist of Criticism and Translations." *Modern Fiction Studies*, IV, 3 (Autumn, 1958).

Beletskii, A.I., "Dostoevskii i natural'naia shkola v 1846 g.," *Nauka na Ukraine*. Khar'kov, 1922. N. 4, pp. 332-42.

Belinskii, V.G. *Selected Philosophical Works*. Moscow: Foreign Languages, 1956.

Belinsky, Chernyshevsky and Dobrolyubov: Selected Criticism, ed. R.E. Matlaw. N.Y.: Dutton, 1962.

Belyi, Andrei. "Gogol'." *Vesy* N. 4 (1909). English translation by E. Trahan in *Russian Literature Triquarterly*, N. 4 (Fall 1972), pp. 131-44.

Belyi, Andrei. *Masterstvo Gogolia*. Moscow, 1934.

Bem, A.L. "En face de la Mort: 'Le Dernier Jour d'un Condamné' de Victor Hugo et *L'Idiot* de Dostoevski." *Mélanges P.M. Haškovec*. Brno, 1936. Pp. 45-64.

Bem, A.L., ed. *O Dostoevskom; sbornik statei*. 3 vols. Prague, 1929, 1933, 1936.

Bem, A.L. "Pervye shagi Dostoevskogo (Genezis romana *Bednye liudi*)," *Slavia*, XII (1933), pp. 134-61.

Bocharov, S. "Pushkin i Gogol' ('Stantsionnyi smotritel' ' i 'Shinel' ')" in *Problemy tipologii russkogo realizma*, ed. N.L. Stepanov and U.R. Fokht. Moscow, 1969. Pp. 210-40.

Bowman, Herbert. "The Nose," *Slavic and East European Journal*, XXXI, 76 (December 1952), pp. 204-11.

Briusov, Valerii, "Ispepelennyi–k kharakteristike Gogolia." *Vesy* (1909). English translation "Burnt to Ashes" by R. Maguire, *Russian Literature Triquarterly*, N. 3 (Spring 1972), pp. 108-27.

Brodskii, N.L., ed. *Tvorcheskii put' Dostoevskogo: sbornik statei*. Leningrad, 1924.

Chirkov, N.M. *O stile Dostoevskogo*. Moscow, 1963.

Chizhevskii, D. "The Unknown Gogol," *Slavonic and East European Review*, XXX (June 1952), pp. 476-93.

Chizhevskii, D. "Gogol: Artist and Thinker," *Annals of the Ukrainian Academy in the U.S.*, N. 4 (2) (1952), pp. 261-78.

Chizhevskii, D., "Golyadkin-Stavrogin bei Dostoevskii," *Zeitschrift für Slavische Philologie*, VII (1930), Nn. 3-4, pp. 358-62.

Chizhevskii, D., "The Theme of the Double in Dostoevsky," in *Dostoevsky*, ed. René Wellek. Englewood Cliffs: Prentice-Hall, 1962.

Chulkov, Georgii, "Dostoevskii i utopicheskii sotsializm," *Katorga i ssylka*, LI-LII (1929), pp. 9-35 and 134-51.

Debreczeny, P., "Nikolay Gogol and his Contemporary Critics," *Transactions of the American Philosophical Society*, New Series, v. 56, Prt. 3 (April 1966), pp. 5-68.

Dolinin, A.S., ed. *F.M. Dostoevskii: stat'i i materialy*. 2 vols. Petrograd, 1922, Leningrad, 1925.

Dostoevskii, F.M. *Polnoe sobranie sochinenii*. Ed. V.G. Bazanov, et al. Leningrad, 1972. Vols. I and II.

Dostoevsky's Occasional Writings. Sel., tr. and intro. D. Magarshack. N.Y.: Random House, 1963.

Driessen, F.C. *Gogol as a Short-Story Writer: A Study of his Technique of Composition*. The Hague: Mouton, 1965.

Erlich, V. *Gogol*. New Haven: Yale University, 1968.

Erlich, V. *Russian Formalism: History—Doctrine*. The Hague: Mouton, 1955.

Erlich, V., ed. *Twentieth-Century Russian Literary Criticism*. New Haven: Yale, 1975.

Evdokimov, P. *Gogol et Dostoievsky ou la Déscente aux Enfers*. Paris: Desclée de Brower, 1961.

Fanger, D. *Dostoevsky and Romantic Realism: A Study of Dostoevsky in Relation to Balzac, Dickens and Gogol*. Cambridge: Harvard University, 1965.

Fanger, D., ed. *O Dostoevskom: Stat'i*. Providence: Brown University, 1966.

Field, Andrew, comp., *The Complection of Russian Literature: A Cento*. N.Y., 1971.

Frank, Joseph. *Dostoevsky: The Seeds of Revolt 1821-1849*. Princeton, 1976

Fridlender, G.M. *Realizm Dostoevskogo*. Moscow-Leningrad, 1964.

Gerhardt, Dietrich. *Gogol' und Dostoevskij in ihren Künstlerischen Verhältnis*. Leipzig, 1941.

Gibian, George. "The Grotesque in Dostoevsky," *Modern Fiction Studies*, IV, 3 (Autumn 1958), pp. 262-70.

Gippius, Vasilii. *Gogol'*. Providence: Brown, 1963. (Reprint of Leningrad 1924 edition.)

Gippius, Vasilii. *Ot Pushkina do Bloka*. Moscow-Leningrad, 1966.

Gogol, N.V. *The Collected Tales and Plays*, ed. L.J. Kent. N.Y. Random House, 1964.

Grossman, L.P. *Biblioteka Dostoevskogo*. Odessa, 1919.

Grossman, L.P. *Dostoevskii*. (Zhizn' zamechatel'nykh liudei: seriia biografii.) Moscow, 1962.

Grossman, L.P. "Dostoevskii-khudozhnik," in *Tvorchestvo F.M. Dostoevskogo*, ed. N.L. Stepanov. Moscow, 1959. Pp. 330-416.

Grossman, L.P. "Gofman, Bal'zak i Dostoevskii," *Sofiia*, V (1914), pp. 87-96.

Grossman, L.P. *Poètika Dostoevskogo*. Moscow, 1925.

Grossman, L.P. *Seminarii po Dostoevskomu: materialy, bibliografiia i komentarii*. Moscow-Petrograd, 1922.

Grossman, L.P., ed. *Tvorchestvo Dostoevskogo 1821-1881-1921 gg. Sbornik statei i materialov*. Odessa, 1921.

Gukovskii, G.A. *Realizm Gogolia*. Moscow-Leningrad, 1959.

Gustafson, R.F. "The Suffering Usurper: Gogol's 'Diary of a Madman'," *Slavic and East European Journal*, IX (1965), pp. 268-80.

Hartland, Reginald W. *Walter Scott et le Roman 'frénétique': contribution a l'étude de leur fortune en France*. Paris: Champion, 1928.

Holquist, J.M. "The Devil in Mufti; The *Märchenwelt* in Gogol's Short Stories," *Publications of the Modern Language Association*, 82 (October 1967).

Iakubovich, D. "Predislovie k 'Povestiam Belkina' i povestvovatel'nye priemy Valtera Skotta" in *Pushkin v mirovoi literature: sbo nik statei*. Leningrad, 1926.

Jackson, R.L. *Dostoevsky's Quest for Form: A Study of His Philosophy of Art*. New Haven: Yale University, 1966.

Kalinine, Paul. "L'école frénétique et la prose romantique en Russie (1831-1836)," in *Communications de la Délégation française, VII Congrès International des Slavistes*. Paris: Institut d'Ètudes Slaves, 1973, pp. 231-41.

Kalinine, Paul. "Pouchkine, Gogol et le passage à la forme prosaique dans les années

1830 en Russie," in *Actes du XIIe Congrès de la Fédération International des Langues et Litteratures Modernes.* Cambridge, 1972.

Kayser, Wolfgang. *The Grotesque in Art and Literature.* Tr. U. Weisstein. Bloomington: Indiana University, 1963.

Kirai, Diula. "Khudozhestvennaia model' rannikh romanov F.M. Dostoevskogo (K voprosy o razgranichenii pozitsii avtora i positsii geroia v romane *Bednye liudi*)," *Studia Slavica*, II, 3-4 (Budapest, 1968), pp. 221-41.

Kirai, Diula. "Kompozitsia siuzheta romana *Dvoinik. Prikliucheniia gospodina Goliadkina,*" *Acta Litteraria Academiae Scientiarum Hungaricae*, II, 3-4 (Budapest, 1969), pp. 351-78.

Kirai, Diula. "Siuzhetnyi parallelizm romana Dostoevskogo *Dvoinik,*" *Studia Slavica*, XVI (Budapest, 1969).

Komarovich, V. *Dostoevskii. Sovremennye problemy istoriko-literaturnogo izucheniia.* Leningrad, 1925.

Komarovich, V. "Peterburgskie feletony Dostoevskogo," in *Feletony sorokovykh godov*, ed. Iu. Oksman. Moscow-Leningrad, 1930. Pp. 89-126.

Kuleshov, V.I. *Natural'naia shkola v russkoi literature.* Moscow, 1965.

Lapshin, I.M. *Èstetika Dostoevskogo.* Berlin, 1923.

Linner, Sven. *Dostoevskij on Realism* (Acta Univ. Stockholmiensis, Stockholm Slavic Studies, 1). Stockholm: Almquist and Wiksell, 1967.

Maguire, Robert A., ed. *Gogol from the Twentieth Century.* Princeton: Princeton University, 1974.

Mann, Iurii. "Èvoliutsiia gogolevskoi fantastiki," in *K istorii russkogo romantizma*, ed. Iu. Mann, I.G. Neupokoeva, U.R. Fokht. Moscow, 1973. Pp. 219-58.

Mann, Iurii. "Filosofiia i poètika 'Natural'noi shkoly'," in *Problemy tipologii russkogo realizma*, ed. N.L. Stepanov and U.R. Fokht. Moscow, 1969.

Mann, Iurii, *O groteske v literature.* Moscow, 1966.

Matejka, L. and Pomorska, K., eds. *Readings in Russian Poetics: Formalist and Structuralist Views.* Cambridge: MIT, 1971.

Mersereau, John Jr. *Baron Delvig's "Northern Flowers," 1825-1832.* Carbondale: Southern Illinois University, 1967.

Mirsky, D.S. *A History of Russian Literature*, ed. F.J. Whitfield. N.Y.: Knopf, 1949.

Mochulsky, Konstantin. *Dostoevsky: His Life and Work*, tr. Michael A. Minihan. Princeton: Princeton University, 1967.

Mossman, Elliott D. "Dostoevskij's Early Works: The More than Rational Distortion," *Slavic and East European Journal*, X, 3 (Fall 1966), pp. 268-78.

Nabokov, Vladimir. *Nikolai Gogol.* N.Y.: New Directions, 1944.

Nilsson, Nils Åke. *Gogol et Pétersbourg.* Stockholm, 1954.

Odoevsky, V.F. *Russian Nights,* tr. O. Olienikov and R.E. Matlaw. N.Y.: Dutton, 1965.

Oksman, Iu., ed. *Feletony sorokovykh godov.* Moscow-Leningrad, 1930.

Passage, Charles. *Dostoevsky the Adapter: A Study in Dostoevsky's Use of the Tales of Hoffmann.* Chapel Hill: University of North Carolina, 1954.

Passage, Charles. *The Russian Hoffmannists.* The Hague: Mouton, 1963.

Pereverzev, V.F. *Tvorchestvo Dostoevskogo: kriticheskii ocherk.* Moscow, 1925.

Praz, Mario. *The Romantic Agony.* N.Y.: Meridian, 1956.

Proctor, Thelwell. *Dostoevskii and the Belinskii School of Literary Criticism.* The Hague: Mouton, 1969.

Proskurina, Iu. M. "Povestvovatel'-rasskazchik v romane F.M. Dostoevskogo *Belye nochi,*" *Nauchnye doklady vysshei shkoly. Filologicheskie nauki*, 2 (1966), pp.123-35.

Roberts, Spencer E., ed. and tr. *Essays in Russian Literature. The Conservative View: Leontiev, Rozanov, Shestov.* Athens: Ohio University, 1968.

Rodzevich, S.I. "K istorii romantizma: È.T.A. Gofman i 30-40 gg. v nashei literature,"

Russkii filologicheskii vestnik, LXXVII, 1-2 (1917), pp. 194-237.

Rozanov, Vasilii. "How the Character Akaky Akakiyevich Originated," pp. 369-85, and "Pushkin and Gogol," pp. 357-68, in Roberts, S.E., ed., *q.v.*

Russian Literature Triquarterly, issue on Russian Romanticism, 3 (Spring 1972).

Seduro, Vladimir. *Dostoyevski in Russian Literary Criticism 1846-1956*. N.Y.: Octagon, 1969.

Setchkarev, Vsevolod. *Gogol: His Life and Works*, tr. R. Kramer. N.Y.: NYU, 1965.

Shklovskii, Viktor. *Za i protiv. Zametki o Dostoevskom*. Moscow, 1957.

Slonimskii, Aleksandr. *Tekhnika komicheskogo u Gogolia*. Providence: Brown University, 1969. (Reprint of the 1923 edition.) Cf. English tr. in R. Maguire, ed., *q.v.*

Stilman, Leon. "Gogol's 'Overcoat'—Thematic Patterns and Origins," *The American Slavic and East European Review*, 1952, p. 138 ff.

Terras, Victor. *The Young Dostoevsky (1846-1849): A Critical Study*. The Hague: Mouton, 1969.

Trubetskoi, Nikolai S. *Dostoevskij als Künstler*. The Hague: Mouton, 1964.

Trubetskoi, Nikolai S. "O metode izucheniia Dostoevskogo," *Novyi zhurnal*, 48 (1957).

Trubetskoi, Nikolai S. "O dvukh romanakh Dostoevskogo," *Novyi zhurnal*, 60 (1960).

Trubetskoi, Nikolai S. "Rannii Dostoevskii," *Novyi zhurnal*, 71 (1963).

Trubetskoi, Nikolai S. "The Style of *Poor Folk* and *The Double*," *American Slavic and East European Review*, VII , 2 (April 1948), pp. 150-71.

Tseitlin, A. *Povest' o bednom chinovnike Dostoevskogo, (K istorii odnogo siuzheta)*. Moscow, 1923.

Tseitlin, A. *Stanovlenie realizma v russkoi literature*. Moscow, 1965.

Tunimanov, V.A. "Nekotorye osobennosti povestvovaniia v 'Gospodine Prokharchine' Dostevskogo," in *Poètika i stilistika russkoi literatury*. Leningrad, 1971. Pp. 203-12.

Vinogradov, V.V. *Ètiudy o stile Gogolia*. Leningrad, 1926.

Vinogradov, V.V. *Èvoliutsiia russkogo naturalizma; Gogol' i Dostoevskii*. Leningrad, 1929.

Vinogradov, V.V. *Gogol' i natural'naia shkola*. Leningrad, 1925.

Vinogradov, V.V. *The History of the Russian Literary Language from the 17th Century to the 19th*, tr. and ed. L.L. Thomas. Madison: University of Wisconsin, 1969.

Vinogradov, V.V. *O iazyke khudozhestvennoi literatury*. Moscow, 1959.

Vinogradov, V.V. "Turgenev i shkola molodogo Dostoevskogo," *Russkaia literatura*, 2 (1959), p. 49.

Wellek, René, ed. *Dostoevsky: A Collection of Critical Essays*. Englewood Cliffs: Prentice-Hall, 1962.

Woodward, James B. "The Threadbare Fabric of Gogol's 'Overcoat'," *Canadian Slavic Studies*, I, 1 (1967), pp. 95-104.

293

294